D1603205

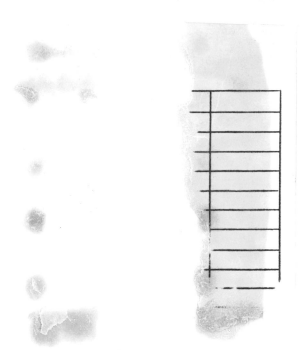

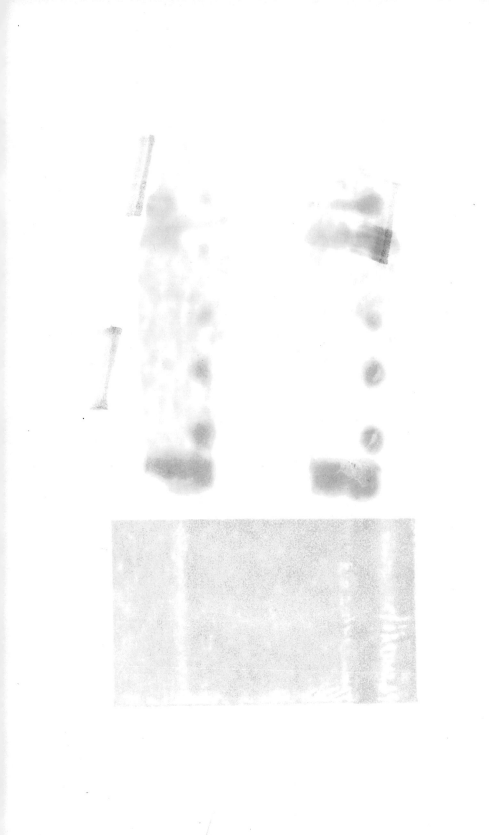

Contributions to the Sociology of Language

4

Editor

Joshua A. Fishman

MOUTON · THE HAGUE · PARIS

Perspectives on Black English

Editor

J. Dillard

MOUTON · THE HAGUE · PARIS

Cover design by Jurriaan Schrofer

ISBN 90 279 7811 5

Contents

Contents 7

J. L. DILLARD

GENERAL INTRODUCTION: PERSPECTIVES ON BLACK
ENGLISH

Despite the controversial and even polemic nature of much of the publication on the subject, it is now generally recognized that there is a language variety called Black English (less frequently Negro Non-Standard
English, or even Merican). This variety is spoken by the great majority of
poor ("disadvantaged") Black citizens of the United States, the descendants
of the plantation field hands, although not by many middle-class Negroes,
descendants of house servants and freedmen. Recognition of the relationship of this variety to the pidgin and creole varieties of West Africa and
of the Caribbean (including Surinam, Honduras, etc.) is also becoming
general.
   This variety is, in the terms of Stewart (1968), a vernacular: it has a
large body (perhaps 18 to 20 million) of living speakers, its history is
traceable (see Dillard 1972), and its rules are essentially autonomous
(regarded only by the linguistically naive as "distortions" of other varieties of English). It has not undergone standardization — in the familiar
sociolinguistic sense of codification and legitimization — although some
first steps in this direction have been taken by those who are concerned
with the plight of the Black child in the U.S. school system (Stewart
1964, 1965; Baratz and Shuy 1969).
   The recent resurgence of interest in Black English can easily lead to
the faulty impression that it has been recently discovered, or even that
it has newly "sprung up". That this is far from true is easily shown by
citing a work so supposedly well known as Leonard Bloomfield's *Language* (1933:474). In the same year, C. M. Wise's "Negro Dialect"
appeared in the *Quarterly Journal of Speech* (vol. 19,522-28). Explicit
statement in popular sources goes back at least as far as N. S. Dodge's

"Negro Patois and Its Humor" (*Appleton's Journal*, 1870,160-61). The articles by Harrison (1884) and Payne (1903), included in this collection, indicate that there was never a complete lapse of observation. Less explicit statements, often merely quotations of Negro speakers of pidgin or creole English, can be found as early as the first years of the eighteenth century. Yet the topic, as a matter for serious study, can be said to have been brought to the attention of the scholarly community by Melville J. Herskovits (*The Myth of the Negro Past*, 1941). The term itself, *Black English*, seems to be first attested from 1734 (Cohen 1952).

At the present time, the date at which West African Pidgin English — based probably on a Maritime Pidgin English, which may derive from the Mediterranean Lingua Franca (Sabir)[1] tradition — came to the British

---

[1] This is the point of view of Hancock (1972). An earlier personal communication suggested "an earlier Panguinean (Manding?) pidgin underlying it". In many respects, especially in phonology and lexicon, this must be true. Something must explain the great West African language influence on the Atlantic English Creoles (Hancock's term [1969]). There remain, however, striking similarities to English varieties in the Pacific, like that of Pitcairn Island. I believe that it is impossible, even absurd, to explain away these similarities in ecological terms, as has frequently been done (e.g. by Cassidy 1971). If similarities between Altantic (African-based or influenced) and Pacific pidgins can be explained away in terms of "linguistic universals" in a simplistic sense, then why cannot the similarities between the Atlantic varieties be so explained as well?

There remains the important consideration of the possible nautical English-based Lingua Franca, a kind of English-lexicon Sabir. (This would be what is called Maritime Pidgin English in Dillard 1972.) Unfortunately, there is not the kind of documentation for this nautical variety which can be found for French-, Portuguese-, and even Italian-based varieties. Matthews (1935) reports seventeenth century comments on the "notorious ... strangeness of their [sailors'] speech". Ned Ward, in *Wooden World Dissected* (1757), asserted the need of sailors ashore for an interpreter. Matthews expresses the traditional view when he interprets this as meaning that "this dialect probably consisted largely of seaterms which the sailors when ashore applied to land objects" (p. 193). Matthews's purely phonological analysis of the attestations could hardly show more. But, if there were syntactic differences at a deeper level than the nautical vocabulary, explanation of the genesis of the maritime variety would at least have a more nearly solid foundation.

More basically, my reason for preferring the Sabir hypothesis to a direct explanation from African language interference is the same as that which motivated this collection: a preference for the use of texts over internal reconstruction, whenever the former alternative is possible. A "panguinean" pidgin, however it came into being, can hardly be postulated except on the basis of reconstruction; there are travellers' reports (e.g. Barbot) of the presence of Lingua Franca in the slave trade, and seventeenth century suggestions of a British nautical variety.

It soon becomes perfectly clear, however, from any kind of approach, that the language contact situation — in West Africa, in the New World, and at sea between the two — was more complex than it has hitherto been acknowledged to be. Simple copying of the European languages by the "inferior" population is not an adequate explanation; neither is the theory of conscious simplification by the European speakers. The complex

colonies on the continent of North America must remain a conjecture. It can hardly have been earlier than 1619 — the date for the first slaves in the colonies. Nor can it have been later than 1692 — the date at which Justice Hathorne recorded the partly pidgin speech of Tituba at the Salem witch trials. Given the fact that West African pidginists are now placing the development of Pidgin English in that area at least as early as the beginning of the seventeenth century,[2] it seems likely that at least some African slaves using Pidgin English came to what is now the United States by the middle of that century. Attestations begin to be common-place around 1710-1720, but the variety may well have been around for the greater part of a century before anyone bothered to write it down.

At any rate, academic studies lagged, in the Americas as in Africa. West African records of the use of Pidgin English go back at least as far as Atkins (1732), but Grade (1892 — reprinted here) is one of the earliest formal studies. Many American attestations were collected by Krapp (1925). Krapp, like the group which would soon found the *Linguistic Atlas of the United States and Canada*, hardly knew what to do with these indications of a dialect with social (ethnic) distribution patterns. Krapp decided to refer to the West African Pidgin English, and to its creolized successor, as a "literary dialect". He also chose to treat the well-attested and authenticated American Indian Pidgin English as a literary creation,[3] although many of the sources which he cited for the English varieties of both the Black and the Indian are not fictional.[4] Until very recently, dialectologists have apparently followed Krapp, un-critically and apparently without reconsidering the issue.

West African language situation may have given rise to solutions to contact problems which were more sophisticated than the Europeans gave the Blacks credit for being able to perform. The speculations about "groping for communicative methods", attractive as they are in a commonsense way, do not take into account the serious tradition of pidgin studies.

[2] On the dating of Pidgin English, see Hancock (1969), Dalby (1969), and Schneider (1967).

[3] For a different attitude toward AIPE, see Leechman and Hall (1955), Miller (1967), and Dillard (1972: chapter IV).

[4] As Krapp points out, sources as diverse as Madam Knight's *Journals* (1704-1705) and James Fenimore Cooper's *Redskins* (1846) contain references to and examples of what Krapp chose to label "Indian dialect" and "Negro dialect". Krapp consistently judges his sources as deficient because they indicate little difference between the two. The possibility that an essentially uniform pidgin variety was being reported apparently did not occur to Krapp; he apparently thought that the authors' sole purpose was to indicate racial characterization through the words given to the characters. It is easy to excuse Krapp because of the early date of his work, but Cooper had been perceptive enough to make the suggestion of a pidgin (calling it rather a *lingua franca*) nearly eighty years earlier. Krapp's objection (1925:266) that "if this *lingua franca* existed, of which Cooper speaks, certainly Cooper made little effort to use it" seems singularly obtuse. This very sentence comes at the end of a long series of citations of Cooper's

Because of the general preoccupation with finding regional — to the virtual exclusion of other — variation and with drawing isoglosses and finding isogloss bundles, the traces of Black English which were found even through the questionable methodology of the *Worksheets of the Linguistic Atlas* were treated in contradictory and illogical fashion. Atwood's *A Survey of the Verb Forms of the Eastern United States* (1953), for example, recorded four "characteristically Negro" expressions in a context of denying any difference between Negro and white speech patterns. The creolist Robert A. Hall, in *Pidgin and Creole Languages* (1966), pointed out, as had Bloomfield, that most American Negro dialects were the result of "decreolization" (merger of the creole with other, more nearly standard dialects), and that the existence of a creole presupposed the prior existence of a pidgin. But Hall asserted that there were no records of that pidgin. Thus, he apparently followed Krapp in assigning the abundant surviving records to the "literary dialect" scrap heap. Accordingly, Hall seems to offend against the principles of parsimony by postulating

---

use of Pidgin English for Negro and Indian characters. Strangely enough, it seems never to have occurred to Krapp that Cooper's "lingua franca" and his own "literary dialects" were the same thing.

Cooper's materials, although imbedded in fiction, were accompanied by a footnote comment in *Redskins* which was obviously intended to be factual. Although Cooper wrote of a time earlier than his own, he probably has as much claim to being a serious student of historical records — where Indians and Blacks are concerned, anyway — as Krapp or any of his colleagues. For non-fictional attestations of Black and Indian uses of Pidgin, Creole, and partly decreolized English which closely parallel what one finds in Cooper and other writers of fiction, one may easily cite many sources. Besides those referred to elsewhere, they would include

George Catlin, *Illustrations of the Manners, Customs, and Conditions of the North American Indians* (London, 1866, 2 vols.).

A. D. Richardson, *Beyond the Mississippi* (1865).

James F. Rusling, *Across America: or, the Great West and the Pacific Coast* (New York, 1875).

Alex. Mackay, *The Western World* (London, 1850).

The Reverend Josiah Pratt, *The Life of David Brainerd* (London 1856) [based on Brainerd's journal of the early eighteenth century].

Lawrence Foster, *Negro-Indian Relationship in the Southwest*, University of Pennsylvania dissertation in Anthropology (1935).

Elisha K. Kane, "The Negro Dialects Along the Savannah River", *Dialect Notes* V, 1925.

and many others. Necessarily incomplete citations of the very many available sources may be found in Stewart (1967, 1968 — reprinted in this collection) and Dillard (1972).

In order to continue to regard either Black English or American Indian Pidgin English as a "literary dialect", one must apparently assume that writers like the missionary Brainerd and the New York Supreme Court member Daniel Horsmanden (*The New York Conspiracy*, 1744) deliberately chose to pass off these "literary dialects" as reported speech.

(1) A pidgin, for which there are no records.
(2) Records, for which there was no pidgin.

Dialect geographers, in keeping with their preconception (almost, at times, an obsession) that the dialects of American English must be basically regional in distribution, continued to assert that Black dialects were — or, at least, had been in earlier times — identical with those of Southern whites. Since any specifically Black forms must represent "archaisms", the pidgin-creole tradition was felt to be unnecessary as an explanation of Black dialects in the United States. But the dialect geographers further asserted that these differences were solely a matter of a few relics, hardly enough to constitute a true dialect difference. The historical records did not, of course, bear them out. Neither did the evidence of listener perception tests (Baratz 1969, Lambert and Tucker 1969). The desire to submerge Black dialects in Southern regional dialects led to the identification of American Blacks as an exclusively Southern group. In some extreme cases, this preconception led to the absurd statement that no Negroes had been in the Northern states (not to mention colonies!) before World War I.[5]

It is hardly necessary to enter into detailed refutation of a glaring demographic error. Although the great concentration of Black slaves in the Southern colonies and states is historically commonplace, the very early presence of smaller numbers of slaves in the North is almost equally commonplace. Greene (1942) and Ottley and Weatherby (1967) show the continuous presence of Blacks in New England and New York since at least as early as 1635. Winks (1971) shows a continuous history of Negroes in that area, especially in Nova Scotia, since 1628.

Nor do the records show a major linguistic break between North and South, at least in the early period. Winks quotes an occasional scrap of Pidgin English like

No Work, No Yam. (p. 84).

from the Halifax Blacks. Dillard (1973) traces the records of Pidgin/Creole in the Halifax area from about 1790 to the present.[6] Justice Daniel P. Hors-

---

[5] The statement is "... all Black people in the North have a common origin — and an origin less than two generations old". (Davis 1971: 50). Davis's context makes it clear that he means by "common origin" the Southern states — not Africa, invasion from some remote planet, change of color within the last two generations, or any other of a conceivably infinite number of equally implausible alternatives. Against this kind of fantasy we can cite historical statements like the following: "New York, at the end of the seventeenth century, had a larger percentage of Negroes in its population than did Virginia" (Alexander C. Flick, ed., *History of the State of New York* [New York, 1933], p. 407).
[6] The Pidgin English quotation from Winks is attributed to the Maroons, as is the following:

manden's *The New York Conspiracy ... 1741-42* reports of Jack, one of the ringleaders in the alleged conspiracy:

his dialect was so perfectly negro and unintelligible, it was thought it would be impossible to make anything of him without the help of an interpreter. (p. 127).

Horsmanden gives one major example of Jack's speech:

His master live in tall house Broadway. Ben ride de fat horse. (p. 128).

The author also uses individual lexical items like *backarara*, a variant used by Benjamin Franklin among others, for *buckra* or *bakra* 'white man'. It is a considerable assumption that all of these reflect simply literary imagination, particularly since the records quoted are not from writers of fiction. Dillard (1971) traces some of the subsequent evidence for the continuity of the language variety in the New York area.

Among the many ignored topics on the New World language picture is the English of the group of about two hundred American Negro freedmen who migrated to Santo Domingo in 1824, according to Work (1940). Now in the Samaná area, this group is reported by Hoetink (1962) to be

---

"Top lilly bit; you say me must forsake my wife. Only one of them. Which that one? Jesus Christ say so? No, no, massa, Gar A'mighty good; he tell somebody he must forsake him wife and children. Somebody no wicked for forsake him wife? No, massa, dis here talk no do for me." (Campbell 1873:207).

This may well be a traditional text. R. C. Dallas, *History of the Maroons*, quotes a somewhat different version. But the following was attributed (by Fyfe, *History of Sierra Leone*, 1962) to a period before the coming of the Maroons to Nova Scotia: "Massa Governor no mind King, he no mind You." (Add. MS41262B, fol. 9, British Museum).

Among the group (not necessarily all Maroons) whom John Clarkson recruited for the trip from Nova Scotia to Sierra Leone in 1791 was one who "came originally from the coast of Africa and spoke English indifferently" (Clarkson, MS diary, Howard University collection). From the attestation quoted, this "indifferent" English is clearly Pidgin: "No, massa, me no hear nor no mind. Me work like slave can not do worse Massa in any part of the world, therefore am determined to go with you Massa, if you please."

Many attestations of a creole or decreolized variety are available from nineteenth century Nova Scotian texts (see Dillard, 1973). Greaves (1930), who believes that language could not possibly have any part in the educational difficulties of Nova Scotian Blacks, cites the "old Negro proverb": "When buckra tief, he tief plantation; when nigger tief, he tief piece of cane." (p. 71).

There remains a (largely unstudied) Black English dialect spoken in the Halifax area, especially by the New Roaders of the North Preston area. I am indebted to Norman Whitten (personal communication) for most of my information on this population, and to John Hogan for the initial suggestion that Black English varieties might be found in Nova Scotia. A popular article, Edna Staebler's "Would You Change the Lives of These People?" (*McLean's Magazine*, May 12, 1956), gives enough examples of the speech of the New Roaders to make it relatively certain that it is a (partly) decreolized variety. The article is, however, anthropologically insensitive and naive even to the point of racism.

divided into two parts, one of which speaks "better" English ("somewhat archaic perhaps and with an elaborate use of biblical parables", p. 20) than "that of the isolated farming people in the surrounding area". Hoetink quotes a boy from the latter group:

They said white man never speak English.

While it would obviously be impossible to draw any conclusions from so brief an utterance, the grammar (uninflected verb) of that utterance is at least consistent with what we know of Black English elsewhere.

Considerable work remains to be done on this population, and field-work is in its beginning stages. Work (1940:17) specifies that "the colony voluntarily remained isolated from the surrounding islanders and thus preserved its dialect". Hoetink's studies show how resistance to the local culture of the Dominican Republic and to Spanish have characterized the more prestigious descendants of the original immigrants. Tentative field studies tend to show, however, that the less prestigious members of the community today, who might be expected to have preserved the Plantation Creole of the field slaves, have acquired not only a great deal of Spanish but an appreciable amount of Haitian Creole. Admittedly inadequate field recordings suggest that, in intonation at least, the Samaná dialect is closer to West Indian English than anything now spoken in the United States.

Much is suggested from a broader context of study of the English of Black populations that is not apparent from geographically restricted investigations. Additional insights may be provided by looking away from English, to the language varieties spoken by Blacks but associated lexically with other European languages.

BLACK SPANISH

There have been many suggestions in recent years that certain dialects of Caribbean or South American Spanish belong in the Creole tradition. Max Leopold Wagner, in *Lingue e Dialetti dell' America Spagnola* (1949), made that suggestion, although it met with a very poor reception from Spanish dialectologists. Papiamentu has usually been the central issue in this debate; but Hispanists have often chosen to isolate Papiamentu, just as American dialectologists have traditionally isolated Gullah. Creolists have often dealt with Papiamentu while ignoring or avoiding the issue of whether it stands in any close relationship to other American varieties, especially of Spanish.[7] The issue might, however, well arise, because of

[7]   There are early sources like P. Alonso de Sandoval, S. J., *De Instauranda Aethiopium Salute* (1627):

the great amount of African vocabulary which survives in certain dialects of Caribbean Spanish (Álvarez Nazario 1961). Cabrera (all references) and other folklore collectors provide texts of apparently recognizable West African languages in Cuba, along with "non-standard" Spanish which has suspiciously Creole features. For bibliography on the subject, see De Granda (1968a).

The most striking evidence for this theory has recently come to light in the works of De Granda, Escalante, and Bickerton. As the last two point out, in El Palenque de San Basilio, Colombia, there are some two or three thousand speakers of a clearly Creole-related language variety — most of them also users of a certain amount of Colombian Spanish. Apparently, they and their ancestors have lived there and spoken earlier versions of the same dialect for three or four centuries (Bickerton and Escalante 1970). Since there are striking resemblances to Papiamentu and to Portuguese Creole, and since direct contact has clearly not been their source, it seems unavoidable that they go back to some contact-variety source.

Puerto Rico and Santo Domingo have been almost completely ignored so far. Puerto Rican language policy has been overwhelmingly concerned with the acquisition — or, in the case of some *indepentistas*, avoidance — of English and with the attendant problems of bilingualism. A little attention has been paid to the interesting hybrid sometimes called Spanglish (M. E. Jones 1962, Dillard 1969b); and there has been bitter, politically-oriented debate over the issue. But all too little attention has been given to the historical implications of the speech of Blacks, especially in past centuries. There are strong indications in the speech of José, the *Negro bozal* in *La Juega de Gallos o el Negro Bozal* (excerpted in Álvarez Nazario 1961), that creole-like features were present in the speech of Puerto Rican Blacks as late as the mid-nineteenth century. (This is quite

---

"Y los que llamamos criollos y naturales de San Thomé, con la communicación que con tan bárbaras y recónditas naciones han tenido el tiempo que han residido en San Thomé, las entienden casi todas con un género de lenguaje muy corrupto y revesado de la portuguesa, que llaman lengua de San Thomé, al modo que ahora nosotros entendemos y hablamos con todo género de negros y naciones con nuestra lengua española corrupta como comúnmente la hablan todos los negros" (Spanish translation, translator unidentified, Bogota, 1956, p. 94).

This is seemingly closely matched by Father A. Schabel's statement (1704): "De Negerslaven van Curaçao spreken gebroken Spaans." Antoine J. Maduro, who quotes this passage (*Papiamentu, Origen i Formacion*, Corsou, 1965), is highly skeptical of the accuracy of Schabel's statement. Maduro seems, however, to be unaware of Sandoval's very similar statement and perhaps even of the implications of both texts for general creole language history. An artificial handicap which Maduro, like other investigators, imposes upon himself is to limit his historical investigation to the Papiamentu-speaking islands and not to look at other areas where Portuguese or "Spanish" was used in the slave trade.

apart from the presence of Papiamentu-speaking immigrants.) The features of José's dialect in that drama are rather unlike Palenquero, but they are very similar to some features of Papiamentu. Vestiges of the creole are especially prominent today in the Loiza Aldea-Guayama area, but the conventional arguments about the provenience of features (e.g. /l/ for /r/ in final or pre-consonantal position) continue.

In this context, it seems increasingly important that pockets of Black speakers of non-standard Spanish keep turning up in scattered isolated areas in both North and South America. Gonzalo Aguirre Beltran (1958) provides evidence of the same *l* for *r* in Mexico. He also shows etymological *s* becoming *j* and has even more interesting replacements of *d* by *l* (*Lalo*, diminutive of *Eduardo*, p. 213). Aguirre Beltran quite conventionally traces these factors to the Spanish of the sixteenth century, but there are reasons to suspect that pat answer with its ubiquitous application.

The same problems are encountered in the study of the Spanish of Blacks in coastal South America. The most prominent specialist in Ecuadorean Spanish, Toscano Mateus (1953:36), writes

Buena parte de los carácteres del habla costeño (por ejemplo, el relajamiento de la *l* y la *r*) se encuentran también en Andalucía, pero no son menos peculiares del español hablado por los negros.

Andalucía, for Spanish dialect geographers, serves about the same function as Scotland and Ireland for their American English counterparts: largely unstudied, it can be claimed as a source for any New World dialect form which would otherwise prove embarrassing to the Eurocentric theory. But Toscano Mateus is guilty of no such simple appeal to the unknown; he makes specific comparison to coastal forms which are "de origin español y náutico" (p. 36), in what may be a striking parallel to what English Creolists are finding out about the historical importance of Maritime Pidgin English. In fact, he quite specifically attributes a language-contact cause to Ecuadorean dialect variation:

Pero los Andes ya la presencia del indio quichua en la Sierra y del negro en la Costa han diferenciado bastante el habla de las regiones occidental e interandina. (p. 36)

Obviously, studies have not gone very far when our only information about large areas and populations must consist of such impressionistic and anecdotal material. But it has now come to be realized that, wherever there are large pockets of descendants of West African slaves, the effects of the language contact factors of slavery may still be observable. A still more controversial issue may be the possible influence of the language of those descendants of slaves upon the American Indian- and even Spanish-descended population of South America. A great deal of Hispanic blood will boil at the very suggestion.

Nevertheless, there is now reason to doubt that New World Spanish dialectology can still be framed, historically, in terms of migration of European "regional" dialect features to the New World. Catalán (1958) makes the outright suggestion of a *koiné*, and there is abundant reason to believe that the leveling of "regional" features of the European languages was the rule rather than the exception. Historically, at least, Spanish dialectology may be in for as much of a revision as English dialectology where the New World dialects are concerned. And a strong case for a change in synchronic procedures is made in Resnick (1968).

BLACK FRENCH

So far, there seems to be no reason to claim such widespread influence of Creole on New World French dialects as upon English and Spanish; but, then, New World French itself is by no means so widespread a phenomenon as New World English or Spanish. Interesting Canadian varieties, like Zoual, are strikingly un-Creole in structure and history. French Creole is known, however, in Haiti, Martinique, Guadaloupe, Marie Galante, Dominica, St. Lucia, French Guyana, and Louisiana. There are, in addition, such relatively well-studied varieties as Cajun, of Louisiana, and such not-so-well studied non-Creole varieties as the French of Frenchtown, Charlotte Amalie, St. Thomas (Virgin Islands) and that of St. Barth's.

It is, however, also known that Creole has influenced the French of the Caribbean and of Louisiana. Pompilus (1961) has studied Creole influence on the Standard French of Haiti, and Stewart (1962b) has shown the switching phenomena which provide a sociolinguistic background for that influence. In *Conjonction*, vol. 116 (1971), Pompilus and Gaillard ("Debat sur le Destin du Français en Haiti") discuss such matters. Pompilus maintains something of an enlightened purism (insisting, for example, that typical Haitian Creole loss of post-vocalic /r/ in *froid* may damage communication by producing homophony with *foie*), whereas Gaillard constantly maintains the complete autonomy of the Haitian varieties and lack of danger of "loss of communication". But even Pompilus does not deny the influence of Creole upon Haitian French.

In Louisiana, where French Creole (Gombo) coexists with Cajun and a relatively standard variety, intermediate varieties are not unknown. Morgan (1959, 1960) has studied decreolization in St. Martin Creole. Cajun and Creole interact enough so that folklore collectors can confuse the two.

In Louisiana and in Southeast Texas, where French Creole speakers can be found, the terminology gets confused. French- and creole-speaking informants whom I studied in Beaumont, Texas, gave me, when asked for "Creole", the most standard French of which they were capable. Asking for *mo couri, mo vini* (literally, 'I run/ran, I come/came') was the quickest way to get what the linguist calls Creole. And in Port Arthur, Texas, where the average white citizen is blatantly racist, asking a person if he is Cajun can motivate the furious answer, "Can't you see that I'm white?"

The early spread of Pidgin and Creole French, even in the United States, has not been investigated. The assumption has been that it was always limited to the Louisiana area. But Edward Larocque Tinker ("Gombo Comes to Philadelphia", *American Antiquarian Society Proceedings* 67, 1957, 50-76) provides what may be some counterevidence. *Idylles et Chansons, ou Essais de Poésie Créole, par un Habitant d'Hayti* was printed in Philadelphia in 1811. As Tinker points out

Long before gombo was printed in Louisiana, it had already appeared in type in Philadelphia ...

BLACK DUTCH

Perhaps least well known among the creoles, Dutch Creole (Negerhollands) has the most obscure history. Hancock (1969) has speculated that it is based upon Pidgin English, through supra-lexification; and there is evidence that he is correct. Hesseling (1905) quotes sentences like

Cabay ka saddel kaba, 'The horse has just been saddled'

wherein the subject and the 'function word' marker of recently completed action are obviously Romance — if not indisputably Portuguese. Crucial to this argument is, obviously, the thesis that Pidgin English is a re-lexification of the Portuguese Trade Pidgin (Stewart 1962a, Whinnom 1965).

The Virgin Islands Dutch Creole is reasonably well attested and described (Hesseling 1905, Josselin de Jong 1924). The so-called Danish Creole was — or is, perhaps, for a few surviving speakers — most likely Negerhollands with a few Danish lexical loans. Most treatments assume that the Dutch Creole was strictly confined to the Virgin Islands.

In "The Jersey Dutch Dialect" (1910), however, Prince clearly pointed out that members of the Dutch-speaking community in the New York-New Jersey area could distinguish Black speakers from white and could specify features of the Black dialect. The few sentences provided, from one aged Black informant, like

äk kän nît fässe xjesterdâx, 'I could not (lit. can not) fish yesterday' (p. 468), are at least consistent with what are generally accepted to be common creole structures. Prince reports that his informant "knew no past forms at all". This is, of course, often reported by investigators who examine a creole superficially while concentrating (as was Prince) upon a different variety of the 'same' language. Prince also points out that his other informants characterized many of the same informant's usages as *nêxer däuts*, and Prince believed that this evidence showed that "the negro slaves of the old settlers used an idiom tinged with their own peculiarities" (p. 460). Vanderbilt (1881) and Loon (1938) provide evidence, even somewhat less professionally linguistic, to the same effect.

It appears, thus, quite likely that Dutch Creole — whether or not originally on a Pidgin English base — was a vehicle of contact between Dutchmen and their Negro slaves, both in the Virgin Islands and in the New York-New Jersey area. The Pidgin-Creole tradition thus seems to have played an important part in the verbal repertoire of African-derived slaves everywhere in the New World. Insofar as the slaves had influence on the children of the master caste, their language varieties must have influenced other language varieties of the New World. So far, that influence has not been taken into account in the language history of the Americas.

Dutch Creole is the least likely of all the creoles to be significantly represented in surviving Black dialects within the continental United States. But its historical role is not necessarily so insignificant. Many of those cute Dutch words so characteristic of the Hudson valley area may have had transmission at least partly by Blacks, speakers of Negerhollands. Even *yankee* may be from Dutch — it has often been traced to *Jan Kees*. Early reports, like that of James Fenimore Cooper (*Redskins*, 1846) which called *yankee* part of a frontier *lingua franca* (see footnote 4 for discussion), associated it with American Indian Pidgin English. AIPE, in turn, seems to have been transmitted to the Indians by Black slaves (Dillard 1972: chapter IV).

In a part of the North, including the New York-New Jersey area and a part of Pennsylvania, AIPE and/or the frontier *lingua franca* shared a language of wider communication relationship and mutual influence with a variety of either German or Dutch. Beadle (*Western Wilds and the Men Who Redeem Them*, 1878) linked Black English, Pennsylvania "Dutch", and Pidgin English in a "Hoosier" contact language which extended as far as Indiana. Whether the New York-New Jersey Dutch, including *nêxer däuts*, was completely separate from Pennsylvania German has not really been investigated. If the reports of observers like Beadle can be substantiated, the pundits of dialect geography will have to reckon with more contact language influence and with more Black influence in the United States than they have wanted.

BLACK PORTUGUESE

To some extent, the failure to treat Black Portuguese directly is a function of the lack of experience of the writer. The weak excuse can be offered that, except for a small colony on Cape Cod, there is little direct evidence of the use of a contact variety of Portuguese within the continental United States, upon which this collection focuses. In the broader sense, according to one still-controversial theory (Voorhoeve 1973) all creoles — and, therefore, all the "Black" varieties under discussion — figure in the Portuguese Trade Pidgin and Portuguese Creole tradition (see the two articles by Christophersen, pp. 202-215). As indicated above, some of these (Palenquero, Papiamentu) are now considered to be varieties of Spanish. Portuguese Creole is spoken in Cape Verde (with the above-mentioned small colony in Cape Cod), Senegal, São Thomé, and Annabon. The "non-Black" varieties are of course omitted (see Hancock 1971). There is considerable evidence concerning what is probably a Creole or a decreolized variety in Brazil (Raimundo 1933, Neto 1950); but, for special reasons, it is beyond the scope of this book. The general study of the spread of the contact variety of Portuguese around the world has been given a firm foundation by David Lopes (*A Extensão do Português na Oriente*, Lisbon, 1936), but there has been little following up of this excellent beginning. Lopes does not identify his many attestations as pidgin and creole Portuguese, but they are obviously that.

THE "BLACK" LANGUAGE VARIETIES AND NEW
WORLD DIALECTOLOGY

The use of pidgin varieties, with rather frequent creolization, has played a much greater part in the development of New World varieties of European languages than has been admitted in conventional dialectology.[8] Much that has been conveniently lumped under "archaism" must now be reconsidered. It is, in fact, doubtful that anything in the "Black" varieties is meaningfully to be called a survival of archaic dialects.

If the Black dialects go, will the "white" varieties remain long behind

---

[8] See Dillard (1972: chapter IV; also "Language Contact in the American West", *Revista Interamericana*, 1972). Survivals of the contact languages tend to show up unexpectedly in special vocabularies, such as that of Northwestern loggers. McCulloch, *Woods Words, A Comprehensive Dictionary of Loggers' Terms* (1958), shows many terms from "Indian", which must mean Chinook Jargon. But he also includes *cumshaw*, which was widespread in the Pacific and which has been traced to a Chinese source. Although much work remains to be done, it is now clear that the contact languages (including Chinook Jargon and Pidgin English) were much more widespread and influential than is generally believed, even among professional historians of language.

for European archaism? Although more privileged migrants than the Blacks and the Indians, the whites were migrants (as well as immigrants) in the Americas. Fairly elaborate studies have been made of the European IMMIGRANT populations of the nineteenth and twentieth centuries. But the consequences of the MIGRANT status which the Europeans shared even with the aboriginal Indians (who WERE set to migrating) have not really been examined.

There seem to be special language varieties normally associated with migration, especially when there is a great deal of mixing of populations. If pidgins are normal in multilingual migrant situations, *koinés* are equally normal in multidialectal situations (Nida and Fehdereau 1970). A *koiné* for Spanish immigrants to the New World has been suggested by De Granda (1968b). There is a great deal of reason to believe that the "good" English and "English of astonishing classical purity" reported of the Americans by travellers (some of whom are cited in Reed 1933) indeed represented a *koiné*.[9] The same process has been reported for Australia (Bernard 1969), although of course the American and Australian *koinés* could not have been identical.

How can American English non-standard dialects (and perhaps those of American Spanish, etc.) be explained if not in terms of transmission of European "regional" dialects? Since Kurath (1928), workers on American English dialects have by and large assumed that all forms can be traced back to some part of the British Isles. This means, however, that some dialects (especially Black English) are, in the traditional formulation, strange amalgams. The very ingenuity of the system by which Form F_1 of Dialect D_1 can be traced to Yorkshire, Form F_2 of the same dialect to Scotland, and Form F_3 of that dialect to Ireland is in the end self-defeating.

Let us consider, however, the not especially innovative procedure of taking into account, for language history, first of all the reports of those who were on hand. If, as they report, the American colonists spoke English "of great classical purity", it seems unlikely that that English was formed from promiscuous mixing of forms from British "regional" dialects. This seems especially unlikely, since the early colonists formed their unions in terms of religious or political beliefs, rather than in terms of regional allegiance.

If we are to believe other reports — and, again, there is hardly any

---

[9] A few more such statements are cited in Read (1935). A typical statement is that of the Reverend Jonathan Boucher in a letter to the Reverend Mr. James Paddington, 23 December 1777: "It is still more extraordinary that, in North America, there prevails not only, I believe, the purest pronunciation of the English tongue that is anywhere to be met with, but a perfect Uniformity." ("Letters of Rev. Jonathan Boucher", *Maryland Historical Magazine* X, 1916:30).

other way of knowing what went on — the frontier was a special locus of "bad" English. We have statements like that of (later General) Ethan Allen Hitchcock, *A Traveller in Indian Territory*, recounting his experiences in the mid-nineteenth century, about the "prominent defects among our border people, West and South" in language. Now, the pidgin contact varieties were prominent in just those border areas; Hitchcock cites a great deal of American Pidgin English and tells of his Black Seminole interpreter Sambo. In "Our Provincialisms" (*Lippincott's Monthly Magazine*, March 1869, pp. 318-19) we find an impressionistic statement about the relationship between border English and AIPE:

"Heap," much used in the West for "a great many," or "very much," has naturally passed to the Indian tribes beyond the border. "He is a big man — heap big," says the Indian.

Since *heap* as a general intensifier belongs originally to the pidgin (*hipi* is still in English Creole usage in Surinam), the opposite historical relationship was probably true: western white English probably got it from the Indian.

Blacks were a large part of the border population in both South and West, bringing words like *buckaroo* into the cowboy language (Mason 1960). Pidgin and Creole languages have almost always been regarded by popular observers, like Hitchcock and the *Lippincott's* writer, as "bad" versions of European languages; every stage of Black English has been stigmatized as "bad" English by non-professional observers. Mixing of the pidgin and creole varieties with the "good" (here interpreted as *koiné*) English of the colonists may have been the greatest single factor in the development of American English non-standard dialects. Like the anonymous *Lippincott's* author, Eurocentric observers have always been disposed to see influence FROM the mainstream varieties TO the contact variety rather than VICE VERSA.

Outside of English, hardly any of the requisite research seems to have been done; but it may be that equivalent reports of "good" colonial usage can be found for other European languages in the New World, especially Spanish. See Toscano Mateus (1953) for a statement at least consistent with such an interpretation.

If these broad generalizations are substantially accurate (and there is reason to believe that they may be), then the received opinion about the history of New World dialects will need to be altered greatly. It may be necessary to deal in the social dynamics of migration, in mutual influences between the *koinés*, the pidgin/creole and other contact varieties, and the languages spoken by the aboriginal populations of the New World. Instead of expecting to find reflection of white settlement history, we may rather need to look for the cultural ties which survived into — and, especially, were forged in — the Americas. Except in the works of Herskovits and his followers, such ties, particularly as they involved African slaves, have been completely ignored. The fact that West Africans were thrown into *ad hoc* communities with members of other tribes who had been traditionally either strangers or enemies means that the studies of ties and survivals are especially difficult where that population is concerned. But difficulty is not impossibility, nor does it excuse the serious student from the effort involved.

Influence of Black language varieties on those of the European-derived population has been sporadically discussed (Dalby 1972, Dillard 1972: chapter V). Liberation of the Black dialects from Eurocentrism may be the first step in the eventual reevaluation of the white varieties. It may be possible to know the white speech communities of the New World better through the insights which we gain from studying the Black communities.

But the influence from the maritime pidgin tradition is not identical, by any means, to African influence. Tristan da Cunha is fairly safely outside the West African orbit, and Zettersten (1969) felt safe in judging its dialect "archaic". But as LePage's review (1971) points out, neither British archaic survivals nor "island universals" (Zettersten's term) explains away the many features held in common not only with St. Helena but also with Guyana and British Honduras. LePage admits that he has "attempted the same task for Jamaican Creole myself, and committed many of the same sins". What one learns from Afro-American situations may well apply elsewhere.

European dialectology itself may not be entirely unaffected. The Sabir/ Portuguese Trade Pidgin tradition which was so important in West Africa could not have failed to influence the Mediterranean. Bloomfield (1933: 330-31) quotes Kloeke (1927) on the influence of the Hanseatic League, strong enough to effect a major break in the German isoglosses based on settlement patterns. This maritime activity could be expected, *a priori*, to develop a trade language, somewhat like Sabir, for the North Sea. Barbot wrote of "Low Dutch" among the languages (including Lingua Franca) which one should learn before going to Africa and the Caribbean. Was that Low Dutch in some way related to the trade language of the Hanseatic League? Recent research has suggested that Negerhollands may have been based on Pidgin English (Hancock 1969 and discussion above). A Hanseatic-North Sea variety might, however, force some complication — even sophistication — in that evaluation. There are older, almost forgotten but still accessible studies like Baumann (1877) tracing the influence of the maritime trade language on dialects like Cockney.

Did the Mediterranean Lingua Franca itself come to the New World? There are tantalizing bits of evidence like

Nickaleer, no comerradoe Englishmen were not his friends

in Jonathan Dickinson's *Journal* of 1696-97 (p. 51), an account of his suffering among the Florida Indians on a disastrous trip from Port Royal, Jamaica, to Philadelphia with a load of slaves. This (except of course for *Nickaleer*) seems obviously Romance, but hardly Spanish. So does "totus (or all) Nickaleer" (p. 32), the words of the "Casseeky" (obviously *cacique*). Dickinson specifically relates how his success in communicating with the Indians was in direct relationship to their knowledge of Spanish. It may well be, however, that Spanish was simply the superposed variety in terms of which the contact variety ("bad Spanish") was evaluated.[10]

Survivals of African languages have been sternly minimized in our language histories since the beginning of the study of New World language. In a sense, African language influence would be a stronger threat to the formulation of migrating "regional" dialects than even the Sabir-Pidgin-Creole theory. Turner's *Africanisms in the Gullah Dialect* (1949) made it perfectly clear, however, that Africanisms could not be completely excluded, even from the continental United States. Dalby (1972) shows how such influence spread far beyond the Sea Islands.

Considering the unfavorable conditions under which the African languages had to exist in the New World, the aggregate evidence of the survivals is very great. Cabrera (all references) shows survivals of African language forms in ritual texts — not always intelligible, even to the reciter — in Cuba, and there are some hints of the same kind of usage in the *santería* ceremonies of Puerto Rico. Turner (1949:256-59) shows Mende and Vai recitations in the Sea Islands, however fragmentary their nature. More African survivals keep turning up. Maureen Warner ("Trinidad Yoruba — Notes on Survival", *Caribbean Quarterly*, 1971) cites considerable use of Yoruba on Trinidad, even at the present time. She considers (and this is most probable) that dialect mixing and leveling took place in the Yoruba of the New World. Yoruba survivals have also been reported in Brazil (Pierson 1967). It seems probable that the Yoruba

---

[10]   For further evidence of a contact variety (probably pidgin or creole) popularly, in its day, associated with Spanish, one might consider such American Southwesternisms as *lariat* (Spanish *la reata*) and *alligator* (*el lagarto*). Although these etymologies have long been known, there has apparently been no explanation of the process whereby the Spanish article became part of the noun stem (*the lariat, the alligator* being non-tautological in English). The same process is well known, however, to be involved in the relationship between creole languages and etymons derived from European source languages (Papiamentu *lareina* 'queen', not 'the queen'; Haitian Creole *lakay* 'house', not 'the house'). The same process produced the Louisiana term *lagniappe*, ultimately from Quechua *yapa* and the Romance article; again, *the lagniappe* is perfectly normal English. In the case of *lagniappe*, creole origin is perfectly clear (see entry in *Dictionary of Americanisms*).

varieties (and perhaps the Twi underlying the survivals in Jamaica reported by Cassidy 1961) represented non-native use of a coastal language by slaves brought in from the interior or from smaller coastal tribes.

The influence of the forces that work on languages in migration are everywhere in evidence in the New World — even in those relatively limited West African varieties which survive. Tracing back to a specific 'regional' dialect is — as Warner found — almost always impossible. The harsh but seemingly inevitable measure would be the elimination of the European-area-to-New-World procedures dear to the philological and reconstructive traditions. A few sputtering beginnings at the study of migration phenomena have been made in the past; the immediate future seems the ideal time to take those studies to the level of real accomplishment.

The decisions that the Blacks were imitators of European immigrants and that the Europeans themselves brought 'regional' varieties to the New World were made in dialectology before any appreciable part of the Black evidence was in. From these hastily formulated theories, it was deduced that investigation of Black populations would turn up no evidence contrary to the Eurocentric picture. Studies of Black language varieties were, therefore, not undertaken, except as Eurocentric or "whitewashing" operations (Brooks 1935; Williamson 1961, 1968). The creolists constituted the only exceptions to this rule; and their studies, for the most part, were safely distant, out in the islands.

But the application of the creolist techniques to the continental dialect picture brings about a strong contradiction of the conjectures made by the Eurocentrists. The most cautious statement which could be made at the present time would at least acknowledge that, if varieties like Palenquero and Cuijla keep turning up, a very different overview will be necessary. In North, South, and Central America, not to mention the Caribbean islands, there are still very many unexplored Black population groups.

THE SOCIOLOGICAL BACKGROUND OF BLACK SURVIVALS AND
DEVELOPMENTS IN THE NEW WORLD

It is not necessary to dwell on the more abstruse areas of sociolinguistics and of sociology in order to point out the errors which characterized the pitifully little and absurdly restricted study which had been devoted to the English of the Negro in the United States (always excepting Turner's Gullah studies) before the mid-1960's. Pickford (1956) (the first selection reprinted here) deals with some of the relatively technical deficiencies of American dialect geography, which, until recently, dominated American dialect studies. But simple blunders — like Davis's assertion, cited above, that all Northern Blacks are in that geographic area because of migration from the South in the past two generations — abound.

Perhaps the most basic misorientation of all has been due to the idealism which substituted for research and for the attitudes basic to research. Krapp's "The English of the Negro" (1924) congratulated (!) the Black on having attained exactly the same dialects as the white. There is, of course, considerable question as to whether the Blacks should feel flattered. But Krapp was basically guided not by a desire to be ingratiating to Blacks nor by the results of any research but by a simple-minded assimilationism which assumed that the melting pot MUST have been effective. At that, Krapp was not the worst of the students of the English of the Negro; his historical studies, collecting attestations of what he would continue to call "literary dialect", had made him suspect that it had not always been so. More naive students simply assumed, in the absence of any evidence except the somewhat ambiguous advertisements for escaped slaves, that the West African slaves had acquired an exact copy of the speech of their masters without a trace of the interference or contact language phenomena which are found in other such occasions of language shift and which are abundantly attested in the records, fictional and nonfictional.

The source of this attitude is Kurath (1928 and 1936, repeated in 1965) who imported the notions of internal reconstruction and of basically geographic distribution to the United States at about the time of the founding of the *Linguistic Atlas of the United States and Canada*. Although he can be partly excused on the grounds that studies like Dollard (1937) and Berreman (1961) were not available when his first articles were published, Kurath (1936) presents what is surely one of the most naive suppositions ever made in any professional statement:

Since folk speech and cultivated speech are very close together in recently settled and democratically organized America and since there is a constant give and take between the ill-defined class dialects ... (p. 19).

There seems, however, to be reason to believe that the *Linguistic Atlas of the United States and Canada* acted from the first in accordance with Kurath's belief in "democratically organized America" and that it assumed that the "constant give and take" of social equals took place between Black and white from the eighteenth century to the present.

To point up the flaw in this reasoning, it is hardly necessary to cite more than the most commonplace facts about American racial history. "Democratically organized America" was the locus — primarily, but by no means exclusively, in the South — of a Black/white caste division in many ways as clearly demarcated as those of India. Since Gumperz (1958) has shown how caste factors can sustain dialect differences, even

in conditions of great density of communication, there seems to remain
no theoretical objection to the possibility of cultural and linguistic differences between ethnic groups in the United States. Historians of jazz
and the blues (LeRoi Jones, Marshall Stearns, Frederick Ramsey, Harold
Courlander, Paul Oliver, and many others), folklorists (Roger Abrahams,
Alan Lomax, Arthur Huff Fauset, Zora Neale Hurston, and many others
including the great Melville J. Herskovits), and historians of the dance
(Stearns 1968) have shown how Black cultural differences in many areas
have remained until the present time. Language studies have lagged
dreadfully.

The sociopolitical reasons for such a lag have been given exemplary
description in Stewart's "Sociopolitical Issues in the Linguistic Treatment
of Negro Dialect" (1970). There is probably no need to recapitulate them
here. The one unanswered question seems to be why such inhibitions
have been more repressive in the area of language than in other areas like
folklore and music. It may be impossible to answer such a question
without making embarrassing statements about the relative talents of the
researchers in the respective fields.

But many sociological, historical, and sociolinguistic questions remain
to be asked. There is, always, the question of the relationship of Blacks
to other disadvantaged immigrant groups in the Americas like the Chinese
— or about the relationship of both to the Indians.[11] Pidgin languages,
and such common social factors as enslavement, were shared, in the early
days, by Black and Indian. The Chinese who came later used Pidgin
English, and the status of the poorest of them was little better than slave
labor. Intermarriage (including the broader, common law sense of that
term) was also more commonplace between these 'colored' populations
than between them and the whites. Use of Pidgin or Creole English
between Blacks and Indians (in this case, the Trio) is attested from Surinam (Goeje 1906) to Nova Scotia.

A priori considerations have greatly hindered research. Writers like
Pfaff (1971) have assumed that no general Plantation Creole could have

---

[11] See Dillard (1972: chapter IV). Concerning the minority groups, there are revealing
statements in the works of historians like Jack D. Forbes, *Nevada Indians Speak*
(1967) and Samuel Eliot Morrison, *The Maritime History of Massachusetts* (1961).
The latter quotes Chinese to Bostonians: "You and I olo flen; you belong honest man
only no get chance ... Just now have settee counter. All finishee; you go, you please"
(p. 65). "Too muchee strong gale; sea all same high mast head — no can see sky" (p.
78).

Foster Rhea Dulles, *The Old China Trade* (1930), says explicitly: "During this period
[1784] the sole medium of communication between the Chinese and their visitors was
that queer jargon known as Pidgin English."

Dulles's footnote is even more revealing: "The dialect largely made up of English
words, with some Portuguese and Chinese embellishments" (p. 20).

developed in the continental United States, on the grounds that the slave owners would not have permitted interaction between Blacks on different plantations. Against this, we have specific documentation like the letter of Governor Nicholson on 20 August 1668 (quoted in Henry F. Thompson, "Maryland at the End of the Seventeenth Century", *Maryland Historical Magazine* II, 1907:165):

... Their [the Negro slaves'] common practice is on Saturday nights and Sundays, and on 2 or 3 days in Christmas, Easter and Whitsuntide is to go and see one another tho' at 30 or 40 miles distance. I have, several times both in Virginy and here met negros, both single and 6 or 7 in Company in the night time. The major part of the negroes speak English, and most people have some of them as their domestic servants & the better sort have 6 or 7 in those circumstances, and may be not above one English. And they send the Negro men and boys about the Country where they have business: and they wait on them to all publick places, so that by these means they know not only the public but private roads of the country and circumstances thereof.

There is much more evidence of the same type, both from the United States (continental colonies)[12] and from the West Indies.[13]

Other well-known phenomena, like the marriages of slaves from different plantations,[14] show how false a viewpoint is which makes each plantation separate and a law unto itself. Cruelty and repression were all

[12] For interesting stratagems used by slaves on adjoining plantations to communicate without the knowledge of their masters, see the notes to *Ethnic Folkways Library Album* no. FE 4417. The classical reference for the slaves' assembling in public and engaging in African behavioral patterns is of course George Washington Cable's "The Dance in the Place Congo" (*Century Magazine*, 1886, reprinted many times). That slaves were regularly required to have passes to leave their plantations, that the infamous "paterollers" pursued those who did not have them, and that many injustices were associated with the system is too commonplace to need documentation. (See collections like Botkin, *Lay My Burden Down*, 1945, p. 6 *et passim*.)
[13] There is a convenient collection of such documents in Jerome S. Handler and Charlotte J. Frisbie, "Aspects of Slave Life in Barbados: Music and Its Cultural Context", *Caribbean Studies* 11 (1972): 5-46. See also Elsa V. Goveia, *Slave Society in the British Leeward Islands at the End of the Eighteenth Century*, especially pp. 235-40.
[14] Documented examples are superabundant, but not everyone who has written on the subject has bothered to consult the documents. This lack is especially characteristic of the speculative psycholinguists who have written about Black English.
Harriet Beecher Stowe's *The Key to Uncle Tom's Cabin* (Arno Press reprint, 1968, part III, chapter VI) cites the case of Milly Edmondson, a slave, married to Paul, a freedman, at the insistence of her owners. In the life story of Josiah Henson (reprinted in Harvey Wish, *Slavery in the South*, 1964), we read "After the sale of my father by Newman, Dr. McPherson would no longer hire out my mother to him. She returned, accordingly, to his estate." There are many such accounts of marriage of slaves to freedmen and to slaves on other plantations in the accounts of ex-slaves in collections like Botkin's *Lay My Burden Down* (1945). Greene (1942) has a great deal on intermarriage of Negro slaves and Indians.

too much a part of slavery, but the serious student cannot afford to ignore other relationships and other processes.[15] Yet, in recent years, it has been the tendency of enthusiastic but misguided liberalism to factor out everything except repression from the study of slavery. Such institutions as the Underground Railroad were possible at least partly because of widespread Black communication networks not shared with whites. We have excellent studies like those of Fisher (1953), but too many of our studies of slavery and its results substitute preconception for history.

As yet, distressingly little is known about the Black use of the contact varieties of European languages in communicating with other minority groups like the Indians. Thanks to Taylor's excellent study (1951), much is known about that interesting mixed group the Black Carib of Honduras and about its associated groups; but we still know too little about linguistic relationships between Blacks and Indians in the early days on St. Vincent, from which the slaves came to Honduras. The priority of attestations of the use of Pidgin English (Leechman and Hall 1955) and Pidgin French (Goodman 1964) by Indians in the New World has been used as support of the argument that typical European patterns of communicating with "inferior" populations were of primary importance in the development of the creoles (see, especially, Hall 1966), but that evidence may simply indicate the degree of linguistic sharing between Blacks and Indians. Even in New York, cooperative resistance by Black and Indian was high on the list of problems faced by slave owners (Ottley and Weatherby 1967: 21-22). For the Florida Seminole-Black relationships, see Dillard (1972: chapter IV). Although a really thorough study devoted entirely to this matter does not seem to exist, Greene's "The Negro in Colonial New England" (1942) contains excellent and revealing materials on Black-Indian social relationships. Even Prince's (1910) *nêxer däuts* New Jersey informant was part Minsi Indian.

In Puerto Rico, where (as sketchily indicated above) the study of the possible Black Spanish variety remains almost entirely to be done, it has often been asserted that the Indians died out within the early years of the sixteenth century. Yet Puerto Rican folk belief persistently ascribes "Indian" heritage to a certain part of its population. "India" is a popular nickname for girls who have Amerindian features, and virtually any Puerto Rican can confidently point out people whom he regards as being Indian in appearance. It may well be that population mixture like that reported by Greene (1942) for colonial New England complicated the

---

[15] Cultural contributions to the New World by African slaves were noted as early as 1721 (Cotton Mather, *The Angel of Bethesda*). Occasional references to such contributions can be found even in very traditional works like Philip A. Bruce, *Economic History of Virginia in the Seventeenth Century* (1896).

"extermination" of the Puerto Rican aborigines. *Tainismo* and *Africanismo* have long been competitors on Puerto Rico, as their equivalents have been elsewhere in Latin America; but they could easily become allies within the Pidgin-Creole tradition. Needless to say, the necessary work on this synthesis remains to be done.

But the most pressing need of all is for a general overview.[16] As long as individual geographic areas, like the American South, are considered without reference to other sections into which essentially the same slave population was brought, like the Caribbean, the linguistic developments peculiar to the slave community can be lost in European archaism because more attention by far is given to the language of the white majority. But it is the merest commonplace that slaves brought to the United States (or to the continental colonies) often went through staging areas in the West Indies. In fact, it should not be forgotten that slavery in the early United States was a relatively minor branch of a trade which extended from Brazil to Nova Scotia, coming from West Africa and including the Caribbean.[17] Concentration on the South, without reference to other areas, also allows for the unsubstantiated assumption that any Black language varieties must be exclusively Southern phenomena. Only through the exaggeration of such tendencies can it be sustained that British 'regional' varieties were transferred to the South, where the Negroes first imitated the whites exactly and then maintained that imitation (still, apparently, in an unaltered state) after its forms had become archaic or even obsolete in Southern white speech. Lack of knowledge of demographic patterns permits the further assumption that those 'archaic Southern' patterns were then carried to the Northern ghettos.

We have seen the shaping of the linguistic myth, which is still a lively one. Replacing it with more accurate formulations is still largely a job for the future. Some of the groundwork for the more responsible formulation has been done by the scholars whose work is represented in the following pages. There are, obviously, omissions. It is especially regretted that nothing from the works of Lorenzo Dow Turner or of Melville J. Herskovits could be included. Perhaps the latter could be considered to be represented in some way by the inclusion of my own

---

[16] Herskovits's *The Myth of the Negro Past* (1941), the book which did most to establish the need for such an overview, is, almost paradoxically, the work which comes closest to accomplishing it. Szwed and Whitten (eds.), *Afro-American Anthropology: Contemporary Perspectives* (1970), carries on the Herskovitsian approach. Unfortunately, dialectology has nothing even roughly comparable to those works.

[17] For onomastic reflexes of cultural continuity in the slave trade in the Americas, see Dillard "The West African Day Names in Nova Scotia", *Names* (1971). Among other things, interchange of slaves between Nova Scotia and Surinam (with two-way traffic in at least a few cases) is documented.

(1964) paper, a kind of appreciation of the work of the then recently deceased Herskovits. If Turner does not have that much direct representation, it still should be remembered that none of this would have been possible without his *Africanisms in the Gullah Dialect*.

Yeshiva University

Section I: Black English Dialectology: Theory, Method

INTRODUCTION TO SECTION 1

Academically, the chief barrier to the recognition of Black American English has been the influence exerted by the dialect geographers who, following Kurath (1928, 1936, 1965), have insisted that variation in American English MUST be more closely correlated with regional than with other factors. Upon examination, one must conclude that this preconception, no matter how influential it has been upon American academic life, is simply false. In fact, those who have worked on Black English and its relationship to other dialects have come increasingly to assign less importance to regional factors. In terms of general theory of dialect variation, there has been the important work of Gumperz (1958) and Labov (1965). But Gumperz, who has some claim to priority in the study of dialect and social stratification, acknowledged an important debt to a predecessor, Glenna Ruth Pickford.

Pickford's fine critical article finds the *Linguistic Atlas* work deficient in significance, validity, and reliability. She points out that the assumption that variation in American English is primarily regional, based as it is on prior work with long-settled European populations, simply does not take into account what sociologists have found out about American behavioral patterns. She is especially critical of *Atlas'* failure to take advantage of great advances in sampling theory. Perhaps the only lack which another avowed critic of *Atlas* techniques can point out in Pickford's criticism is her failure to note that cartographic techniques could be developed which were much better than the old isogloss maps. (More recently, such new techniques have been used in studies like Resnick 1968.) In sum, Pickford provided an almost complete theoretical background for the study of dialects of American English which correlated with social factors like ethnic group membership. Although she said nothing about Black English, work in that area would have been much more difficult without her contribution.

No direct rebuttal to Pickford's criticism was ever attempted by the *Atlas* group, beyond claims like that of Davis (1971) that Pickford had confused population sampling techniques with dialect sampling techniques. Assertions like that of Davis that recognition of representative informants could be left to the judgment of dialect geographers are, of course, counter to all sociolinguistic theory. Failure to profit from Pickford's criticism may be the single greatest indication of the poor state of American dialect geography in the mid-twentieth century.

Meanwhile, aside from the researchers into Black English and the few others mentioned above, scholars like Hattori (1964), Blanc (1964), and Bernard (1969) have been providing examples of how dialectology need not be merely a spatial matter — and how, further, it need not be merely a propping up of "horizontal" geographic factors with "vertical" factors of social stratification. A more modern dialectology will seemingly have to consider factors like age, sex, class/caste, professional and religious affiliation, topic, interlocutor, and ethnic group membership — each of these at least potentially as important as narrowly geographic considerations.

Although she said nothing about the American Black population, Pickford provided the theoretical framework within which creolists like Stewart and syntactic dialectologists like Loflin and Luelsdorff could establish the autonomy (in Luelsdorff's words, independence) of the dialect of a great majority of the Black population in the United States. Stewart's public lectures, beginning around 1964, made very forcibly the point that not only an ethnically-related dialect (which he called Negro Non-Standard English and which has more recently been called Black English) but also a media-related dialect (which he called Network Standard) could exist in the United States. Most of the controversy has, of course, centered around the former; but the latter concept is no less revolutionary as an approach to social dialectology.

Loflin, Luelsdorff, and Fickett have been concerned with the technical details and theoretical considerations involved in writing a grammar of Black English. Loflin, particularly, was involved, as a transformational-generative linguist, in the controversy over whether a dialect of English could differ from other dialects by syntactic — and not only by phonological — rules. Loflin steadfastly maintained the possibility of syntactic differences (1967, 1969, 1970), even in the face of what was at one time considerable disapproval from the mainstream of transformational grammarians. Although Loflin took no sides in the creolist controversy, his conclusions did agree with those of creolists like Stewart in many general ways. The common parts of their otherwise often highly divergent positions held that, while "mainstream" English (including white non-standard) dialects probably had not diverged from each other syntactically since Middle English times, the pidgin/creole related Black English (belonging to what Stewart, 1965, called a "quasi-foreign language" tradition) had diverged greatly. No one who is aware that Saramaccan is called an English-based Creole could be surprised that there are rather deep differences within that tradition.

Joan G. Fickett approached the problem of the language of inner city children from neither a creolist nor a transformational-generative position. An anthropological linguist in an older American tradition, she concentrated on internalizing the language structures before analyzing them. In this she agreed, by and large, with Stewart, except that she worked in the classrooms and halls of her junior high school (Fickett 1970), whereas Stewart depended upon even less formal contact with younger children. It is amazing that the work of Stewart and of Fickett agrees as often as it does with that of Loflin and Luelsdorff, since their theoretical orientations were so greatly different.

Luelsdorff, like Loflin, insisted upon working with one informant in an office interview situation, although of course he "soaked up intuition" by contact with the Black community in less official capacities. Loflin, Luelsdorff, Stewart, and Dillard — members of the Urban Language Study of the District of Columbia — have thus been left open to charges of laxity in sampling procedures — a situation which, on the surface, seems to contradict their function within the post-Pickford tradition. Labov, Cohen, Robins, and Lewis (1968) and Shuy, Fasold, and Wolfram (all references) were able to utilize more thorough sampling procedures. Although there are differences, their results in many ways resemble those of the original *Urban Language Study* group. And if that group was more naive statistically than Fasold (1972), it was far beyond his data collection procedures, relying as they do upon adult informants in an ultra-formal situation.[1]

[1] Fasold reports that "The interviews were conducted in a variety of circumstances, all of them rather formal" (1972:27) and that "The studio-recorded interviews may have caused some speakers to use a more formal style than they would have in a field-recorded interview, but such an effect was not obvious" (1972:27).

Such impressionistic statements accord poorly with the claims often made by Fasold and his associates that their works are "technical" whereas works of others (especially Stewart) are "non-technical". In a dialect situation in which the importance of child informants has frequently been stressed, it is disconcerting to read "Children were not included in these comparisons ... because children can be expected to be the least sensitive to the social effects of language" (Fasold 1972:26-27). Again, one cannot help being reminded of the tendency of the *Linguistic Atlas* projects to seek out adult and even elderly informants.

The analytical procedures of all the linguists mentioned in the last paragraph were all superior to the lackadaisical taxonomy of the *Linguistic Atlas of the United States and Canada*, and thus all of them add something to American dialectology. The older system is woefully represented by Williamson (1968). Although her data include, on two representative pages

> It be kind of complicated
> They're made their mistake
> They be doing
> If you be talking
> He going
> They coming
> If you trying to
> If you telling a story (p. 39).
> We do be out
> It don't be enough
> I don't be paying attention
> They be done cut your head off[2]
> Everybody done seen you
> I done forget (p. 40).

Williamson found that

Most of the grammatical patterns which they [Negro high school students in Memphis, Tennessee] use are found in standard or substandard [sic!] Southern English. (Documentary Resumé)

With fourteen control sentences like those above, Loflin could write rules which would show very clearly the differences between Black English and other varieties. And Fickett (1970) could have told Williamson a great deal about the differences between even junior high school students and those "bilinguals" who had found their way to the dizzy level of high school. The only way in which these scholars would have agreed with Williamson is that they all found it necessary to collect data from some source other than the records of the *Linguistic Atlas of the United States and Canada*. Thus all of the investigators herein discussed (even Williamson) are to some degree Pickfordians.

---

[2] Williamson describes the sequence *be done cut* as one of "three instances of *done* being used as an auxiliary" (1968:40). Thus, the complex situation in which both *be* and *done* are preverbal auxiliaries escapes her analysis.

 Williamson has frequently, in this and other works, responded to amateur (or straw man professional) observers who would assert that Negro speech is structureless. Ironically, by ignoring the structural complexity of such verb phrases — as well as by utilizing impossibly outmoded models of linguistic analysis — she provides some ammunition for just those observers.

GLENNA RUTH PICKFORD

AMERICAN LINGUISTIC GEOGRAPHY:
A SOCIOLOGICAL APPRAISAL

Long-term research projects cannot escape the risk of becoming antiquated in design before their completion. Some linguistic atlases are
notorious examples. The linguistic atlas of Germany, data for which
were collected from 1879 to 1888 on a scale that practically ruled out
publication, did not see the appearance of the first printed maps until 1926,
and after not very many fascicles, its publication is now being suspended,
with the method of the work a good two generations behind the times.

The *Linguistic Atlas of the United States and Canada*, being a human
enterprise, has not been immune to the same dangers. Conceived in 1929,
it began with New England, and the impressive tomes devoted to that
region appeared, together with a useful handbook, in the latter 1930's.
Field work has also been completed for the entire Eastern United States
and, though unpublished, has been utilized for concrete studies (Kurath
1949, Atwood 1953); the remainder of the area is still to be covered. We
are dealing, then, with a time span of at least 27 years, a period in which
sociological techniques and the understanding of American society has
advanced in a decisive way. Consequently, it is not too surprising that
while many linguists are dismayed by the pre-structural design of the
American *Atlas*, a sociologist is beset by grave doubts as to the validity
and reliability of procedures used in it.

There is another source of misgiving. While the science of language
may be entitled to theoretical and methodological autonomy, it will be
granted that such branches of linguistics as dialect study are motivated
and evaluated by the contribution they can make to the understanding

Reprinted with permission from *Word* 12 (1956), 211-29.

of broader sociocultural diversities and unities (Weinreich 1954:397f.). In Europe, dialect study has helped to supply answers to important questions of human geography (Dominian 1915:401-39; Roedder 1926:281-92; Bloomfield 1933: 321-45; Bottiglioni 1954:375-87). But geography is only one factor reflected in linguistic diversity (Hertzler 1953:115); in America, it is NOT the most important (Dieth 1948; Shevky and Bell 1955: 22). The preoccupation with geography at the expense of other dimensions of dialectal diversity makes one suspect that American linguistic geography originated as a somewhat mechanical imitation of European approaches. To put it bluntly, American linguistic geography has expended vast energies in order to supply answers to unimportant, if not to nonexistent, questions. Is it surprising that the social scientists who were expected to take an interest in the findings of the *Atlas* have been so unresponsive (McDavid 1946:168)? If the study of American English is to contribute to the knowledge of America, it must address itself, as McDavid seems to suggest (1946:168-72), to such questions as the political structure of American society, differences and interrelationships between rural and urban communities, changes in the size and organization of the family, linguistic snobbery, and a wealth of other aspects of American social life (see e.g. Hertzler 1953). In other parts of the world comparable questions are also coming more and more to outrank regional diversity in importance, so that the potential methodological achievements of a modernized, sociologically-minded American dialectology would find important applications in other languages as well.

1. IMPROVING RESEARCH PROCEDURE

In its procedures, existing American linguistic geography falls short of the standards of social-science inquiry. Geographers of language are vulnerable to the charge that they have failed to use the best available methods for testing theories. The technique of sampling, developed within the past twenty years into a highly responsible scientific method, offers a number of lessons for dialect study. Linguists, like sampling theorists, agree that it is seldom possible to gather or manipulate a complete body of information, and therefore it has become customary to utilize a partial count and to reach conclusions about the whole from analysis of the small representative selection, or sample. But sampling theory has gone a long way in refining its concepts and techniques (Hagood 1941; Cantril 1944; McNemar 1949; Garrett 1953; Cochran 1953). It has been demonstrated that the success of a sample survey depends greatly upon disciplined control which linguistic geographers have not always exercised; this has resulted in error. Existing dialect studies are full of the two main types of mistakes in sample surveys, errors of validity and errors of reliability, despite the fact that sampling experts and statisticians have designed techniques to eliminate or reduce such errors (Deming 1944).

Validity, in this context, has to do with the initial problem of asking the right questions. When planning a survey, experts with deep and thorough knowledge of the subject must decide exactly what is wanted. The scientific method of sampling emphasizes that the very first step is to determine the significance of the study, for to elicit irrelevant information is a waste of effort and money. "The requirement of a plain statement of what is wanted (the specification of the survey) is perhaps one of the greatest contributions of modern theoretical statistics" (Deming 1950:3). Many a proposed survey has not gone beyond the planning stage because valid questions were not being asked.

Secondly, validity involves the problem of how to draw out the needed information. This problem is the joint province of the statistician, the psychologist, and the expert in the subject (the experienced observer and the man of judgment), who must work together to determine the construction of the questionnaire, the technique of the interview, and the administration of field work. Biases arising from the interview or the questionnaire can be eliminated by skillful planning and preliminary testing (Deming 1950). American linguistic geographers have failed to employ indispensable technical assistance in the formulation of their survey plans, and invalidity is the unfortunate result.

Reliability is concerned with gathering a representative, unbiased selection of data, and procedures used in linguistics to this day justify an elementary review of the subject. To achieve a reliable sample two general procedures of sampling are in use. The random, or probability, sample is an automatic plan which virtually eliminates biases of selection, nonresponse, and estimation. Statistical formulae, based on the mathematical theory of probability, have been devised to calculate the sampling errors. The other procedure, the judgment sample, is an attempt to gather representative data by using informed judgment to determine which units are typical. In this procedure biases and sampling errors cannot be calculated mathematically; they must be estimated. It is important not to confuse the two types of sampling procedures, as linguists, it will appear below, do. For the judgment sample is not amenable to statistical analysis as is the probability sample. Each is an accepted method in its own right; each has its own proper uses and checks. The probability sample is reliable only if conducted faithfully and rigorously, and it is the type predominantly used in large-scale government surveys. The judgment sample is only as reliable as is the combined judgment of those who plan and execute it, and it is the type ordinarily used in small surveys of a preliminary nature (Deming 1950).

Basically, of course, all surveys partake indispensably of judgment, of knowledge and wisdom in the choice of the problem, in the wary design of the questionnaire, and in the final assessment. The difficulties of achieving validity are the same for both types of sample survey. Only in the search for reliability do the two types diverge: the automatic sample vs. the judicious selection.

Errors of Validity

From the point of view of validity, the questionnaire, interview, and evaluation of the surveys of the American *Atlas* are defective (Dieth 1948). The dialectologists' own cautions do not save their work from this criticism.

The needlessly formidable length of the questionnaire, by discouraging participation, has increased the important problem of nonresponse. Bloch (1935) gives an account of the difficulties of inducing persons to grant an interview ten to twelve hours long. Alexander in his discussion of similar difficulties (1940:42) remarks that one informant became deaf during the interview and one died.

Ambiguity of definition, where the use of a pictorial device might have clarified the meaning (see e.g. Sapon 1953:65), has resulted in erroneous answers (Reed 1954:9-10).

The wording of the items in the work sheets ... to some extent determined the method of inquiry and hence, also, in a measure, the response ... All distortions of the material due to formulation of the item are scrupulously noted in the commentaries (Kurath 1939:47).

The lack of systematic checks has permitted wrong answers to go undetected, except as the individual interviewer has happened to notice them. Questionable responses

... ... must be viewed with skepticism, since memory, politeness and the desire to appear to best advantage play tricks with informants, especially with older people. Sometimes an affirmative answer is given to a suggestion merely to get the matter out of the way, and the field worker is left in doubt (Kurath 1939:46).

Particularly important has been the failure to design a questionnaire adequate to the "double standard" (Alexander 1940:44) problem. The bias of the auspices has called forth a self-conscious speech, "English teacher's English", which technical precautions might have controlled by skillful checks. The precautions of the *Atlas* have gone no further than this:

Conversational forms are especially valuable ... for certain sounds or words on which the schools and the educated or would-be educated have focused their attention and which therefore pass as social shibboleths. In such cases direct inquiry may put the informant on guard and lead him to use the 'better' pronunciation instead of his natural and habitual one (Kurath 1939:45).

On the contrary, conversation is necessarily kept at a minimum in an interview requiring roughly ten hours for the questionnaire alone. While no questionnaire is expected to be perfect, and all are difficult to design, it is not too much to expect routine precautions. For the future, professional assistance of sampling experts is available (Deming 1947, 1950).

Interviewing for the *Atlas* failed to obtain valid information, not only because a faulty questionnaire was used, but because field workers lacked professional training in interviewing techniques. The planners of the New England Atlas tried to avoid biases due to the interviewer by issuing detailed "Instructions for Field Work". The lack of professional guidance is apparent in some of the instructions:

5. Do not suggest a response by asking, 'Do you say so-and-so?' until all other methods are exhausted. If the response is secured by direct suggestion, prefix *sug.* to it ... If the informant lacks the information, ask someone else in the house or in the community. *All responses secured from an auxiliary informant must be starred* ... (Kurath 1939:48).

Any suggestion to the person being interviewed introduces a bias, not to just one question, but to the whole interview (Cantril 1944). The inclusion of response from a person other than the selected informant also introduces a bias in the returns (Deming 1944). The *Atlas* designers have failed also to appreciate the importance of other errors of the interview arising inadvertently from the interviewer, such as "fatigue bias, or dilution bias, whereby an interviewer... fails to note a characteristic that appears infrequently..." (Deming 1950:29). Since sampling experts anticipate these and try to provide checks for them, consultation with them might favor future work.

Variations arising from different interviewers in a corps were recognized by the editors of the New England *Atlas*, who found that their precautionary training was insufficient protection against this type of error:

A common training period of 6 weeks in the summer of 1931 did much to standardize the practice of field workers, but it would be wrong to assume that earlier habits of observation and notation and the effects of earlier differences in training were actually eliminated (Kurath 1939:52).

The editors did not realize that training sometimes introduces a mass bias instead of eliminating the presence of error (Deming 1950:43). Accredited techniques of instruction and control, determined by consultation with sampling authorities and psychologists, should have been employed instead of amateur advice. It has been characteristically narrow of linguistic geographers to insist on training in phonemics and transcription (Frank 1948), while ignoring other at least equally necessary qualifications.

Errors of administration, in both the planning and execution of the *Linguistic Atlas*, have been numerous. Dieth (1948) questions the comparability of the collected data. Interpretation of the findings would not be so complicated if the planning period had ironed out many ambiguities of approach and question, so that the final data would be subjected as little as possible to error.

Field workers differ considerably in their efforts to record synonyms and semantically related terms. Some are content with the first response ... others suggest additional terms rather freely ... others again secure additional terms by talking about the subject matter .... Moreover, the field workers' practice varies from item to item .... The seeming uniformity ... must not be taken at face value, but must sometimes be interpreted in the light of observations made by the editors in the commentary (Kurath 1939:47).

A survey must be planned and executed throughout in anticipation of the evaluation (Deming 1950). Yet a linguistic geographer has ventured the excuse that analysis and interpretation are not properly the subject of an *Atlas* survey (DeCamp 1953:5f.). Failing to plan for a consistent analysis, the editors of the *Atlas* have attempted to evaluate many variables impressionistically. In one survey it was admitted that evidence which could not be easily accounted for was avoided (DeCamp 1953: ch. IX).

The complexity of linguistic problems makes desirable the use of random sampling, in which the techniques of multiple and net correlation would allow comparison of relationships between many variables, such as age, sex, class, occupation, education, region, etc. (Garrett 1953). It cannot be arbitrarily assumed that linguistic features are distributed regionally or by educational levels, when other social factors, probably more influential, have not been controlled, analyzed, and correlated. (See the twelve-way breakdown of such factors in Kinsey 1948:ch. III.)

Errors of Reliability

The professed purpose of the investigators of the *Linguistic Atlas* is to determine scientifically the regional and social variations in American English (Kurath 1949:Preface). Later appended to this purpose is an intention of providing an index to American speech useful to the revision of educational curricula (Marckwardt 1952). To accomplish these large aims, it is necessary that the language samples be accurately representative of the speech of the total population. Unfortunately, the samples of the *Linguistic Atlas* have not achieved this reliability. The linguistic geographers are not measuring what they seek to measure.

The samples of the *Linguistic Atlas* project suffer chiefly from biases of selectivity. As shown below in section II, there has been selection of culturally subordinate communities for investigation, so that the data gathered are insufficiently representative of the dominant urban centers of America. There has also been selection of the elderly strata of the population, so that the data tend to be archaic and provincial, not in present currency. There has been selection of the most stable element of a population which is characteristically mobile. And there has been selection from three educational levels, so that existing social classes are not proportionately represented. These biases of selection are important enough to invalidate the results of the surveys.

As is well recognized, information obtained from one segment of the population may not be valid for another segment .... Ascription of the characteristics and opinions of the people interviewed to the people not interviewed is dangerous if selection of the sample is influenced by willingness to respond, convenience of the interviewer, or the fulfillment of quotas (Deming 1947:152).

The conclusion, therefore, that regional variations are strongly entrenched in American speech does not rest on scientific proof but is a mere projection of the ill-judged presupposition with which the *Atlas* surveys began. The surveys of linguistic geography distort the picture of American speech by selecting communities, informants, and data which magnify the degree — and thus the importance — of regional variations.

The biases of availability in the *Linguistic Atlas* are evident in various accounts of the difficulties in finding qualified informants and in persuading them to cooperate. Skilled assistance of psychologists in the planning period would have avoided such biases as choosing only persons of "sympathetic intelligence", who were "hospitable, honest, self-confident in personal character" (Bloch 1935:3-4). It has become an axiom of anthropology that the unusual informant responds, for the anthropologists are aware, although the linguists are not, of distortion of data from unrepresentative informants. Sampling experts at the same time would have guarded against the chains of contact which were usual in finding informants: town clerk, welfare department officials, school teachers, ministers, physicians, librarians, storekeepers, idlers (Bloch 1935:5). Some awareness of this particular bias is seen in the cautions exercised in recent *Atlas* research, in which no two informants are taken through the same source and no three even indirectly (DeCamp 1953:10-11).

A common misconception among linguistic researchers is that sampling biases can be compensated for by increasing the size of the sample (Davis 1949:44; Reed and Spicer 1952:359; Atwood 1953:Preface). This practice is again the result of thoughtlessness or unfamiliarity with sampling theory. Most biases are not removed or diminished simply by increasing the size of the sample. The important specification in a sample survey, to insure reliability, is not how many, but how, informants are selected (Deming 1947:152; 1950:17).

Although the judgment sample is especially liable to biases which affect reliability, major error can be avoided during the planning period by employing mathematicians, sociologists, and persons who know the community by experience to correct the grossest misunderstandings of stratification. Of course the fact is that no selection by stratification can take the place of automatic selection. While it is possible to lay out even a judgment survey with provision for measuring the sampling error empirically (Deming 1947:154), a statistician must be consulted. Each sample design has its own mathematical formula.

Unfortunately, no single formula exists, even for random sampling, and still less for the quota method or any biased procedure of selection .... The development and even the use of formulas and charts for quantitative measures of sampling tolerance are professional problems in the province of mathematical statistics (Deming 1947:153-54).

The fruitless application of the statistical method of standard of error, to adjust for errors of reliability in linguistic samples of the judgment type (Reed 1949:246; 1954:6), again suggests insufficient familiarity with current progress in a related science. The original sample must be representative if quantitative analysis is to be used (McNemar 1949). Reed's references are all to out-of-date statistical sources, such as Yule (1922), Fisher (1936), and Garrett (1939).[1] Important advances have been made in statistics within the past decade which could help avoid such serious mistakes in linguistic surveys.

Random sampling has often been hastily rejected for proposed surveys because of its reputed high cost of execution, but a probability sample need not be large to be useful; furthermore, the cost can be estimated in advance. By comparison, the expenses of a closely controlled judgment survey are often as great as those of a random sample. Judgment methods are frequently used where appropriately designed probability methods would give greater reliability at equal cost (Hansen and Hurwitz 1949). It might be possible to utilize in linguistic surveys the typology evolved by Shevky and Bell in their social area analysis of San Francisco (1955), in which correlations are determined from census tract averages. Their typology is based on three social dimensions — social rank, urbanization, and segregation — and they themselves suggest that it could be used with the city as the unit of analysis, for the study of regions, or even for the study of countries.

[1] Omission of these three sources from the Bibliography characterized the original article in *Word*. [Ed.].

While correlations based upon census tract averages must be used with caution, the typological analysis for a particular city offers an efficient method for studying the attitudes and behaviors of individuals living in the various types of neighborhoods in the city. Again the geographical distribution of a particular attitude or behavior would not be of primary interest. Rather, the relationship between the attitude or behavior and type of community as to social rank, urbanization, and segregation would be of primary importance (Shevky and Bell 1955:22).

No recommendation is here intended, for only consultation of linguists with sampling specialists could determine the best method to be used for a particular research problem.

2. EXTENDING THE SCOPE OF INQUIRY

While American linguistics has, to a large extent, been working the treadmill of European dialectology, the other social sciences have been studying American society inductively and developing theory to explain its behavior. American linguistics has unfortunately ignored much of the developing theory in sociology, anthropology, and psychology. Important anomalies developed in the course of geographic research have consequently remained unaccounted for. Here are briefly presented some of the postulates of the social sciences which are related to unsolved problems in American linguistics.

Group Affiliations of the Individual

Out of the multiple factors which sociologists entertain as explanation of human behavior, American linguistic geographers have elected to examine region and education primarily (Kurath 1939:41). Yet sociologists do not find reason to believe that Americans identify only, or mainly, with region and educational level.

The cavalier assumption that 'most of the people in the United States identify themselves with their community' is not demonstrated; it is rather belied by the extreme geographic mobility of the American people. It seems far more likely that the individual is oriented primarily toward his occupational group ...,

suggests Goldschmidt (1950:485). Other identifications must also be considered: age, sex, church, political party, social class, etc. (Centers 1949). In an up-to-date study of human behavior, none of these factors can be neglected; none can be subsumed under others arbitrarily.

Sociologists have noted that these social groups have their own conventions of behavior, some of which are linguistic. Indeed, that groups help to establish and maintain their exclusiveness by erecting systems of communication intelligible only to members is commonly acknowledged;

46   *Glenna Ruth Pickford*

this clique talk may extend from the smallest social grouping of two persons to great ideological groups. In other societies anthropologists have observed significant differences in the conventions of speech between the sexes (Sapir 1951:206-12); in our society there are also linguistic conventions attached to sex, such as that, in some social classes, men who among themselves speak obscenely and profanely observe in the presence of women a special decorum. Occupational identity may be accompanied by language peculiarities, not only of vocabulary but — notoriously — of style. Religious affiliation may be signaled by speech differences of some importance; it may be, for instance, that middle-class Protestants omit colloquial references to their religious beliefs which come spontaneously into the talk of Catholics of all classes and of lower-class Protestants. Age groups also manifest conventions of linguistic behavior, such as teen-age slang (Hertzler 1953:112-6).

Group affiliation may account for the distribution of some linguistic forms which linguistic geographers have been unable to explain geographically. "Some forms — phonetic, morphological and especially lexical — have a distribution pattern completely at variance with the settlement pattern, often cutting across the major settlement boundaries" (Kurath 1939:22). Group affiliation may help to explain the "astonishing" variety in speech between communities and individuals noted by Alexander (1940:47). Linguistic analyses should at least consider such explanations as group affiliation for data which are at variance with geographic patterns of distribution. They should do more. They should ask which are the most important factors in American speech, allowing regionalism to find its proper place.

Conflicts and Cross-Affiliations

Some social groups seem frequently to go together, such as the usual combination of social class and occupation with political party affiliation. Combinations occur in some of the examples of group conventions cited above. However, these normal patterns of affiliation are sometimes disturbed by changing or competing interests. Studies of behavior have noted the effect of conflict, where groups compete for individual loyalty or where mobility among groups exists. Lazarsfeld, Berelson, and Gaudet (1948:ch. 6 *et passim*) discuss the effect of conflicting affiliations on voting behavior. Kinsey, Pomeroy, and Martin (1948:chs. III, XI) are concerned with the stability of sexual patterns between generations and where there is present the complicating factor of vertical mobility; use is made of a twelve-way breakdown in analyzing the effect of specific factors, such as the above-cited social conventions, on sexual behavior. Students of our society observe that group identification is marked by this instability.

Cross-affiliation is a result of the mobility and heterogeneity of our urbanized society (Sorokin 1927; Warner 1953).

The conflict and mobility of group affiliations may be expected to show in an individual's speech (Hertzler 1953:113, 114, 116; Martinet 1954:10). Linguistic geographers have encountered contradictions between the conscious and spontaneous speech of persons interviewed (Alexander 1940: 44). Linguists determined to make a geographic analysis insist upon trying to elicit only spontaneous speech.

Persons who speak two dialects (say, an urban and a rustic dialect) may furnish important leads, but they are not desirable informants unless they command both dialects equally well and are in the habit of setting one off against the other. They are apt to be opinionated. The ideal informant is one who cannot help talking the way he does (Kurath 1939:49).

Linguists are deliberately ignoring contradictory responses which may be evidence of conflict and mobility of individual affiliation with social groups.

The Factor of Social Class

American linguistic geographers have not only ignored some of the influences affecting speech but have oversimplified some that they have recognized. Their efforts to analyze differences among social classes, for instance, have been naive by sociological standards. American linguists have obscured the nature of American social classes by defining them chiefly in terms of educational level, leaving other important attributes of social class to be evaluated less consistently. Thus Kurath writes (1939: 44):

For any treatment of social differences in speech and for any attempt to determine trends of change, the lives of the informants ... must be consulted. For ready reference, the accompanying rough tabulation of all informants by types should prove serviceable.

TABLE OF INFORMANTS BY TYPES

Type I: Little formal education, little reading, and restricted social contacts.

Type II: Better formal education (usually high school) and/or wider reading and social contacts.

Type III: Superior education (usually college), cultured background, wide reading and/or extensive social contacts.

Type A: Aged, and/or regarded by the field worker as old-fashioned.

Type B: Middle-age or younger, and/or regarded by the field worker as more modern.

Recent sociological studies indicate that education is only one of numerous important criteria for social class placement and not an index that can be used singly (Centers 1949). In the definition of social classes in America, sociologists are beginning to reject as unsound the emphasis of any single criterion, seeking instead a controlled concordance among several criteria: education, economic level, occupation, explicit statements of identification, patterns of attitude and behavior, etc. (Goldschmidt 1950:491; Shevky and Bell 1955:9,10). None of these taken singly can explain the multiplicity of affiliations and cross-affiliations observed. Sociology has not completed its analysis of class, but it is proceeding critically and it needs the help of linguistics — language certainly looks like one of the clues (Hertzler 1953:113; Sapon 1953; Currie 1952). The recent study of Putnam and O'Hern (1955), remarkable for its sociological awareness, is a significant attempt to establish the importance of speech as a mark of social status. In England, Alan S. C. Ross has pioneered inquiry into the speech of different social classes (1954).

Sociology, indeed, may be unduly preoccupied with the concept of social class; but linguistics has failed to take account of the relevant scholarship on it. For instance, linguistic geographers assume three social classes in America. Yet an important school of sociologists uses a seven-point scale of social stratification (Warner, Meeker, and Eells 1949; Eells, Davis, Havighurst, Herrick, and Tyler 1951:ch. XI). Other sociologists are more parsimonious in their estimates of classes in our society. The studies of Bell (1934), Anderson (1937), Dollard (1937), Powdermaker (1939), Useem, Tangent and Useem (1942), Whyte (1943), Withers (1945), and Goldschmidt (1947) utilize two, three, or five classes in their analyses. A recent consensus of the evidence, however, points toward the existence of at least four social classes in this country. These four classes are (1) a small elite class which (and this is crucial to regionalism) is not found in each community or even in most communities; (2) a large middle class, perhaps 40% of the population, part of which acts as the elite in most communities; (3) a working class which lacks definitude of size; and (4) a low and dispirited sector whose size is not determined but is probably small (Goldschmidt 1950:494-95). The informants interviewed for American linguistic atlases do not present a proportionate or representative cross-section of apparent social classes. The linguists select communities with regard to settlement history and geographic location rather than their relationship to the class composition of the region or nation. They choose informants from these communities on the bases of age, length of residence, and education, ignoring or dabbling with their social ranking and its relationship to the structure of the community (Kurath 1939: 41-44). Typical is the statement about one informant that he "occupies low social position in community" (Kurath 1939:202), as if it mattered not at all how this ranking was arrived at — on the opinion of his fellow townsmen, his own estimate, or the impression of the field worker, all three of which estimates should be correlated with other sociological aspects of social rank (Centers 1949). Both the elite and lowest social classes are being neglected in the surveys, with the result that linguistic data are distorted toward the center classes of the sociological scale.

Linguistic geographers have suspected that some linguistic features which are not distributed geographically may be distributed by social class. Investigators of the *Linguistic Atlas* have tried to establish the variant pronunciations of the /r/ in South Carolina as conventions of social classes (McDavid 1948a). As the analysis is based on an incomplete approach to social class, however, it has little scientific value. If linguistics is to assist the social sciences in ascertaining the distinctions of social classes, it must first avail itself of the experience and data of previous scientific inquiries therein.

Urbanized Society of America

American linguists are radically at variance with contemporary sociologists in assuming, or seeming to assume, that America is basically a rural society: only about one fifth of communities selected for the *Linguistic Atlas* were cities (Kurath 1939:41; McDavid 1948b:233f.). Students of our society believe that with the industrialization of agriculture even traditionally rural areas are rapidly becoming urbanized (Hertzler 1953: 115; Goldschmidt 1947). This change has important consequences. In the American countryside, as in the city, the facility of transportation and communication and the consequent multiplication of contacts make for rapid social mobility, both vertical and horizontal. The result is a heterogeneity approaching that of the city. But only approaching. The city is still preeminently mobile and heterogeneous — cosmopolitan (Gist and Halbert 1947). The analysis of the country town is more complex than it used to be (Withers 1945); the analysis of the city is so complex that sociologists have had to sophisticate their statistical techniques to cope with it (Shevky and Bell 1955).

By using techniques developed for some of the most stable peasantries of Europe, American linguistic geographers have come to confusion in the country and chaos in the city. They have tried to muddle through the manifest linguistic heterogeneity by limiting observation to a restricted segment of the total linguistic material. In the selection of lexical features for investigation, for instance, no attempt was made to obtain either a random or representative selection of the total vocabulary (Kurath 1949: 9f., 49). Instead, a vocabulary was selected which would be most likely to accent regionalism.

Regional differences within New England, as elsewhere, are greater in the homely vocabulary of the family and farm than in the vocabulary of 'society' and of urban areas (Kurath 1939:1).

No consideration is here included regarding the selection of features of morphology or pronunciation. Informants who are likely to give trouble have been avoided. "Persons who have traveled a good deal or have attended college outside their section of the country must be avoided" (Kurath 1939:49). The result is a collection of data biased to make regionalism appear to be more entrenched than general sociological evidence indicates.

Even with the application of their selective techniques to rural communities, linguistic geographers have discovered numerous features that disregard regional boundaries (Alexander 1940:43,47). They explain them as national terms used side by side with local and regional terms.

The neutral expression *illegitimate child* and the blunt term *bastard* are known and used everywhere. Playful and veiled terms, on the other hand, are regional and local in character (Kurath 1949:77).

They acknowledge, that is, that regionalism is diminishing in the country (Kurath 1949:50; Davis 1949:93; Clough 1954:32-35). But they do not take the positive step which is to ask how important urbanization is in the country. Their regions fail them in a still more important way. Linguistic features in the cities do not justify the inclusion of the cities within the regions they delineate. Hubbell (1950:11) concludes that there is no evidence of purely geographical distributions of speech patterns in New York City. Thomas (1947) observes that New York City speech is not equivalent to that of New England. The cities remain anomalies of linguistic geography.

To the degree that it is urbanized, the countryside, like the city, is not amenable to the geographic approach. California, where urbanization has reached an extreme, will serve as an example of the difficulties confronting *Atlas* investigators who are contemplating little modification of techniques as they extend their survey throughout the West Coast states (Reed 1954:6).

Sociological studies of California have demonstrated the high degree of urbanization throughout the state, even in the great agricultural areas and small towns (Goldschmidt 1942, 1946, 1947; McWilliams 1949; Shevky and Bell 1955). These studies illustrate the extreme mobility and heterogeneity of the population of California. The population has always been unstable; the migrant influx has been a constant fact in its social history. Although incoming groups at first tend to settle in pockets, they scatter in time and recombine in other patterns. The periodic resettlements are further complicated by the heterogeneous origins of greatly diverse elements. All the states of the union and all the countries of the world contribute to the mounting flow of immigration. Fresno County alone, though rural, numbers 139 ethnic groups (*The Fresno Bee*, April 21, 1953 10-A). The backgrounds of immigrants to Fresno are, furthermore, inordinately tangled. Some of the Fresno Armenians left their homeland (a community made up of Armenian, Greek, Syrian, Arabic, and Slavic elements, under Turkish domination), came to Mexico or Boston, and finally migrated to Fresno. The whirlpool caused by the continual mixing, moving, and intermarriage of peoples of heterogeneous origin renders a sociological analysis by groups of common origin patently impossible. Reed (1954:5), expecting to find dialect differentiation in California by patterns of settlement, apparently overlooks the intense degree of intrastate migration which mixes up original settlement patterns.

Neither have natives in California anything like the status of natives in an old European village. Native Californians are an unrepresentative minority of the state's population. In 1946 only about one third of the residents were native-born, and most of these were in the younger age groups. There has never been enough stability of population or homogeneity of origin in California to establish the cultural dominance of an aged native sector (McWilliams 1949:76). A Fresno State College graduate seminar in English Language (Spring 1953) attempted a preliminary survey for the Pacific Coast Atlas. Out of fifty-three interviews completed, where aged, life-time Fresnans of American stock were sought, only six qualified — from a community of 150,000 population first settled by white men in 1849. These six showed a complete lack of homogeneity in their individual backgrounds. Their parents and grandparents migrated from over sixteen states, in varying proportions and combinations. The fact that these six were unacquainted with one another further demonstrates that native Californians do not necessarily comprise a cohesive group — do not, indeed, comprise a group at all.

Proposed corrections (increasing the number of informants and permitting the inclusion of first-generation natives) for California's linguistic atlas (Reed and Spicer 1952:359; DeCamp 1953:ch. I) are useless, for they continue to limit the survey to an unrepresentative, uncohesive, minor segment of the state's total population, selected by an arbitrary criterion corresponding to no known or probable reality. Even this "intentionally biased" (Reed 1954:7) selection of informants inevitably reflects the urbanization of California. California vocabulary as Reed describes it appears to be not so much regional as national — the urban speech of most of the rest of the United States. The lack of Southern terms is probably due to the cultural prestige of Northern urban centers in establishing national speech.

Movements of population and continuing immigration are characteristic not only of California but also to an important degree of the whole United States (McWilliams 1949; U.S. Census 1950). Even in the supposedly most stable, old areas of New England, it has been impossible for linguistic geographers to adhere fully to the policy of sampling only natives of native stock:

... the field worker's final choice of a community was made after a visit to the area and was prompted largely by his success in finding suitable informants .... The field workers tried to find these types but did not always succeed equally well (Kurath 1939:39-41).

Thus they report a profound failure and ignore its procedural implications.

Cultural Hierarchy of American Society

Because of their methodological predilection, linguistic geographers deliberately confine most of their research to life-time residents of culturally subordinate communities (McDavid 1948b:233f.). This selection, refusing even an equal recognition to what may be the most influential communities, is ignorant of or biased against the sociological theory of urbanization discussed above. The theory specifies centers of influence which dominate the society and spread forth cultural change (Hertzler 1953:112; Martinet 1954:10; Muntz 1938). Among the urban centers, also, there is thought to be a hierarchy, with some cities definitely more influential than others of approximate size (Goldschmidt 1950:486). This theory is too prevalent to be ignored; it should be tested against linguistic data. At the very least, it should be entertained as a procedural *caveat.* It is no longer permissible to assume that a random community is typical of its locality or region or is representative of the whole culture.

From time to time the sponsors of the *Linguistic Atlas* glance at the theory of a hierarchy of communities:

Under the dominance of urban centers, local expressions and pronunciations have been replaced in the countryside by new expressions and pronunciations radiating from them ... (Kurath 1949:2).

See also McDavid (1948b:202). Nevertheless, the linguistic geographers continue to expect regional typicality of data gathered from the most conservative informants of the most culturally subordinate communities:

In the *Atlas* survey, nearly every county in the Eastern States is represented by two speakers .... In addition, most of the larger cities are represented by one or more cultured persons. This systematic record of the usage of more than 1200 persons gives us full information on the geographic and social dissemination of the words and phrases selected for this study (Kurath 1949:v).

By their selectivity, the cartographical surveys would deny the extent of the spread of urbanization in America.

The *Atlas* surveys are not constructed to examine American speech even geographically. Neither the findings of the geographic surveys nor the interpretations can be trusted. For instance, some of the terms given as typical of an area, such as *piece* (for "to eat between meals") in the Pennsylvania Midland, do not appear to be in present currency (Menner 1950:125). More important are the errors of interpretation, such as the statement that the rate of change in rural dialects is very slow in spite of the influences of standardization (Alexander 1940:47). Such conclusions cannot be sustained by data slanted toward seeking out surviving archaisms. If the linguists are primarily interested in contributing to a collection of provincialisms (McDavid 1948a:238), their surveys are needlessly tedious, elaborate, and expensive (Martinet 1954:2). If, on the other hand, they indeed wish to relate linguistics to the other social sciences (McDavid 1946:172), their surveys are of doubtful value, for the data they gather are unrepresentative of American English.

We have tried to show that the surveys of the *Linguistic Atlas of the United States and Canada* and related studies are not on the highest level of scientific research. They lack significance, validity, and reliability. Even at the time of its launching, the project was not sensitive enough to the complexity of American speech. Had the pilot study of New England been subjected to a battery of the criticism that is usual for contemporary scientific research, its errors need not have been repeated. The relative insignificance of a geographical study causes the *Atlas* project to be ignored by the very social scientists whose cooperation would be most salutary. It is hoped that future research in American speech will be used to determine the more significant questions and will bring the professedly sociological branch of linguistics up to date on social theory and scientific method.

BIBLIOGRAPHY

Alexander, Henry
1940 "Linguistic Geography", *Queen's Quarterly* 47:38-47.
Anderson, Elin L.
1937 *We Americans* (Cambridge, Harvard University Press).

Atwood, E. Bagby
  1953 *Survey of Verb Forms in the Eastern United States* (*Studies in American English Series*, II) (Ann Arbor, University of Michigan Press).
Bell, Earl H.
  1934 "Social Stratification in a Small Community", *Scientific Monthly* 38:157-64.
Bloch, Bernard
  1935 "Interviewing for the Linguistic Atlas", *American Speech* 10:3-9.
Bloomfield, Leonard
  1933 *Language* (New York, Henry Holt).
Bottiglioni, G.
  1954 "Linguistic Geography: Achievements, Methods, and Orientations", *Word* 10:375-87.
Cantril, Hadley
  1944 *Gauging Public Opinion* (Princeton, Princeton University Press).
Centers, Richard
  1949 *The Psychology of Social Classes* (Princeton, Princeton University Press).
Clough, Wilson O.
  1954 "Some Wyoming Speech Patterns", *American Speech* 29:28-35.
Cochran, William G.
  1953 *Sampling Techniques* (New York, John Wiley and Sons, Inc.).
Currie, H. C.
  1952 "A Projection of Socio-Linguistics", *Southern Speech Journal* 18:28-37.
Davis, A. L.
  1949 "Word Atlas of the Great Lakes Region", unpublished dissertation, microfilm, University of Michigan.
DeCamp, David
  1953 "The Pronunciation of English in San Francisco", unpublished dissertation, University of California.
Deming, William
  1944 "On Errors in Surveys", *American Sociological Review* 9:359-69.
  1947 "Some Criteria for Judging the Quality of Surveys", *Journal of Marketing* 12:145-57.
  1950 *Some Theory of Sampling* (New York, John Wiley and Sons, Inc.).
Dieth, Eugen
  1948 "Linguistic Geography in New England", *English Studies* 29:65-78.
Dollard, John
  1937 *Caste and Class in a Southern Town* (New Haven, Yale University Press).
Dominian, Leon
  1915 "Linguistic Areas in Europe: Their Boundaries and Political Significance", *American Geographical Society Bulletin* 47:401-39.
Eells, Kenneth, Allison Davis, Robert J. Havighurst, Virgil E. Herrick, and Ralph Tyler
  1951 *Intelligence and Cultural Differences* (Chicago, University of Chicago Press).
Frank, Yakira H.
  1948 "The Phonology of New York City Speech", unpublished dissertation, microfilm, University of Michigan.
Garrett, Henry E.
  1953 *Statistics in Psychology and Education* (New York, Longmans, Green and Company).
Gist, Noel P. and L. A. Halbert
  1947 *Urban Society* (New York, Thomas Y. Crowell Company).
Goldschmidt, Walter R.
  1942 "Social Structure of a California Rural Community", unpublished dissertation, University of California.

1946 "Small Business and the Community", Washington, U.S. Government Printing Office.
1947 *As You Sow* (New York, Harcourt, Brace, and Company).
1950 "Social Class in America — A Critical Review", *American Anthropologist* 52:483-98.
Hagood, Margaret Jarman
1941 *Statistics for Sociologists* (New York, Henry Holt and Company).
Hansen, Morris H. and William N. Hurwitz
1949 "Dependable Samples for Market Surveys", *Journal of Marketing* 14:363-72.
Harris, Z. S. and C. F. Voegelin
1953 "Eliciting in Linguistics", *Southwestern Journal of Anthropology* 9:59-75.
Hertzler, J. O.
1953 "Toward a Sociology of Language", *Social Forces* 32:109-19.
Hubbell, Allen F.
1950 *The Pronunciation of English in New York City* (New York, King's Crown Press).
Kinsey, Alfred C., Wardell B. Pomeroy, and Clyde E. Martin
1948 *Sexual Behavior in the Human Male* (Philadelphia, W. B. Saunders Company).
Kurath, Hans
1949 *A Word Geography of the Eastern United States* (Ann Arbor, University of Michigan Press).
Kurath, Hans, with the collaboration of Marcus L. Hansen, Julia Bloch, and Bernard Bloch
1939 *Handbook of the Linguistic Geography of New England* (Providence, Brown University).
Lazarsfeld, Paul F., Bernard Berelson, and Hazel Gaudet
1948 *The People's Choice* (New York, Columbia University Press).
Marckwardt, Albert H.
1952 "Linguistic Geography and Freshman English", *The CEA Critic* 14:1.
Martinet, André
1954 "Dialect", *Romance Philology* 8:1-11.
McDavid, Raven Ioor Jr.
1946 "Dialect Geography and Social Science Problems", *Social Forces* 25:168-72.
1948a "Postvocalic /r/ in South Carolina: A Social Analysis", *American Speech* 23:194-203.
1948b "Linguistic Atlas of the South Atlantic States: its history and present status", *Southern Folklore Quarterly* 12:231-40.
McNemar, Quinn
1949 *Psychological Statistics* (New York, John Wiley and Sons, Inc.).
McWilliams, Carey
1949 *California: The Great Exception* (New York, A. A. Wyn, American Book-Stratford Press).
Menner, Robert J.
1950 "An American Word Geography", *American Speech* 25:122-26.
Muntz, Earl E.
1938 *Urban Society* (New York, Macmillan).
Powdermaker, Hortense
1939 *After Freedom* (New York, Viking).
Putnam G. N. and Edna M. O'Hern
1955 "The Status of an Isolated Urban Dialect", supplement to *Language* 31, no. 4.
Reed, David W.
1949 "A Statistical Approach to Quantitative Linguistic Analysis", *Word* 5:235-47.
1954 "Eastern Dialect Words in California", *American Dialect Society* 21:3-15.

Reed, David W. and John L. Spicer
    1952 "Correlation Methods of Comparing Idiolects in a Transition Area", *Language* 28:348-59.
Roedder, E. C.
    1926 "Linguistic Geography", *The Germanic Review* 1:281-92.
Ross, Alan S. C.
    1954 "Linguistic Class Indicators in Present-Day English", *Neophilologische Mitteilungen* 55:20-56.
Sapir, Edward
    1951 *Selected Writings of Edward Sapir*, ed. David G. Mandelbaum (Berkeley, University of California Press).
Sapon, S.
    1953 "A Methodology for the Study of Socio-Economic Differentials in Linguistic Phenomena", *Studies in Linguistics* 11:57-68.
Shevky, Eshref and Wendell Bell
    1955 *Social Area Analysis* (Stanford, Stanford University Press).
Sorokin, Pitrim
    1927 *Social Mobility* (New York, Harper and Brothers).
Thomas, C. K.
    1947 "Linguistic Geography: Place of New York City in American Linguistic Geography", *Quarterly Journal of Speech* 33:314-20.
Useem, John, Pierre Tangent, and Ruth Useem
    1942 "Stratification in a Prairie Town", *American Sociological Review* 7:331-42.
Warner, W. L.
    1953 *American Life* (Chicago, University of Chicago Press).
Warner, W. L., Marchia Meeker, and Kenneth Eells
    1949 *Social Class in America* (New York, American Book-Stratford Press, Inc.).
Weinreich, Uriel
    1954 "Is a Structural Dialectology Possible?", *Word* 10:388-400.
Whyte, William F.
    1943 *Street Corner Society* (Chicago, University of Chicago Press).
Withers, Carl (pseud. James West)
    1945 *Plainville, U.S.A.* (New York, Columbia University Press).
Anonymous
    1952 "1950 Population Census Report P-B 1", preprint of vol. II, part I, ch. B: General Characteristics, U.S. Summary, Washington, U.S. Government Printing Office.
    1953 "139 Ethnic Groups Broaden Fresno County Cultural Base", *The Fresno Bee*, April 21:10-A.

WILLIAM A. STEWART

OBSERVATIONS (1966) ON THE PROBLEMS OF DEFINING
NEGRO DIALECT

POSTSCRIPT 1971

In their present written form, these "observations" are an edited version
of remarks made in April of 1966 at the Conference on the Language
Component in the Training of Teachers of English and Reading, held
in Washington D.C. by the Center for Applied Linguistics and the National Council of Teachers of English. Although it was originally the intention of the former organization to publish the proceedings of that conference, this was never done. At the same time, however, my "observations" were written up and distributed on mimeograph to a limited number of linguists. For this reason they are sometimes found cited in the
linguistic literature. These citations have in turn caused increased demand
for access to the "observations", which explains why they are finally
being submitted for publication at this late date. When they were originally made, my "observations" formed part of a growing doubt —
particularly among creolists (Caribbeanists and Africanists) — concerning
the validity of a belief then held by most American English specialists
and dialectologists that the nonstandard speech of American Negroes
was no different from the nonstandard speech of at least southern American whites, and that designations like "Negro dialect" or "Negro speech"
were accordingly inaccurate, misleading, and socially mischievous. In
fact, the motive for my making these "observations" at the Language
Component Conference was that a linguist had been strongly criticized

Reprinted with the permission of *The Florida FL Reporter* and the author from vol. 9,
nos. 1 and 2 (Spring/Fall 1971): 47-49, 57, Alfred C. Aarons, ed.

by a dialect geographer for using one of these terms. Of course, debate on the existence of Negro-white speech differences had begun decades before the Language Component Conference, just as it has continued through the present. The ideological and theoretical convolutions of this debate have been traced in my "Sociopolitical Issues in the Linguistic Treatment of Negro Dialect" and "Historical and Structural Bases for the Recognition of Negro Dialect", both in James E. Alatis, editor, *Monograph Series on Languages and Linguistics*, 22 (Georgetown University, 1969). Although they may have sounded highly speculative at the time, my "observations on the problems of defining Negro dialect" were the direct product of extensive observations of American Negro speech. Thus, it was not surprising that subsequent research validated the structural differences I had suggested. Significantly, this was so even in the Deep South. See, for example, the results of research done in Mississippi as written up in Walt Wolfram, "Black-White Speech Differences Revisited", *Viewpoints*, 47, 2 (1971). Because of this, I suspect that the main interest in these "observations" will be historical. Therefore I have added the date of their original formulation to their present title. In this regard, it would seem that they contain the first linguistic reference to the use of uninflected *be* in an iterative or durative sense in Negro dialect — a feature which has come to loom large in the points of structural difference which distinguish white and Negro nonstandard speech in research that has been done so far. This mention of iterative or durative *be* predates slightly the first published reference to it, which was in my paper "Social Dialect" in the *Research Planning Conference on Language Development in Disadvantaged Children* (Yeshiva University, Ferkauf Graduate School, June 1966).

TEXT OF 1966

In advocating the validity of terms like "Negro dialect" and "Negro speech", it is indeed difficult to generalize uncontroversially about so sensitive a topic as social dialect variation. Yet, because of the fact that Negroes make up such an important part of our nation's socio-economically disadvantaged population, any attempt to deal with the language problems of the disadvantaged in general must certainly involve dealing with the language problems of the disadvantaged Negro in particular. For those whose local language problem involves remedial English teaching primarily to disadvantaged Negroes, knowledge about the details of their language competence and performance will be of the utmost importance.

Essentially, acquiring this knowledge means answering the question:

what is the linguistic behavior of uneducated Negroes like, and how does it compare with that of educated Negroes and both uneducated and educated whites? Since this means isolating analytically the dialect features of a particular socio-economic stratum of a particular ethnic group, the answer will require extensive sociological and anthropological research, as well as linguistic research. And such research can really only be considered to have just begun, so that no final conclusions will be arrived at in the immediate future. However, enough data have been reported so far to permit me to indicate what, in general terms, some of the final conclusions are likely to be.

In the process, I hope to be able to place the discussion in a broader perspective — one which will be more useful for understanding a wider range of alternative hypotheses than previous ones seem to have been, at least when taken by themselves and interpreted literally. For their arguments, those who oppose the concept of "Negro dialect" or "Negro Speech" rely heavily upon the evidence produced by traditional *American Dialect Atlas* elicitation procedures. Yet most of these procedures were developed before very many of the English-based pidgin and creole languages had been studied, so that the special ways in which these types of languages deviate from the normal kind of English dialect variation were not taken into account. Now, if the non-standard speech of Negroes were to differ from the non-standard speech of whites in any of these special ways (due, presumably, to substrate influence from a slave pidgin which seems formerly to have been used along the Eastern Seaboard), the differences might well be overlooked by field workers using the *ADA* questionnaires. Furthermore, much of the development of the *ADA* tradition preceded the most important substantive studies of the American Negro (such as the pioneering works of Myrdal and Herskovits). Thus, although American dialectologists have done a wonderful job of condemning racist interpretations of the nature of Negro dialects, they have not really appreciated the extent to which the sociology and anthropology of Negro "ethnicity" could encourage the development and maintenance of unique behavioral patterns to be used overtly or in secret. (I will never forget my experience with the Negro community in Bloomington, Indiana. At first sight, it seemed to me that the native born Negroes in that city spoke only a dialect which was virtually identical to that of the local whites. But I later came to find out that most Bloomington Negroes also had a distinctly "ethnic" dialect, which was used at in-group gatherings, etc.)

This last point brings up the all-important distinction which must be made when talking about "racial" groups between race in a purely physical sense and race in a primarily social sense. It is in the former sense that the term "Negro" is used in most of Latin America. To say there that so-and-so is a Negro transmits some rather specific information about the way he looks, but not much about his social relationship to other people. In the United States, on the other hand, being a Negro is first and foremost a social classification. Although genetically determined physical traits may be used by Americans as an aid in identifying each other as "white", "Negro", etc., they are by no means the sole identifying factors. Thus, to say here that so-and-so is a Negro tells us almost nothing definite about the way he looks, but nevertheless transmits some rather specific information about his social relationship to other people. This is why it is possible in the United States for many people who are clearly of predominantly European descent to be considered just as much Negroes as others who have few if any European ancestors.

Now, the implications of this fact for the controversy at hand ought to be quite clear. For if it is true that much of the hostility which has been directed toward terms like "Negro dialect" and "Negro speech" has been based on the assumption that such terms link language behavior with genetic traits, then the hostility is unjustified. Rather, these terms turn out to link language — a kind of social behavior — with other kinds of social behavior.

Once it is understood that such terms as "Negro dialect" and "Negro speech" are, at the present time, intended to suggest cultural relationships between social identity and language usage, rather than causal relationships between, say, skin color and certain linguistic features, then it should be obvious that such terms are predicated on a hypothesis which, though it could turn out to be either right or wrong, is in any event too reasonable to be rejected *a priori*. It's certainly the case that some social groups have developed special ways of speaking in other parts of the world. In the Arabic speaking countries, for example, Christians and Jews often speak dialects of Arabic which are both different from each other and different from the Arabic of the Moslems in the same country. And in Amsterdam, Jews retained social dialect features in their Dutch for generations after they had become native speakers of the language. And in India, people of different castes usually talk differently, even though they may have lived in the same village for centuries and speak, in a general sense, the same language.

The use of special dialect features by the members of certain well-defined social groups in other cultures (sometimes in addition to, and sometimes instead of the more characteristic regional and social class dialect features) is important to know about, because it shows that the correlation of linguistic features with ethnic identity is by no means an unknown phenomenon in the world. In fact, these foreign situations may well turn out to be rather typical with respect to the relationship they show between dialect variation and social group membership. Certainly they suggest that we should at least look for social dialect behavior in the American Negro who, with respect to the white majority, is in something of the same situation as the other social groups mentioned previously. Indeed, if anything, some of these other social groups are much less socially isolated from the surrounding majorities than American Negroes are from American whites.

But although foreign sociolinguistic situations may suggest what we might look for in the American sociolinguistic situation, only impartial observation, fed into a scrupulously honest theoretical framework, will provide any sure answers. In particular, we must be on guard against any temptation to select our facts to fit pre-determined social ideals. Dialectologists often cite the common "r-lessness" of the speech of many Negroes as evidence that Negro dialect traits are nothing more than southern white dialect traits. But what about the rather striking pronunciation of prevocalic /l/ with the center of the tongue spread and high up in the mouth? What about the pronunciation of /b/, /d/, and /g/ as fully voiced and imploded stops? What about the pronunciation of intervocalic /f/ and /v/ as bilabial spirants? What about the neutralization of final /m/ and /n/, with the result often realized merely as nasalization of the preceding vowel? And what about the special kinds of syllable dynamics, as well as unique uses of extra-high pitch, over-loudness, falsetto, breathiness, creaky voice, and quaver? None of these features are mentioned by the dialectologists, nor is any specific attempt made in the usual *Dialect Atlas* questionnaires to test for the existence of even the straight phonological ones. Yet these phonological and paralinguistic features seem to be markers of Negro social dialect. In addition, there are a number of syntactic constructions which also seem to have a suspiciously ethnic distribution. Among them are the so-called zero copula (e.g. *he a farmer* 'he is a farmer'), possession indicated without a possessive morpheme (e.g. *the lady hat* 'the lady's hat'), and the use of the verb *be* as a time extension auxiliary (e.g. *he be busy* 'he is habitually busy' in contrast to *he busy* 'he is momentarily busy').

Now when I say that such features seem to be Negro social dialect markers, that does not imply that they are always to be found in the speech of all American Negroes. Rather, it means that their occurrence seems to be in large part restricted to the speech of Negroes. Although some of these features may be used — or aimed at — by whites when imitating Negroes, they do not seem to be normal features of white dialects. As to their distribution within the Negro population, most of these features turn up in the normal discourse style of large numbers of uneducated persons. In the case of educated persons, the situation is more interesting. For, although some educated Negroes may never use any of these social dialect features, many others seem to use some of them in special styles. Such persons often have a "public" style which is more-or-less free of specifically Negro dialect features, and in addition, an "ethnic" style in which the same speaker will use Negro dialect features (especially the pronunciation of /l/ and the paralinguistic features referred to earlier) as well as current in-group vocabulary.

The recognition of the fact that the language competence of a particular individual may encompass several styles or kinds of language performance (sometimes involving rather different configurations of dialect features) is as crucial to the assessment of the validity of concepts like "Negro dialect" or "Negro speech" as is an understanding of the difference between race as a genetic and race as a social entity. For, in their preoccupation about their personal and racial public image, many educated Negroes neglect to "tell it like it is" about their OWN dialect switching capabilities. When engaged in public debate about the validity of "Negro dialect" or "Negro speech" (which they usually challenge), such a person is likely to use a style of speech which is devoid of ethnic markers, saying in effect: "Listen to my speech; I'm an example of a Negro whose speech has none of the features which you associate with Negro dialect." Yet, at an in-group party, the very same person may switch automatically into a style which does indeed have many of the features which are associated with Negro dialect. If caught doing this (and a tape recording may be required to convince people that they really talk the way they sometimes do), the individual may claim that the ethnic-less style represents his or her normal dialect, while the ethnic dialect is only a special "put on" style. But, if a person knows two dialects equally well, and one of them is appropriate in one kind of situation while the other one is appropriate in another situation, then which can be considered to be that person's "normal" dialect?

It is precisely because that question is impossible to answer that an individual's total style and dialect range must be taken into account before any really valid statements about people's linguistic likes and differences can be made. For if a person's linguistic competence is largely determined by his region of origin, socio-economic status, ethnic identity, sex, age, and education, his performance within this competence will vary with his role as speaker, his relationship to the person spoken to, the topic, and the situation in which the discourse takes place. Now that newer research techniques are sophisticated enough to take this kind of variability into account, I think it will become evident that American Negroes are often linked by overlapping styles into one or more cohesive sociolinguistic speech communities, even though members of such a community may exhibit very different ways of behaving in certain selected styles. This would justify the use of a term like "Negro speech" in reference to a range of dialect behavior, wherein some features are shared with whites, but others are not.

Finally, I would like to apply what I have said to the problem of teaching English to disadvantaged Negroes. In one sense, the existence of ethnically associated linguistic differences may be pedagogically trivial. That is in the sense that purely structural differences between the speech of the student and standard English account for language learning problems. From this point of view, it is the linguistic remoteness of a particular dialect from standard English which is taken as determining the degree of difficulty which the student may experience in acquiring the school language. In such terms, it is quite conceivable that some whites may find it more difficult to become fluent in "correct" English than some Negroes, if the native speech of the whites is more non-standard than that of the Negroes.

On the other hand, it is pedagogically important to know whether or not the majority of American Negroes make up one or more cohesive sociolinguistic speech communities and, if so, what the specific nature of these communities is. For the development of remedial English materials must proceed in different ways, depending upon whether pedagogically problematic linguistic differences are more characteristic of geographic distance, socio-economic distance, or ethnic distance. For example, if it turns out that the non-standard speech of Negroes in any particular part of the country is structurally closer to the non-standard speech of Negroes in other parts of the country than to the non-standard speech of the local whites, then this fact will have a very direct effect on the way remedial materials will be organized and distributed.

Although the clearest examples of dialect conflict in the learning of English which have been noticed so far are purely structural ones, there is growing evidence of cases in which very minor structural differences between dialects can also be pedagogically problematic — particularly if the dialects are associated with disparate social values. Such may be the case with those southern Negro students who strongly reject the standard dialect of the local educated whites, preferring as a model some more "northern" standard dialect — even if this is structurally more remote from their own dialect than the local (white) standard is. Or, some of these students may even reject the standard dialect of the local whites in favor of a less standard "correct" dialect used by local educated or semi-educated Negroes.

The fact that these students have been able to discriminate between the speech of local whites and Negroes in even purely auditory tests shows that they are reacting to features which must be in the stream of speech. And these features must mark either the speech of the local Negroes, or the local whites (if, as is probable, there are white social dialect features, too), or both of these. The implications which the existence of such features in even standard dialects has for the selection of linguistic models in remedial English teaching should be obvious.

In trying to ascertain the durability and effort of social dialect features, however, linguists and language teachers must take into account the possibility that reaction to them may vary both regionally and ethnically, so that the reaction of a northerner to a given speech pattern may be different from that of a southerner, or the reaction of a Negro different from that of a white in any particular region. Failure to take this kind of variability into account can easily lead to inadequate interpretations of the data. For example, cases in which northern whites have mistaken southern whites for Negroes over the telephone are often cited as evidence that Negro dialects in the north are nothing more or less than southern white dialects (presumably used by Negroes, too). Now, even leaving aside the problem of whether or not the acoustic limitations of the telephone channel make it a suitable medium for testing the perception of dialect differences, these anecdotes leave unresolved a key question: does the fact that northern whites hear no difference between the speech of southern whites and the speech of Negroes necessarily mean that no difference exists? To most Americans, "broad" Australian and Cockney sound the same, although these dialects are perceptually quite distinguishable to an Australian or a Briton. Even with respect to American dialects, many northerners hear southern speakers as using the same vowel in words like *walk* and *on* as in words like *woke* and *own*. Yet the southerner uses — and perceives — different vowels in these two sets of words.

American social dialectology has now left the stage in which personal anecdote can be offered alone as sufficient evidence. As the field enters the stage of well-planned research, testing, and analysis, many cherished beliefs and assumptions, now enjoying unquestioned popularity, are liable to be challenged.

Education Study Center

Editor's Note (in the *Florida FL Reporter*): At one point in his 1966 "Observations", Stewart referred to the possibility that an early slave pidgin, which would have been spoken in the plantations along the Eastern Seaboard, might have provided Negro dialect with some of its unique structural characteristics. This thesis was subsequently developed, with documentation, in two articles of Stewart's which were published in the *Florida FL Reporter*. These are: "Sociolinguistic Factors in the History of American Negro Dialects", vol. 5 (1967) and "Continuity and Change in American Negro Dialects" vol. 6 (1968). [Both reprinted in this volume.]

MARVIN D. LOFLIN

BLACK AMERICAN ENGLISH
AND SYNTACTIC DIALECTOLOGY

An aggregate of persons can be identified not only by language features
but by physical, geographic and social features as well. In fact, although
it has long been recognized that people who apparently speak the same
language are different physically from each other and are distributed in
social space differently, until recently few had taken the steps to prove
it by correlating specific language variables with social and physical facts.
There is a new trend afoot, however, which suggests things are changing
in this regard.[1] Correlation studies of this sort define a language community in any of several different ways. Usually, three or four different
characteristics such as age, sex, income level, race, residence within a
given geographic area, and education are lumped together and used to
delimit the boundaries in terms of which language variation will be studied. In studies devoted to clarifying the correlation between language
forms and non-linguistic information, the assumption is made that in the
past scholars inadequately portrayed the language variation actually existing in the community. With this viewpoint little fault can be found.
Variation exists and the community of scholars might profitably seek
techniques to increase the ability to describe it. However, this trend to
recognize variation seems preoccupied with the overt to the neglect of the
covert (usually in these studies the assumption is made that the variance
in the outward features is not matched by an equal variance in cognitive
or covert forms; that is, in a study of standard and non-standard dialects
it is presumed that two randomly selected informants, one a standard

This trend is most evident in the work of William Labov, Dell Hymes, Joshua[1]
Fishman and others whose works should be consulted for more detailed bibliography.

66   *Marvin D. Loflin*

speaker and one a non-standard speaker, have identical cognitive structures [grammatical deep structures] but slightly different overt realizations
of these inner forms). In the case of Black American English it is especially important to ascertain whether or not members of the community
share cognitive structures with the larger dominant community.

If we decide that everyone in the population whose speech we are
studying speaks the same language, our statements of variation will be
different from those we would make if we determine that the people who
contributed to our speech sample speak different languages. Let us suppose that all the rules we might use to describe a language can be divided
into two categories, those that deal with deep structures[2] and those that
deal with surface structure. We could assume that as long as there are
no differences in the rules of different grammars dealing with deep structures those grammars represent the same language. Ascertaining whether
or not all the people who provide speech samples for a study of speech
variation share the same deep structure (that is, speak the same language
and belong to the same language community) then becomes a matter of
constructing grammars and comparing them to determine deep structure
sameness. Variations among deep structurally nondistinct language varieties are dialectal variations. Thus, the theoretical and methodological
assumptions which give rise to postulating deep structure entities are
crucial to the study of language variation and the determination of the
formal distinctions to be made between languages.[3]

In traditional dialect studies there has been a tendency to make an
assumption about the language of the group being studied: everyone in
the sample speaks the SAME language. Once this is assumed it is relatively
easy to identify independent social, physical, and geographical features
which can be correlated with dependent language variables, dependent
language variables which, it is assumed, are matched with a single set
of cognitive elements. That is, variation in the surface forms is presumed
not to match with variation in the meaning forms. Often these studies
correlate geographic facts with language facts, an exercise which does not
deal directly with the problem of establishing and comparing deep structures. For example, one scholar, E. Bagby Atwood, undertook *A Survey
of Verb Forms in the Eastern United States*[4] and interviewed both Negroes
and non-Negroes. But, in presenting his results, wherein he associated
verb forms with the locales from which they were taken, he excluded the

[2] See the discussion on deep and surface structure in Noam Chomsky, *Aspects of the
Theory of Syntax* (Cambridge, MIT Press, 1965).
[3] The term "deep structure" means many things to many people, but as far as I can
determine, all claimants to a linguistic theory use it, whatever interpretation they impute
to the term (Chomsky, 1965; Fillmore, 1966; McCawley, 1968; and Lakoff, 1968).
[4] *Studies in English* 2 (Ann Arbor, University of Michigan Press, 1953).

samples taken from Negroes. Because the samples taken from Negro respondents were surprisingly deviant, given the prior notion of SAME language, and because they were homogeneous over a wide area, it was fairly obvious that he could not include his Black English examples and maintain that some non-standard usages were regional, as he expressed the desire to do. In my opinion, Atwood encountered the difficulties he did with Black American English because he was dealing with different language communities which not only could be differentiated on the basis of geographical, physical and social characteristics but also had to be differentiated on the basis of non-shared grammatical deep structures.

Our image of dialects in the United States is a product of the theory and methodology subscribed to by dialectologists. Actually, four methodological assumptions and no theory seem to have guided dialectologists in the construction of their elicitation procedures and materials:

(a) Is the response to a question likely to be quaint or archaic?
(b) Can it be easily elicited?
(c) Will anything more than a list be needed to report on it?
(d) Does it fit within the domains of morphology, lexicon or phonology?

It may appear unduly harsh to claim that little or no theory has guided the work of dialectologists; however, looking at the last ten years in linguistics, during which time questions centering upon the nature of the metatheory (its form and goals), rules (their form), etc., have come to the fore, we must admit that dialectology seems to have been little affected by these changes of emphasis. No one in the mainstream of dialect work seems to be asking questions such as: what systems of hypotheses are required to describe and account for differences between dialects? Still to be answered is the question: where are dialectal differences to be accommodated in the grammar?

Obviously, the most fundamental problem confronting dialectology is that of determining the relevance of statements of variation; that is, what are the theoretical and methodological assumptions which give rise to deep structure hypotheses? When are the variables apples and when are they pears? Except for intuitive criteria, the present state of affairs is such that it is impossible to provide principled reasons of appropriateness (or relevance) for the inclusion or exclusion of any given variable in a dialect study.

What is important is not the particular brand of deep structure that McCawley proposes or that Chomsky proposes, but the justification provided for the categories and relations postulated. "Justification" is taken to mean to argue for. Once it is clearly understood how the deep structure component is justified for one language it should be possible to argue for the deep structure in another language using the same kinds of arguments. If same argument types lead to same deep structures, then any other variation whether phonological, lexical or functional (in the anthropologist's sense) is dialect variation. On the other hand if same argument types lead to different deep structures the difference is a language difference.

At the present time it is fairly easy to discuss mode of argumentation in a generative syntactic framework. It is not so easy in the case framework or in generative semantics. This state of affairs may change soon. Until it does we have the example of Chomsky and others arguing for the deep structure of English with a mode of argumentation that is both explicit and applicable to any language. The mode of argumentation entails explicit rules and independent motivation for those rules. For good examples of this mode of argumentation cf. Chomsky (1964), Lakoff (1968), Koutsoudas (1971), and Sanders and Tai (1972).

Linguistically, speakers of BAE are those whose speech is demonstrated to have underlying it a BAE deep structure which has been independently argued for with an explicit mode of argumentation.

In Loflin (1972) I presented an auxiliary hypothesis growing out of auxiliary co-occurrence relations in conjoined (*and, or, but*) sentences. There I argued that the hypothesis was to some degree independently motivated; it reflected generalizations in its category structure which increased the generality of the input conditions in transformational rules. The providing of independent syntactic motivation was defined as the demonstration that more than one phenomenon is accounted for by the postulated symbols and relations. Stated in another way, a rule which describes corpus$_x$ is motivated only by the facts of corpus$_x$. An independently motivated rule is one which is not only motivated by the facts of corpus$_x$ but also by the facts of corpus$_y$.

Here the intention is to present data which provide additional independent syntactic motivation for the auxiliary hypothesis presented in the earlier paper. The rules presented there are the following:

(1) *Auxiliary Hypothesis for Black American English*

    a. AUX   → $\left\{\begin{array}{l}\text{PRES}\\\text{INDEFPAS}\\\text{NONINDEFPAS}\end{array}\right\}$

    b. NONINDEFPAS → $\left\{\begin{array}{l}\text{A-TEMP}\\\text{TEMP}\end{array}\right\}$

    c. TEMP   → $\left\{\begin{array}{l}\text{DEFPAS}\\\text{GEN}\end{array}\right\}$

    d. DEFPAS   → $\left\{\begin{array}{l}\text{DFPS}\\\text{PERF}\end{array}\right\}$

Auxiliary Co-occurrence in Conjunction

(2) OR

$$W - AUX - X - OR - Y - AUX_d - Z \Rightarrow$$
$$W - AUX - X - OR - Y - AUX - Z$$

(3) AND

$$W \begin{bmatrix} GEN \\ \begin{bmatrix} PERF \\ DFPS \end{bmatrix} \\ A\text{-}TEMP \end{bmatrix} X - AND - Y - AUX_d - Z \Rightarrow$$

$$W \begin{bmatrix} GEN \\ \begin{bmatrix} PERF \\ DFPS \end{bmatrix} \\ A\text{-}TEMP \end{bmatrix} X - AND - Y \begin{bmatrix} NONINDEFPAS \\ TEMP \\ DEFPAS \end{bmatrix} Z$$

(4) BUT

$$W \begin{bmatrix} GEN \\ PERF \end{bmatrix} X - BUT - Y - AUX_d - Z \Rightarrow$$

$$W \begin{bmatrix} GEN \\ PERF \end{bmatrix} X - BUT - Y \begin{bmatrix} \begin{Bmatrix} GEN \\ PERF \end{Bmatrix} \\ TEMP \end{bmatrix} Z$$

The auxiliary labels given in the Auxiliary Hypothesis are to be matched with surface forms in the following way:

(5)

jump + ∅ = GENERIC	= GEN	
jump + ED = PERFECTIVE	= PERF	
BEEN + jump + IN = INDEFINITE PAST	= INDEFPAS	
WAS + jump + IN = DEFINITE PAST	= DFPS	
BE + jump + IN = A-TEMPORAL	= A-TEMP	
IS + jump + IN = PRESENT	= PRES	

Other symbols in the hypothesis reflect the imposition of postulated structure. Without this auxiliary hypothesis, (1), that is, if the rules for auxiliary co-occurrence in conjunction, (2), (3), and (4), are formulated without the benefit of the structural hypothesis in (1), the number of symbols is increased from 53 (including symbols in the auxiliary hypothesis and cover symbols) to 62. In the less general alternative formulation, the OR rule would be the same. However, the AND rule would have the form:

(6)
$$W \begin{bmatrix} \text{GEN} \\ \begin{bmatrix} \text{PERF} \\ \text{DFPS} \end{bmatrix} \\ \text{A-TEMP} \end{bmatrix} X - \text{AND} - Y - \text{AUX}_d - Z \Rightarrow$$

$$W \begin{bmatrix} \text{GEN} \\ \begin{bmatrix} \text{PERF} \\ \text{DFPS} \end{bmatrix} \\ \text{A-TEMP} \end{bmatrix} X - \text{AND} - Y \begin{bmatrix} \begin{Bmatrix} \text{A-TEMP} \\ \text{GEN} \\ \text{DFPS} \\ \text{PERF} \end{Bmatrix} \\ \begin{Bmatrix} \text{GEN} \\ \text{DFPS} \\ \text{PERF} \end{Bmatrix} \\ \begin{Bmatrix} \text{DFPS} \\ \text{PERF} \end{Bmatrix} \end{bmatrix} - Z$$

and the *BUT* rule would have the form:

(7)
$$\begin{bmatrix} \text{GEN} \\ \text{PERF} \end{bmatrix} X - \text{BUT} - Y - \text{AUX}_d - Z \Rightarrow$$

$$W \begin{bmatrix} \text{GEN} \\ \text{PERF} \end{bmatrix} X - \text{BUT} - Y \begin{bmatrix} \begin{Bmatrix} \text{GEN} \\ \text{PERF} \end{Bmatrix} \\ \begin{Bmatrix} \text{GEN} \\ \text{DFPS} \\ \text{PERF} \end{Bmatrix} \end{bmatrix} - Z$$

Thus, the rule set, (3) and (4), is more general than the rule set, (6) and (7). We will now assume that rule sets, (2), and (3) and (4), are hypotheses based on a corpus of conjoined sentences, which we will label CORPUS$_c$. We now wish to turn to auxiliary co-occurrences in matrix and constituent sentences where the constituent sentences are relativizations and that-complements and which we will label CORPUS$_d$. We will argue that the facts of CORPUS$_d$ provide independent motivation for the auxiliary hypothesis of (1) as reflected in auxiliary agreement rules (2), (3) and (4) as well as (9) and (11) below.

(8) (A) *TEMP* occurs with any other *TEMP* so that we find
     (a) An' you *know* cat da' us'lly *carry* all de key? GEN: GEN
     (b) I *got* a frin' name Abraham da' *broke* 'is arm. GEN: PERF
     (c) He was singin' "Luv", a reco'd, da' reco'd he *know* call "Luv". DFPS: GEN
     (d) I *seen* one boy look like, *look* like his son aroun' nere. PERF: GEN
     (e) An' so we saw one, we *saw* a couple of dead bodies da' *were* over dere da' fell off a cliff. PERF: DFPS

Thus, every instance of an auxiliary in a matrix sentence in these data is dominated by TEMP and every instance of an auxiliary in an associated relative is also dominated by TEMP.

A co-occurrence hypothesis would be:

REL

(9) $W - TEMP - X - Y - AUX_d - Z \Rightarrow$
$$W - TEMP - X - Y - TEMP - Z$$

It is apparent that the auxiliary hypothesis for BAE given above makes it possible to formulate this co-occurrence statement without requiring that additional structure be postulated. Thus, the auxiliary hypothesis growing out of a consideration of conjoined data is independently motivated by the formulation needed to describe relations between auxiliaries in matrix and constituent sentences where the constituent sentence is a relative.

THAT COMPLEMENTS

(10) (B) In "that" complement embedding, *GEN* co-occurs with NON-INDEFPAS and *PRES*
  (a) She always *tell* evrbody she *beat* me three games. GEN: GEN
  (b) 'An he *say* dey *had* it in de window. GEN: PERF
  (c) I *mean* it *was* after nine o'clock. GEN: DFPS
  (d) Ey *say* dey *be* countin up you' food, man, see how much you ha'. GEN: A-TEMP
  (e) "You *know* da' your frien's *are* givin' you a bad mark, make you git a bad mark." GEN: PRES

  (C) PERF co-occurs with *TEMP*
  (a) An' so de man *tol'* my muvah she *need* a new starter. PERF: GEN
  (b) So he *said* I *did* it 'n I ain't do it. PERF: PERF

  (D) A-TEMP co-occurs only with *GEN*
  (a) Ev'rytime I *come* over to my gran'muvah house, she *be* washin'. A-TEMP: GEN

  (E) PRES co-occurs only with *PRES*
  (a) De man *is signifyin'* da' de boat *is bein'* attack. PRES: PRES

Applying our auxiliary rule set, we obtain the following rules:

Tob that-Complement

(11)

$$W + \begin{bmatrix} \text{GEN} \\ \text{PERF} \\ \text{A-TEMP} \\ \text{PRES} \end{bmatrix} + X + \text{that}_c + Y + AUX_d + Z \quad \Rightarrow$$

$$W + \begin{bmatrix} \text{GEN} \\ \text{PERF} \\ \text{A-TEMP} \\ \text{PRES} \end{bmatrix} + X + \text{that}_c + Y + \begin{bmatrix} \begin{Bmatrix} \text{NONINDEFPAS} \\ \text{PRES} \end{Bmatrix} \\ \text{TEMP} \\ \text{GEN} \\ \text{PRES} \end{bmatrix} + Z$$

It is crucial to note the congruence of co-occurrence relations for the conjoining rules and the relativization and complement rules. Almost any other auxiliary hypothesis would have increased the number of symbols required to construct the structural descriptions and changes in these rules.

Thus, not only does this auxiliary hypothesis capture generalizations for the conjoining structures and the REL/COMP structures separately but it also provides an analysis which suits the needs of both sets of rules. There is then some reason for the auxiliary structure given here: the auxiliary structure contributes to two sets of transformational rule statements which state the co-occurrence relations between conjoined, relative and that-complement sentences and whose formulation is more simple and more general because of that auxiliary structure.

Department of Linguistics
University of Wisconsin-Milwaukee

BIBLIOGRAPHY

Chomsky, Noam
  1964 *Current Issues in Linguistic Theory* (The Hague, Mouton).
Fillmore, Charles J.
  1966 "A Proposal Concerning English Prepositions", *Monograph Series on Languages and Linguistics*, no. 19, 17th Annual Round Table, edited by F. P. Dineen (Washington, D.C.: Georgetown University Press).
Koutsoudas, Andreas
  1971 "Gapping, Conjunction Reduction, and Coordinate Deletion", *Foundations of Language* 7:337-386.
Lakoff, George
  1968 "Instrumental Adverbs and the Concept of Deep Structure", *Foundations of Language* 4:4-29.

1969   "On Derivational Constraints", in Robert I. Binnick, *et al.* (eds.), *Papers from the Fifth Regional Meeting, Chicago Linguistic Society: April 18-19, 1969*, University of Chicago, Department of Linguistics: 117-39.
Loflin, Marvin D.
1972   "Black American English: Independent Motivation for the Auxiliary Hypothesis", Technical Report No. 2, Institute for the Study of Urban Linguistics (University of Wisconsin, Milwaukee).
McCawley, James D.
1968   "Lexical Insertion in a Transformational Grammar without Deep Structure", in Bill J. Darden, *et al.* (eds.), *Papers from the Fourth Regional Meeting, Chicago Linguistic Society*, University of Chicago, Department of Linguistics: 77-93.
Sanders, G. and James Hau-Y Tai
1972   "Immediate Dominance and Identity Deletion", *Foundations of Language* 8:161-198.

PHILIP A. LUELSDORFF

DIALECTOLOGY IN GENERATIVE GRAMMAR

0. SUMMARY

In the present paper I examine several past approaches to the theory of syntactic and phonological variation within generative grammar. The general conclusion of this recent work is that dialects of the same language may differ in their deep structures. This unanticipated conclusion, if correct, entails an approach to the study of intrapersonal and interpersonal variation considerably more individually, i.e. clinically, oriented than past approaches have in fact been.

In §1 I examine several contributions to the theory of syntactic dialectology. In §2 generative contributions to phonological dialectology are reviewed and a distinction is drawn between grammars underlying the speech behavior of individual speakers and grammars which relate the speech behavior of individual speakers. In §3, I formulate the principle on which the present study is based and, in §4, present seven examples from the phonology of Black English which, when analyzed on the basis of the principle stated in §3, entail underlying phonological representations different from those of Standard English.

1. SYNTACTIC DIALECTOLOGY

Contributions to the theory of syntactic dialectology are, unfortunately, extremely few in number and, typically, very poor in quality. Exceptions to this rule are the recent contributions of Klima, Rosenbaum, and Loflin.

Klima (1964) approaches the relationship between grammatical systems and their differences in the following way. The syntactic structure of each system is considered revealed by the set of rules which most economically generates the sentences of the system:

That set of rules will be designated as its grammar (G). The relationship between one style (L_1) and another (L_2) will be thought of in terms of the rules (E_{1-2}) that it is necessary to add as an extension to the grammar (G_1) of L_1 in order to account for the sentences of L_2. A convention will be adopted regarding the place where extension rules may be added to the grammar. They may not be added just anywhere, but must come at the end of certain sets of rules; e.g. extension rules dealing with the case forms of pronouns must come after the set of grammar rules for case in the previous system. By this convention, extension rules are prevented from superseding previous rules. Fundamental structural difference, varying in structure and degree, will be considered to exist between systems L_1 and L_2 when the set of rules G_2 for most economically generating the sentences of L_2 is not equivalent to G_1 plus its extension E_{1-2}.

From the point of view simply of relating coexisting systems, the particular pairing and the direction chosen in extending the grammar of one system to account for the sentences of another are those representing the shortest extension rules, that is, L_1 is compared with L_2, and L_2 with L_3, rather than L_1 with L_3, because E_{1-2} and E_{2-3} are each shorter than a hypothetical E_{1-3}. Similarly, L_1 rather than L_2 is taken as primary in comparing L_1 and L_2 because E_{1-2} is shorter than a hypothetical E_{2-1}.

Although motivated by a purely synchronic principle of simplicity (shortness of rules), Klima points out that the order in which the styles are considered does, in fact, recapitulate comparable aspects in the historical development of the English pronouns.

Rosenbaum (1964) calls for a characterization of the notion DIALECT in terms of transformational theory and the determination of the level on which dialects differ from one another. Due to the then lack of transformational research in the area of syntactic dialectology, Rosenbaum leaves the problem of deep structural differences between dialects of the same language an open question. He concludes by stressing the need to develop a motivated methodology for describing and relating different linguistic systems and investigating the constraints on dialect divergence.

In 1965 Beryl Bailey advanced the bold and exciting hypothesis that the speech of the Southern Negro differs in deep structure from the speech of the Southern white. In support of this hypothesis, Loflin (1967) presents evidence that certain copulative sentences with *be* are ambiguous in Non-standard Negro English (NNE) and that in order to disambiguate such sentences an HABITUATIVE category must be postulated in the grammar of NNE not found in the grammar of Standard English. The HABITUATIVE category appears to have the function of representing a recurring activity engaged in at specific times. Loflin further observes that there is no perfective form in NNE comparable to the one posited for Standard

English (*have* + *en*): surface realizations of *have* + *en* in simple sentences, yes/no questions, tag questions, and nominalizations are totally lacking.

2. PHONOLOGICAL DIALECTOLOGY

Applegate (1961) presents a description of the speech of two children whose "subdialect" deviates from Standard English. It was the only language of the children, and they used it to communicate with English-speaking adults, with each other, and with their playmates. The children's brother served as a translator in situations where the children could not communicate effectively with adults.

Although Applegate refers to the children's dialect as an "autonomous system", he describes it in terms of its deviant relationship to Standard English. One relevant passage is worthy of quotation *in extenso*:

At this point reference to the language of the community is helpful. In adult speech, the form of the plural morpheme, the possessive, and the third-person singular verb morpheme is [s] alternating with [z] in those places where the children have [t] and [d]. Further examination of the children's speech shows that all fricatives are missing. /f/ is articulated as /p/, /v/ is /b/, /s/ is /t/ and /z/ is /d/. The interdental fricatives are also articulated as stops, and /c/ and /j/ are /t/ and /d/ respectively. The two series of stops in the children's language are then related in the same way that stops and fricatives are related in adult speech. A rule of the following form, again in terms of distinctive features, can be used to describe this phenomenon.

$$\begin{bmatrix} +\text{consonant} \\ -\text{vocalic} \\ +\text{continuant} \\ X \end{bmatrix} \rightarrow \begin{bmatrix} +\text{consonant} \\ -\text{vocalic} \\ -\text{continuant} \\ X \end{bmatrix}$$

The application of this rule results in the change of all fricatives, i.e., continuants, to noncontinuants, or stops.

This rule, rather than describing the dialect as an autonomous system, describes it in terms of its deviation from Standard English. The children have no fricatives in their speech, yet underlying fricatives are postulated for their dialect in the interests of relating it to Standard English.

While rules of this type may in fact reflect the way in which the dialect was acquired and the knowledge a speaker of the Standard language would have to internalize in order to speak the dialect, they are unjustified in the description of the dialect because there are no forms in the dialect which would support their postulation.

A sharp distinction must be made between grammars underlying the speech behavior of individual speakers and grammars relating the speech behavior of individual speakers. The goal of the former is the accurate and complete description of the linguistic competence of selected members of the speech community. The goal of the latter is to relate these descriptions to one another in a maximally simple and illuminating way. The former are statements of the linguistic competence of individual language users; the latter are statements of the similarities and differences in the linguistic knowledge of individuals in the community.

Exemplary of the generative approach to dialectology is a study by Halle (1961) in which he considers a hypothetical dialect of English — a dialect with almost exactly those features as described by Applegate in the above-mentioned publication — differing from the standard language in the following two respects:

When the standard language has a continuant consonant in non-initial position, the dialect has the cognate non-continuant (stop) consonant.

When the standard language has several identical non-continuant consonants in a word, the dialect replaces all but the first of these by a glottal stop. Examples:

I			II		III	
cuff	(cup)	[kʌ́p]	*puff*	[pʌ́p]	*pup*	[pʌ́ʔ]
gave	(Gabe)	[géb]	*brave*	[bréb]	*babe*	[béʔ]
sauce	(sought)	[sɔ́t]	*toss*	[tɔ́t]	*taught*	[tɔ́ʔ]
lies	(lied)	[lájd]	*dies*	[dájd]	*died*	[dájʔ]

Note that the dialect admits words with several identical non-continuant consonants (cf. column II), but that in every one of these examples the second non-continuant corresponds to a fricative in the standard language.

Halle handles the phonetic peculiarities of this dialect by the following two ordered rules, which do not function in the standard language:

1. If in a word there are several identical non-vocalic, consonantal non-continuants, all but the first become non-vocalic, non-consonantal non-continuants (i.e. glottal stops in distinctive feature terminology). Examples in column III.

2. In non-initial position, non-vocalic, consonantal continuants become non-continuant.

Halle comments on this solution as follows:

I believe that this solution, proposed by Applegate, is preferable to the alternative of postulating a different phonological system for the dialect than for the standard language. It seems to me intuitively more satisfactory to say, as we have done here, that the dialect differs from the standard language only in the relatively minor fact of having two additional low-level rules, rather than to assert — as we should have to do if we rejected the proposed solution — that the dialect deviates from the standard language in the much more crucial sense of having either a different phonemic repertoire than the standard language, or of having a strikingly different distribution of phonemes. It must be stressed that in the proposed solution the ordering of the rules is absolutely crucial, for if Rule (1) is allowed to operate after Rule (2) the noncontinuants produced by Rule (2) would be turned into glottal stops by Rule (1); i.e., the examples in Column II could not be accounted for. Without ordering of the rules we are forced to accept the unintuitive alternatives mentioned above.

Halle (1962) characterizes recent work in dialectology as focusing attention on the facts of the utterance and concerning itself primarily with questions of mutual intelligibility of two dialects, the similarities and differences of cognate utterances, of their phoneme repertoires, distributional constraint etc. Instead of following this procedure, Halle proposes to focus on the grammars of the dialect, that is, on the ordered set of statements that describe the data, rather than on the data directly.

Halle considers the case of Pig Latin in order to show that these two approaches are different in fundamental ways. The former approach entails noting the distributional differences of the phonemes of Pig Latin and General American, that infixation is the major morphological device in Pig Latin, and that Pig Latin is incomprehensible to the uninitiated speaker of General American. On the basis of such observation we would be led to falsely conclude that Pig Latin and General American were at best remotely related tongues. The latter approach, involving a comparison of the grammars of General American and Pig Latin, results in the observation that Pig Latin contains a morphophonemic rule that is absent in the more standard dialects, namely, the shift of initial consonant clusters to the ends of words and the addition of /ē/. Since this rule is the only difference between the grammars of Pig Latin and General American, we conclude that Pig Latin is a special dialect of General American, a conclusion which is obviously right. Halle states that this result follows only if instead of concentrating on utterances, we shift primary attention to the grammars that underlie the utterances.

Saporta (1965) offers evidence from Spanish dialects to support the view of Halle that the grammatical description of a given dialect may be converted into an adequate description of a related dialect by the addition, deletion, and reordering of a relatively small number of rules.

Saporta stresses that the choice of underlying forms and rules is motivated by the desire to account for the greatest number of facts in a manner as straightforward as possible. This desire, however, leads Saporta to postulate underlying representations for a given dialect which are unsupportable on the basis of the primary data of that dialect.

As an example, consider Saporta's treatment of the morphophonemics of pluralization in Latin American Spanish:

Castilian (C)	Latin American (LA)	
lúnes	*lúnes*	'Monday'
lúnes	*lúnes*	'Mondays'

lápiθ	*lápis*	'pencil'
lápiθes	*lápises*	'pencils'

For C there is a general rule for the plural expressed in (1).

(1)

$$\text{pl} \rightarrow \begin{cases} \text{s} \ / \ \text{V} \_\_\_ \\ \text{é} \ \_\_\_ \\ \emptyset \ / \ \text{Vs} \_\_\_ \\ \text{es} \end{cases}$$

This rule states that the plural is represented by /s/ in the environment after all unstressed vowels and after stressed /é/, by $\emptyset$ after unstressed vowels followed by /s/, and by /es/ elsewhere. Thus the plural of *lunes* /lúnes/ with final /s/ is also /lúnes/, but the plural of *lápiz* /lápiθ/ with final /θ/ is *lápices* /lápiθes/. Saporta notes that /θ/ and /s/ have fallen together in LA and concludes that some modification must be made in the grammar. One alternative is to list for LA all words like *lápiz* /lápis/ as exceptions to the rule — that is, to say that the plural is represented by zero after unstressed vowel plus /s/ except for a list of words, when this list corresponds exactly to words where C has /θ/. The other alternative is to keep (1) unaltered, but to add a rule like (2) for LA.

(2) $\begin{Bmatrix} \theta \\ s \end{Bmatrix} \rightarrow [s]$

Saporta adapts the second alternative, arguing that linguists presumably agree that rules are preferable to lists, even short lists. This presumption, however, even if correct, is irrelevant to the justification of underlying representations.

Assuming rule (1) to be correct, it is an adequate expression of the morphophonemics of pluralization in Castilian Spanish. A rule like (2), in addition to (1), might be found, perhaps in an optional form, in the grammar of a bidialectal speaker of Castilian and Latin American Spanish. But rule (2) is totally unmotivated on the basis of the data of Latin American Spanish alone. Given these data alone, there is no alternative between a list and a rule: a list must be given.

A speaker of C learning the morphophonemics of pluralization in LA must internalize a rule of the sort given in (2). A speaker of LA learning the morphophonemics of pluralization in C, however, is confronted with a different task. First, he will have to learn that the list of exceptions including /lápis/ in his grammar consists of forms ending in /θ/ in Castilian Spanish. The underlying representation of the final consonants of these forms will change from /s/ to /θ/ and he will internalize (2) as an optional rule. The end products of these two different processes of second dialect acquisition will be the same: identical underlying representations with identical optional rules. The native speaker of Castilian has added

an optional rule to his grammar with the acquisition of Latin American
Spanish as a second dialect. Having formed the plural of /lapiθ/, he
applies an optional rule, converting /lapiθes/ to /lapises/. The native
speaker of LA has changed his underlying representation and learned an
optional rule. Interestingly enough, he must apply more rules in speaking
his native dialect after he has learned Castilian than when he was a mono-
dialectal speaker of Latin American Spanish.

3. PRINCIPLES AND PROCEDURES

The essential feature of the above approaches to phonological dialectology in generative grammar is the principle that the description of a
given dialect may be converted into an adequate description of a related
dialect by the addition, deletion, and reordering of a relatively small
number of rules. Call this the Dependence Principle. In each case examined, however, this principle has led to the postulation of underlying
representations for a dialect identical to those of the system from which
it is derived irrespective of whether or not those representations are
justifiable on the basis of the dialect data alone. THIS PRINCIPLE HAS THE
UNDESIRABLE RESULT OF MAKING THE ADEQUATE DESCRIPTION OF A DIALECT
IMPOSSIBLE WITHOUT RECOURSE TO THE DATA OF SOME OTHER VARIETY OF
THE LANGUAGE. Since generative grammars are representations of the
linguistic competence of individual speaker-hearers, this principle must
be rejected.

In its stead, I offer the principle that each dialect may be adequately
described in its own terms, i.e. without reference to the data of related
dialects. Call this the Independence Principle. The associated procedure
is to produce such descriptions for individual speaker-hearers. These
independently motivated individual descriptions may then be compared
with an eye to pointing out their similarities and differences, leaving the
extent and nature of dialect differences an essentially empirical question.

4. UNDERLYING PHONOLOGICAL DIFFERENCES

In this paragraph I present several examples of Black English phonetic
data which, when analyzed on the principle that each dialect may be
adequately described on its own terms, result in systematic phonemic
representations for Black English which are different from those of
Standard English.

Example A. In Black English there are no examples of lax [ɛ] occurring
in the environment of an immediately following nasal consonant. Cor-

responding to Standard English words in which lax [ɛ] occurs in the
environment of a following nasal are Black English words in which lax
[I] occurs in the environment of a following nasal. Examples:

	SE	BE
pen	[pɛn]	[pɪn]
hem	[hɛm]	[hɪm]

According to the Dependence Principle, the phonology of Black English
would differ from the phonology of Standard English in that it would
contain a rule which rewrites *e* as [I] in the environment of a following
nasal consonant. According to the Independence Principle, Black English
would have an underlying *i* before nasals in just those words in which
Standard English has an underlying *e* before nasals and the phonology
of Black English would contain a Sequence Structure Condition stating
that if a non-Tense, non-Back, non-Low true vowel occurs in the environment of an immediately following nasal consonant, then the vowel
will also be specified High. Thus, according to the Dependence Principle, the underlying representations of Black English and Standard
English are the same, and the phonology of Black English differs from
that of Standard English in that it contains an additional phonological
rule. According to the Independence Principle, the underlying representations of Black English and Standard English are different and the
phonology of Black English contains a sequence structure condition which
the phonology of Standard English does not. Since I accept the Independence Principle and reject the Dependence Principle, I conclude that
there are underlying differences in the phonologies of Standard and Black
English.

It might be argued that the analysis that I am proposing fails to express
the relationship between Standard and Black English. But this relationship is expressed by the rule which rewrites *e* as *i* in the environment of
a following nasal. This rule is of a formally different character from
phonological rules, it does not occur in the phonology of either dialect,
and is postulated in order to account for the differences between the two
dialects.

Example B. In Black English there are several words which contain
[ə] before [r] which have Standard English counterparts with either [ɛ]
or [æ] before [r]. Examples:

	SE	BE
very	[vɛri]	[vəri]
fairy	[fɛri]	[fəri]
carriage	[kærɪǰ]	[kərɪǰ]

This correspondence between Standard English and Black English is not completely regular, however, for there are some words which contain [ɛ] and [æ] before [r] in both language varieties. Examples:

	SE	BE
hairy	[hɛri]	[hɛri]
Larry	[læri]	[læri]

According to the Dependence Principle, the same underlying representations would be postulated for Black English and Standard English, and a rule would be added to the phonology of English which would have the effect of rewriting ɛ and æ before *r* as phonetic [ə] in the case of words like *very, fairy, carriage, Mary, merry,* etc. and words like *hairy* and *Larry* would be marked as exceptions to this rule. According to the Independence Principle, different underlying representations would be postulated for Standard English and Black English in the case of *very, fairy, carriage,* etc., but not in the case of *hairy* and *Larry,* other things being equal. The two systems would be related to one another by a rule which maps the underlying representations with *æ* and *e* before *r* in Standard English onto Black English underlying representations with *a* before *r,* with certain words being marked as exceptions. This rule would not be a phonological rule in either Standard English or Black English, but would merely serve to relate the two systems in an economical and revealing way.

Example C. In Black English there is a large number of words which do not contain an [r] where an [r] is present in Standard English prevocalically and postvocalically in consonant clusters. Examples:

	SE	BE
wizard	[wɪzərd]	[wɪzɪt]
custard	[kəstərd]	[kəstɪt]
protect	[prətɛkt]	[pətɛk]
professor	[prəfɛsər]	[pəfɛsə]

Following the Dependence Principle, an underlying *r* would be postulated in those environments in which it is phonetically absent in Black English but phonetically present in Standard English, and a rule would be added to the phonology of Standard English which would delete the *r*'s in Black English in the appropriate environments. According to the Independence Principle, on the other hand, no underlying *r*'s would be postulated for Black English in these environments and the relationship between the two systems would be expressed by a rule which deletes underlying Standard English *r* in the appropriate environments. Again, this rule would not be a phonological rule in either Standard English or Black English, but would merely serve to relate the two systems in an economical and revealing way.

Example D. In Black English the word *bulb* is pronounced [bɤːp]; and, in some varieties of Black English, the word *help* is pronounced [hɛp]. According to the Dependence Principle, underlying *lb* and *lp* clusters would be postulated for these words and the Black English pronunciation would be derived by introducing a rule which would delete underlying *l* in the environment of a following bilabial stop. According to the Independence Principle no underlying clusters would be postulated for these two words, even though there is an *l*-deletion rule operative in Black English which is independently motivated, and especially frequently operative in the environment of a following bilabial stop. For if we were to posit underlying clusters for *bulb* and *help* on the basis of the independently motivated *l*-deletion rule, there would be nothing preventing us from positing underlying clusters for *cub*, *sub*, *pep*, etc. except the correct but irrelevant observation that *bulb* and *help* end in clusters in Standard English, whereas *cub*, *sub*, *pep*, etc. do not. Note that the irrelevance of this observation is a direct consequence of my acceptance of the Independence Principle. Thus, even in the case of underlying representation by means of the application of independently motivated phonological rules, these representations are rejected if they necessarily entail considering Standard English data.

Example E. It is well-known fact that Black English is *r*-less. Among other things, this entails the absence of phonetic [r] in word-final position. Examples:

	SE	BE
sister	[sɪstər]	[sɪstə]
father	[faðər]	[favə]
bother	[baðer]	[bavə]
smother	[sməðər]	[sməvə]

According to the Dependence Principle, the Black English phonetic representations would be derived from underlying representations containing final *r*. According to the Independence Principle, however, the Black English pronunciations of *bother* and *smother* are derived by a rule which deletes word-final *r*, where the positing of an underlying *r* for these words is justified on the basis of the forms *bothering* and *smothering* in which [r] is present. Thus, with respect to the feature under discussion, Standard English and Black English would have the same underlying representations. Since *father* and *sister* do not have related forms which contain an [r], the only justification for positing an underlying *r* for these words is the correct but irrelevant observation that they end in *r* in *r*-full varieties of Standard English. Thus, the systematic phonemic representations for *sister* and *father* differ from those of the *r*-full varieties of Standard English in that they do not contain an underlying final *r*, even though if

there were an underlying final *r* it could be deleted at no extra cost by
the r-deletion rule which is in the grammar anyway.

Example F. In Black English there are several dozen monosyllabic and
a few polysyllabic words which phonetically contain the low front lax
unrounded vowel [a] in the environment of a single voiceless stop.
Examples:

[nat]	*not*	[lat]	*lot*
[pat]	*pot*	[tap]	*top*
[hat]	*hot*	[fəgat]	*forgot*

In addition, the word *knot* is pronounced [nɑt]; and the words *heart* and
part are pronounced [hɑt] and [pɑt], respectively. According to the
Dependence Principle, an underlying *r* would be postulated for the systematic phonemic representations of *heart* and *part*; *heart* and *part* would be
marked as exceptions to a general rule for *r*-less dialects which lengthens
the vowel preceding underlying *r*, and the underlying *r* would be deleted
by a general rule for *r*-less dialects deleting *r* preconsonantally after
lengthening. According to the Independence Principle, on the other hand,
no underlying *r* would be postulated for the Black English pronunciations
of *heart* and *part*, and the underlying representations of *heart* and *part*
differ from the underlying representations of *hot* and *pot* solely in their
vowels, i.e. /hāt/ *heart*; /pāt/ *part* vs. /hæt/ *hot*, /pæt/ *pot*. The postulation
of an underlying *r* in these words can only be justified by recourse to
Standard English data, but the consideration of standard English data is
ruled out by the Independence Principle.

Example G. A variety of considerations lead to the conclusion that
the underlying representations for the Standard English plural and preterite must be /Vz/ and /Vd/, i.e. that the phonology of these aspects of
Standard English inflection must be treated by a deletion rule rather
than an epenthesis rule and that these inflectional suffixes end in voiced
rather than voiceless consonants in their underlying representations (for
justification and discussion cf. Luelsdorff 1969). The same arguments in
support of handling the phonology of the plural and preterite by means
of a deletion rule in Standard English may be adduced to support handling the phonology of the plural and preterite by means of a deletion
rule in Black English, but the underlying representations of the consonants of these suffixes are different in Black English. The Black English
phonetic manifestation of the plural after noun stems ending in [+Coronal, +Strident] consonants is [ɪs] and the phonetic manifestation of the
preterite after verb stems ending in [+Coronal, −Continuant] consonants is [ɪt]. According to the Dependence Principle, underlying voiced
final consonants would be postulated for Black English and, by appropriately extending the utterance-final devoicing rule discussed in chapter

III, these voiced consonants would devoice. According to the Independence Principle, underlying voiceless consonants would be postulated for the dialect, and Standard English would be related to the dialect by a rule which maps certain underlying voiced consonants onto certain underlying voiceless consonants.

REFERENCES*

Applegate, Joseph R.
  1961 "Phonological rules of a subdialect of English", *Word* XVIII, 186-93.
Bailey, Beryl L.
  1965 "Toward a new perspective in Negro English dialectology", *American Speech* XL, 171-77.
Halle, Morris
  1961 "On the role of simplicity in linguistic descriptions", In *Structure of language in its mathematical aspects* (Providence, R.I.: American Mathematical Society), 89-94.
  1962 "Phonology in generative grammar", *Word* XVII, 54-72.
Klima, Edward S.
  1964 "Relatedness between grammatical systems", *Language* XL, 1-20.
Loflin, Marvin D.
  1967 "A note on the deep structure of Nonstandard English in Washington, D.C.", *Glossa* I, 26-32.
  1967 "On the structure of the verb in a dialect of American Negro English" (Columbia, Mo.: Univ. of Missouri, Center for Research in Social Behavior).
Luelsdorff, Philip A.
  1969 *Standard English for urban Blacks: pronunciation* (Programs in English Linguistics, The University of Wisconsin, Madison) and Linguistics Associates International, Department of Linguistics, The University of Wisconsin, Milwaukee, 1971, under the title *Black American English to Standard American English: exercises in phonology.*
Rosenbaum, Peter S.
  1964 "Prerequisites for linguistic studies on the effects of dialect differences on learning to read" (Project Literacy Report no. 2, Ithaca, New York: Cornell Univ.), 26-30.
Saporta, Sol
  1965 "Ordered rules, dialect differences, and historical processes", *Language* XLI, 218-24.

* For a fairly comprehensive bibliography of primary and secondary sources for the study of Black English, cf. my *Interim bibliography of Black English*, distributed at The First Wisconsin Symposium on Black English, Historical Society, The University of Wisconsin, Madison, May 1-3, 1970, by the Programs in English Linguistics, Department of English, The University of Wisconsin, Madison. The taped proceedings of this conference, comprising the presentation and discussion of papers by Daisy Crystal, Suzan Houston, Mary-Louise Kean, Burr Angle, Joey L. Dillard, Marvin D. Loflin, John B. Mack III, Philip A. Luelsdorff, and William A. Stewart, are available from the Programs in English Linguistics.

JOAN G. FICKETT

AIN'T, NOT, AND *DON'T* IN BLACK ENGLISH

Ain't, not, and *don't* play interesting roles in the syntax of Black English, particularly in the relationship to the tense system. Multiple negation, on the other hand, is shared by non-standard dialects of English and in this sense is less interesting than the operation of *ain't, not,* and *don't* in Black English.

Briefly, Black English can talk about four degrees of "pastness" and two degrees of "futurity" in relationship to a present (or "now") which is morphologically identifiable. The reference point for the present (or "now") is the point in time at which people are talking to each other. Meanings such as "a little while ago" or "momentarily" or "in a little while from now" are carried in the verbal system of Black English.

There are six such tenses in Black English which may be "phased" to the present. These, moving from present into the past, are the INCEPTIVE, the PRE-PRESENT, the RECENT PAST, and the PRE-RECENT PAST:

	Present	She singing.	'She's singing right now.'
(1)	Inceptive	She do sing.	'She just started to sing.'
(2)	Pre-present	She did sing.	'She just finished singing.'
(3)	Recent	She done sung.	'She sang recently.'
(4)	Pre-recent	She been sung.	'She sang a long time ago.'

Moving from the present into the future we have the IMMINENT and the POST-IMMINENT:

	Present	She singing.	
(1)	Imminent	She's a-sing.	'She will sing momentarily.'
(2)	Post-imminent	She's a-gonna sing.	'She will sing soon.'

Negative counterparts of the tenses are carried by distributions of *ain't*, *not*, and *don't*. The patterns are complex, involving the interplay of pitch, stress, and juncture, as well as the juxtaposition of form with form. Certain stress patterns overlay the combination of forms in phrase. A form occurring in a pattern where it has weak or tertiary stress, and its syntactic partner form has primary stress, is said to occur in MICROFIX. A form occurring with secondary (stronger) stress where its syntactic partner has primary stress is said to occur in MACROFIX. A typical microfix pattern for Black English may be noted as ($\diagdown + \diagup$). A typical macrofix pattern may be noted as ($^\wedge + \diagup$). *Ain't, not,* and *don't* all occur in microfix patterns:

(ain't + verb), (not + verb), and (don't + verb). *Ain't* and *don't* also

occur in macrofix: (ain't + verb), (don't + verb). In addition both *don't* and *ain't* may receive *emphasis* which means that as they occur in combinations with verb forms, *ain't* and *don't* (1) show primary stress, (2) high pitch, and (3) are separated from their syntactic partners by a juncture (pause phenomena).

Ain't and *don't* in microfix patterns will be noted as ain't and don't.

In macrofix they will be noted as ain't and don't. If they receive emphasis, they will be noted with a superscript ε: ain't, don't. In English, emphasis has no syntactic significance; in Black English contrastive syntactic structures may be signalled by emphasis in certain cases. In other cases, EMPHASIS carries only the same non-significance that it does in English.

A number of Black English sentences are presented and their negative counterparts juxtaposed.

(1) Negation of the present
    She singing.   'She's singing right now.'

    She not singing.   'She's not singing right now.'

    She ain't singing.   'She's not singing right now.'

(2) Negation of the inceptive
    She do sing.   'She just started to sing.'

    She don't sing.   'She hasn't started to sing yet.'

(3) Negation of the recent
    She done sung.   'She sang recently.'

    She ain't sung.   'She hasn't sung recently.'

(4) Negation of the imminent
    She's a-sing.   'She will sing momentarily.'

She ain't a-sing. [^]   'She won't sing right away.'

She ain't a-sing. [ε]

(5) Negation of the post-imminent
    She's a-gonna sing.   'She will sing soon.'

    She ain't a-gonna sing. [^]   'She won't sing soon.'

    She ain't a-gonna sing. [ε]

We note that both *not* and *ain't* operate in negating the present tense. *Not* is basic and *ain't* the emphatic. Where *ain't* occurs with a form such as *singing* (*She ain't singing*) it must be glossed as 'She's not going to sing, She doesn't intend to sing.' If *ain't* receives emphasis, (*she ain't singing*) it becomes homophonous with the emphasized present. In the absence of emphasis, *not* + *V-ing* and *ain't* + *V-ing* are clearly separate structures, with *not* + *V* unambiguously marking the present negative.

Analogously, *don't* + *V* (don't sing) sets the inceptive negative apart from the general negative:

The bell don't ring.   'The bell hasn't started to ring.'

The bell don't ring.   'The bell doesn't work.'

The bell don't ring.

A pre-present negative, *didn't* + *V*, does not occur, nor does a negative for the pre-recent, *She been sung*.
A contrast between the recent negative and a general past negative is carried by the different forms of the main verb in conjunction with *ain't*:

She ain't sing.   'She hasn't sung recently.'

She ain't sung.   'She didn't sing, hasn't sung at any time in the past.'

Not all dialects have a form *sung*.
    Speakers who contrast *ain't sing* and *ain't sung*, use the item *never* only with the latter, that is, *ain't never sung*.
    The negation of the future is a simple matter. The phased futures are clearly marked by either *a-V* or *a-gonna* + *V* and *ain't* may occur as *ain't* or *ain't*. For the general punctuative future, *She gonna sing*, 'She will sing', *ain't* may occur as *ain't* or *ain't*.

The meaning of *ain't* depends upon the forms with which it is distributed. *Don't* signals the inceptive negative and is in contrast with *don't* and *don't*, which signals a non-tensed negative. *Not* clearly signals a present negative. *Not* also marks certain topic comment sentences unambiguously as *present*:

He not here.   'He's not here right now.'
She not nice.   'She's not being nice right now.'

The negative structures, like their matching tenses, may be arranged along a time line. They are shown along with those tenses in figure 1.

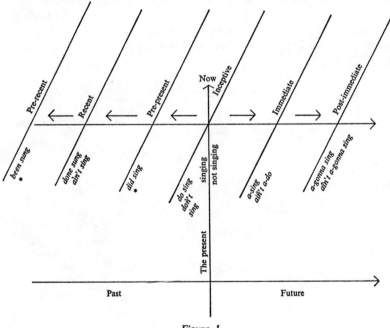

Figure 1

Ain't sung does not appear on the chart, but could be placed at a point anywhere along the line labeled PAST, as a general past negative. *Ain't gonna sing* could appear at any point along the line labeled FUTURE. *Ain't singing* could be placed between any two points along the line labeled FUTURE. *Ain't singing* and *ain't gonna sing* differ in aspect, where *singing* indicates imperfective aspect and *sing* indicates PUNCTUATIVE aspect. *Don't sing*, or the general punctuative negative, can occur at any point along the line which includes both PAST and FUTURE.

In its use of *not*, *don't*, and *ain't* Black English does not completely support its optional tense system. It does distinguish between general negatives and time limited negatives. Under continued pressure toward a more standardized language, we cannot expect further elaboration of either the tenses or their negatives, and probably the negatives will go first. On the other hand, structures which explicitly convey messages only inexplicitly or indirectly conveyed in English may become part of acceptable colloquial English. There are many Southerners, black and white, who distinguish between *I ain't a-gonna do it*, 'I'm not going to do it soon', and *I ain't gonna do it*, 'not at all'.

Like all languages, Black English can talk about things that don't happen or things that aren't going to happen. Because it has a system of tenses which indicate degrees of pastness and degrees of futurity, it can talk about how long ago things didn't happen, or how far ahead they aren't going to happen. English does not do this in its verb system; Black English does.

Section II: The History of Black English

INTRODUCTION TO SECTION II

Although it is reasonable to assume that any language variety has a legitimate history (the entire discipline of linguistic reconstruction being built upon that premise), historical explanation seems more crucial in the case of Black English than of other varieties to which attention is currently being directed. Almost any statement about Black English seems to imply something about its history. And for virtually no other variety can there have been so many explanations lacking legitimate bases consistent with linguistic relativism. The "thick lips" explanation was once so widespread, in fact, that it almost rendered taboo all inquiry into Negro dialect forms: any linguist, particularly a white one, who dared to deal with the matter was subject to automatic accusation of believing in a physiological cause of language differences. More recently, the environmentalist orientation of the educational psychologists (John 1963, Bereiter and Engelmann 1966) found a deficient language traceable to the supposedly restricting influence of a slum environment. These have by now been largely dismissed (see Stewart 1969, Baratz and Baratz 1969, Labov 1969a). But there lurks one more rationalization of deficit origin, ready to be articulated by physicalist psychologists in support of their pet early childhood intervention programs: protein deficiency!

Opposition to these premature psychological explanations probably motivated the long-time insistence upon phonological change as the causative factor. This theory was held by many linguists who were aware of the autonomous nature of Black English, like Labov (1969b). These linguists looked to Labov's zero copula rule (contraction as in Standard English, with Black English-specific deletion of /z/ representing "underlying" *is*) as an alternative to the racist belief that there was something strange about Black dialect, phonological change as "normal" change having been accepted in principle from the beginnings of historical linguistics.

In addition to the immediately obvious objection that all historical change ought to be considered "normal", however, there were other criticisms of the position that the relationship had to be expressible in terms of phonological rules. The "zero copula" (including, here, the zero form of the auxiliary comparable to a Standard English *is* in a phrase like *is going*) did not always co-occur with a present-tense (or, in terms of some linguistic descriptions of Standard English, non-past) form. There were data like

> I stayed in that hollow teeth [sic] until the storm over
> (Rich Amerson, Ethnic Folkways Record P 471A).
>
> He was scared and he holding his mother's hand
> (a Washington, D.C., informant).
>
> One day the ghost trying to scare me. And when the ghost
> try to scare me, he was coming past the house.
> (Turner 1949:279, cited as transliterated by Turner).

Besides seeming to be outside the contraction-deletion sphere (since the deletable underlying form would have to be *was* or *were*, not *is*) these sequences agreed strikingly with what is commonplace in West Indian English. The sharing of the zero copula by Gullah and urban Black English fits into the pattern suggested by the creolists, in which structures in which other Black varieties differ from Gullah represent greater decreolization in those varieties. (On the possibility of some decreolization in Gullah, see section III and the material on Guinea, below.)

Phonological change would apparently also be invoked to explain other relationships, like that of zero (or unmarked) possessive to the inflectionally marked possessive (Black English *the lady hat*, Standard English *the lady's hat*). Such usages in the Black community have been frequently observed, as by prescriptive-minded teachers (Loban 1967). Reasoning analogous to that relating the "zero copula" to *is* phonologically virtually dictated that the possessive rule also be considered to be phonological in nature. As the copula had to be realized in "exposed" position:

> John not working? Yes, he is!
> *Yes, he!

so the possessive could not always be zero

> Dat he book? Yes, it his.
> *Yes, it he.

In this requirement of overt marking in "exposed" position, Black English agreed with Standard English, and perhaps with language universals. But

there were explanations of the agreement which did not demand derivation of Black English from Standard English, conceived as some kind of
super-language.

The various English Creoles, to which Black English seems to be
related, also require "fillers" in such exposed positions. In the terms of
one grammatical theory, they would have the category present in deep
(or underlying) structure and delete it by later rules — in some systems,
phonological rules. For example, in Gullah one version of the possessive
is

him grandfather (Turner 1949:268).

Obviously, some other form would be required in "exposed" position,
making impossible (as a possessive absolute)

*Yes, it him.

In this case, however, Gullah (including somewhat decreolized versions
of urban Gullah) utilizes *own* rather than the possessive "'s" inflection
of Standard English:

me own (Turner 1949:275).

Black English basilect (in the sense of Stewart 1964) would have

Yes, it he own.[1]

The creolist theory (the two articles by Stewart in this section, Bailey
1965, Dillard 1972) would hold that Black English

Yes, it his.

involves historically a relexification of

Yes, it he own.[2]

which can hardly take place as a PHONOLOGICAL process, although it
is certainly both a natural and a normal linguistic change.

There are many other developments in Black English which are
clarified in terms of this relationship to Gullah. For example, simple
phonological observation establishes the use of /bowf/ for BOTH in the
Black English of inner city children. But closer observation will disclose
the basilect form *all bofe*. Gullah has, of course, *all two*. Decreolization,
taking the form of relatively within-awareness lexical imitation without
equal success in the area of out-of-awareness grammatical factors, easily

[1]   There is some evidence from hypercorrection. Loman (1968:21) reports "An' mine's
ain' bout no ghos'".
[2]   Ambrose Gonzales, *The Black Border*, lists "me own 'mine, my'" (p. 314); "you'
own 'your own, yours'" (p. 340). Gonzales also has, of course, unmarked possessives

explains how *all bofe* arises in a dialect which is intermediate between Gullah and Standard English. The phonological change (/θ/ to /f/) is irrelevant. It does not even matter whether the sound change took place before or after the lexical replacement of *two* with *both*.[3]

There are many analogies to the decreolized varieties of the West Indies. On many of the islands, the form

You coming (affirmative statement).

is questioned merely by intonation:

You coming?

However, some speakers, interested in switching to a more prestigious variety of English, produce

Is you coming?

"Joe maussah duh him Jedus" (p. 24); "Him wife" (p. 107).

Loman (1968:8) presents an interesting form: "Well, le's see your one."

Stewart (personal communication) regards the ultimate source as *Pn one*, of which the Loman form might be a survival. Hancock (personal communication) cites Krio *yes, na ī yon*.

For the use of data from writers like Gonzales, who, despite his obvious racism, was proficient in Gullah from childhood, see Stewart "Continuity and Change" (reprinted in this section). A subtler problem, which is actually more difficult to deal with, concerns the transcription practices of writers like Gonzales. Does *own*, at least in some cases, in his transcriptional practices represent what would be *one* in another transcriptional system? Unfortunately, the much more sophisticated transcription of Turner (1949) is concerned with a corpus which in many ways is more limited than that of Gonzales, Charles Colcock Jones, Jr., and other dialect writers.

[3] The nature of the decreolization process — and, therefore, of the relationship between Black English and Gullah — is frequently misunderstood. For example, Davis (1969) observes:

"Getting back to the /θ, ð > f, v/ shift, it is notable that in Gullah, an undisputed creole, these interdental fricatives become /t/ and /d/, respectively, and not /f/ and /v/. I find it odd that, if all Black dialects supposedly contain this shift because of a creole substratum, Gullah does not also contain it" (in Wolfram and Clarke 1971:93).

If Davis had consulted his creolist sources carefully enough, he would have observed that they specify forms with /t, d/ as ONE stage of Black English. Insofar as forms realized in Standard English with /θ ð/ are concerned, this stage is roughly identical to Gullah. The realization with /f, v/ is, in fact, an elegantizing pronunciation, ranking in acropetal shift at about the same level as /θ, ð/ (Stewart 1964). Elegantizing his basilect /t, d/ pronunciation, the Black English speaker "spirantizes" his pronunciation without much regard as to whether the end product is /θ, ð/ or /f, v/. Perhaps because of the data collection procedures, the full alternation /d ~ v ~ ð, t ~ f ~ θ/ is absent from Luelsdorff (f.c.) and only hinted at in Williamson (1968).

Peripheral evidence for the relationship between Black English and Gullah lies in the widespread use of GEECHEE as a designation of the language forms regarded as most aberrant. Hancock (personal communication) reports it from Texas, and it is well known in Florida and on Cape Cod.

The same thing happens, of course, in U.S. Black English; in fact, it could be said to be the basilect form. *Is* can become a general question marker, producing (in conjunction with another development in which *I'm*, the contraction of *I am*, is borrowed as a variant of the pronoun *I*) the now almost famous

Miss, is Im failing English?

In both urban Black English and Gullah, *is* may be associated with other than third-person subjects:

You is a fool (Turner 1949:289).

Even more obviously non-phonological (although explainable in terms of some familiar concept like hypercorrection) is the use of *am* as a verbal auxiliary with all persons. (For examples, see Brewer, all entries.)

There has not been any real denial of the participation of Gullah (and Louisiana French Creole) in the area of creole languages. Establishing a continuum between Gullah and the Black dialects of other parts of the United States, including the urban North, obviates the need to explain the historical development of those dialects in terms of any special, new processes. It also eliminates the formerly apparent moral necessity to explain their development in terms of phonological change, since another explanation in terms of "natural" and "normal" change has been found. This also apparently means that the investigator of language variation who uses data from Black English is not thereby making any claim about the psychological processes of the speakers of that variety — beyond the modest one that they are the same psychological processes involved in the production of any language or dialect.

The relationship of Black American English to the creole tradition has long been recognized by specialists in that field (Bailey 1965, Dalby 1969). This means that a dialect of English exists in the United States which is historically related to Krio and Saramaccan, not Yorkshire and Scottish dialects. Because it reopens the entire issue of language contact within the continental United States (see General Introduction), this interpretation has been bitterly contested by some historical linguists, especially those who have thought that American English dialects could be traced exclusively in terms of British English settlement patterns (Kurath 1928, 1965; Davis 1969, 1971).

Against this, the creolists have been able to offer not only the evidence of structural correspondences with West Indian and West African varieties of English, but documentation going back at least as far as 1692. The rebuttal expressed by defenders of the traditional position has been to deny the validity of the documents (Krapp 1925, Stockton 1964). In one extreme case, the validity of all documentation has been denied (Davis 1969).[4]

If historical dialectology in the continental United States has shown a strange preference for the suppositions of the internal reconstructionists over documentation (and for reconstruction over history, despite the tremendous mass of recorded attestation), the same has not been true of the Caribbean or of West Africa. In the Caribbean, there have been Taylor (1961, in press), Cassidy (1962, 1971), Voorhoeve (1961), and many other students of recorded attestation. In West Africa, there have been Jones (1962), Schneider (1967), Hancock (1969, 1971), Dalby (1969), and others. One of the earliest and most noteworthy, although virtually ignored, was Paul Christophersen, whose 1953 and 1959 articles are reprinted here. As Christophersen showed, documents like the reports of John Barbot, John Atkins, William Smith, and other travellers clearly show the use of Pidgin English in the West African slave trade. They also demonstrate its connection to Portuguese Trade Pidgin — which is one reason why the whole issue is a confusing one to conventional-minded historical dialectologists whose experience has been limited to English (or perhaps English and German).

Since the earliest Plantation Creole in the United States was very closely linked to the West African and West Indian slave trade and its language contact situation, the nature of that creole on the early plantations (especially in the eighteenth century) becomes an issue again. Was it merely a more widespread Gullah? Even that modest suggestion has been a red flag to the more conventional. But is it possible that what was spoken by the field hands on the big plantations was closer to Saramaccan (i.e. with, in addition to much Portuguese vocabulary, such African features as imploded stops and tonal contrasts)? It is worth examining the evidence.

In J. F. D. Smyth's 1775 account, it is asserted that

> ... many of the others also speak a mixed dialect
> between the Guinea and the English. (p. 39).

It is widely assumed (e.g. Dillard 1972) that "Guinea" (geographically a

---

[4] Davis asserts "... by using the first part of his *Confessions*, one could "prove" that St. Augustine was a profligate. Or, by looking at only a segment of *Elijah*, one could also conclude that the prophet was viciously anti-Semitic."

In short, Davis apparently believes that he has reduced documentation (as in the two articles by Stewart, reprinted in this section) to absurdity. It is, however, not quite true that "anything" can be proved even by selective documentation. For example, Davis is invited to "prove" by selective quotation, that the women of the West African-derived American slave population spoke Tagalog whereas the men spoke Cheremis. Even more relevantly, he might try to "prove" by such quotation, from contemporary or near-contemporary sources, that members of the slave population learned British dialects.

term, at that time, for anything African) must have meant African languages. This is, however, implausible: if many African languages had been around, there would hardly have been any reason to call them in the singular; and observers could hardly have been so obtuse as to take many African languages for one. There is, further, the well-known problem of language mixing by the slave dealers.

Because of his explicit statements, as well as for his relative objectivity as a visiting Englishman, Smyth would seem to provide valuable evidence. He was very closely associated with at least two slaves, whom he bought while on his trip. Of the first he reported

> ...for he scarcely understood a single word that
> I said to him, nor did I know one syllable of his
> language (I, 79).

It is virtually inconceivable that this slave, purchased by Smyth in Petersburg, Virginia, was not able to communicate with other members of the slave community. Probably, also, such speakers of English Creole could communicate with whites who had learned the variety. Other assumptions make it difficult to understand how the slaves could have survived. The hypothesis that this particular slave spoke only the equivalent of Saramaccan would explain (although of course there are other explanations, as that the slave didn't WANT to understand and be understood) why Smyth — in only a slight exaggeration — "didn't know one syllable" of his language. Smyth's other slave Richmond (bought in North Carolina) spoke something which is obviously Creole (quoted in Dillard 1972:87), and was capable of discourse tactics, like copping a plea, which are familiar from recent investigations of ghetto verbal strategies.

Provisionally, let us assume that there were at least two varieties represented in the slave community of the continental colonies around 1775:

(1) "Guinea", so heavily Africanized (and possibly with non-English vocabulary from another source) that it was unintelligible to those who had not learned that specific variety.
(2) A variety already somewhat merged with white varieties, but still too deviant from any British dialect to be regarded as anything but Creole (perceivable, although of course not nameable, as such by any observer).

If this was the situation in Virginia and North Carolina around 1775, and there is other evidence to support it,[5] it may be especially instructive to consider the situation in the North at an earlier period.

---

[5] Another possibility, far more deviant from the traditional language history of the Americas, would be that many whites learned an African language, or languages, in the

On Manhattan Island, in the city of New York, in 1741, Justice Daniel Horsmanden reported how the language of Jack, the leader of an alleged slave plot, had to be interpreted for the court by two young (white) men who had conversed with him enough to understand his dialect. (The passage is quoted in the General Introduction, p. 14.) Jack's testimony, which does not bulk very large in the trial report, took three days. Jack, if he was a leader, could hardly have had a speech impediment.[6] In the brief passage cited by Horsmanden, nothing seems especially strange except

---

early period. This is what seems to be suggested by J. Graham Cruickshank: "Probably every planter of the day — certainly every experienced and sensible one — knew a little African himself ... Many a planter before-time could have compiled a very creditable Kongo or K'romanty dictionary..." (*'Black Talk', Being Notes on Negro Dialect in British Guiana, with (inevitably) a Chapter on the Vernacular of Barbados*, Demarara, 1916).

This is, however, an unsupported assertion. The data which Cruickshank himself presents (*A-we country, pull 'Nancy story*) is obviously Creole. Cruickshank reports "ten or twenty dialects [i.e. African languages] heard in the West Indies" (p. 2), but does not identify them or give any evidence. It is probably significant that he specifies the ability of the "before-time" planter to compile a DICTIONARY, since that planter is much more likely to have learned some West African vocabulary incorporated into the contact language than to have acquired one or more West African languages. Cf. the Liberian English of Cape Palmas (Hancock, this volume, Appendix).

[6]   The use of *Guinea* as a descriptive term, and of course the hypothetical approximation to Saramaccan, is most characteristically eighteenth-century. In Samuel Low's drama *The Politician Outwitted* (1788), it is said of a Frenchman who speaks with an almost incomprehensible accent that "He talks as crooked as a Guine niger" (III:1). In this context, it is clear that *crooked* refers to unintelligible English and not to dishonesty. In the same play, set in New York City, there is a Negro with the day name Cuffy who has one long speech: "Tankee, massa buckaraw; you gi me lilly lif, me bery glad; — disa ting damma heby ... An de debelis crooka tone in a treet more worsa naw pricka pear for poor sona bitch foot; and de cole pinch um so too!" (V:1). There is no application of the term *Guinea* to Cuffy or to his speech, and no indication that it is unintelligible to white New Yorkers. In terms of my hypothesis (above), he would be a speaker of variety (2); other New York City Blacks of the time, of variety (1) ("Guinea").

The tradition of the use of the term survived into the nineteenth century, as in the quotation from Olmsted above and in Frederick Douglass's *My Bondage and My Freedom*: "There is not, probably, in the whole south, a plantation where the English language is more imperfectly spoken than on Col. Lloyd's. It is a mixture of Guinea and everything else you please" (Arno Press edition, 1968, p. 76).

The citations by Douglass, like *Lloyd Bill* 'Lloyd's Bill', *Oo you dem belong to?* 'Whom do you belong to?' and *Oo dem got any peachy?* 'Have you got any peaches?' suggest neither an extremely "deep" Creole nor linguistic observation by Douglass which was very different from that of the plantation novelists. He specifies that the users of such language were "from the coast of Africa" and that "I could scarcely understand them when I first went among them, so broken was their speech." Again, the absolute correlation of "deep" Creole forms and African provenience does not hold perfectly true: there are, today, varieties of Cameroonian Pidgin/creole which are much less "bizarre" to speakers of British or American English than Saramaccan.

for the phonology of *fat* 'white'.[7] But Horsmanden very possibly cited that segment just because it was a rare part of the speech of Jack which he was able to understand. Otherwise, Horsmanden rather proudly displayed what he knew of "the Negroes'" — not Jack's — dialect. He cites the day names, although of course not with that interpretation. The people of New York seem to have been familiar with that dialect — or with ONE Negro dialect — but not with the dialect of Jack. Jack, as a leader, may have been more closely identified with "African" culture than other slaves — as happened frequently in the early history of slave revolts. Is it a considerable supposition that Jack spoke "Guinea" and that some of the other New York slaves spoke variety (2) — the situation that would prevail in Virginia-North Carolina thirty years or so later?

Seventy-five years later, Yankee historian and reporter Frederick Law Olmsted found a lot of Plantation Creole in the South in which he had a professional interest. He reported of one slave that she

> ... was a native African, having been brought when a
> girl from the Guinea coast ...

Here, as elsewhere, Guinea obviously means nothing more specific than (West) Africa. Olmsted also reported that, in her talk with her master in Olmsted's presence, she produced

> ... some conversation, in which I had not been able
> to understand a word ...

Again, both the slave and the white master spoke and understood SOMETHING which the Northerner Olmsted was unable to follow. (His "not ... a word" may of course be a humorous exaggeration.) He also reported some conversation from the same slave woman which he was able to understand:

> I lubs 'ou, Mass'r, oh I lubs 'ou. I don't want go
> 'way from 'ou.

Like Jack in New York, this slave woman was able to produce some sentences which an outsider could not understand without interpretation.

---

[7] The form *fat* (cited by Horsmanden and here interpreted as [ɸa·t]) is at least potentially ambiguous. It can of course be argued that 'a fat horse' is meant, in spite of the greater probability of 'a white horse' (i.e. horses are more usually identified by color than by weight). But the spelling *f-* for an initial consonant which is spelled *wh-* in non-dialect writing abounds in the plantation literature of the late eighteenth century and a little later, as in the speech attributed to Cuff in Hugh Henry Breckenridge's *Modern Chivalry* (1792): "Oh! Fat dey call it all tone." "Oh! What name do they give to something that's all stone?"

The plantation literature frequently records forms like *a fite man* (obviously, 'a white man').

   Pidgin English, in West Africa today, is not the monolithic thing which it may appear to be to those who have no experience with it beyond reading a description or two. (This holds true, even if we leave aside the considerable problem as to whether certain varieties, as in the West Cameroon, should be called pidgin or creole — or whether some new designation is necessary.) Some indication of the kind of variety which exists can be found in an appendix to Schneider (1966). Pidgin English speakers can occasionally make themselves intelligible to Europeans, but there are styles and registers of Pidgin which the un-initiated white can not follow at all. It may well be that this kind of variation existed on the plantations of the continental colonies, the early United States (including some Northern states), and the slave-owning South before the Civil War.

   For these reasons, it seems reasonable to conclude that the linguist who has no perspective on the "English" varieties of West Africa and of Surinam has essentially no perspective on the Black English of the United States. Knowledge of Gullah is important — and all too rare — but not sufficient. Fortunately, there are now available studies on the varieties spoken in Surinam, Sierra Leone, the Cameroons, and the West Indian islands.[8] Liberia, which should in many ways be closest to the historical pattern in the United States because of the obvious ties, remains, unfortunately, very poorly and sketchily studied. Hancock's article (reprinted here) represents essentially the viewpoint of a Krioist, with some comparison to New World varieties.

   There is also, fortunately, some historical depth in the study of the West African varieties. Some of the early studies, like Grade's (reprinted here), even approach the kind of formality which characterized early modern linguistics. Grade, it will be noted, makes comparison to American literary representations like those of Joel Chandler Harris — comparisons which regularly strike anyone who is familiar with the West African varieties. The *Religious Intelligencer* excerpts, far less professional than the others, are nevertheless interesting indications of on-the-spot observation in West Africa. And one section represents the reporting of Pidgin English in use by West Africans by another West African whose English is itself not perfectly standard.

   Observers like Harrison and Payne obviously represent a level of sophistication somewhere between that of the *Religious Intelligencer* and that of Hancock and Christophersen. They are included partly to document the continuity of observation of Black English in the United States.

---

[8] Especially valuable are Hancock, "A Study of the Sources and Development of Sierra Leone Krio" (London University dissertation, 1971) and "A Provisional Comparison of the English-derived Atlantic Creoles", *African Language Review* VII (1969): 7-22.

Wise was, of course, a reputable scholar and a totally different kind of observer. It is noteworthy that both he and Payne point out the influence (further documented in Dillard 1972) of Black English on Southern white dialect.

But the two articles by Stewart carry the burden of proof of historical relationship between Black English of the United States/continental colonies and the West African and West Indian varieties. They were controversial articles when printed, and they remain pace-setting and controversial. In these articles and elsewhere, Stewart has produced enough documents of the speech of slaves in the United States (see also Dillard 1972) to leave the denial of documentary significance as the only recourse of those who would deny the creolist hypothesis. Stewart's articles (like that printed in the first section) also contain educational recommendations — which were in general excluded from this collection. It was felt, however, that the articles were important enough to be reproduced in their original form.

Detailed internal comparisons between the articles here reprinted (and other interesting sources), an ambition of the editor in the beginning, have proved beyond the scope of this collection. One could note, however, such common elements as *palaver* in Christophersen's first article (pp. 206-208) and in Harrison's (p. 187). To these could be compared Fisher's (n.d.) citations proving that the semantic shift from Portuguese 'word' to Southern Black English 'argue or talk' had begun in West Africa as early as 1704.[9] It is also interesting to note that Harrison (p. 187) cites *bimeby* 'after a while', well known as a Pidgin English futurizer, and not only in the West African-related varieties.

[9]   See Fisher (n.d.) and Dillard, "Creole Portuguese and Creole English: The Early Records", *Center for African and African-American Studies, CAAS Papers in Linguistics*, no. 3 (1971).

THE RELIGIOUS INTELLIGENCER
FOR THE YEAR ENDING MAY, 1821 (VOL. V)
CONTAINING
THE PRINCIPAL TRANSACTIONS
OF THE VARIOUS
BIBLE AND MISSIONARY SOCIETIES,
WITH PARTICULAR ACCOUNTS OF
REVIVALS OF RELIGION

New Haven:
Conducted and Published Weekly
by Nathan Whiting
1820

[Most of the West African Pidgin English materials in the *Religious Intelligencer* come from a group at Regent's Town, Sierra Leone. It is briefly described in the following passage:

Natives of twenty-two different nations were here collected together; and a considerable number of them had been but recently liberated from the holds of Slave Vessels; they were greatly prejudiced against one another, and in a state of continual hostility, with no common medium of intercourse but a little broken English. (Excerpt dated March, 1820, from p. 658.) — Editor.]

EXCERPT I (from p. 40) [dated June, 1820]

The power of the Word of God is striking displayed in the following cases of some Female Communicants, all of whom, except one, are of the Ebo Nation, which is the most savage of the tribes that arrive in the Slave Vessels: —
    E. II. "My heart trouble me too much. Sometimes me heart so hard, that it will not let me pray. I hope the Lord Jesus Christ will teach me, more and more, to love him, and to serve him. I, poor guilty sinner, thank God for send Jesus Christ to save poor sinners."

M. A. "My heart remember, this time, all them bad thing me do before. Me bad too much. Me heart trouble me too much. Me pray Jesus Christ have mercy upon me poor sinner! make me to love you more, more, more!" — I asked, "Do you understand this time when I talk God-palaver?" [that is respecting Religion] — she said, "Yes! me understand this time: first time me hear, when you talk, Massa, sometimes me afraid too much: me afraid me no love Jesus Christ."

M. M. "Wicked thing trouble me too much. Me want to do good, but me wicked heart can't let me. Me heart run away all this week — run all about." — "What do you mean, Mary, when you say your heart run all about?" Suppose me pray, my heart run to my country — to Sierra Leone — all about. Sometimes them things me no want to remember, come in my heart; and then me can't say no more, but 'Jesus Christ have mercy upon me, poor thing!' I no sabby what we must do. I hope Jesus Christ will save me. Suppose he no save me, me sabby lost for ever. Sometimes you preach, Massa — me think you only talk to me: me say in my heart, 'That me! me been do that thing!' Me fraid me no love Jesus Christ yet. Me want to love and to serve Him too much; but me bad heart! Me think sometimes me have two hearts — one want do good; that other always want do bad. Oh Jesus! have mercy upon me, poor sinner!"

I. A. "My husband trouble me too much, Masa. He no pray: he no serve God. Suppose me talk to him about God-palaver, he take whip and flog me. Me have trouble too much, trouble too much! but the Lord Jesus help me to take all trouble. But Massa, sometimes me fraid he no love me, and me no love him. Oh may he teach me for good! Suppose, Massa, you no been come in this country, we all sabby go fire — we be sabby nothing: [that is, we now know that we should have perished — we know nothing of ourselves]. We thieve — we lie — we do all that is bad. I thank God for send you hear, for teach us poor sinners!"

M. C. "My heart too wicked. Me can't love Jesus Christ. Me want to love him, but my wicked heart won't let me. When I pray, my heart tell me, 'What you pray for! Jesus Christ no hear your prayer! You too bad!' Me no love my Brethren in the Lord: me do not know what to do to love them. Sometimes my husband tell me something, me heart no like it — it raise up. May Jesus Christ give me a better heart! for my heart bad past all hearts."

S. I. "Me been sick, Massa. Me think me die. Me fraid too much. Me think me no belong to Jesus Christ. Me want to love and to serve him too much; because he die for me, poor sinner. Me heart love this world too much. Me pray that Christ may teach me more and more, to love and to serve him."

(*To be concluded.*)

EXCERPT II (from p. 51) [dated June, 1820]

REGENT'S TOWN (SIERRA LEONE)

Another school-girl, about sixteen years of age, gave him [Mr. Johnson, a missionary] a most interesting account of the state and conflicts of her mind: —

"About three months past, you talk to the school girls. When you done talk, plenty girls go and tell you what they been hear on Sunday. You pass me, and ask me what the matter that me no hear something. Me no answer; but me shame too much. You tell me that you think, and be fraid, that me never pray to Jesus Christ; but be careless and prayerless, and going down to hell. When you say this, me no like it at all. You done. Me go home. Me begin to fear too much. Me try to pray; but my heart came like stone. Me consider all them bad things me do before. Me fear more, more. Me no sleep, me fear me die and go to hell. Since that time me no feel rest; me think nobody be bad past me; me worst, past all. But me think how that Jesus Christ be strong enough to save me. But me sorry too much that my bad heart is always against me: it will not let me serve the Lord Jesus Christ. Me no sabby what to do with my bad heart."

(from p. 52)
We shall close these extracts respecting the young of Mr. Johnson's flock, by his account of the death of one of the school girls, about fifteen years of age: —

She always complained greatly of the depravity of her heart. I was called up this morning about one o'clock, by the woman who attends the sick in the Female Hospital. I found this poor girl in great distress of mind. She cried aloud — "Massa, what shall I do! what shall I do! I am going to die now; and my sins be too much — I thief — I lie — I curse — I do bad too much — I bad past all people; and now me must die! — What shall I do!"

EXCERPT III (from pp. 265-66) [dated September, 1820]

WEST AFRICA
Sierra Leone

We continue some further extracts from communications from Christian Negroes at Regent's Town. They derive their principal interest from the fact, that they are the production of native Africans, who not long since were liberated from slave-vessels. During the rains of last year, when

Mr. Johnson, their minister, was absent, and a number were sick, one of these Christian converts gives the following representation of their troubles:

I staid at Charlotte Town, when Mr. Taylor was sick; and I speak to the people the Word of God. One time we meet together for Missionary Prayer Meeting. Oh, that time many White People sick! and many of them die!

And, that time, we lose one of our ministers, Mary Moddy. She was brought to bed, and the child died, and herself caught cold; and I went to see her; and I asked her "How you do?" she said, "I fear too much." — I asked her, "What you fear for?" and she said, "I done sin" — and I said, "Pray to the Lord Jesus Christ: He only can do you good" — and I prayed with her; and the next day I went again, and I say unto her, "How do you feel in your heart?" and she said, "Oh, my heart too wicked;" and I said, "Do you pray to Jesus Christ?" she said, "Yes! to whom should I pray, if I not pray to the Lord Jesus Christ?" — and I talked with her, and then I prayed with her, and went away. The next day I went again, and she could hardly speak: I prayed with her, and stop with her; and, by and by, she died.

That time Mr. Cates sick, and Mr. Morgan sick; and poor Mr. Cates die. I think the journey to the Bassa Country, which he take, that too much for him: the sand so long to walk, and the sun so hot — yet I cannot prove that. But I think his work done, and his time up. When he was sick, I went to see him. "How you do, Mr. Cates?" and he said "I shall certainly die:" — and, by and by, he got down to Freetown, and he sick very much: all his strength gone; but he was a man of faith; and he die on Friday about five o'clock; and, on Saturday, we go to bury him four o'clock, and we look upon him: and then we went to Mr. Jesty's house; and Mr. Jesty tell us, and say, he think God would leave this place, because White People die fast; and when I hear that, I fear too much, and I consider many things in my mind, and I think Hypocrites live among us, and God want to punish us; but I trust again in the Lord: He knows his people; He never forsake them.

EXCERPT IV (from pp. 729-31) [dated April, 1821]

REGENT'S TOWN
(SIERRA LEONE)

CHURCH MISSIONARY SOCIETY
Influence of Religion on the Negroes
Continued from page 709

After service, several of the communicants expressed great joy. One, an old man, said, "Massa, my heart sing: me glad too much." I asked,

"What makes your heart sing?" — "Ah! Massa! you see that poor thief you talk about — he no be good at all — he be bad, when they hang him on the cross, God teach — He shew him bad heart — He make him pray to Jesus Christ: he say, *Lord remember me!* Jesus no say, 'Me no want you — you too bad — you be thief too much.' No! He no say so: but take him, and tell him, *To-day thou shalt be with me in Heaven.* I see Christ take poor sinner: that make me glad too much. Ah! my heart sing. True, me bad — me very bad — me sin too much: but Jesus Christ can make me good. He take poor thief — He take me — me the same. Thank God! Thank God!"

One night a house caught fire, and was burnt down. The alarm bell was rung, and the people rose and ran to the spot. One of the communicants, who had not heard the alarm, was much distressed, and said —

"Last night that house burn — the bell ring — all people got up, and go to the fire; but I no hear it. I sleep all night until this morning — then the people tell me — this make me fraid too much. Jesus Christ shall come in the same fashion, and me fraid he find me sleep." The same tenderness of conscience is manifested by the young. A girl said —

"Massa, last Sunday you say that God's people have no business to keep company with the wicked. On Monday morning I go with one bad girl down to the brook, and I have no business to go with her. When I walk with her a stick cut my toe. I think about them words you talk in Church — my heart strike me — I come home — and cry; but, Massa, I no cry about my toe, that time, when you see me, but I cry about my sins."

The following conversations with persons who are not yet communicants, shew the manner in which it pleases God by His grace to awaken the minds of these people.

"Massa", said an Ebo man, one of the people naturally most savage, "I come to you to talk about God palaver. Me heart trouble me too much — me want to pray, but me no sabby how to pray." — "What do you want to pray for?" "Me want to pray to God to save me — me too bad." — "What makes you bad?" "Me remember me thief — me lie — me curse — me do bad thing too much; and no remember me do good ["]; He appeared to be convinced of sin. I questioned him on the Saviour's ability to save him, but found him not clear on that head. I gave him such instructions as will relieve him, if blessed by the Holy Spirit. "Massa", said a second, "I can't get rest at all — my wicked heart trouble me. None can do me good, except the Lord Jesus Christ. He only can do me good." — "If you are persuaded of that, then go to Him: He says, *Whosoever cometh unto me, I will in no wise cast out.*" "I cannot go to Him by my own strength, Massa." — "Did you ever pray to Him?" "Yes, I pray;

but I can't tell if God hear my prayer. Sometimes, when I pray, I feel glad; but sometimes, when I pray, my heart run all about, and then I feel no peace." "What makes you feel glad sometimes?" "Because Jesus Christ been hang on the cross for poor sinners — He shed His blood to save sinners."

"Once, Massa", said a school girl, who appeared much distressed in her mind, "you say in the Church, "Every one who dies without believing in Jesus Christ would go to hell!" Them words, Massa, live always before my ear — make me afraid too much — and again me do bad very much. Every day me heart plague me — me get bad more and more — me don't know what to do." She wept bitterly. "How long is it you feel so?" "Before you go to England, and since that time me heart trouble me — no good thing live in me heart. I hope the Lord Jesus Christ will have mercy upon me. Suppose he no save me, I must go to hell. I want to pray to Him, and sometimes me pray; but me think He no hear me. I have no strength, but I trust the Lord help me."

We shall close these extracts with an affecting narrative.

March 4, 1820. Several people spoke in such a manner this evening, that I felt what I cannot express. One woman, who has been in my school, and is now married, said, "When I very young, my mother die. Soon after, bad sick come in my country. People look quite well, and all at once they fall down and die. So much people die, that they could not bury them. Sometimes six or seven people stand at one place, and all at once three or four fall down and die. My father take me, and run to another country, because he fraid of that bad sick. My father got sick, but he no die; me got sick too. One day father send me to get some cassada; two men meet me in the road, catch me, and carry me to the Headman, and tell the Headman that me thief: the Headman say that they must sell me. Massa, me no been thief that time; but they wanted to sell me, therefore they tell that lie. Just when they wanted to carry me away my father come — he very sick — he look me, and they tell him me thief, and they go and sell me. My father begin to beg them, but they no hear. My father stand and cry; and, Massa, since you talk that Palaver about Missionary, and about our fathers and mothers, me no have rest." Here she burst into tears, and said, "My father always stand before my eyes. O poor man! he no sabby anything about Jesus Christ." She wept very loud, after a little she continued her sad tale. "After they carried me two days, they sold me. I do not know what they got for me. I stop there a little, and then people carry me to another place, and sell me again with plenty more people. Me very sick that time: oh! me so poor, me nothing but bone. After the man that buy me look me, he say, 'This girl no good — she go to die. I will kill her — she no good to sell.' A woman live there (I think it was one of him wife): she beg the man not to kill me." She here wept again bitterly, and said, "O massa, God send that woman to save my life. Suppose that woman no come and beg for me, what place I live now?" She wept again, and could not proceed with her tale.

P. GRADE

DAS NEGER-ENGLISCH AN DER WESTKÜSTE VON AFRIKA

§1. Mensch und sprache, das sind zwei begriffe, von denen jeder selbständig für sich ohne den zweiten nicht vorgestellt werden kann; eng
verflechten sie sich mit einander und ergänzen sich gegenseitig, stets in
harmonischer wechselwirkung. Seine sprache wächst mit dem menschen
auf, entwickelt und vervollkommnet sich, sie wird des individuums
ureigenstes eigentum, zugleich aber der ausdruck seines ganzen seins.
Und was wir bei dem einzelnen menschen beobachten, das geschieht
auch in den gemeinschaften jener, den grösseren völkerverbänden. Der
sprache des kindes fehlen die bezeichnungen abstrakter begriffe, aber
reichlich vorhanden sind solche, mit denen die fassbaren gegenstände der
umgebung bezeichnet werden und bilder, welche die einfachsten vor-
kommnisse des lebens darstellen können. Verfolgen wir den entwicklungs-
gang der sprache eines ganzen volkes, so stossen wir überall auf genau die
gleichen erscheinungen. Ueberall haben wir im ersten stadium des seins
und werdens eine ausserordentliche mannigfaltigkeit der formen und der
bezeichnung concreter gegenstände. Die ganze sprache ist musik; wolklang
der worte und des ganzen satzgefüges, poetischer und freier ausdruck und
bildlichkeit der gedanken charakterisieren sie und mit ihr den, der sich
ihrer bedient. Hier ist alles gefühl und herz. Aber das alter ist nüchterner,
kühler und erkennt nur den verstand allein als seinen richter und leiter an.
Die vollen, tönenden formen, welche einer schnellen gedankendarstellung
hinderlich oder beschwerlich sind, sie fliegen über bord und werden an-
fangs noch durch schwache anklänge ersetzt, bis am ende auch diese
schwinden. Was einerseits die sprache an poesie und der davon unzer-

Reprinted from *Anglia* (1892) with the permission of Max Niemeyer Verlag.

trennlichen, grösseren schwierigkeit des ausdrucks und des verständnisses und andrerseits an umständlichkeit einbüsst, das gewinnt sie jetzt an klarheit, schärfe und kürze. Die epische behaglichkeit, welche ihre freude an langatmigen schilderungen und wiederholungen findet, die den begriff der zeit nicht kennt, denn zehn jahre sind vor ihr wie ein tag, an dem des menschen alter kaum zugenommen, sie muss vor dem harten, materiellen "time is money" weichen.

Das goldene zeitalter entfloh auf ewig, zurück blieb das eiserne. Wenn irgendwo, so kann man die reihe solcher erscheinungen in dem entwicklungsgange der englischen sprache deutlich beobachten.

Das Altenglische zeigt einen reichtum an unterschiedlichen formen, wie wir sie in den stammverwandten sprachen, dem Gotischen und Altdeutschen, im Griechischen des Homer und in anderer weise in den altsemitischen sprachen finden. Singular, plural, dual, männliches, weibliches und sächliches geschlecht werden genau unterschieden, da giebt es noch eine declination der substantiva, sowie der adjectiva,und ihrer nicht nur eine, sondern zwei. Wortzusammensetzungen sind in erster linie den gesetzen harmonischen wolklangs angepasst, wie wiederum das Gotische und Altdeutsche auch hier gleiches leisten.

Das Mittelenglische stellt sich nun als eine fast neue sprache dar. Das verständniss für die alten kräftigen und ausdrucksvollen endungen, welche wol schon am ende der altenglischen periode ausser gebrauch zu kommen begannen, ist völlig verloren gegangen. In einem reste von anhänglichkeit an des "gute alte" werden sie zwar nicht überall verworfen, doch treten sie entstellt und verstümmelt, oft kaum noch erkennbar uns entgegen. Von jenen feinen unterschieden in der declination und conjugation sind jetzt nur noch schwache spuren festzustellen.

Die moderne zeit, zwar eine geistige blüteperiode, doch der beginn und die fortsetzung des ruhelosesten hastens und ausnützens des augenblicks, räumt mit dem letzten in pietät bewahrten gründlich auf. Jetzt ist die sprache fertig. Sie noch einfacher zu gestalten scheint kaum denkbar. Wo aber hierauf gerichtete bestrebungen zu tage treten, da müssen ungeheuerlichkeiten notwendig herauskommen, welche ihr fast den ganzen charakter rauben. Eine derartige sprache aber giebt es in der tat. Immer noch ist sie Englisch zu nennen, wenn sie auch auf den ersten blick als ein gesetz- und charakterloses slang erscheinen mag. Aber nicht das englische volk schuf sie, sondern seine pflegekinder: die neger.

Ich habe hier nicht die sprache der amerikanischen neger im auge, welche ebenfalls auf der ersten stufe einer solchen weiterbildung des modernen schriftenglisch zu einem besonderen und eigentümlichen dialekte steht,[1] sondern jenes idiom, wie es sich bei den negern an der westküste von Afrika herausgebildet und festen bestand gewonnen hat.

[1] Vgl. J. A. Harrison, "The Negro-English", *Anglia* VII (1884).

Weit entfernt aber eine schriftsprache zu sein, hatte dieses Negerenglisch keinerlei beachtung gefunden; es blühte im stillen, ein unscheinbares blümlein im waldesdickicht, noch weniger aber war es beobachtet und auf seine gesetze hin untersucht worden. Und wer wollte es leugnen, das solche vorhanden sind! Kann doch eine jede sprachliche verständigung zweier und mehrerer menschen nur auf grund ganz bestimmter, wenn auch weniger grammatischer regeln und gesetze zu stande kommen. Solche haben sich in jenem idiom ausgebildet, und werden unbewusst wol, aber doch mit einer so grossen genauigkeit beobachtet, dass es möglich ist, sie herauszufinden.[2]

Das interesse, welches die sprache an sich bietet, wird vielleicht noch durch die teilnahme erhöht, welche für unsere colonialen erwerbungen an der westküste von Afrika, im besonderen Togo und Kamerun, wach gerufen ist. Die frage, in welcher sprache dortselbst mit den schwarzen verhandelt werde, wird häufig gestellt und vielfach ist der wunsch lebhaft, jene näher kennen zu lernen. Daher erscheint es vielleicht nicht unwillkommen, dieselbe einer eingehenderen behandlung zu unterwerfen. Während eines langjährigen aufenthaltes in jenen gegenden lernte ich dieses idiom kennen. Es sei mir daher gestattet, in einer kurzen systematischen darstellung einen überblick über dasselbe zu geben.

2. *Das sprachgebiet*

Das Negerenglisch an der westküste von Afrika ist lediglich eine verkehrssprache. Es giebt kein sich ihrer bedienendes individuum, welches nicht eine andere muttersprache besässe. Analog der *lingua franca* der küsten des mittelmeeres und dem Pitchin'englisch der chinesischen hafenplätze, ist es eine art volapük, dessen kenntniss ein jeder, der nach der afrikanischen westküste kommt, sich aneignen muss, gleichviel ob schwarzer oder weisser, ob Deutscher oder Engländer. Der grammatisch geschulte Deutsche und der die formen der in der guten gesellschaft üblichen schriftsprache beherrschende Engländer, sie müssen sich zu der einfachen sprechweise bequemen, wenn sie sich verständlich machen und nicht gar bald von den schwarzen, die ja der festen meinung sind, sie sprächen allein ein gutes Englisch, zu hören bekommen wollen: *him no be proper english* oder *him no be right englishman.* Diesem charakter entsprechend kann die ausdehnung des sprachgebietes auch nur eine beschränkte sein.

Die nördlichste grenze bildet der Senegal, also etwa der 17. grad nördlicher breite. Nur bis hierher gehen die arbeiterstämme der küstenneger, die Kru- und Weileute, die als die rechten träger unserer sprache

---

[2] Dr. M. Buchner veröffentlichte eine kurze notiz in der *Münchener Allgem. Ztg.* no. 318 (1886), s. 4683.

anzusehen sind. Gehen wir südlicher, so kommen wir zu den englischen
besitzungen, Sierra Leone, Freetown u.s.w. und nach Liberia, wo die
quellen unseres idioms entspringen, alsdann bald zu deutschen, wiederum englischen, französischen und portugiesischen besitzungen in Ober-
und Nieder-Guinea, bis im süden der Kongo, also etwa der 7. grad
südlicher breite, die grenze bildet; ebenfalls der südlichste punkt, bis zu
welchem die erwähnten arbeiterstämme ihre fahrten ausdehnen. (Noch
weiter südlich werden sie durch die Kabindaleute vertreten).

Verstanden und gesprochen aber wird die sprache von allen weissen,
die mit der schwarzen bevölkerung zu verkehren haben, von allen eingeborenen jener küste, die mit weissen oder Kruleuten in unmittelbare
berührung kommen, endlich von fast sämmtlichen angehörigen der
arbeiterstämme, die zugleich die mission erfüllen, den der sprache eigentümlichen charakter unverfälscht zu erhalten. Besonders zu erwähnen
ist aber der umstand, dass gegen die endpunkte ihres gebietes zu es
weniger dieser sprache mächtige giebt, als in den dem centrum näheren
distrikten. In die ersteren gegenden haben die Franzosen ihre herrschaft
getragen, und diese, sei es aus mangel an talent, sei es aus bequemlichkeit
oder patriotismus, enthalten sich anscheinend grundsätzlich unseres
idioms. Sie sehen mit strenge auf den gebrauch ihrer eigenen sprache, die
allerdings hier denn auch ihre eigene entartung zeigt.

3. *Alter und geschichte der sprache*

Das Negerenglisch der westküste von Afrika ist die jüngste von allen
modernen sprachen, wie seine geschichte und entwicklung erkennen
lassen. Als die heimat der sprache ist das land der freien neger, die
küstengegenden von Sierra Leone und besonders von Liberia zu bezeichnen; sie ist mithin zwischen dem 6. und 8. grad nördlicher breite zu
suchen.

Es war im jahre 1787, als die ortschaft Sierra Leone gegründet wurde.[3]
Durch die englische regierung wurden vierhundert neger und sechzig
weisse dorthin geschafft. Erstere waren teils freigelassene sklaven aus
Nordamerika, die sich in den strassen Londons als bettler umhertrieben,
widerwärtig dem auge eines jeden durch ihre zerlumptheit und ihr ekel-
haftes wesen, teils aber schwarze soldaten, die früher in englischen
diensten gestanden und nun nach dem friedensschlusse im jahre 1783
dem volke eine lästige bürde waren.

Wir haben also hier schon drei verschiedene gruppen der sprechweise
zu unterscheiden: das Englisch der amerikanischen neger, das vulgäre

---

[3] Vgl. *African Repository* (Washington 1826ff.); *Oberländer*, *West-Africa* (Leipzig
1874); Valdez, *Six years of a traveller's life in Western Africa* (London 1861); W.
Winwood Reade, *Savage Africa* (London 1863).

Englisch der soldaten und bettler, und endlich das schriftenglisch der leiter der expeditionen.

Diese drei elemente vermischten sich naturgemäss durch den stetigen, unmittelbaren verkehr der einzelnen individuen miteinander.

Zu einer consolidierung der sprache aber konnte es noch nicht kommen. Die colonie war noch nicht fertig. Im jahre 1792 wurden elfhundert freie neger aus Neu-Schottland dorthin geschafft, welche jedenfalls auch einen gewissen einfluss auf die sprache ausübten. Von der grössten bedeutung war aber das in den folgenden jahren der bevölkerung aufgepfropfte element.

England begann seine mission: die unterdrückung der sklaverei. Alle schwarzen, die in den aufgebrachten sklavenschiffen sich in jammervoller bedrängniss befanden, wurden nach Sierra Leone gebracht, welches seit 1808 unter englischer regierung stand. Tausende der armseligen befreiten wurden dorthin geschafft: leute der verschiedenartigsten stämme und völker Afrikas, von denen jeder seine eigene sprache mitbrachte. Behauptet doch der missionar Kölle zweihundert verschiedene sprachen und dialekte gezählt zu haben.[4]

So sehen wir hier ein wildes chaos, aus welchem heraus sich erst eine allen verständliche sprache herausbilden musste.

Die vorgänge in der schwestergründung Liberia sind denen in Sierra Leone analog, wenngleich auch einfacher. Die gründung geschah im jahre 1821. Als in den vereinigten staaten von Nord-Amerika sich das bedürfniss fühlbar machte, sich der unmenge von negern, die auch hier als vagabunden die strassen der städte durchzogen und unsicher machten, zu entledigen und zugleich der humane wunsch sich regte, jenen ein eigenes heim zu geben, da schaffte man eine anzahl derselben nach dem festlande von Afrika, zuerst nach Sherbro und später von dort weg nach Monrovia. Zuzug erhielten sie fast ausschliesslich aus Amerika. Allmählig verbreiteten sie sich an der ganzen küste entlang und siedelten sich hier und dort fest an. Ehe aber hier die zustände zur festigung und sicherheit kommen konnten, bedurfte es noch mancher kämpfe, ja, erlangt wurde dieses ziel erst mit der, zwar nur nominellen, unterwerfung der eingeborenen stämme jener landstrecken, der Kru-, Wei- und teilweise Mandingoneger. Wenn nun auch die herrschaft nicht als eine wirkliche aufgefasst werden durfte, so waren doch immer nahe wechselbeziehungen der unterworfenen zu den Liberianern geschaffen worden, durch welche sich ein sprachlicher verkehr bedingte. Wie wenig aber den eingeborenen daran gelegen war, das ihnen eigenartige, aus der amerikanischen heimat mitgebrachte wesen zu bewahren, geht aus einem berichte der African Colonization Society von 1870[5] hervor. Die amerikanischen neger übten

[4] Ritter, *Zeitschrift für Erdkunde* (1853); Koelle, *Polyglotta africana*, London (1854).
[5] *African Repository* (Washington 1870-71).

nach diesen angaben so gut wie keinen civilisierenden einfluss auf die eingeborenen aus, es war keine seltenheit, dass leute die kleidungsstücke civilisierter menschen, die sie eben aus Amerika herüber gebracht, von sich warfen, sich in der busch begaben und hier ein leben wie die wilden führten. Was für eine gestaltung die sprache da annehmen musste und annahm, kann man sich leicht vorstellen. Trotzdem aber war und blieb doch in Liberia sowol als wie in Sierra Leone ein stamm von leuten, die von gebildeten missionären unablässig zum gebrauche einer sprache herangezogen wurden, welche sich von negroïsmen und sonstigen idiotismen ziemlich frei hält und auch in grammatischer hinsicht ein leidliches Englisch genannt werden kann. Die leute, welche dieser sprache sich mächtig wissen, halten viel darauf, sich durch ihren gebrauch auszuzeichnen. Sie bilden eine art aristokratie, die sich mit vorliebe "coloured gentlemen" nennen lässt, wogegen die übrigen schwarzen mit dem namen "bushnigger" von ihnen bezeichnet werden. Ihrer ist aber naturgemäss nur eine kleine zahl, und da auch sie im verkehr mit den "bushniggers" sich des eigentlichen westafrikanischen Negerenglisch bedienen müssen, so ist ihr einfluss auf die entwicklung dieses idioms mit der zeit verschwunden.

Ein element, welches nicht ohne bedeutung für unsere sprache geblieben, ist das matrosenenglisch. Die wichtigkeit desselben darf aber nicht überschätzt werden. Die schiffer, welche jene küsten besuchen, haben einerseits selbst mit den eingeborenen und arbeitern wenig zu tun, und dann wird die zahl der englischen schiffe und englisch redenden schiffer von derjenigen der deutschen übertroffen.

Fassen wir nun kurz die sprachen zusammen, aus welchen sich wie eine *quinta essentia* das Negerenglisch gebildet, so haben wir:

(1) das moderne schrift- und vulgärenglisch;
(2) das amerikanische Negerenglisch;
(3) die sprachen der Kru-, Wei- und Mandingo- etc. neger.

Das zu (1) genannte giebt den wortschatz und einiges für den grammatischen bau, das zu (3) vieles für den grammatischen bau und sehr wenig worte, während das unter (2) aufgeführte sich nur noch in einzelnen verbindungen und redensarten als vorhanden nachweisen lässt.

Für die consolidierung der sprache ist wol kaum eine frühere zeit als die vierziger jahre dieses jahrhunderts anzunehmen. Früher konnte das amerikanische Negerenglisch seinen einfluss noch nicht verloren haben, denn es ist in der tat das schwinden eines solchen sowol in der sprache der gebildeten Liberianer als in der unsrigen äusserst beachtenswert. Es beginnen ferner erst seit den fünfziger jahren die wanderungen jener arbeiterstämme und werden erst allgemeiner und systematischer, als einigermassen regelmässige dampferverbindungen mit den verschiedenen küstenplätzen geschaffen wurden.

Aus der tatsache, dass die kenntniss unseres idioms sich in dem kurzen zeitraume von weniger als fünfzig jahren über die weiten obengenannten länderstrecken verbreitete, ist deutlich erkennbar, wie gross überall das bedürfniss war nach einer leicht und möglichst allen verständlichen sprache. Ein solches aber wird immer bestehen bleiben, denn das sich langhin ausdehnende sprachgebiet umfasst eine ausserordentlich grosse menge sehr verschiedener sprachen und dialekte,[6] und diejenigen, welche für die verbesserung jener verkehrssprache oder für einen ersatz für dieselbe mitwirken könnten, nämlich die weissen kaufleute, die sich so gern die pioniere der civilisation nennen lassen, verschmähen es, lehrer ihrer untergebenen zu sein. Besonders sind es aber gerade die Deutschen — und etwa 90 procent aller weissen an der westküste von Afrika sind Deutsche —, welche, sobald sie in jene gegenden kommen, sich sofort das Negerenglisch aneignen und sich fast möchte man sagen ihrer muttersprache schämen. Eine änderung dieser zustände ist in absehbarer zeit nicht zu erwarten. So wird denn unserem Negerenglisch noch ein langes dasein und blühen beschieden sein; und wenn auch bisher keinerlei schriftliches denkmal, welches in dieser sprache verfasst ist, existiert, was sich leicht aus charakter, mangel an anlage oder bildung der sie verstehenden individuen erklärt, so möchte ich doch nicht die möglichkeit eines zukünftigen entstehens solcher durchaus bestreiten, hat doch auch die *lingua franca* sogar einige lyrische produkte aufzuweisen.

Diesem mangel einer schriftlichen fixierung aber ist es zuzuschreiben, dass die formen und wendungen nicht absolut feststehen und dass hin und wieder solche, die dem modernen schriftenglisch näher stehen, vorkommen. Indessen sind diese doch von zu geringer bedeutung und nur individuell, um den allgemeinen charakter der sprache alterieren zu können.

4. *Die sprache*

Die hier behandelte sprache gleicht besonders darin der von den amerikanischen negern gesprochenen, dass sie, wie Harrison es nennt, *an ear language* ist. Wenn dieser spricht von *the indescribable intonation and shades of intonation with which the sounds are uttered*,[7] so ist dieses urteil für einen Engländer oder Amerikaner zutreffend, welche an eine reichliche differenzierung der vocale in ihrer sprache gewöhnt sind; das ohr eines Deutschen, für den der laut das ist, was er darstellt, würde nur ein annähern an die uns natürlich scheinende aussprache darin entdecken.

Es ist der neger nicht im stande, jene der englischen sprache so eigen-

---

[6] Cast, *Modern african languages* (Oxford); Lepsius, *Nubische Grammatik*, "Einleitung".

[7] J. A. Harrison, "Negro-English", *Anglia* VII, einleitung.

tümliche trübung der vocale mit seinem gehör aufzufassen, wie denn
auch keine der hier in betracht kommenden negersprachen derartige laute
aufweist, wie viel weniger also vermag er sie mit ungelenker zunge wieder-
zugeben! Da das amerikanische Negerenglisch aber sehr wol ähnliche
getrübte vocale kennt, so ist umbildung derselben in andere dem ohre und
dem munde der afrikanischen neger mehr passende laute, dem einflusse
ihrer landessprachen allein zuzuschreiben, wie eine betrachtung der
lautlehre am deutlichsten veranschaulichen wird.[8]

5. Orthographie

Von einer der sprache eigens angepassten orthographie muss aus dem
grunde abgesehen werden, weil eine litteratur nicht existiert. Diejenigen
schwarzen, welche lesen und schreiben können, haben dieses von christ-
lichen missionären gelernt, welche die englische sprache beherrschen und
die keine veranlassung haben, um einer als barbarisch und nicht eines gebildeten menschen würdig geltenden sprache willen von der gelernten und
zu lehrenden schreibung der wörter abzuweichen. In dem näheren verkehr
mit weissen bekommen die schriftkundigen schwarzen ebenso wenig
andere schreibungen der wörter als im classischen Englisch zu sehen. Diese
gründe im verein mit der eitelkeit des schwarzen, der auf den vorzug ein
"scholar" und damit in die reihen der "coloured gentlemen" eingerückt zu
sein, nicht wenig stolz ist, und der, um nicht dieses idealen vorzugs
unwürdig zu scheinen, auch nie die gelernte schreibart der wörter,
wenigstens nicht im prinzip, verlassen würde, erklären das fehlen einer
dem Negerenglisch der westküste von Afrika besonders angepassten
orthographie, wie eine solche sowohl in dem slang des Londoners wie in
dem Englisch der amerikanischen neger bekannt ist. Ich werde demnach
in den anzuführenden beispielen mich ebenfalls der schreibweise bedienen, wie sie die elegante büchersprache verlangt.

LAUTLEHRE

6. Vocale

Während sich sowol im Londoner *slang* und *cant* als auch in der sprache
der amerikanischen neger alle jene dem Englisch der gebildeten klassen
eigentümlichen mischlaute unter den vocalen finden, haben diese in dem
Englisch der neger Westafrikas mannigfache veränderungen erleiden
müssen.

[8] S. W. Koelle, *Outlines of a Grammar of the Vei language* (London 1854); Kru-
Sprache: Fr. Müller, *Sitzungsbericht der phil.-histor. Klasse der Wiener Akademie*
(1877), 85-120; Mandingo (Mande): Steinthal, *Mande-Negersprache* (1867).

Den negersprachen der westküste fehlen derartige laute so gut wie gänzlich, hierdurch sowie durch die bequemlichkeit, faulheit und mangel an schulung des schwarzen erklärt es sich, dass dieselben nunmehr so gesprochen werden, wie die ihnen am nächsten stehenden vollen vocale oder diphthonge. Es vollzieht sich eine unwandlung, die nur dem amerikanischen negerenglisch nicht fremd ist.

In betreff der einzelnen vocale ist zu bemerken:

â hat die aussprache wie

1. ê in leder: *take, shame* spr. *têk, schêm.*
2. â in vater: *answer, arm* spr. *ànfser, â(r)m.*
3. óó in sohn: *fall* spr. *fôhl.*

Dagegen ist die aussprache wie òò unbekannt, es wandelt sich in:

1. â: *water, salt* spr. *wàter* und *fsâlt.*
2. óó: *all* spr. *(h)ôhl.*

Zu bemerken ist, dass â oft verkürzt wird, und zwar geschieht dies in der aussprache wie â, óó und è: *father* spr. *fäder, want* spr. *wŏnt, snake* spr. *fsnĕk.*

In der Londoner vulgärsprache begegnet man nicht selten einer ähnlichen kürzung der langen vocale und diphthonge, wie z.b. *babby* für *baby, craddle* für *cradle.*[9] *ship* statt *sheep* (Thackeray, *Vanity Fair*, edit. Tauchnitz I, 107).

Auch das Englisch der amerikanischen neger kennt diese verkürzung:

nater für *nature* (cf. *Anglia* VII, 261).
massa für *master* (cf. *Anglia* VII, 257).

ă wird gesprochen wie

1. ă in gatte: *what* spr. *wăt, bad* spr. *băt.*
2. ä in hätte: *hat* spr. *hăt, man* spr. *măn.*

Bemerkenswert ist die aussprache des *a* in *bad*, ebenfalls häufig wird auch *hat* wie *hăt* gesprochen. Neben diesen formen finden wir noch solche mit gedehnten *a*, so dass *bad* und *hat* lauten *bât* und *hât.*

ê wird gesprochen wie
î in vier: *me, here* spr. *mî* und *hîr.*
ê lautet wie
ĕ in wette: *yet, them.* — ĕ vor *r* wird mit diesem zusammen wie â, seltener wie ă gesprochen.

Die erklärung haben wir in mehreren tatsachen zu suchen. Die für die entwickelung der hier behandelten sprache in betracht kommenden

---

[9] Vgl. Baumann, *Londinismen, Slang und Cant* (Berlin 1887), s. XCII.

negersprachen besitzen bis auf ganz wenige ausnahmen kein *r* (vgl. hierzu das unter *r* gesagte in §9). Dem bestreben, ein solches durch einen mundgerechten, leicht aussprechbaren laut zu ersetzen, kommt nun der umstand zu hülfe, dass sich im Englisch der gebildeten klassen worte finden, in denen die aussprache des *er* wie *ar*, wobei das *r* kaum noch hörbar ist, neben der gewöhnlichen vorkommt, wie z.b. *clerk* spr. *klâ(r)k* neben dem schlechteren *klĕrk*, oder das dem vulgärenglisch angehörige *sarve* für *serve*.

Das amerikanische Negerenglisch macht nun schon die aussprache wie *ar* zur allgemein gültigen, wenn auch nicht gerade zur alleinigen.

presarves Uncle Toms Cabin, edit. Tauchnitz I, 105.

Das afrikanische Negerenglisch aber kennt überhaupt nur noch diese aussprache mit gänzlicher ausstossung der *r* oder ersetzung desselben durch einen schwachen hauchlaut, über welchen das zu *r* gesagte zu vergleichen ist.

Dazu tritt alsdann noch die ersatzdehnung des *a*: *clerk* spr. *clâ*$^{(h)}$*k*, *servant* spr. *fsâ*$^{(h)}$*went*, *kernell* spr. *kâ*$^{(h)}$*ₑl*, *preserve* spr. *prîsâ*$^{(h)}$*f*.

Dagegen ohne ersatzdehnung *german* spr. *djăm*$^{?}_e$*n* und *jăm*$^{?}_e$*n*.

î sprich wie *ei*: *fine* spr. *fein*.
ĭ sprich wie *ĭ*: *ship, fish, live*.
ô hat die aussprache wie
    1. *óó* in not: *more, hope, no, go*.
    2. *û* in mut: *move* spr. *mûf, do* spr. *dû*.
ŏ wird nur gesprochen wie *ŏ* in nord: *God, chop, for*.

Die aussprache des *o* als eines zwischen *ă* und *ŏ* liegenden lautes wie in *come* des schriftenglisch ist unbekannt.

Dem allgemeinen gesetze folgend tritt die wandlung dieses mittellautes in den ihm am nächsten stehenden vollen vocal, nämlich *ŏ* ein, also *come* spr. *kŏm, hot* spr. *hŏt, son* spr. *fsŏn*.

û wird gesprochen
    1. im anlaute wie *jû*: *use* spr. *jûfs*. Die aussprache wie *ô*, welche in manchen wörtern das vulgärenglisch liebt, z.b. *sure* spr. *schôr*, ist unbekannt.
    2. im inlaute wie *ŭ*: *stupid* spr. *stŭpit* oder *tŭpit*. Im Englisch der gebildeten Nordamerikaner, sowie besonders in der sprache der niederen volksklassen Englands ist dies durchaus gebräuchlich.

Das amerikanische Negerenglisch zeigt dagegen noch spuren der correcten aussprache *jû* auch im inlaute. Also

Chuseday = Tuesday (cf. Anglia VII, 237).

ŭ lautet wie

1. *ŭ* in busch: *full, pull, bush.*
2. *ŏ* als wiedergabe des zwischen *ŏ* und *ŏ̄* stehenden lautes in *but, sun* (diese spr. *bŏt, ʃsŏn*), so auch in *hungry* spr. *hŏngri* neben *hŭngri.*

Die abschwächung und trübung der vocale, sobald sie in unbetonter silbe stehen, ist auch im afrikanischen Negerenglisch zu beobachten: *suppose* spr. *ʃsₑ́pŏss, village* spr. *willₑ́dj, fashion* spr. *fĕschₑ́n, kernel* spr. *kânₑ́l.*

7. Diphthonge

au Die aussprache ist gleich derjenigen des *ô*, also *because* spr. *bĭkôhʃs*, es lautet nie wie *ŏò*; es hat also wiederum der mittellaut seine eigentümliche wandlung erfahren.

Gleiches können wir im amerikanischen Negerenglisch beobachten (cf. *Anglia* VII a.a.o.). Daneben aber kommt dort noch die aussprache wie *â* vor. Also *because* ergiebt *'case.*

ai, ay spr. *ê* in ehre: *chair* spr. *tschêhr*, so *pay, Friday.*

ei gesprochen wie

1. *ê* in ehre: *eight.*
2. *ei* in *either*, welches nie *îther* lautet wie im Am. N.E. *eeder* (cf. *Anglia* VII, 256).

ey 1. gesprochen wie *ê*: *obey.*
2. wie *î*: *key, money* spr. *monî* neben *monêh.*
3. wie *ei* in *eye.*

ea hat die aussprache

1. *î*: *peace, sea, guinea-fowl.*
2. *â*: *heart* spr. *hâ(r)t.*
3. *ê*: *swear* spr. *ʃswêhr.*
4. *ĕ*: *leather* spr. *lĕder.* Vgl. AE. *leder.*
5. *ŭ* in *steady* gesprochen *stŭddi*, ebenso wie im Am. N.E.

Das matrosenenglisch legt die betonung auf die letzte silbe, wodurch das *ea* seinen wert als voller vocal verliert und fast tonlos wird. Diese betonung, welche neben der correcten besteht, erklärt sich aus der natur des wortes, als eines commandorufes; solche verlegen gern den ton auf die letzte silbe. Hier hat es die bedeutung 'geradeaus' bekommen.

ee spr. *î*: *three* spr. *trî.*
eu spr. *jû* in *Europe.*

Die aussprache, welche die beiden vocale trennt, wie z.b. das Am. N.E. sie hat in dem verstümmelten *'spe'unce* gleich *experience* ist so unbekannt, wie dieses wort selbst.

ew spr. *û* in *stew* wie im Englisch der Amerikaner. Worte mit diesem anlaute kommen im W. Afr. N.E. nicht vor.

oo wird gesprochen wie
1. *û* in schule: *moon, cooper.*
2. *ô* in tor: *door*, wo das Am. N.E. *dû* ohne *r* spricht.
3. *ŏ* in stöcke: *bloody*, wo somit eine wandlung des mittellautes in den vollen vocal stattfand.

Bemerkenswert ist, dass die vulgärenglische aussprache des *oo* wie *ô* in worten, in denen der laut *û* der gewöhnliche ist, wie z.b. in *poor*, durchaus unbekannt ist. Solche wörter lauten im W. Afr. N.E. wie im guten Englisch, also *poor* spr. *pûhr.*

oe spr. *ô*: *toe*, auch in *shoe.*
oi spr. *eu* wie in eule: *boil, hoist. poison* nicht zu sprechen wie das Am. N.E. es tut: *pĭzen.*
oy lautet ebenso: *boy.*
oa wird gesprochen wie *ô* in ofen: *goat.*
ou lautet
1. *au* wie in auge: *mouth* spr. *mauss, house* spr. *haufs.*
2. *ŏ* wie in nord: *country*, auch hier hat wieder die wandlung des mittellautes in einen vollen vocal stattgefunden.
ow hat die aussprache wie
1. *au* in faul, so *fowl, how.*
2. *ô* in ohr: *morrow, show.*

Das Am. N.E. kennt noch die aussprache *er* z.B. in *morrow* spr. *morrer*, wovon keine spur im W. Afr. N.E. zu entdecken ist. Vergleiche hierzu unter *r* §9.

uy hat seine regelmässige aussprache bewahrt: *buy* spr. *bei.*
eo nimmt die natur der abgeschwächten und getrübten vocale an: *pigeon* spr. *pitsch'n*, und ist nicht gleich dem im Am. N.E. gebräuchlichen *pidgin* zu sprechen.
ue wird gänzlich unhörbar und hat nicht einmal mehr so viel kraft, um den vorhergehenden consonanten weicher gesprochen zu machen.

ague spr. *êhk*, während hier das Am. N.E. noch ein *r* anhängt, wodurch der diphthong zu einem abgeschwächten vocal wird, also für *ague* spricht man *agur.*

8. *Der halbvocal* **w**

Der halb vocal **w** hat seinen charakter als solchen verloren. Die sitte des Londoner pöbels, *w* gleich *v* d.i. gleich unserem deutschen *w* zu sprechen, findet hier ihre nachahmung, nur mit dem unterschiede, dass diese aussprache nunmehr die alleinige ist. Also *well* spr. *well, water* spr. *wat'_er, what* spr. *wat.*

Die vocalische aussprache des *v*, die im slang beliebt ist, hat im W. Afr. N.E. keine nachahmung gefunden.

w wird gesprochen in *one* spr. *won.*

9. Consonanten

Gleich den semitischen und hamitischen sind die reinen negersprachen und die mischsprachen der beiden letzteren ausserordentlich reich an gutturalen.[10] Dem bedürfniss der kehle des negers an der westküste von Afrika, möglichst viele consonanten dieser klasse zu sprechen, kam die vorliebe des Irländers und der niederen volksklassen Englands, vor dem vocalischen anlaute öfters ein *h* hören zu lassen, ausserordentlich entgegen. Wo nur irgend möglich wird in unserem Negerenglisch dieses nachgeahmt:

> *irish stew* spr. *heirisch stû*
> *all right* spr. *hôhl leit*
> *ask* spr. *hax* und *hask.*

Das gegenteil, die verstümmelung der worte durch die apokope eines anlautenden *h*, regel des Londoner *slang*, findet nie statt. So bleibt *hot* stets *hŏt, house* sprich stets *hauss.*

Auch das Am. N.E. zeigt dieselben umgestaltungen wie das Vulg. Engl. (vgl. *Anglia* VII, 240), aber auch hier gilt die fortlassung des anlautenden *h* nicht als regel.

Eine dem W. Afr. N.E. eigene, sich durchgängig zeigende neigung, besteht darin, die weichen und tönenden consonanten am ende des wortes, hinter vocalen und consonanten, hart und tonlos zu sprechen, eine erscheinung, welche uns im Deutschen auf schritt und tritt begegnet. So haben wir in solchen fällen

d zu sprechen wie *t: stupid* spr. *stŭpit* und *tŭpit.*

Im Vulg. Engl. ist teils das gegenteil hiervon der fall, indem das hinter consonanten anlautende *d* kaum hörbar wird, also statt *husband husbin* zu sprechen ist, teils aber sich auch formen finden, die dieselbe verhärtung jedoch nur hinter vocalen aufweisen: *goot* statt *good* (vgl. Ainsworth, *Jack Sheppard* 'the well hole', *Epoch the third*).

Das Am. N.E. kennt ebenfalls eine ähnliche verhärtung: *to git ur holt* statt *hold* (cf. *Anglia* VII, 261).

[10] Lepsius, *Nubische Grammatik.*

Ebenso wird

f sets gleich dem deutschen *f* in 'für' gesprochen.

v lautet diesem *f* entweder völlig gleich oder ist wie *w* in *wenn* zu sprechen. *surf* spr. *ſsörf* und *ſsâf*, *knife* spr. *neif*, *live* spr. *lĭf*, *palaver* spr. *pălâwâ*.

g am ende lautet wie *k*: *flog* spr. *flŏk*, *pig* spr. *pik*, *big* spr. *bĭk*.

In der Londoner volkssprache wird *g* bisweilen, und zwar nur hinter *n* durch *k* ersetzt, wie *nothink* für *nothing*, *anything* (Thack., *Van. Fair* I, s. 102).

Das W. Afr. N.E. aber hat für die endung *ng* nur eine andere aussprache. Das *g* wird unhörbar, übt aber auf das *n* noch so viel einfluss aus, dass dieses seinen nasalen klang behält, wodurch es sich vom Vulg. Engl. unterscheidet, welches wie das Am. N.E. gewohnheitsmässig einen solchen nicht hören lässt. In Vulg. Engl. *morning* spr. *mornin* etc., so Am. N.E. *tryin'* und *springin'* spr. *triin* und *springin* (*Uncle Tom's Cab.* I, 89), W. Afr. N.E. *morning* ist zu sprechen *mornin(g)*.

s Der unterschied zwischen tönendem und tonlosem *s* ist bekannt, am ende jedoch des wortes hinter einem vocal ist es stets tonlos.

t wird im Vulg. Engl. sowie im Am. N.E. und W. Afr. N.E. im auslaute öfters abgeworfen: *breakfast* giebt *brĕkfŏs*. Dagegen schwindet es im inlaute im W. Afr. N.E. nicht: *coloured gentleman* ist stets zu sprechen *djentle'men*, nic wie im Vulg. Engl. *djenl'm'ₑn*.

th mit seinen nüancen im Englisch der gebildeten volksklassen hat mehrere veränderungen erfahren. So lautet es vor einem vocale wie *d*: *them* spr. *dĕm*, *there* spr. *dehr*. Diese aussprache ist dem Vulg. Engl. nicht ganz unbekannt — vgl. die formen *furder* statt *further*, *farden* statt *farthing* (Thack., *Van. Fair* I, 103) — und im anlaute wird es hin und wieder gar nicht gesprochen, also *them* spr. *'em*. Das Am. N.E. schliesst sich dem Vulg. Engl. hier völlig an. Es kennt die form *them* spr. *dem* und *'em*, welch' letztere im W. Afr. N.E. auch bekannt ist. Dagegen finden wir hier nicht das abwerfen dieses buchstabens im auslaute wie *sou' wester* für *south wester*, oder *wi* statt *with* (Vulg. Engl. und Am. N.E.).

Vor consonanten lautet *th* im W. Afr. N.E. wie *t*: *three* spr. *trî*, in zusammensetzungen *trĭ*.

Das Vulg. E. kennt die aussprache *trĭ penss* für *three pence*, doch im Am. N.E. ist eine solche schon zum gesetz geworden:

> *troo = through* (*Anglia* VII, 242).

th am ende des wortes oder der silbe ist wie *ſs* zu sprechen: *tooth* spr. *tŭſs*, wo der neger eine sibilante, nicht aber eine dentale heraushörte.

Andere aussprachen etwa wie *r* oder *f*, welche man im Vulg. E. in einigen wörtern trifft, kommt nicht in unserer sprache vor.

r Der umstand, dass die meisten negersprachen der westküste Afrikas ein *r* nicht besitzen, bewirkt lautliche veränderungen, welche sich in keiner der muttersprachen des hier behandelten idioms wiederfinden.

Am häufigsten findet ein ersetzen des *r* durch *l* statt: *carriage* spr. *cǎllǐdj brother* spr. *blŏdder*, wie wir es im Spanischen häufig treffen: *marmor* ist span. *marmol*; baum lat. *arborem*, span. *arbol*... .

Der von G. Ellis "vanish r" genannte, im Vulg. E. nicht seltene laut, wie in *feller* statt *fellow* (Thack., *Van. Fair* I, 92) ist hier gänzlich unbekannt. Das Am. Engl. kennt ebenfalls dieses *r*: *feller* (*Uncle Toms Cab.* I, 295) neben *fellow* (ebenda I, 290).

Bemerkenswert ist die öftere einschiebung eines *d* zwischen *n* und *r*. *Henry* spr. *Hendri*.

l Das umgekehrte von der eben behandelten vertauschung des *r* in *l* findet sich in vielen distrikten, wo *l* in *r* beziehungsweise den dem letzteren entsprechenden gutturallaut verwandelt wird, eine erscheinung, die nur unserem W. Afr. N.E. eigentümlich ist: *place* spr. *prêfs, flag* spr. *frag, gentleman* spr. *djentremen, play* spr. *prêh*.

Vgl. hierzu im Spanischen *franela* = unserem *flanell*.

er hat, wie wir §6 unter *e* gesehen, die aussprache *â* mit folgendem, ganz schwachem hauchlaute bekommen. Durch dieses aufgeben des *r* unterscheidet sich das W. Afr. N.E. wesentlich von dem Am. N.E., wo *r* hinter *e* oder einem der anderen vocale gesprochen, ja sogar dort eingeschoben wird, wo ein reiner vocal mit einem consonanten zusammentrifft, wie z.b. *merlettler* für *mulatto, marter* für *matter*.

ir Die bildung und aussprache des Vulg. E. *gal* für *girl* hat keinen eingang gefunden. Dieses wort wird immer *gŏ*[(h)]*$_e$l* gesprochen, ebenso *first* spr. *fŏ*[(h)]*st*; dagegen lautet *Sir* immer *ſsâh*.

ur folgt in der aussprache sowol dem *er* wie dem *ir*: *surf* sprich *ſsörf* und *ſsâf, surgeon* sprich *ſsâ*[(h)]*lj'$_e$n* und *ſsö*[(h)]*lj'$_e$n*.

10. *Lautliche veränderungen in den wörtern*

Aus dem bestreben, die aussprache eines wortes sich nach möglichkeit bequem zu machen, erklären sich einige erscheinungen, für welche sich nur hie und da analogieen im Vulg. E. und im Am. N.E. finden.

METATHESIS ist ziemlich häufig, die form des Vulg. E. *perfessor* für *professor* wird hier im W. Afr. N.E. gesprochen *pûfessǎ*, Am. N.E. *poofessor*. Vulgär und provinc. E. *pervide* für *provide, ax* für *ask* finden sich ebenfalls. Daneben kommen noch eigentümlich bildungen vor: *floget* für *forget*.

PROTHESIS. Das hinzufügen eines buchstabens im anfange eines wortes beschränkt sich auf *h* bei vocalisch anlautenden worten: *all* spr. *hôhl, ask* spr. *hax*. Zu erwähnen wäre die hinzufügung eines *a* in namen z.b. *a-William, a-Jone,* eine bildung, welche den negersprachen entlehnt ist, im besonderen hat die Ewe-sprache: *a-Queité, a-Kotowi*.

EPENTHESIS kommt vor in *nigger,* so auch in *calcrooch* für *cockroach, Hendry* für *Henry*.

EPITHESIS. Das hinzufügen eines buchstabens am ende eines wortes ist im Vulg. E. sowol als im Am. N.E. sehr beliebt. Vgl. Vulg. E. *acrost* für *across, drownd* für *drown,* Am. N.E. *drownded; clifft* für *cliff (Anglia* VII, 237; Baumann, *Londinismen* s. XCIV). Das W. Afr. N.E. aber kennt solche formen nicht. Das einzige hier zu nennende wort, das jedoch auch nur hier und da gehört wird, wäre *clăki* für *clerk*. Dies könnte an die bemerkung in Defoe, *Robinson Crusoe* s. 396 (Edition of the Society for Promoting Christian Knowledge, London) erinnern, wo von den indianern Westindiens, sowie den eingeborenen Afrikanern gesagt wird: "When they learn English allways they use to add two e's at the end of the word where we use one", ein vorwurf, der schwerlich seine volle berechtigung hat.

APHAERESIS. Auch hier unterscheidet sich das W. Afr. N.E. vorteilhaft von den beiden an wortverstümmelungen reichen muttersprachen, welche durch abstossen oder verschlucken eines buchstabens am anfange eines wortes hervorgebracht werden; nur ganz wenige werden gefunden. So die form *'em* für *them,* wie sie auch das Vulg. E. und Am. N.E. hat ferner das auslassen des *s* in den *st* anlautenden worten: *steamer* spr. *tîmer, stupid* spr. *tŭpit, stick* spr. *tick,* indessen sind diese formen auch nicht einmal allgemein üblich.

SYNKOPE ist etwas häufiger, sie ist sehr beliebt im Vulg. E. und im Am. N.E. So haben wir:

Vulg. E., Am. N.E. und W. Afr. N.E. *thanky. Christmas* giebt im Am. N.E. *Chrismus,* W. Afr. N.E. *Chrism̦s*.

Vulg. E. und W. Afr. N.E. *ha'penny* für *half-penny*.

Vulg. E. *threepence* spr. *trĭpence,* W. Afr. N.E. *trĭp̦nce*.

Am. N.E. *șpote (support),* W. Afr. N.E. *șpô^{(h)}t*.

Eigentümlich ist das W. Afr. N.E. *sissence* für *subsistence* mit der bedeutung lebensunterhalt; *good morning* W. Afr. N.E. *gŏ mornin'(g)*.

APOKOPE. Ueber das verschlucken eines buchstabens am ende des wortes, wie im Am. N.E. und Vulg. E. in der aussprache der *ing* auslantenden worte, vgl. §9 unter *ng*. Sonst ist diese art der wortverstümmelung im W. Afr. N.E. unbekannt.

Andere lautliche veränderungen tragen mehr einen individuellen charakter und sind nicht derartig, dass man sie unter ein allgemeines gesetz bringen könnte.

11. *Formenlehre*

Während die einflüsse der negersprachen in der lautlehre nicht bedeuten-
dere sind, als diejenigen des Vulg. E. und des Am. N.E., machen sie sich
in der formenlehre fast mit aufdringlichkeit geltend. Ihnen sind die meisten
oft recht seltsamen, originellen vereinfachungen zuzuschreiben. So ist
vor allem hier zu gedenken, dass die negersprachen einen grammatischen
geschlechtsunterschied nicht kennen. Ein solcher ist dem naturmenschen
von seinem standpunkte aus, wo er alles ihm gegenüberstehende oder
entgegentretende nur als ihm feindlich oder freundlich betrachtet, durchaus unwichtig.[11] Er hat wol verschiedene worte für mann und weib,
sie aber, wenn er sie ersetzen will, durch nicht ein und dasselbe wort zu
bezeichnen, oder, dass ein "begriff" gar ebenfalls ein seiendes mit gramma-
tischem geschlecht sei, dafür fehlt ihm gänzlich das verständniss. Aus
dieser vorstellungswelt vermag sich der neger nicht herauszulösen und
so müssen hierdurch schon allein eine ganze reihe von erscheinungen
erklärt werden, welche uns nunmehr zu beschäftigen haben.

12. *Der artikel*

Der bestimmte artikel ist für alle geschlechter und zahlen stets *them*
spr. *dĕm*, wie diese form ebenfalls für alle geschlechter und zahlen im
matrosenenglisch vorkommt (vgl. Baumann, *Londinismen*, s. XCVIff.,
them sly manoeuvres). Auch das Am. N.E. wendet sie an, wenn auch
nicht so häufig als die englischen matrosen. Dagegen ist die form *one*
für den unbestimmten artikel *a* und *an* nur dem W. Afr. N.E. eigen.

> *them man, them wife, them house,*
> *one man, one wife, one house.*

Häufig findet die auslassung sowol des bestimmten, als des unbestimmten
artikels statt.

> *palaver come* 'ein ding kommt',
> *palaver finish* 'das palaver ist zu ende'.

13. *Das substantivum*

Sämmtliche wörter sind eines geschlechtes: *them man — them wife —
them child — he come.*

Selbst das Am. N.E. unterscheidet die grammatischen geschlechter der
einzelnen wörter: *The old nature hath its way* etc. (*Uncle Toms Cabin* I, 280).

Ohne jede analogie aber steht die art da, wie der pluralis ausgedrückt
wird. Vulg. E. und Am. N.E., sowie auch die negersprachen nehmen zu

---

[11] Lepsius, *Nubische Grammatik*, s. XXII u. XXXIII.

diesem zwecke änderungen jeglicher art mit den singularformen der
wörter vor: das W. Afr. N.E. aber hat keine vom singularis verschiedene
form des pluralis. Nur wenn man ausdrücklich hervorheben will, das
mehrere individuen einer gattung vorhanden sind, so fügt man *plenty*
'viele', *all* 'alle', oder *some* 'einige' hinzu: *two child, three house; plenty
woman, some girl, all ship.*

Hieraus folgt, dass unregelmässige pluralbildungen nicht vorkommen
können: *two woman, three child, plenty man* u.s.w.

Abgesehen von dem als einen einzigen begriff mit der vorstehenden
zahl aufgefassten *pence,* wie *three pence, six pence, nine pence,* bilden
eine ausnahme, und zwar nur wenn sie in der anrede stehen, die beiden
wörter *Sirs* spr. *ſsörſs* und *boys:*

> *Good morning Sirs — Pull away boys*

sonst heisst es *plenty boy.*

14. *Das genitivverhältniss*

Hier macht sich der einfluss der negersprachen allein geltend. Die formen
des sächsischen genetiv oder die umschreibung durch die praeposition
of, wie sie auch das Am. N.E. noch gebraucht, sind unbekannt. Die
sämmtlichen negersprachen drücken dieses verhältniss durch eine art
status constructus aus, wie ihn die semitischen sprachen besitzen. Bei
diesen letzteren steht das logisch bedeutsamste wort voran, während das
bestimmende, spezialisierende folgt und den haupton erhält unter be-
wirkung von mehr oder weniger geringen formveränderungen des nomen
regens. Hierdurch werden beide worte zu einem, aber aus zwei durch
schrift und aussprache gesonderten teilen bestehenden, logischen ganzen
verbunden, z.b. psalm 1, 1 רְשָׁעִים כַּעֲצַת im rate — nämlich der gott-
losen.[12]

Die negersprachen setzen aber das nomen regens zuerst, das nomen
rectum alsdann, ohne beide durch irgend etwas, sei es praeposition oder
änderung der form eines der beiden, zu verbinden, oder ohne die beiden
worte zu einem einzigen begriff zu verschmelzen, wie es z.b. im Deutschen
geschieht, wenn wir sagen *vaterhaus.* So ist in der Ewe-sprache vaterhaus
to home, W. Afr. N.E. *(me) father house,* königspalast Ewe Spr. *fio home,*
W. Afr. N.E. *king house.*

Da eine notwendigkeit, die existenz eines genetiv-suffixes in den negersprachen und somit ein fehlen eines solchen in derartigen verbindungen

---

[12] Vgl. Gesenius, *Hebräische Grammatik* (Leipzig 1885), §89; Strack, *Hebr. Gramm*
(Leipzig 1885), §21; Heinrich Ewald, *Ausführliches Lehrbuch der hebräischen Sprache
des Alten Bundes* (Göttingen, 1870[8]), §208ff.; A. Dillmann, *Grammatik der Aethio-
pischen Sprache* (Leipzig 1857), §144, IIIa.

anzunehmen, nicht eine absolut zwingende ist, so sei es mir gestattet, mich mit dieser erklärung in gegensatz zu Lepsius zu stellen, welcher in seiner *Nubischen Grammatik*, s. XXXIV, diese construction durch den ausfall des genetiv-suffixes erklärt: nubisch *fofo afo* vaters fuss. Bestärkt werde ich noch durch den umstand, dass der neger in derartigen zusammenstellungen den hauptton in der aussprache auf das ende derselben zu verlegen pflegt, wie *fio hóme*, was sich auch im W. Afr. N.E. nicht verleugnet.

Wenn wir ausdrücken wollen 'meines váters haus', so heisst es im W. Afr. N.E. *me father hoúse*, soll *father* aber im gegensatz zu einem anderen gestellt werden, so sagt man: *them house for mé father*, noch lieber wählt man eine weitere umschreibung, etwa *them house wo belong for me father*.

15. Das adjectivum

Ebenso wenig wie in allen englischen dialekten ist das adjectiv irgend welchen veränderungen bei seiner declination unterworfen.

Die steigerung wird bewirkt durch vorsetzung von *more, most* vor den positiv und zwar wird diese art der steigerung auf alle adjectiva ausgedehnt: *big, more big, most big*.

Die steigerungssilben *er* und *est* sind unbekannt. Ausnahmen nur *better, best* und *more, most*, und ich möchte bezweifeln, dass man sich der natur dieser als comparative und superlative bewusst ist. Indessen findet sich für erstere formen sehr häufig *more good, most good*.

Findet eine vergleichung statt, so hat sich eine ausdrucksweise herausgebildet, welche ohne analogie in den anderen sprachen dasteht. In consequenter durchführung der unveränderlichkeit des adjectivs wird dort, wo im correcten Englisch die vergleichspartikel *pass* auf die comparativform folgen würde, die letztere durch den positiv ersetzt, der rest aber unverändert belassen.

than als vergleichspartikel ist unbekannt.

he is greater than oder *pass me* giebt *him he big pass me*. Diese ausdrucksweise ist ausserordentlich beliebt und man ersetzt durch sie, wo nur irgend angängig, die zusammensetzungen mit *more*.

Auch die superlativbildungen mit *most* sucht man zu vermeiden, indem man sich einer ähnlichen umschreibung wie beim comparativ bedient. Man lässt auf den positiv *pass all* folgen.

he is the largest giebt *him he big pass all*.

16. Die pronomina

Da das matrosenenglisch schon die verwechselung der formen des casus rectus und obliquus der pronomina personalia liebt, so wird es nicht

wunder nehmen, wenn das W. Afr. N.E. noch einen schritt weitergeht
und die formen des casus rectus nur noch als ausnahmen gebraucht.

Verringert sich hierdurch schon die anzahl der formen, so tritt eine
weitere reduction durch die vorher schon erwähnte nichtachtung allen
grammatischen geschlechtes ein.

So haben wir:

a. PRONOMEN PERSONALE

1. pers. sing. *me* für alle fälle, selten *I*, jedoch auch für casus rectus
   und obliquus.
2. pers. sing. *thou* ist unbekannt.
3. pers. sing. *him* für alle fälle und geschlechter, selten *he*.
   she und *it* sind unbekannt.
1. pers. plur. *we* einzige form für alle fälle, ebenfalls nach praepositionen, wie es auch das matrosenenglisch kennt. Vgl. die verse:

   > *What's cunning and such quivication*
   > *And them sly manoeuvres to we?*

2. pers. plur. *you*. Die form *ye*, welche sich auch im Am. N.E. häufig
   findet (*Uncle Tom's Cab.* I, 106) ist nur in *thanky* noch bekannt.
3. pers. plur. *them* für alle fälle und geschlechter. Die form *they* ist
   unbekannt. Das sich enklitisch anschliessende *'em* des Vulg. E.
   (vgl. Thack., *Van. Fair* I, 102), sowie des Am. N.E. (vgl. *Uncle
   Toms Cab.* I, 107) ist, wenn auch selten, doch nicht unbekannt.

Beispiele:
> *him be for me* (*I*) 'das ist für mich'.
> *him never look we* = *he did not see us.*
> *them come for we* = *they went to us.*
> *he be him* = *that's it.*
> *he be him sister* 'das ist seine schwester'.
> *he kill them all together* 'er tötete sie alle insgesammt'.

Zu bemerken ist, dass auch umschreibungen dieser pronomina durch
ein substantiv, verbunden mit einem pronomen demonstrativum, wie sie
das Am. N.E. z.b. in *this nigger* liebt durchaus unbekannt sind.

b. PRONOMEN POSSESSIVUM

Auch hier hat sich das W. Afr. N.E. von den mutterdialekten freigemacht.
Die formen jener für das pronomen conjunctivum, regelmässige oder
entartete, wie *yer* u.s.w. (*Uncle Tom's Cab.* I, 106), *hisn, ourn, theirn* u.s.w.,
oder gar eine ausdrucksweise wie *mine own eyes* (*Uncle Toms Cab.* I, 106)
sind sämmtlich durchaus ungebräuchlich. Der possessivbegriff wird hier
in der gleichen weise zum ausdruck gebracht, wie bei den substantiven,
welche im verhältniss eines genetivus possessivus zu einem anderen

worte stehen: das pronomen personale wird einfach neben das wort gestellt, dessen besitz angezeigt werden soll. Diese verwerfung des pronomen possessivum kann also als eine weitere durchführung des in §14 über den status constructus gesagten angesehen werden.

Bemerkenswert ist, dass in diesem falle die formen *I* und *he* nie angewendet werden.

me father, you house, him sister; we country; them brother.

Dasselbe gilt auch vom pronomen possessivum absolutum: *them knife be me* 'das messer ist mein'.

c. PRONOMEN DEMONSTRATIVUM

Von den zahlreichen formen des schrift-, vulgär- oder Am. N.E. hat sich fast nichts erhalten. Der neger der westküste Afrikas begnügt sich mit dem deutewort, welches er auch für den artikel anwendet, nämlich *them*, um damit alle demonstrativen verhältnisse auszudrücken:

them house ist dieses, jenes, dasjenige, dasselbe haus, diese, jene, diejenigen, dieselben häuser u.s.w.

Der einzige fall, in welchem *that* gebraucht wird, ist in der stereotypen redensart *that's all*.

d. PRONOMEN INTERROGATIVUM

Auch hier verringert sich die anzahl der formen, so dass für das pronomen absolutum nur *whom*, für das conjunctum nur *what* übrig bleibt. Indessen ist auch, wenngleich selten, *whom* für letzteres zu beobachten:

whom kill him? 'wer tötete ihn?'

whom you look? 'wen sahen sie?'

for what (whom) country you come? 'aus welchem lande kamen sie?'

Das interrogativum *why* und *wherefore* wird durch die redensart *what's the matter* wiedergegeben, die daneben aber noch einen anderen sinn hat, nämlich den eines kernfluches.

e. PRONOMEN RELATIVUM

Das beim pronomen interrogativum gesagte gilt auch hier; die für dieses gebrächlichen formen sind auch die für das relativum allein bekannten:

One soldier what come for steamer live for die for sea 'ein soldat, welcher vom dampfer kam, ist ertrunken'.

Das relativum im accusativ oder in der verbindung mit einer praeposition wird stets ausgelassen:

them steamer you come for,

them t'other night, we live for Bagidá, we get plenty rain 'in der zweiten nacht, da wir in Bagidá waren, hatten wir u.s.w.'

f. PRONOMINALIA

Auch die anzahl dieser wird eingeschränkt.

every ist zwar bekannt, doch liebt man es durch *all* zu ersetzen.

all, spr. *hôhl*, wäre durch die aussprache nicht von *whole* zu unterscheiden, dieses ist indessen nicht bekannt, denn die bei diesen gebräuchlichen constructionen, wie z.b. *the whole people* kommen nie vor, dagegen sehr häufig redensarten wie *all them people, all people, all house* 'jedes haus'.

many wird ersetzt durch *plenty: plenty soldier; we get plenty fowl* = *many soldiers; we have many hens.*

'Niemand; jemand' ist *no man; some man, some people.*

other in verbindung mit dem bestimmten artikel giebt *them t'other* (*one*). Die im älteren Neuenglisch noch gute form *tother, t'other* für *other* und *the other* hat sich sowol im Vulg. E. als im Am. N.E. erhalten (*Uncle Toms Cab.* I, 107), dem neger Westafrikas trat die form *t'other* als eine constante entgegen. Da er sie sich nicht zu erklären vermochte, als eine den artikel schon enthaltende, indem ihm wiederum die form *the* für den artikel nicht bekannt ist, er aber doch andererseits das bedürfniss fühlt, denselben zu dem begriff des 'anderer' hinzuzufügen, so bildet er sich *them t'other*. In verbindung mit einem substantiv *them t'other: them t'other steamer*. Absolut: *them t'other one*, worin nunmehr der bestimmte artikel zweimal enthalten ist, eine bildung, wie sie ähnlich in dem franz. *le lierre* geschehen ist.[13]

17. *Das verbum*

Vollständig emanzipiert von dem klassischen schriftenglisch hat sich die hier behandelte sprache bei der bildung der verbalformen. Ganz originell haben sich diese entwickelt und festgesetzt. Mag auch das niedere volk Altenglands, ähnlich wie die kinder, grundsätzlich eine menge von formen in der flexion der verba nicht achten, bestehen bleibt doch stets die art, wie jene bewirkt wird: nämlich durch anhängung von endungen an den stamm der schwachen, beziehungsweise durch lautliche veränderungen im stammvocale der starken verba.

Eine verringerung dieser mannigfaltigkeit der formen hat das Am. N.E. erstrebt (vgl. *Anglia* VII, 249 ff.) und durch schaffung einer selbständigen conjugationsart bis zu einem gewissem grade auch erreicht. Aber bis auf das einfachst mögliche die flexion der verba zurückgeführt zu haben ist dem W. Afr. N.E. vorbehalten geblieben.

Es finden sich für die art der formenbildung analogieen in keiner der für die entwicklung unseres idioms in betracht kommenden sprachen. Diese haben sogar eine reiche conjugation, person und zahl sind unterschieden, ebenso giebt es dort drei bis vier tempora (vgl. die oben genannten grammatiken).

[13] Vgl. G. W. Moon, *Common errors in speaking and writing* (London 1875) und R. C. Trench, *On the study of words* (1872[14]).

Die infinitivform der verba bleibt im W. Afr. N.E. als das stamm-
hafte bestehen, niemals irgend welchen veränderungen unterliegend.
Daraus folgt, dass starke und schwache conjugation nicht unterschieden
wird. Die tempora aber werden durch hinzufügen von hilfsverben gebildet.
Person und zahl wird dagegen nur durch die dabeistehenden pronomina
oder durch den zusammenhang erkannt. Partizipien sind ganz geschwun-
den. Vom passiv endlich sind ebenfalls nur noch schwache spuren vorhanden.

18. *Paradigma*

PRAESENS

1. pers. sing.   *me done take* oder *me live for take*
2. pers. sing.   *you done take* oder *you live for take*
3. pers. sing.   alle geschlechter *him (he) done take* oder *he live for take*
1. pers. plur.   *we* ⎫
2. pers. plur.   *you* ⎬ *done take* oder *live for take.*
3. pers. plur.   *them* ⎭

Indicativus und conjunctivus sind nicht verschieden.

Die formen *we take* u.s.w. für das praesens kommt hin und wieder
vor, sie sind die allein gebräuchlichen in der frage oder mit der verneinung.

Auffällig ist die form *me done take*, welche jedenfalls aus dem bestreben hervorgegangen ist, eine dem *I don't take*, dessen entstehung man
sich nicht erklären konnte, welches man aber oft zu hören bekam, ent-
sprechende positive form zu bilden, wobei das weitere missverständniss
unterlief, das *n* des *not* als zu *do* gehörig zu betrachten. Man könnte
vielleicht annehmen, dass die form aus dem Am. N.E. *done* hervorge-
gegangen sei, welches mit dem participium perfecti verbunden wird: *Lirrys'
done gone* (*Uncle Toms Cab.* I, 105). Hiergegen spricht, dass die form *done*
im W. Afr. N.E. nie für ein anderes tempus gebraucht wird, als für das
praesens, während im Am. N.E. sie stets nur für das perfectum angewendet wird und dass ferner participia im W. Afr. N.E. gänzlich unbekannt
sind. Dem *live* in *me live for take* liegt der verallgemeinerte und erweiterte
begriff "leben" zu grunde. Ein solcher ist dem cant nicht fremd, wir finden
in Thomas Middleton and Thomas Decker, The Roaring Girle or Moll
Cutpurse das verb *lib* als liegen, sich befinden, allerdings nicht mit
folgendem *for*.[14] Diejenigen Engländer, welche die kenntniss des W. Afr.

---

[14] Vergleiche die stelle:
Oh, I would lib all the lightmans
Oh, I would lib all the darkmans
By the sollamon under the Ruffemans etc.

N.E. sich aneignen müssen, pflegen auffälligerweise *lib* in den fällen zu sprechen, in denen *live* als hilfsverb gebraucht wird.

PRAETERITUM

me, you etc take, ebenso in der frage und mit der verneinung.

FUTURUM

me, you etc go take. Daneben noch *me live for take* oder *me go for take*, wenn auch seltener. Die conjugatio periphrastica wird ersetzt durch den indicativ praesentis: *me live for take*.

Hiermit sind die bildungen erschöpft. Für perfectum, plusquamperfectum und futurum II giebt es keine besonderen formen. Es folgt hieraus, dass auch unregelmässige bildungen nicht vorkommen können.

Wenn sich hin und wieder *me have wrote* findet, so ist diese dem matrosen- und vulgärenglisch angehörige form ebenso wie *got* part. perf. von *to get* ganz einzig in ihrer art und wird nur von individuen angewandt, welche sich als "gebildete" betrachten.

Das passivum wird umschrieben, meist durch verwandlung der construction in eine aktive, wodurch das für den sprecher logisch bedeutsamste zum subjekt wird. Dasselbe geschieht auch in der häufigen umschreibung des passivs durch -*get*. *him get flog* er wurde geprügelt.

Auch das Am. N.E. kennt die wiedergabe des passivs durch *get: to git kilt* (*Anglia* VII, 261).

19. *Die hilfsverba*

to have ist nicht gebräuchlich, es wird ersetzt durch *get*.

me get one fish ich habe einen fisch. *to get*, besonders das participium perfecti *got* ist mit der bedeutung von 'haben, besitzen' oder zur verstärkung des *to have* im Vulg. E. nicht unbekannt.

to be ist gebräuchlich nur in verbindung mit einem substantivum oder adjectivum. Seine conjugation entspricht der des regelmässigen verbums, mit dem unterschiede, dass *me, you* etc. *be* für praesens und imperfectum dient. Andere formen kommen mit ausnahme des *is* in den beiden redensarten *what's the matter* 'warum oder donnerwetter!' und *that's all* überhaupt nicht vor.

Um 'sein' absolut auszudrücken, bedient man sich des verbs *live: he is here* wird gegeben durch *him live*. Ueber dieses *live* vgl. §18.

Auch die anzahl der hilfsverba wird verringert. Ohne analogie in allen für die entwickelung des W. Afr. N.E. in betracht kommenden sprachen erhalten einzelne verben bedeutungen, welche ihnen ursprünglich nicht oder doch nur in geringem masse innewohnen, während wiederum ihre eigentliche bedeutung mehr zurücktritt.

will, shall und *may* wird ersetzt durch *can* bezw. *must*. Vgl. auch die bildung des futurums § 18.

he will not die 'er wird nicht sterben' ist *him never can die.*
he will die ist *him can die.*

you shall come }
you may come } ist *you must come.*

must behält seine bedeutung, *you must come* kann also auch sein 'sie müssen kommen'.

can 'können', im sinne von möglich sein, wird gegeben durch *can:* *he can come* 'es ist möglich, dass er kommt'.

Dagegen in der bedeutung 'im stande sein' heisst es *fit* oder *be fit*. *him fit* oder *him be fit for kill him* er ist im stande: er kann ihn töten.

ought wird ersetzt durch *must*.

20. Das adverbium

Das Vulg. E. sowie das Am. N.E. lässt häufig das adjectiv die stelle des adverbiums vertreten. *Anglia* VII, 243 wird zwar behauptet, dass das Am. N.E. jedes adjectiv ohne *-ly* als adverb gebraucht, doch haben wir neben *drefful* statt *dreadfully fatigued* auch *'markably (remarkably)* (*Uncle Tom's Cab.* I, 105). Im W. Afr. N.E. indessen wird dieses zum allein giltigen gesetz gemacht: es kommen formen mit der bildungssilbe-*ly* überhaupt nicht vor.

Vulg. E. *Well nigh dead* (Thacker., *Van. Fair* I, 103) oder *he talk foolish* (*Mrs. Brown on the Turf*) = W. Afr. N.E. *him talk foolish.*

Kenntlich als adverbien bleiben nur diejenigen, welche eine besondere adjectivform nicht besitzen.

much wird meist in verbindung mit *too* gebraucht und bedeutet sehr oder zu sehr. Es ersetzt *very*, das äusserst selgen ist.

> *me be hungry too much = I am very hungry*
> *him be big too much = he is very tall.*

Negation: für *not* gebraucht man ohne unterschied *no* und *never*, in denen somit nichts von ihrer ursprünglichen bedeutung nein bezw. nie oder durchaus nicht zurückbleibt:

> *him no live = he is not here.*
> *me never get power.*

Die einzige ausnahme ist das seltene *not yet*, hier *not* jedenfalls aus euphonischen gründen.

once einst, und ein mal und einmal (*at once* ebenso) wird stets gegeben durch *one time.*

me kill him one time = I killed him at once oder *once.*
me come one time ich kam einst, einmal, ein mal, zugleich.

21. *Praepositionen*

Die summe der im Englischen gebräuchlichen praepositionen ist auf das niedrigst mögliche herabgedrückt worden.

Eine praeposition ist gleichsam eine universalpraeposition geworden, um die verschiedensten wendungen auszudrücken, nämlich *for.* Dieses steht für *to, into, at ago, before, against, from, of, till,* häufig für *by* und *through.*

Beispiele, *for* steht für:
to: me done go for them town.
into: me go for them t'other factory.
in: me live for him house.
at: he live for Berlin.
ago: ⎫
before: ⎬ *for ten years.*
against: them fight for him foe = they fought against his foe.
from: we come for Bagida.
of: him be stick for king = it is the stick of the king.
by (lokal)*: for you house = by your house,* dagegen nie, um 'von' nach einer construction mit passivem sinn zu geben, da steht stets *by: me never get power by me master* 'ich bekam keine erlaubniss von meinem herrn'. *me get plenty flog by them people* 'ich wurde sehr von jenen leuten geschlagen'.
through: you must pass for lagune suppose you want come for Gridji = you must walk through the lagune if you etc.

Ebenso wird das dativverhältniss durch *for* ausgedrückt: *you do bad for me* 'sie tun mir übles'.

Von anderen praepositionen ist nur noch zu erwähnen: *with, by, downstairs* und *for downstairs* (ohne unterschied im gebrauch) = *down,* ebenso *upstairs* und *for upstairs = up, upon,* dafür aber auch *for top for.*

for top for them house = upon that house.

Eine eigentümlichkeit, welche unsere sprache vor dem Vulg. E. und dem Am. N.E. voraus hat und welche auf diese armut an praepositionen zurückzuführen ist, ist die construction derjenigen verba, welche eine praeposition regieren. Hier lässt man einfach dieselbe fort:

me want come = I want to come.

22. *Conjunctionen*

Auch von diesen ist nur eine mässige zahl im gebrauch. Besonders *and, too, but, or, because, if* mit der bedeutung 'ob' im indirekten fragesatze, nie als conditionale conjunction, letztere giebt man durch *suppose*:

suppose you go = if you go.

23. *Interjectionen*

what's the matter 'donnerwetter, der tausend' u.s.w., *oh, ye, for God, oh God.*

Als schimpfwörter werden ganz besonders die dem niedrigsten matrosenenglisch entlehnten redensarten gebraucht: *bloody fool* und *stinky nigger* (*stinky* abgeleitet von *to stink* hat die bedeutung 'schmutzig, schmierig, filzig, stinkend', in verbindung mit dem an sich schon an der westküste von Afrika (nicht im Am. N.E.) als grobe beleidigung aufgefassten *nigger* giebt eines der schwersten schimpfwörter).

Die schwarzen unter sich nennen sich nicht selten *black devil*.

Anreden sind: *Sâ* = Sir, *Massa* = *Master, Captain, Miss, Mistress, Sirs* (vgl. oben).

Antworten: *thank, thanks, thanky* = im Vulg. E. ganz besonders *thank for yesterday*, was die bedeutung hat: (1) nochmaliger dank für eine sache, die man gestern bekommen, (2) willkommengruss an jemand, der am vergangenen tage den wirt durch sein kommen und seinen aufenthalt im hause geehrt hat.

Endlich *yessă* und *nossă* = *yes Sir* und *No Sir!*

24. *Die syntax*

Bei einer so grossen einfachheit der sprache ist eine compliziertheit des satzgefüges nicht zu erwarten.

Der satz, den Lepsius einleitung zur *Nubischen Gramm.*, s. LXXXIII ausspricht, nämlich, dass in den negersprachen ursprünglich überall im einfachen satze des verb zwischen subjekt und objekt stand, gilt auch für alle für die entwickelung unserer sprache in frage kommenden negersprachen in vollem masse. Da auch für das Englische diese art des satzbaues angemessen ist, so kommen im W. Afr. N.E. andere constructionen im einfachen satze nicht vor.

Fragesätze: die frage wird weder durch die umschreibung mit *to do*, wie es im Vulg. E. und Am. N.E. regelmässig geschieht, noch etwa durch eine umstellung der worte wie im Deutschen, sondern lediglich durch den tonfall bemerkbar gemacht: *you father go for them town?* 'geht ihr vater nach der stadt?'

Negative sätze: auch hier findet die umschreibung mit *to do* nicht statt, die negation und zwar *no* oder *never* tritt unmittelbar zum verbum. *I do not come to the village* ist *me no come for them town.*

Darüber, dass in frage- und negativsätzen im praesens die bildungen mit *live* und *done* nicht stattfinden vgl. §18.

Ueber die zusammenstellung der worte, um das genetivverhältniss auszudrücken, vgl. §14.

Besonders zu bemerken ist der häufige gebrauch von ellipsen: *Me fear too much, all them t'other Kruboy go flog me proper and kill me* (nämlich wenn er dies oder jenes tut).

25. *Die wörter*

"Es ist geradezu charakteristisch für die afrikanischen sprachen, dass sich der wortschatz derselben und ebenso auch die grammatischen sprachteile mit ausserordentlicher leichtigkeit lautlich verändern, gänzlich umformen und gegen andere vertauschen, sobald die stämme, die sie sprechen, sich gegenseitig äusserlich isolieren oder in veränderte verhältnisse irgend einer art treten", so bemerkt Lepsius, *Nubische Grammatik*, s. XIX. Diese eigenschaft kann aber nicht nur den sprachen, sondern auch der ganzen natur des schwarzen zugeschrieben werden. Zum anpassen an neue verhältnisse besitzt der neger nicht nur grosse befähigung, sondern auch ausserordentliche neigung, ja, heisses verlangen. Dabei aber ist er nicht im stande, allem neuen das richtige verständniss entgegen zu bringen, und so wird das meiste als karrikatur wieder erscheinen.

So ist es auch mit den sprachen. Die neger, welche nach Amerika in die sklaverei wandern mussten, gaben ihre muttersprachen auf und behielten von diesen nur vereinzelte grammatische und syntaktische formen bei. Das Am. N.E. aber wurde nunmehr ihre muttersprache. Diese wurde wiederum nach Afrika versetzt, in neue verhältnisse und in berührung mit anderen, jetzt fremd gewordenen negersprachen gebracht. Die grammatischen sprachteile haben wir gesehen sich lautlich verändern und gegen andere vertauschen. Und gleiches ist auch mit den wörtern geschehen.

Die anzahl der gebräuchlichen wörter ist nur eine kleine. Schwerlich wird die zahl von dreihundert überschritten werden. Die bedürfnisse, welche sprachlich darzustellen sind, sind sehr wenige. Begriffliche, philosophische auseinandersetzungen und erklärungen sind schon deshalb ausgeschlossen, weil dem erst halbzivilisierten neger der hier in betracht kommenden länder solche nicht entgegen treten und er für sie wenig, wenn nicht gar kein verständniss besitzt.

Dagegen liefert das westafrikanische Negerenglisch die worte für die bedürfnisse des täglichen lebens im weitesten sinne, ferner für die arbeit in den faktoreien und besonders zur see, für jagd, fischfang, krieg und handel. Das ist alles.

Und auch hier noch finden beschränkungen im gebrauche der wörter statt.

Da, wo mehrere wörter gleiche oder ähnliche bedeutung haben, bleibt in der regel nur ein einziges. Die begriffe von *to wear, bear, carry* werden alle nur durch das letzte gegeben:

> *me carry one hat.*
> *you carry hammock.*

Von *large, tall, great, big* bleibt nur *big*.
Von *see, look* nur *look*.
Von *vessel, ship* nur *ship*.
Von *chair, stool* nur *chair*.
Von *path, way* nur *way*.

26. *Besondere fälle*

chop: bedeutet 'essen' und 'das essen' (*to eat* ist unbekannt), es wird gebraucht von menschen und tieren, daneben hat es noch die bedeutung von beissen, zernagen, zerfressen, aufzehren, sogar im übertragenen sinne. Die identität der worte für essen und beissen ist aus dem gebrauch der negersprachen herzuleiten, in denen sämmtlich beides durch ein wort wiedergegeben wird. *to chop* ist in dieser bedeutung dem Neuenglischen fremd, nur mit dem sinne von 'zernagen' kommt es selten vor.

Es ist vielleicht richtiger, seinen gebrauch mit der so sehr beliebten speise des Engländers, den *mutton chops*, in verbindung zu bringen, von dem auch das *chop house* als garküche seinen ursprung herleitet. Es ist dann der name einer speise auf den begriff von speise ausgedehnt worden. Das Am. N.E. und Vulg. E. weisen nichts dem ähnliches auf.

dash, spr. *däsch* = schenken und das geschenk (*to present* ist unbekannt), ebenfalls ein wort, das unserem idiom allein eigen ist. Wie das wort zu der bedeutung gekommen, ist mit sicherheit nicht zu sagen. Vielleicht ist es eine weiterbildung der im schriftenglisch seltenen bedeutung 'schmeissen', nämlich als zuschmeissen, wo dann die wandlung des transitiven sinnes in den intransitiven zu bemerken ist. Es erinnert an den in der deutschen vulgärsprache stattfindenden gebrauch von schmeissen mit der bedeutung: ausgeben, ponieren oder traktieren.

what you go dash me? was schenken sie mir?

palaver, spr. *pălâwâ*. Das *palavra* der Portugiesen, häufig im munde der sklavenhändler jener nation, wurde von den amerikanischen negern aufgenommen und ihrer sprache angepasst. So ergiebt es *perláver* (vgl. *Anglia* VII a.a.o.) und *palaver*, z.b. *to sorter palaver on* = *to go on talking*; *to perlaver* = *to talk* u.s.w.

Es kommt nun zu den negern der westküste von Afrika zurück und giebt *palaver*, spr. *pălâwâ*, welches jetzt unzählige bedeutungen erhält. Es ist ein wort, von dem man sagen kann:

"Denn eben, wo begriffe fehlen,
Da stellt dies wort zur rechten zeit sich ein".

Einige solcher bedeutungen sind:

suppose you kill one snake palaver come d.i. 'wenn du eine schlange tötest, so geschieht dir etwas schlimmes'.

him be God palaver 'das steht in gottes hand oder das ist sache der religion'.

make palaver 'zanken, schwierigkeiten machen'.

settle palaver 'streit schlichten'.

some palaver live 'es giebt etwas'.

me go show you them palaver 'ich werde dir schon zeigen, was du zu tun hast'.

him no be me palaver 'das geht mich nichts an'.

one big palaver 'eine grosse ratsversammlung'.

fetish palaver 'alles, was fetisch heisst'.

them pig palaver 'die streitfrage in betreff des schweins'.

them chop palaver 'das essen'.

some big palaver live 'eine schwierige entscheidung ist zu treffen'.

palaver finish 'fertig'.

sabe, spr. *ſsăbĕ* und *ſsăbĭ* = 'wissen', für das unbekannte *to know* gebräuchlich. Dieses ebenfalls dem Portugiesischen bezw. dem Spanischen entlehnte wort findet sich weder im Vulg. E., noch im Am. N.E. Dagegen hat das an den küsten Asiens, besonders Chinas, gesprochene Pitchin'-English dieses wort aufgenommen. Dass im W. Afr. N.E. eine selbständige bildung stattgefunden haben sollte, ist kaum anzunehmen. Das wort ist nach Afrika verpflanzt worden und zwar durch see- und kaufleute, die auf schiffen in den meeren oder in faktoreien an den küsten Asiens jene sprache kennen lernten. Derartige leute, deren abenteuerliches leben sie in alle denkbaren weltgegenden wirft, findet man häufig unter den faktoristen der westküste Afrikas, und auf ihre rechnung sind auch wol viele dem Vulg. E. angehörige formen des W. Afr. N.E. zu setzen.

27. *Wörter und redensarten, welche zu ferneren charakterisierung der sprache dienen*

Von einzelnen dieser lassen sich noch spuren im Am. N.E. finden, wogegen bei anderen unsere sprache wieder zu den guten formen des schriftenglisch zurückkehrt, noch andere aber selbständig bildete:

make book 'schreiben'.

book 'buch, brief, alles geschriebene'.

get out oder *clear out* 'heraus!' (cf. *Grieb. Diction. get thee out of the land*), erstere form ist zwar nicht im schriftenglisch zu verwenden, doch nicht selten in der umgangssprache.

to bad = *to do wrong* und *to treat ill*.

feel good, Am. N.E. *feel good* = *to feel well*.

me reckon, Am. N.E. *reckin* = *I suppose*.

catch man 'leute rauben, um sie zu sklaven zu machen'.

what's the matter 'donnerwetter' und 'weshalb'.

pull away 'rudert munter los?'

catch hold for, Am. N.E. *to git ur holt*, Vulg. E. *ketched 'old on me* 'hand anlegen an jemand'.

nigger ist schimpfwort, Am. N.E. ist es gleich *negro*.

me go flog him proper 'ich werde ihn tüchtig durchprügeln'.

go wash 'baden gehen'.

look proper, *look out* 'pass auf'.

bump for, Am. N.E. *to bump agin* = *to knock against*.

him be strong too much 'das geht über meine kräfte'; z.b. als ein schwarzer den auftrag erhielt, ein kästchen mit einem theodolithen zu tragen, der ihm als "big medecin", grosser zauber, bezeichnet war und den er sich zu tragen fürchtete, machte er diese einwendung.

for sun up, Am. N.E. *fo'sun up early in the morning*.

that's all 'fertig'. *me go kill him one time that's all*, Am. N.E. *that's all* mit der gleichen bedeutung (*Uncle Tom's Cab.* I, 280).

he be him 'das ist er' oder 'so ist es'.

be all right, ebenso im Am. N.E. (*Anglia* VII, 268) *to be in good condition*.

them thing hot me 'das tut mir weh'. *hot* ist im schriftenglisch nur adjectiv, hier ist es gleich (*it*) *hurts* (*me*).

me never get power 'ich habe nicht erlaubniss bekommen'.

mash (spr. *mâtsch*) *corn* 'mais zerschroten'.

cold catch me 'mich friert'.

for now, Am. N.E. *by now* = *by this time*.

fowl, bei Krunegern *chicken*, Am. N.E. *chicken* = *hen*.

he like dram (*rum*) *too much*, Am. N.E. *roll in dram: to be a drunkard*.

beg pardon, Am. N.E. *ax pardon* = *to ask pardon*.

two moon = *two months*.

make farm 'feld bestellen'.

you want him? 'wollen sie es haben?'

when sun come for bed 'wenn die sonne aufgeht'.

them steamer go sleep here for night 'der dampfer wird heute nacht hier vor anker liegen bleiben'.

them steamer him belly be full 'der dampfer ist beladen'.

them steamer be hungry 'der dampfer kann noch ladung aufnehmen'.
me go try me best, Am. N.E. *to try yo' bes'* 'ich will versuchen'.
me go catch you 'ich will dich schon fassen!'
catch Bagidá 'Bagida erreichen'.
him be no use 'der taugt nichts'.
go for bush 'ins innere (nämlich von Afrika) gehen'.
blan für *belong, them knife blan for me.*
king = chief.
brother ist 'bruder', 'schwester', 'verwandter', 'landsmann', endlich
werden leute von gleicher farbe so genannt.
one brother for you live for Porto Seguro 'einer ihrer landsleute befindet
sich in Porto Seguro'.
me brother be girl 'meine schwester'.
country fashion 'landessitte'.
bushman 'ein mensch aus dem innern', dann 'ein dummkopf'.
sash, spr. *ʃsǎsch*, ein wort, welches der Krusprache entnommen ist,
bedeutet 'sehr schlecht', doch nur von der brandung: *them surf be sash.*
me use meself ist entstanden aus dem missverstandenen Vulg. E.
I ease myself 'ich verrichte meine notdurft'.
he get belly 'sie ist schwanger'.
him live for die 'er liegt im sterben'.
be sharp, Am. N.E. *to be right sharp = to be smart* oder *to pay attention.*
hard = difficult.

28

Aus diesen betrachtungen erhellt, dass der unterscheid des W. Afr. N.E.
von der sprache der gebildeten klassen Englands ein recht bedeutsamer
ist. Bewunderungs würdig ist, dass mit diesen schwachen und geringen
mitteln der bedarf an wörtern und formen gedecket werden konnte.
Allerdings stehen ja die formen noch nicht durchaus fest und es kommen
neben den hier gegebenen andere gute und bessere vor; da diese aber
selten und sämmtlich auf individuelle einflüsse zurückzuführen sind,
kann das hier zusammengestellte in seinem grunde nicht berührt werden.
   Es erhellt ferner, dass die einflüsse jener sprachen, welche für die
bildung und entwickelung des W. Afr. N.E. von massgebender bedeutung
waren, nicht überall in gleicher weise wirksam gewesen sind.
   Dasjenige element, welches dem menschen mit der muttersprache in
fleisch und blut übergeht, welches er erst in sich bekämpfen und über-
winden muss, will er ein fremdes, jener nicht verwandtes idiom erlernen,
haben wir in den lauten und in der syntax zu suchen. Der sieg wurde
dem neger nicht; daher haben hier auf diesen gebieten die negersprachen
ihre hauptwirksamkeit ausgeübt.

Die wörter selbst und grammatikalische bildungen hingegen sind das ureigenste eigentum der sprache, abgesehen vom individuum; sie willkürlich zu ändern, heisst der sprache einen ganz anderen charakter aufdrängen. So ist denn auch hier das Englische überhaupt, im besonderen das vulgär- und matrosenenglisch, von durchschlagender, wenngleich nicht alleiniger bedeutung gewesen.

Von dem einflusse endlich, den das Am. N.E. gehabt, sind zwar an allen orten, jedoch nur geringe spuren zu bemerken, nirgends aber sind dieselben entscheidend gewesen.

29

Zum schlusse sei es gestattet, einige gespräche zu geben, wie sie an der küste Westafrikas vorkommen.

Zur freier des geburtstages kaiser Wilhelm's I. im jahre 1886 fühlte sich ein schwarzer zimmermann im deutschen Togogebiete gedrungen, die anwesenden weissen, insonderheit die kaiserlichen beamten, und die "coloured gentlemen" mit folgender rede zu begrüssen und in erstaunen zu setzen:

We all be happy too much, them old german emperor be king for we. All people like him and all man be glad we no blan for Englishman. Them take too much duty for all thing. Massa, you be we father and mother, we never get other. You must look for we and do we good (an uns gut tun). We sabe them german emperor be one old man, him be good man and fight for plenty war for Frenchman.

Me, them chief for Bagidá and all man, whom live here, beg for God, he be him palaver, he must give him long life that he han protect we for Englishman, who will make we fool, and we beg you, Massa, you must make book and tell him all we good wish! —

Ein Kruneger, Friday, und ein eingeborener aus Bagidá, Mensâ, erscheinen vor einem weissen, um ein "palaver" entscheiden zu lassen.

Der weisse (im ersten augenblick sich vergessend): Mensâ, explain the case.

M. Massa, me no fit hear, me no sabe (sprich *ſsăbe* oder *ſsăbi*) you mean.

W. You must tell me them palaver.

M. All right (spr. *hôhl leit*) Sâ! Me live for sleep, when me small boy come and tell me, one pig, who blan for me, live for die for outside for them french factory.

Me go one time for them prace (*place*) for look them palaver. Plenty people live. Me ax him what's the matter you stand for me dead pig. All people say one Kruboy shoot him when him come for them yard and chop kernels. Now me come for you and me beg you, Massa, me beg you, you must help me. Me no fit for help me alone, me fear too much, all them t'other Kruboy go flog me proper and kill me one time. (Nämlich: wenn er sich selbst hilft.)

W. Friday, you sabe, you must never kill pig, who blan for one other man. What's the matter you do bad?

F. Yes Sâ! Massa, me swear for God, me no fit lie (ich kann gar nicht lügen). Me want go for use meself for beach and one pig, big pass all we pig (grösser als alle unsere schweine) come for we yard. Me take one gun and shoot for him. Me look he can die one time and we all Kruboy take him and put him for outside for them fence. For true, Massa, him be them palaver. But me no go pay money for him you sabe, Massa, him be country fashion, people can kill pig who come for him yard but must not pay, suppose he never chop them pig.

Nach anhörung des häuptlings, der das gesetz bestätigt, entscheidet der weisse auf einfache weise die streitfrage:

W. Mensâ, you sabe too them country fashion, Friday must not pay, for he no chop them pig. Palaver finish.

Das im leben an der küste wichtigste ereigniss ist immer die ankunft eines dampfers. Da entspinnen sich ungefähr solche gespräche:

Neger. Massa, one steamer live for come. Me look, him be german (spr. *djämen*).

Weisser. Go, hoist them flag and open them gate for beach.

N. Them key for gate no live; me find him but no look him (ich habe ihn gesucht, aber nicht gesehen). —

W. You make them boat ready?

N. No Sâ, he live for them shed. We no fit for go for sea, them surf be sash (*very bad*) too much.

W. Suppose you go for steamer me go dash you two bottle gin.

N. Massa, no man can go for sea, Them sea be high (*flut*). Suppose you stop one hour he live for dry (*es wird ebbe sein*), and we can go.

Madrid

J. A. HARRISON

NEGRO ENGLISH

INTRODUCTION

The area embraced within the ensuing investigation is the area lying between the Atlantic Ocean on the East, the Mississippi River on the West, the Gulf of Mexico on the South, and the 39th parallel on the North ("Mason and Dixon's line", a name given to the southern boundary of the free state of Pennsylvania which formerly separated it from the slave states of Maryland and Virginia).

This area now contains between 6,000,000 and 7,000,000 Negroes, who speak, in large measure, the English to which attention is drawn in this paper. There are several distinctly marked dialects of this English, prevailing, respectively, in Virginia, on the sea-coast of South Carolina and Georgia, and through the middle Southern States: examples of which are given at the end of the paper.

It has been impossible to register scientifically the varied phenomena of Negro Phonetics or to re-produce the quite indescribable intonation and shades of intonation with which the sounds are uttered; but an effort has been made to approximate a correct re-production of the pronunciation by an imitative orthography and by key-words serving to show the dialectal variations of different localities.

It must be confessed, to the shame of the white population of the South, that they perpetuate many of these pronunciations in common with their Negro dependents; and that, in many places, if one happened to be talking to a native with one's eyes shut, it would be impossible to say whether a Negro or a white person were responding.

Reprinted from *Anglia* (1884) with the permission of Max Niemeyer Verlag.

The humor and *naïveté* of the Negro are features which must not be overlooked in gauging his intellectual calibre and timbre; much of his talk is baby-talk, of an exceedingly attractive sort to those to the manner born; he deals in hyperbole, in rhythm, in picture-words, like the poet; the slang which is an ingrained part of his being as deep-dyed as his skin, is, with him, not mere word-distortion; it is his verbal breath of life caught from his surroundings and wrought up by him into the wonderful figure-speech specimens of which will be given later under the head of Negroisms.

The results of a total abstraction of all means of self-cultivation from the field of Negro life are clearly enough seen in the representations which follow of his treatment of the English tongue. Negro English is an EAR-LANGUAGE altogether, a language built up on what the late Prof. Haldeman of Pennsylvania called OTOSIS, an error of ear, a mishearing, similar to that by which Sirâdyhu-d-daula, a viceroy of Bengal, became in the newspapers of the day, Sir Roger Dowler. (!) The only wonder is how the Negro could have caught the rapidly uttered sounds of the language spoken around him so truly and reproduced them so ingeniously, transmitting what he had learned in a form so comparatively unspoiled. He has simply taken the principle of PARESIS or word-neglect ... a principle by which *maculate* becomes *mole* 'a spot' ... and worked it out to its ultimate consequences, so far as English is concerned. If his masters say *won't, shan't*, why should not he say *dasen't* 'dares not' and use it for every person? If his master says, paroptically, *énjïne* (long *i*), why should not he say *injïne* 'for éngĭne'? If euphemism so dominates the master that, in his oaths, he must say *dad blame* for something much stronger, why should not the Negro catch it and apply it analogically to a whole class of expressions (see *Interjections*)?

Such parasynetic forms as *sparrer-grass* for *asparagus*, due to misunderstanding or misconception of a word, are common enough in Negro; but the African, from the absence of books and teaching, had no principle of *analepsy* in his intellectual furnishing by which a word, once become obscure from a real or supposed loss of parts or meaning, can be repaired, amended, or restored to its original form. He is continually led by analogies, and induced by classes of words like *gift, lift* to add, for example, a *t* to *cliff* if indeed he can be got at all to pronounce this, to him, very difficult final dental.

The process of hybridization both in word-formation and in word-pronunciation (if one may so apply the term) is extensively practiced by him; for not only have we such formations as *smartually* 'smartly' and the like in Negro, but such pronunciations as *ailment, president, obleege* (caught from the Romance settlements in the South) are common enough all over the South among white and black alike.

The opposite principles of education and absorption are actively at work in the processes of Negro speech, giving rise on the one hand to such lengthenings and strengthened forms as corn*d*er drown*d*ed, clos*t*, 'cross*t*, rous*t*, and on the other to such syncopations and contractions as '*spe'unce* (experience), *cu'ius* (curious), *mo'*, 'membunce, etc.

Numerous examples of aphaeresis, apocope, syncope, epenthetic insertion, prothesis, epithesis, and metathesis have been collected and are given under these heads in their special section of this paper.

What has been called DIMORPHISM — a principle according to which a word may appear in the course of time under two forms — is not without suggestive illustration in Negro; e.g. the word *admiration* has not only its usual meaning, but, in the form "to make a great '*mīration*", has gone back to its early meaning of 'wonder, astonishment'; *up* is made to do the duty of a verb in such expressions as, "he *up* en duz"; *allow* comes to signify, additionally, *maintain, insist*; *parade* ("*perrade*") means also 'walk' etc.

The fertility of the Negro dialect indeed is really wonderful, not only in the ingenious distortion of words by which new and startling significance is given to common English words (e.g. a *hant* in Negro means a *ghost*), but more especially in the domain of imitative sounds, cries, animal utterance. To the Negro all nature is alive, anthropomorphized, replete with intelligence; the whispering, tinkling, hissing, booming, muttering, "zoonin" around him are full of mysterious hints and suggestions, which he reproduces in words that imitate, often strikingly, the poetic and multiform messages which nature sends him through his auditory nerve. He is on intimate terms with the wild animals and birds, the flora and *fauna* of the immense stretches of pine-woods among which for generations his habitation has been pitched. His mind is yet in the stage in which ready belief is accorded to the wrangles of shovel and tongs, the loves and hates of dish and platter on the kitchen shelves, the naïve personification of the furniture of his cabin; and for him rabbits and wolves, terrapins and turtles, buzzards and eagles live lives no less full of drama and incident, of passion and marvel than his own kith and kin gathered around the pine-knot or the hickory fire.

The Negro passion for music and for rhythmic utterance has often been remarked; a Negro sermon nearly always rises to a pitch of exaltation at which ordinary prose accent, intonation, word-order are too tame to express the streaming emotion within; the sermon becomes a cry, a poem, an improvisation; it is intoned with melodious energy; it is full of scraps of Scripture in poem-form, and to say that it becomes an orgy of figures and metaphors sobbed or shouted out with the voice of Boanerges is hardly going at all too far. The sermon style naturally exerts a powerful influence on the style of ordinary life; so that it is not remarkable if the utterance and language of the household and the street are largely cast in a rhythmic mould. Nearly every Negro above the average is a hymn-maker, or at least co-operates with others in the production of hymns, songs, plantation-rhymes, "corn-shucking" glees, "joubas", and the like. He invents his own airs and tunes, which are often profoundly touching and musical; his sense of *takt* is delicate, and in congregational singing his voice has a beauty and richness and justness which often exceed the best efforts of the trained choirs of the cities.

In this paper the author has endeavored to give merely an outline of Negro language-usage, an outline far from exhaustive or immaculate, but which, he hopes, will attract the attention of better qualified linguists to a series of phenomena which are certainly not devoid of interest. A life-long residence in the Southern States of North America enables him to say that what is here given is at least approximately correct. It will perhaps be several generations before the American public school system has sufficiently penetrated the wilds of the Negro South to render what is here recorded obsolete.

PHONETICS

1. VOWELS

a

is pronounced

1. *a*: *glad, bad, dad.*
2. *ah*: *ahx* 'ask', *bahskit, rahsberry* (Tide-water Virginia).
3. *o*: *wroppin', strop, flop, wheelborrer, olmanick, stomp, tromp, tossle bobbykew.*
4. *ai*: *pairbile, air* 'are', *pairsel.*
5. *ä*: *känt* (*kaint* 'can't').
6. *u*: *fur, distunce, gizzud, el'phunt, wuz, ruther, Missus, Cris'mus.*
7. *iar, yar* or *yah, iah; kyahnt* 'can't' (Tide-water Virginia), *giard'n, kiar, skiahlit* 'scarlet', *kiards, kiarm* 'garden, car, cards' etc. (cf. Anglo-Saxon ӡ*eard,* etc.).
8. *ee*: *keer, skeer, Jeems*[1] 'care, scare, James'.
9. *i*: *kin shill* 'can, shall'.
10. *y*: (at end of proper and common nouns) *Ameriky, M'lindy, 'Tildy, sody, Georgy;* so, *callyboose.*
11. *e*: *ketch, ez, ken* 'as, can' (Georgia dialect).
12. *er*: *er* (indef. article), *ermongs', erlong, manyer* 'many a'.
13. *au, aw*: *Nauncy, dawnse, awnt, Chawmberlin* (Tide-water Virginia; cf. M.E. phonetic spellings).

---

[1] Cf. Robert of Gloucester's *Gemes*.

e

1. The ordinary sounds in *met, mete.*
2. *a* in *car, thar, whar, dar, Brackenridge, Shanandoa, Latcha, Riddelbarga* (cf. Barkshire, Barclay, etc., in Robert of Gloucester), *sarve.*
3. *ee: eend, peerch, peert* (few words only).
4. *u* (with *r*): *putty* 'pretty', *mussy* 'mercy'.
5. *ai: aig, aidge, kaig, laig* 'egg' etc.
6. *o: fotch, sot, sont* 'fetch, set' etc.
7. *er: ther* 'the' (common among the whites).
8. *i: nigger, trim'le, git, million* 'melon'.

Observations:

1. *ee = i: crick.*
2. *er = u: wuffo', thuffo'* 'wherefore, therefore'.
3. *e* is often dropped: *'nuff, 'b'leeve, b'long, 'spec.*

i

1. The ordinary sounds in *pine* and *pin.*
2. *ai:* (like German *ai* in combinations where a nasal follows: *gwaine, whaine*; uttered with a nasal drawl. The Hibernicism *oi* in *foine* is unknown).
3. *ee:* (in *sheens, teenshy* 'teeny, tiny' *erbleeged, peazzer.*
4. *u* in *fust* 'first', *strucken, wull-o-de-wust* 'Will-o'-the-wisp'.
5. *ah: sah* (for 'sir').
6. *e: ef* (for 'if'), *tell* (for 'till'), *sence* (for 'since').
7. *a: clam* (for 'climb'), *lak* 'like' (Georgia dialect), *gal* 'girl'.
8. *u: burd* 'bird'.
9. *we: twel* 'till' (Georgia dialect).
10. *er: eperdemic.*
11. *j* in contact with *d: Injins* or *Injuns.*
12. *ou: mought* 'might'.
13. *ea* in *eatch* 'itch'.

Obs.: Sometimes omitted: *you k'n* 'you can'.

o

1. The ordinary sounds in *not, note, more.*
2. *u: stummuck, young-uns* 'ones', *fur, dun-no* 'don't, know', *mudder, 'pun* 'upon', *wud* 'word'.
3. *er: banjer, ter* (before infinitives), *Baltimer* (*er* especially in proper names with stress on penult or antepenult), *perlite, terbacca* or *terbacker.*
4. *oa: doan* 'don't' (in some dialects).
5. *a: drap, crap, saf'* 'soft', *jew-drap* 'dew-drop', *'bacca.*

   6. *yu*: *yuther* 'other' (parasitic *y*; cf. Yorkshire dialect).

   7. *i*: *waggin, kivver*.

   8. *aw*: *Gawd, Lawd* (in some dialects).

   9. *oe*: *to* (when stress is laid on it as if spelled *toe*).

10. *ow* or *or*: *cownfown'* 'confound', *Cornfedrit, morck* 'mock', *cornfown'*.

11. *e*: *er* 'or'.

Obs.: 1. Often cut off: *'possum* etc.

      2. Long *o* is sometimes shortened: *chock full* 'choke'.

u

   1. The ordinary sounds in *tube, tub, full, fur*.

   2. Causes peculiar phonetic changes in preceding consonants: *Chusedy* 'Tuesday', *chune* 'tune'.

   3. Replaces *o* in many localities: *lub, lubly, uf, ub, cunjer*.

   4. Becomes *i* in *sich* 'such'.

   5. *e*: *jes'* 'just', *jedge, bresh* 'brush', *sech* or *sich, shet* (sometimes shot).

   6. *a*: *harrycane, tribalation*.

   7. *yo*: *kyo'* 'cure', *pyo'* (with *r* associated).

   8. *o*: in sho (sure), *oneasy, onloose, hongry, ontie* (of O.E.).

   9. *oo*: in *soople, pursooin'*.

Obs.: 1. In some Virginia localities *u* in *put* = *u* in *but*.

      2. Often syncopated: *reg'ler, s'posen, pertick'ler*.

      3. Becomes *er* in *merlatter*.

y

   1. The ordinary sounds: *your, yaller-gal, yo'*.

   2. Sometimes prefixed parasitically: *yuther, yudder* 'other', *year, Yallerbamer, yerbs, yuse, yallergater* 'alligator'.

   3. Often results from final *a*: *Calliny, Virginny, Wally-Wally* (also a Westernism).

2. DIPHTHONGS

Digraphs and Trigraphs

au

   1. Very commonly = *a*: *'kase, 'kase I'se sassy* 'because' etc.

   2. *a*: *hant, jant*.

   3. *ar*: *larf* (Tide-water Va.).

ai

    1. Often simplified into *e*: *'fred, wescut*.
    2. Or becomes *ay*: *Isayah*.
    3. Or *a*: *fa'r trile* 'fair trial'.
    4. *eer* in *cheer, reezins* 'raisins'.

ay

    1. *e*: *sez* 'says' (*saze*, Valley of Va.).
    2. *aw*: *crawfish*.

ei

    i: *height*.

ey

    1. *ay*: *obay*;
    2. *u* in *nuther* 'neither';
    3. *a* in *nary*, or *nare one* (neither, neither one).

ea

    1. The usual sounds;
    2. becomes *ee* in *deep, heerd* (cf. Dr. S. Johnson's pronunciation) *creetur*;
    3. *aa* in *blate*;
    4. broad *a* in *t'ar, b'ar, wa'r*;
    5. *i* in *instid*;
    6. *u* in *studdy* (*keep yo' hed studdy*);
    7. *e* in *gred big, het, pled* 'pleaded';
    8. *ee* in *idee*;
    9. *y* in *ginny-hin* 'guinea-hen'.

ee

    1. Usual sound;
    2. *i* or *e* in different localities: *bin, ben*;
    3. *a*: *quare* 'queer'.

eu

    Result of peculiar syncopation: *'spe'unce* 'experience'.

i

    1. Usual sound in *high*;
    2. *a* in *chany* 'china'.

ie : *ee*

    b'leeve 'believe'.

io(n) : *un*
>   *fashun, nashun.*

oo

>   1. As in *moon, loon*; or
>   2. as in *mow, do', flo'* (door with absorbed *r*); or
>   3. as in *duck, tuck* 'took', *shuck* 'hands'; or
>   4. as in *puff, huff* 'hoof'.

oe

>   As in *toe, roe-buck*.

oi

>   1. *i*: *his't, jis', on-jint, pint, bile, pizened, sile* (cf. last century pro-
>   nunciation);
>   2. *wi*: *gwine, gwine = on*.

oa

>   Simplified to *o*: *bode* 'board', *bote*, "*all abode*", *de chuchbode*.

ou

>   1. As in *soul*; or
>   2. as in *bound* (*bown'*); or
>   3. as *u 'nuff* 'enough', *ruffness*;
>   4. *ow* in *wownded*; or
>   5. *e* in *tetch* 'touch';
>   6. *or* in *trorff*;
>   7. *o*: *do'* 'though'.

ow

>   1. As in *how, found*;
>   2. *er* (in final syllables) *morrer, feller, sorrer, borrer, medder, follerin'*;
>   3. sometimes *u*: *gallus* 'gallows'.

eo(n) = i(n)
>   *pidgins, lunchin.*

ew

>   1. Usual sound in *mew* (*ew* as *oo* [*stoo, doo, noo*] seems to be un-
>   known in genuine Negro); or
>   2. in *sew*.

ue

1. As in *rue*;
2. *ur*: *agur* 'ague'.

ui

1. Result of syncopation: *cu'ius* 'curious';
2. *ee* in *musketeer*.

3. CONSONANTS

b

Usual sound: *b'long, bile* 'boil', *brown, bone, barry* 'barrow', *bounce 'roun', bigrudgin', boss, unbiknownst.*
Obs.: 1. Initial *be* is often omitted: *'kasse, 'gun.*
2. So final *b*: *plum', down, lam, lim'* (cf. O.E.), *jam'.*
3. Sometimes *b* creeps in: *fambly, chimbly-jam.*
4. *mb* sometimes = *ng*: *bung-shell* 'bombshell'.

c

Usual sound: *'coon, creeturs, Cris'mus, cheer* 'chair', *clost* 'close', *cock up, cuss, cackerlatin'.*
Obs.: *ct* often changes (medial and final) to *ck* or *c*: *'speck, d'reckly, fack, specs.*
Obs.: *ch* has the ordinary sound: *chick'n, chile, chowda, chawin' churnin'.*

d

1. Usual sound: *fear'd, done gone, dozin', dast* 'dares n't', *drappin', dis-a-way.*
2. Often added (a) to past part.: *busted, brokend, hurtid, ketched, drownded* (cf. sound *d*); or (b) to infinitives to form p. tense; *seed, run'd* (but often omitted in past tense; *he rush'*).
3. When final or medial it is usually dropped: *min', han'le, fine', kin', boun', soun', ol', mill-pon', stow', en'* or *an', grine-stone, de roun' worl', aint bin use' ter.*
4. Sometimes changes to *t*: *skeert, holt, terreckly* 'directly', *hilt, kilt.*
5. Sometimes omitted or assimilated: *neenter* 'needn't to', *scan'lous, chilluns, scannul, Wensdy, I bin use', 'pennunce* 'dependence'.
6. Sometimes (before an *e*) becomes *j*: *jew* 'dew'.
Obs.: *dv* sometimes = *bv*: *abvertize* 'advertise'.

f

1. Usual sound: *fotch, fust* 'first', *fer, scufflin', far' en' squar', fling, diff'unt.*

2. Sometimes becomes *t* or *r* after preceding broad *a*: *atter, arter* 'after'; *I journey fur, I journey fas', I glad I foun' de place at las'* ... Harris.

3. Sometimes in connection with *o* = er: *sorter, kinder, to put in min' er* 'of'; *little bit er gal.*

4. Sometimes absorbed: *brekfus, brekkus* 'breakfast'.

g

1. Usual sound: *w'at I gits, I gits*; *agin, diggins, golly, goobers, gran'-pa.*

2. Often becomes *ds* or *dz* in contact with following *d*: *obleeds* 'obliged'.

3. Nearly always omitted in pres. part.: *fishin', mornin', goin', so, nuthin', nuffin'* etc.

Obs.: 1. *gn*: *g* here is usually silent, in *gnaw* = *ni*, as, *niaw*.
         2. In *inguns* 'onions' a *g* creeps in.

h

1. As usual: *hallyluyah-holler, hatter* 'have to', *hadder* 'had to', *hem en' haw, hankcher, hankercher* (cf. Shakspere).

2. Often omitted: *make 'ase, w'iles, w'en, w'ot, w'ich, w'ite, 'umble.* So in connected discourse: *grittin 'er toofs, sezee* 'says he', *had 'a bin, dey'd 'a lef'.*

3. Sometimes inserted: *hit* (cf. A.S.), *hain't, rensh* 'rinse', *hits* 'its'.

4. Sometimes replaced by *y*: *year* 'hear', *yer* 'here', *dish yer* etc.

j

1. Usual sound: *jinin', joyin', joggin', jam', Jeemes River.*

2. Becomes *d* in some dialects: *des* 'just'.

3. Replaces *di*: *Injun.*

Obs.: *dj* replaces *s* occasionally: *medjer* 'measure', *pledjer* 'pleasure'.

k

1. Usual sound: *fokes, keer, keerful, ketch, lak* 'like', *kin'lin', hunk, chunk, racket, skittish, skace, erclock, ketch holt, reckin, slick.*

2. Takes the place of *ct*: *'speck, d'reckly, perteck* 'protect', *districk.*

3. *sk* sometimes becomes *sh*: *tush, mush-million.*

l

1. Usual sound: *'low, lak, w'iles, cole, hol'in', lemme 'lone.*

2. Often omitted: *hisse'f, theirse'f, he'p, yokes* 'yolks', *on'y.*

3. Sometimes interchanges with *r*: *gentermans, warkin'.*

4. Sometimes creeps in: *splatter* (cf. could; sputter and splutter).

m

1. Usual sound: *minners, minnit, Marm, mo', mighty mad, Kingdom-come, 'um (them), monst'ous, 'miration, 'mungs, ma'ied, mo'ners, musn't, wom* 'warm', *m'anderin'*.
2. Sometimes creeps in: *disumgree, whatsumever, hoppum-skippum-run-en'-jumpum* 'humorous', *hebumly* 'heavenly', *'levm* 'eleven', *Hev'm*.

n

1. Usual sound: *ondo, 'simmon, w'en, nasty 'nuff, natchul, nigger, nohow*.
2. Often omitted in past part.: *broke', writ'*; so in indef. article; *a' apple, a' arm, a' eench*; or separates and joins the following word; *a nour, a nudder* (cf. aneft, a newt etc.).

Obs.: 1. *nd* sometimes becomes *me*: *behime, bime-by* 'by-and-by'.
2. Initial *in* and *en* are often cut off: *'deed, 'joy*.
3. *n* creeps in in absolute poss. pronouns: *hisn, hern, yourn, ourn, theirn*.
4. Changes to *m* in *rozzum* 'rosin', *'lev'm* 'eleven' etc.

p

1. Usual sound: *pertickler, pone, pumpin', po'ly, patterrollers* 'patrols' *piller-case, de ve'y chap, pester, Pairidise, sperrit*.
2. Omitted in *punkins*.
3. Creeps in in *sump'n*.
4. Sometimes changes to *k*: *turkentine*.

Obs.: *pl* sometimes interchanges with *fl*: *flatform*.

q

Usual sound: *mighty quare noshuns, squall, quile* 'coil', *squar', 'quaintunce, squinch-owl, licker* 'liquor'.

r

1. Usual sound, though weak: *romancin' roun, formd, fr'en', ridem-shun, pie-rootin* ('pirouetting': Valley of Va.).
2. Sometimes inserted (see below) after broad *a*: *Mars John*; but *marter* 'matter'.
3. Often omitted: *thow, thoat, thoo, hick'y nut yan'* ('yonder'), *diffunce, do', flo', mo', fum, sho', sho'ly* 'sure', *fust, dey (dere =* 'there'), *sho'* 'shore', *ku'ius, ve'y, ev'y, wud* (cf. Creole, cf. omission of *r*), *gals, monstus, wukkin, yo'sef, co'se, kyo* 'cure', *pa'tridge, cullud pusson, front-po'ch, so'*.
4. Assimilates to *l* or *b*: *Calliny* 'Carolina', *Calline, puppus*.

5. Becomes *w* or *ah*: in *swawmin'*, *bawn* etc.
6. Initial *re* often cut off: *'fuse, 'ceive, 'spon'*.
7. *r* sometimes creeps in: *terbarker, marster, tergidder, dorg, lorg*.

Obs.: er often represents *of*: *stidder* 'instead of'.

rr and *re* final. Weak; often absorbed or vocalized: *kyar* 'carry', *und'* 'under', *fo', befo', tar'ypin* 'terrapin', *squ'iel* 'squirrel', *pe'ish, slippy, qu'oll* 'quarrel'.

Obs.: *ra* is sometimes transposed: *Abarham* etc.

s

Usual sound: *shot* 'shut', *sech* 'such', *spar', sno', satun, spang, slap-on, sparrer-grass*.

Obs.: *s* is added to the verb through all persons, pres. tense: *I knows, he goes* (cf. North dialect, O.E.).

1. Becomes *z* in *wuz, cuzzun* 'cousin', *bisznis*.
2. Often omitted: *wa'nt, 'twa'n't* 'was not' etc.
3. Becomes *sh* in *dish here* ('this here', leans on *h* following).
4. Is sometimes added initially and finally *splunge* (cf. 'plash and splash', etc.), *squench, squash* 'destroy', *squince* 'quince', *nowhars, sumwhars* (*summers*), *long ways, wharbouts*.

Obs.: *st* sometimes interchanges with *sp*: *superspitious*.

t

1. Usual sound: *turibul, totin', tromplin', 'spute, tarryfyin', tu'nout, tas'e, taller* 'ow', *ter* 'to', *truck* (Georgian for 'thing'), *'twix'* (*tu = chu* in *chune, Chuseday*).
2. Assimilates to *m* and *n*, *lemme, dunno* ('let me' etc.).
3. Is sometimes added: *tother, 'crosst, wisht* 'I wisht'.
4. Often dropped when final: *fas', lif', pas', Jack Fros', trac', las', mus', fus', nex', dreckly*.
5. Becomes *d*: *pardner*.
6. Often becomes *d* by assimilation: *dad-dere* or *g*, *daggal* 'that girl'.
7. Changes to *k*: *mud-turkle*.
8. To *s*: *lissen*.

th

1. As usual in many words.
2. Becomes *d*: *dan, dey, de, dat, dis, wid, furder, bodderin', mudder, fader, brudder* (cf. Chaucer's *fader* and the Scotch dialects etc.).
3. *f* (final): *mouf, trufe, bref, warmf, paf, toofies* 'toothies'.
4. *v*: *smoove*.
5. *t*: *t'ing, troo* 'through'.

6. Often omitted in some dialects (when medial or final): *dem 'ar, brer Fox, ne'er* 'neither'; so very often *'um, 'em*.

Obs.: *ti* = *sh*: *'spishuns, salvashun, nashun*.
gth = *k*: *full lenk* 'length', *strenk*.

v

1. Usual sound: *ven'sun, venjunce, vittles, 'vite*.
2. Sometimes in connection with *h* = dropped, and the syllable left then = *er*: *fo' you cud er* 'have' *sed Jack Rob'son; you moughter* 'have'.
3. Sometimes changes to *f*: *lef* 'leave', *I gif 'im twelf, Ferginny, trafflin'* 'travelling', 'Virginia' etc.
4. Sometimes assimilates to *m*: *gimme* 'give me'.
5. Sometimes changes to *b*: *sebenty, moobe* 'move', *gib, eb'ry, nebber, hab, oberflow, oberload, ribber*.

w

1. Usual sound: *know'd, blow', howdy, 'twant, whar', waller, swaller, wescut, wall* 'well' (Westernism), *wuss, wuff* 'worth', *w'ar*.
2. Often omitted when initial or medial (in connected discourse): *'ud, uz* 'would, was', *'ull* 'will', *ans'er, ole 'oman*.
3. Sometimes absorbed: *todes, allers* 'always', *somers* or *summers* 'somewheres'.
4. Sometimes a variant of *o* or *or*: *Gawd* 'God', *mawnin'*.
5. Changes (rarely) to *b*: *bidout* 'without'.
6. Sometimes creeps in: *twel* (Georgia dialect).

Obs.: *ow* (final) becomes *er*: *shadder, waller, beller, sorrer, yallerjackits*.

x

1. Usual sound: *'twix, extry*.
2. Sometimes *z*: *'zample* 'example' (cf. 'sample').
3. Sometimes results from transposition: *ax* 'ask' (cf. A.S. acsian).

z

1. Usual sound: *'zackly, Zach, 'Ziah, fuzzle, sezee, 'zasperatin'*.
2. Often replaces *s*: *wuz, ez, 'zeeze* 'disease'.

APHAERESIS, SYNCOPE, APOCOPE, PROTHESIS, EPENTHESIS, EPITHESIS, TRANSPOSITION

Aphaeresis (initial clipping)

'Sturbs, 'possum, 'coon, rassel 'wrestle', *'mungs, 'fo', 'twix', 'bleedged*

'obliged', *'tater-slips, 'nudder* 'another', *'gin, 'spishun* (as verb), *'lone,*
'ceppin, 'fuse, 'ny 'deny', *'scuze, 'mazin, 'stracted, 'spress, 'tall, 'uz*
'was', *'a* 'have', *'way off, 'buzin, 'penon, 'pears like, 'um, 'tween, 'oman,*
'umble, 'simmons, 'nounce, 'low'd, 'speshully, 'rested, 'member, 'ciety,
'scurshuntrain, 'spe'unst, 'zamine, 'intment, 'stemper 'distemper', *'seetful,*
'lasses, 'tack, 'ligion, 'ritmertic, 'zackly, smoke-'ouse, co'te-'ouse, 'lowance,
'tickler, 'sprize-party, 'termin', 'our, 'bunnunce, 'skiver, 'spectful, 'sides,
'sprize, 'sist, 'tenshun, 'arly, 'pozzit, 'pennunce, 'cashun, 'splain.

Prothesis (initial addition)

1. *a* is added in innumerable instances to verbs and participles:
   agwinter 'a-going to', *a-stan'in', a-dancin'* etc.; so in *dat-a-way,*
   dis-a-way, aloose.
2. *y: yuther, year* 'ear'.
3. *h: hit, hits, haint.*
4. *fer: fer-given* 'given' (in: *fer-given name*).
5. *dis: dis-remember, dis-commerdate.*
6. *e: eend.*
7. *n: nunicorn* 'unicorn', *Nunited States.*
8. *en: endurin'.*
   Miscellaneous: *a nour, disperlite, a nudder, ye'th, to year* 'hear',
   Djune 'June', *Djuly* 'July'.

Syncope (medial clipping).

Cu'ius, ha'r, Saddy 'Saturday', *w'ite, w'isky, chu'ch, fum, hymes* 'hymns',
mo'ners, Gaberl 'Gabriel', *heav'm, pow'ful, p'inted, allus,* or *allers* 'always',
somers, dreckly, s'po'te 'support', *ca'se, might'ly, everlas'nly, w'en, b'leeve*
ve'y, present'y, hosses, wuss, fo'-mile, w'eat, sassers, w'ip, ska'cely, sodes
'swords', *ma'm* 'warm', *min', kep', skummishin', fe'xy* 'ferry', *toas'n,*
thoo', gal, nuss, w'ar, op'n, funer'l, Cris'mus, ker'ner 'coroner', *reconnize,*
wushup, giner'ly, cullud fokes, a'r 'air', *hyme-book, p'leece-man, po'ke,*
las's 'lasts', *gemmun, bo'dinhouse, mor'l, grum'lin', nas'ness, comp'ny, cle'r,*
gum-bile, kam 'calm', *out'ard, forrard, inst'ument, guv'nment, sassafac,*
fish'man, s'ingletree, go'de, pa'm, bil', intrust 'interest', *atterwuds, res'n,*
endu'unce, sco'ze 'scores', *pra'rs, ho'seness, h'ist, pu's, spile, s'roundid,*
vinyud, fuddermo', prom'nade, w'iss'lin' 'whistling', *confunce* 'conference',
gran'chilluns.

Epenthesis (medial addition)

Disumgree, chimbly, fambly, a-sojourneyin', togyudder, tergyudder,
terbacker, perlite, cowcumber, Mars 'Master', *kwis'hins* 'cushions',

mush-million, ter-morrer, carridge, pidgin, nigger, cornder, muel 'mule',
shin-plarster, britches, tetch, 'kummerlated, figgers, wurril 'world',
stummuck, circuous 'circus', *kyarpet-sack, Ellick* (Alex.), *montykyards,
dosted, termartusses* 'tomatoes', *mebbe, conserlation, sitivation, rickerlec*
'recollect', *kyarvin'-knife, mustarsh, merlasses, innercent gyard* 'guard',
berloon, ter-do 'to do', *juberlee, injuns, um'erella, orffis, orfficer, morckin'-
bird, skyar, twel, drownded, milerterry, kyarkiss, dividjun, langwidge,
leetle, whosomedever, ridjun* 'region', *perlaver, pledjer, orbjeshun* 'objection', *medercine, aggervate, morgidge.*

Apocope (final clipping)

*Spar', skippin', en', an', boun', mo', las', saf', plum', clum' up, sho',
conscrip', fiel', 'fo', name', blame', fattes', settin'-room, ole, feelin',
cole', bus', fus', lissenin', hin', rhoomatiz', mar', kyo', hoar-houn', middlin',
totin', yistiddy, leas'ways, fus'-en-fo'-mus', mout', 'fo' de wah* 'war',
fi' dolla 'five dollars', *po' fokes, was'nes', eave-drappers, strenk, gra'-vines,
do-jam, ilun* 'island', *dey* 'there', *new-fangle', dremp'.*

Usually final *g* and *r, d, p,* and *t* are omitted; sometimes final *m*;
often final *l*.

Epithesis (final addition)

Hearn 'hear', *clost, 'crost* 'across', *oncet, twicet, sorter, kinder, wanter,
gwinter, gotter* (prep. *of* and *to* suffixed), *his'n, her'n, yone* 'yourn', *oune*
'ourn', *earnt* 'earn', *inter, ter, smartually* 'smartly', *hurtid* (p.p.), *busted,
hyeener, spurrers, peazzer, peanner, stunted* 'stunned', *outen* 'of', *bumbler-
bee-stinger, ennywhars.*

Transposition

Hwoop 'whip' (*u* in *full*), *ax, Putmon* 'Putnam', *congergashun, sakerfice,
persidin', keration* 'creation', *ambertype, peckerwoods, hoppagrasse* 'wood-
peckers, grass-hoppers', *peeramble, pervishuns, fier* etc.

THE ARTICLES

1. The Definite article is *de*:
   de man, de chile.
Obs.: The Negro speech-organs are becoming slowly and with difficulty
accustomed to the sound *th*.
2. The Indefinite article is *a* or *an*.
   (a) *A*, unless stress is laid on it, is usually sounded *er* or *ur*: *er
   house, er box, ur yard, ur street.*

158   J. A. Harrison

(b) *A* is often used for *an* before vowels and *h*: *a oven, a ape a hour, a honor* (possibly from a feeling that *a* in the Negro pronunciation is usually = *er, ur*, and contains a consonant element; (cf. *Amelia r, Anne*), though when so used it often has a distinct stress laid on it, and is pronounced *a*).

(c) The *n* of *an* often separates from it and joins a following vowel or *h* form: *a nour, a nudder* (cf. examples in Shakespere).

NOUNS

Formation of Plural

1. The Negro forms the plural regularly by addition of *s* or *z*, usually ignoring irregular plurals like *oxen, children*.
2. Some forms like *men, mice, geese*, however, are in familiar use.
3. *Foots, chilluns, galluses, beastesses (beas's) ghos'es, bredrens*, are examples of double plurals in familiar use. So *umberellases, belluses, hind-footses, oxens, boot'ses, sheeps, deers, fokeses*.
4. The plural sign is often omitted with *mile, pound, gallon, peck, cord*, and other expressions of weight, quantity, and dimension (cf. German and A.S.); *two stran' er ha'r, fi' poun'* etc.
5. *Kind* and *sort* commonly omit the plural sign: *all kinder creeturs* etc.
   Examples: *Dis or dese ashes; fifteen foot squar'; five or fi' barl* 'barrel' *'taters; forty mile a 'our; dat tongs* etc.

Obs.: The verb is usually in the singular no matter what the number of the noun may be.

The Possessive Case

1. The possessive case is either formed by *s, es* or *z*: *Marsters gun, Missuses dress, de bee'z sting*.
2. Or the possessive sign is altogether dropped: *Abarham sakerfice, Dinah book, Molly plate*.

Obs.: The pronouns *his, her, our, your, their*, add *n* in their absolute form: *hisn, ourn (owne)* etc.

Comparison of Adjectives

1. The usual terminations *-er, -est, -r, -st*, changed into *-ur, -ir, -ist, -ust*, are in use: *mo' and mos'* are likewise used.
2. Double comparatives and superlatives, as in Elizabethan English, are exceedingly frequent: *de bes's* 'bestest', *de mos' deepist water I ever seed, mo' trubblesomer, mo' puttier* 'prettier', *de musses' gal*.

3. *Than* after comparatives is usually worked down into *'n: mo' 'n
   me, mo'n jimson weed* 'Jamestown weed'.
4. If there is no verb after *'n*, the case is invariably objective: *bigger'n
   him, her, dem* etc.; thus extending indefinitely the apparent govern-
   ing power of *than* in phrases like *than whom*, etc.
5. Adjectives irregularly compared are often made more irregular by
   recomparison, thus: *wuss* (as quasi-positive), *wusser* or *-er, wussist*;
   so, *leas's', mos's', bes's'*.
6. The forms *bad, good, little* (cf. Shakespere), *well* (adverb) are compared regularly: *littlest, wellest, baddest* etc.
7. The length of the word has nothing to do with Negro comparisons:
   mos' beau'fullest etc. occur.

PRONOUNS

Personal

1. (a) *I, my, mine, me: we* (*we-uns* in North Carolina "Cracker" dia-
       lect), *our, our'n, ours, us.*
   (b) *I* agglutinates with *is* — *Ise* as in Scotch 'I is': *me* agglutinates
       with imper. of *give, let*, and other verbs; *gimme, lemme* etc.
       So *wese* 'we is'.
   (c) *Me* is frequent as a nominative, not alone but with other
       pronouns: *me'n him, him en me* etc.
   (d) Circumlocutions like "*dis darkey*", "*dis nigger*", "*dis chile*" (cf.
       Greek, Provençal etc.), often stand for *I*.
2. *Thou*: exists for the Negro only in prayer or poetry. *You, yo',
   yose, yo'ne* (*your'n*), *yer* (*I tell yer, yur*), *ee* (*lookee yer, thankee*), *y*
   (*howdy do, howdy*). *You* is often "preglutinated" to its verb:
   youk'n = you can, *yule* 'you will' etc.; cf. *dars* 'there is', M.E.
   ichitl, choll etc.
3. (a) *He, 'ee, his, his'n* (*hizzen*), *him* (*'im*). *Dey, deir'n, deir, deirs,
       dem* (*'em, 'um*).
   (b) The objective forms *him* and *dem* are often used as nomina-
       tives: *dem* alone, *him* in connection with other pronouns;
       dem's mine, dem en us wuz dar.
   (c) *He* = *ee* in agglutinated phrases: *sezee* etc.
   (d) *He* is often used in personification of inanimate objects.
   Obs.: The *n* in *his'n, our'n, yo'ne* etc. seems to have been added from
       analogy with *mine* etc.
4. (a) *She, her her'n, hers, her* (*'er*).
   (b) *She, her* etc. are often used of inanimate objects: *let her rip*;
       de house, she's a bakin etc.

(c) *Her* often stands with other pronouns (not alone) as subject: *her'n me gwine-ter come.*

Obs.: *Me, her, him* etc. are the invariable predicates after the verb *to be*: *dat's me* etc.

5. *It, hit, hits* (cf. A.S. and O.E.). The *h* is usually dropped when the form follows another: *I sed 'it.*

Emphatic Pronouns

1. *Self* is *se'f: yo'se'f, myse'f* etc.
2. *Hisse'f, derese'f, dey se'f, dereseves,* are in constant use.
3. *Deyse'f, hisse'f,* are constantly used as objective forms: *dey tole deyse'f* etc.; *'mungs' deyse'f* etc.

DEMONSTRATIVES

1. *Dis,*
2. *dat,*
3. *dish here, dish-yer,*
4. *dad-dare, daddere* 'this here, that there',
5. *dem* 'those',
6. *dis'n,*
7. *dat'n* 'this one' etc.
8. *deze here,*
9. *yan (yan side).*

Obs.: 1. *Yer* 'here' *and dere, dar, da* 'there are usual enclitic accompaniments to the forms *dis, dish, dat, dem.*

2. *Dat* is often used as an intensive: *dey wuz dat imperdent; hit come down ter dat pass dat* etc.
3. *Dis* is often used = 'the present time': *'twix' dis en Cris'mus.*
4. *Dish* has grown out of the constant association of *dis* and *here: dishere = dish-'ere = dish-here.*
5. *Dem* has nearly driven out *doze.* A Negro that knew the difference between these two forms would go a step farther and use *those.*
6. *Yan* is not very common.

RELATIVES

1. *Who, w'at* (often used with personal antecedents: *dem w'ot knows* etc.).
2. *w'ich.*

3. *dat.*
4. *ez* (after *sich, sech*).

Obs.: 1. *W'at often* = that: *de man w'ot I'scribe* etc.
2. *W'ich* is often inserted pleonastically: *w'ich a little mo' 'n one un um*; or used for *dat*: *he say w'ich (dat) 'twuz over dar*.
3. *W'ich his* often stands for *whose*: *er nigger w'ich his brer wuz er witch* etc. (cf. O.E. forms).
4. Generalized forms are made by addition of-uvver, *somuvver, who-uvver, w'atsomuvver* etc.
5. *Whom* is not used by the Negro.
6. *h* (in which, what) is omitted or pronounced without definite rule; probably more usually omitted than pronounced.

Interrogatives

1. *Who? Who dar?*
2. *W'ich* (often used in replies or repeated questions, for what? or how?: *a mighty big w'ich? in dis w'ich?*).
3. *W'at, w'ot?*
   Adverbs: *Whar? w'en? wharbouts? how?*
   The prepositions *at, ter* etc. are often appended: *what you bin at? wharbouts you gwinter?*

Indefinites

The Indefinites are *enny, nun, manyer* 'many a' *sum, all, each, ev'ry (ebry), sum'un, one (wun), sumboddy, sum pusson (person), dey, ennyboddy, er man, sumboddy er nuther* etc.

NUMERALS

1. Cardinals: *wun, 'un — too — three, th'ee (tree) — fo' — five (fi') — six — sevin, sevun, seb'n — eight — nine — ten, teen — 'levin, 'levun, 'lev'n, 'leb'm, 'leb'n — twelve, twelf — thurteen — fo'teen — fifteen — sixteen — sev'nteen, seb'teen — eighteen — nineteen — twenty — thurty — forty — fifty — sixty — sev'nty, seb'nty — eighty — ninety — hundud, thousan', tousan', million* etc.
2. Ordinals: *fuss, — secun' — thurd — fo'th, fo'f' — fif' — six' — sevunf — eight' — ninef* etc.
3. Multiplicatives: *oncet, mennifol' — twicet, hundufol' — thee times* etc. *— thrubble — couple — harf, ha'f.*

Obs.: *Gwine-on* is often prefixed to numbers indicative of age; *gwine on sebenty* etc.

THE VERB

REGULAR

Ter love (luv', lub').

Present:		Imperfect:
I love or *loves* (*lub'* etc.)	*I wuz lovin'*	
he love or *loves*	*he wuz lovin'*	} or *I loved or love'* etc.
we love or *loves*	*we wuz lovin'*	
you love or *loves*	*you wuz lovin'*	} *we loved* or *love'* etc.
dey love or *loves*	*dey wuz lovin'*	

Perfect:

I done loved or *love'*

he done loved or *love'*

we done loved or *love*

you done loved or *love'*

dey done loved or *love*

Future:

I gwinter love or *lub'*
I'm a-gwinter love or *lub*

he gwinter love or *lub*
he's gwinter

we gwinter love or *lub*
we's a-gwinter

you a-gwinter love or *lub*
you's a-gwinter

dey a-gwinter love or *lub*
dey's a-gwinter

Pres. Conditional:
I would love, I'd love (*lub'* etc.)
he would love etc.

Perfect Conditional:
I would ur (a) loved or *love'*
he would (a) loved etc.

The Subjunctive tenses are the same.

Observations:

1. *Thou* is unknown in Negro except in prayers and poetry.
2. The verb form in *-s* is usual throughout the singular and plural.
3. The Negro perfect is most commonly formed by the auxiliary *done* (from *do*) inserted between the pronoun and the past participle; I *done gone*, he *done gimme sump'n* etc. *Have* is also used, though, in pure Negro, not so prevailingly as *done*.
4. *Shall* and *will* as auxiliaries of the future are sparingly used, and when they are used *will* is usually found where *shall* should be. *Gwinter* is the pure future.
5. *Would* takes the place of *should* in the conditionals; and in the perfect conditional *have* is corrupted to *ur*, *'a'*, *'er*, which lean closely on the preceding auxiliary; *woulder* etc. like *to* in *gwinter*.
6. The participles often drop their final letter, the pres. part. almost invariably: *lovin'*, *love'*; *doubtin'*, *doubt'*; *crowin'*, *crow'*.

Obs.: *a* (*er, ur*) is commonly prefixed to pres. part.; he's *apreachin'*, *a-watchin'* etc.

7. Negative sentences in which there are verbs usually contain a double negative: I *dunno* him, *nohow*; he *aint a-gwinter tersee me, nudder*.

8. The ordinary auxiliaries of mood, apart from *shall* and *will*, are; *kin* 'could'; *may* — *mout* (*mought, might*) *mus'* — *mus'*.

Obs.: Negative auxiliary forms are; *das'nt* ('dares not', used in all persons), *won't* (New England pronunciation *wunt* is unknown among the Negroes), *can't, cahnt, kyahnt* (Tide-water Va.), *shan't, shahn't, moutent, mus'nt* (*musen*) or *wahn't* (Virginia), *ain't, hain't, don't* (*doan'*).

9. The *Passive voice* is formed in the usual way: *I is* (*am*), *he is*; *we is* (*ar', air*), *you is* (*ar', air*), *dey is* (*ar', air*) *loved a love'*; *I wuz, he wuz, we wuz* etc., *loveder love'*.

10. The verbs *to be* and *to have* occur in Negro as follows.

1. Ter be

Pres.:	Imperfect:	Perfect:
I am, I'm, I'se, I is	*I wuz, I 'uz*	*I done bin*
he is, he's, hese	*he wuz, he 'uz*	*he done bin*
we is, we'se (*ar', air*)	*we wuz, we 'uz*	*we done bin*
you is, you'se (*ar', air*)	*you wuz, you 'uz*	*you done bin*
dey is, dey'se (*ar', air*)	*dey wuz, dey 'uz*	*dey done bin*

Obs.: *Were* is very rare as a plural. *Gwinter* comes in as usual to form the future. The other tenses are formed as usual. The participles are *bein'* and *bin*. *Am* sometimes runs throughout all persons of pres. tense: *he am, we am* etc.

2. Ter have (ha')

Pres.:	Imperfect:	Perfect:
I have or *has, I'se*	*I had, I'd*	*I done had*
he have or *has, he's*	*he had, he'd*	*he done had*
we has or *have, we've*	*we had, we'd*	*we done had*
you has or *have, you've*	*you had, you'd*	*you done had*
dey has or *have, dey've*	*dey had, dey'd*	*dey done had*

Obs.: 1. The future and conditionals are formed as usual.
2. The participles are *havin'* and *had*.
3. It is a very characteristic Negro trait, when forming a pluperfect tense, to thrust in *ur, er, 'a* (have, between the regular auxiliary *had* and the past part.; I had *ur* (er, 'a) bin, I had *ur* tole him etc. This is not common except after *ef*, in conditional forms: *ef I had ur bin dar* etc.

This seems to have originated from analogy with contracted conditionals like *I'd ur tole him* 'I should have told him', etc.

4. The auxiliary *have*, as the auxiliary of transitive verbs, is in many localities superseded by *is*: *I is got it, we is saunt him* etc.
5. The verb *git* often takes the place of *have* as a principal verb; *I got it* (as a present = 'I (have) got it, I have it').
6. Curious agglutinations or agglutinated phrases like: *I done bin en had my dinna, he done bin en borned agin* etc., *we bin done gone down ter, he done bin had ter* etc., are common.
7. The copula *to be* is constantly omitted especially in questions: *how yo' fokes? whar you gwine?* etc.
8. A favorite Negro representative of the pres. tense is the verb *to be* and a pres. part.: *I aint a-keerin'*, 'I care not, do not care' even when no continuance is involved.
9. The simple imperfect is often insufficient for the requirements of Negro emphasis; hence it frequently inserts the auxiliary *did*; *he did had some peace.*

Obs.: The pres. is often used for past: *he say* (*said*) etc.

10. Various particles are used to soften the positiveness or sharpen the definiteness of a statement; *he kinder* 'kind of' *got me*; *I'll des* 'just' *'bout git dar*; *little mo'n he'd'a bin lef'* 'a little more, and' = 'almost' *he wan't mon gone* 'had hardly gone' etc.
11. The Negro is not content, often, with a single verb; but uses two, and connects them by *en'*, *he done gone an' lef'* 'he has left'; *he up en say* 'he said'; *he tuck en run* 'he ran off'; *he gone an' done it* 'he did it'.
12. In countless instances the infinitive sign *to* (*ter*) leans on a preceding verb; *gwineter, useter, bleegdter* 'obliged to'; so, pronouns are affixed enclitically; *sezee* 'says he', *sheshe* 'says she', *howdy* 'how-do-ye'; or are pre-glutinated; *Ise, wese, deyse, hese* 'I, we, they, he, is'.
13. In many passive combinations the verb *git* takes the place of *to be*; *to git kotch up wid, to git flogg'*; (so, *bin* or *done bin* sometimes takes the place of *have been*; *to bin tuck up* 'to have been arrested'; *to done bin sole out* 'to have been sold out'). Cf. *he like ter fell* etc.
14. The pass. part. of a verb is sometimes used as an infinitive (in a manner analogous to *seen* and *done* used as past tenses, with *have* omitted; *I (have) seen* etc.); *to loss his manners* 'to lose'.

Irregular verbs

To the regular forms of the Irregular verbs as used by the whites, the Negro adds the following forms of his own.

Pres. *(a)rise* — Past. *riz, ris'n (de bred ris'n)* — Pass. Part. *rose.*

Pres. *bear, b'ar* 'bring forth' — Past. *bo', bored, beared* — Pass. Part. *born, borned.*

Pres. *bear, b'ar* 'carry' — Past. *bo', bo'd, b'ared* — Pass. Part. *bo'd, b'ared.*

Pres. *beat* — Past. *beat, beated, beaten, -ened* — Pass. Part. *beated, beatened.*

Pres. *begin* — Past. *begin, beginned, begint* — Pass. Part. *beginned, begint.*

Pres. *behole* 'behold' — Past. *behole* — Pass. Part. *behole.*

Pres. *bine* 'bind' — Past. *boun, 'bined* — Pass. Part. *boun', bined.*

Pres. *bite* — Past. *bitten (he bitten me), -ened* — Pass. Part. *bittened.*

Pres. *blow* — Past. *blowed, blewed* — Pass. Part. *blowed, blewed.*

Pres. *bring* — Past. *brung, bringed, brunged* — Pass. Part. *brung, bringed.*

Pres. *break* — Past. *broked, brokened (he brokened his arm), broken* — Pass. Part. *broked, brokened.*

Pres. *(burst) bu'st, bus'* — Past. *bu'sted, bussed* — Pass. Part. *bu'stid, bussed.*

Pres. *choose* (also = 'wish'; *I don't choose any*) — Past. *choosed, chosen, chosed, chosened* — Pass. Part. *choosed, chosened.*

Pres. *cleave* 'to split' — Past. *cluff (I cluff him in two)* — Pass. Part. *cluff.*

Pres. *cling* — Past. *clinged* — Pass. Part. *clinged.*

Pres. *clime* 'climb' — Past. *clambed, clum* (cf. Milton's "up clomb"), *(he clum up) clam* — Pass. Part. *clum.*

Pres. *come* — Past. *come, comed* — Pass. Part. *come, comed.*

Pres. *do* — Past. *done, doed* — Pass. Part. *done.*

Pres. *draw* — Past. *drawed, drawned (he drawned er prize)* — Pass. Part. *drawed.*

Pres. *drink* — Past. *drinked, drink, drunked* — Pass. Part. *drinked.*

Pres. *drive* — Past. *driv', druv', driven, drivened* — Pass. Part. —.

Pres. *eat* — Past. *eat* — Pass. Part. *eat.*

Pres. *fall (fell: like ter fell)* — Past. *felled, fallen, fall* — Pass. Part. *felled.*

Pres. *fight* — Past. *fit, foute* (pro. like out) — Pass. Part. —.

Pres. *fine* 'find' — Past. *foun', fined* — Pass. Part. *foun', fined.*

Pres. *fling* — Past. *flinged, fling'* — Pass. Part. *flinged.*

Pres. *fly* — Past. *flied, fly'* — Pass. Part. *flied.*

Pres. *fergit* — Past. *fergit, fergotten, -ened* — Pass. Part. —.

Pres. *fersake* — Past. *fersaked, fersaken, -ened* — Pass. Part. —.

Pres. *freeze* — Past. *friz, fruz, frozen, -ened* — Pass. Part. —.

Pres. *git* — Past. *git, gotten* — Pass. Part. —.

Pres. *give, gib, gif* — Past. *give, gib, gif, given, guv (I guv him two cents)* — Pass. Part. —.

Pres. *go* — Past. *goed* (cf. Scotch), *gone* — Pass. Part. —.

Pres. *grine* 'grind' — Past. *groun', grined* — Pass. Part. —.
Pres. *grow* — Past. *growed, grewed, grown* — Pass. Part. —.
Pres. *hang* — Past. *hankt, hunkt* — Pass. Part. —.
Pres. *heave* — Past. *huff, heave* — Pass. Part. —.
Pres. *help* — Past. *ho'pe* — Pass. Part. —.
Pres. *hole* 'hold' — Past. *holt, hilt, helt, holed* — Pass. Part. —.
Pres. *know* — Past. *knowed, knewed* — Pass. Part. —.
Pres. *lay* (for 'lie') — Past. *laid* — Pass. Part. *laid.*
Pres. *lose* 'loss' — Past. *losed, loss* — Pass. Part. —.
Pres. *ride* — Past. *rid* — Pass. Part. *rode.*
Pres. *ring* — Past. *ringed* (cf. A.S. Chronicle), *ring', runged* — Pass. Part.
         —.
Pres. *raise* (for 'rise') — Past. *raised, riz, ris* — Pass. Part. —.
Pres. *run* — Past. *runned* — Pass. Part. —.
Pres. *see* — Past. *seed, see, sawed, seen* — Pass. Part. —.
Pres. *sent* — Past. *sont, saunt* — Pass. Part. *sont.*
Pres. *shake* — Past. *shuck, shake, shaked, shaken-ed* (*I shaken de tree*) —
         Pass. Part. —.
Pres. *sing* — Past. *sing, singed, sunged, singt* — Pass. Part. *sing.*
Pres. *sink* — Past. *sink, sinked, sunked, sinkt, sunken, -ed* — Pass. Part.
         sink.
Pres. *set* (for 'sit') — Past. *set, sot* — Pass. Part. —.
Pres. *skin* — Past. *skint, skunt* — Pass. Part. —.
Pres. *slay* — Past. *slayed, slewed, slain* — Pass. Part. —.
Pres. *sling* — Past. *slinged, slunged, slingt* — Pass. Part. —.
Pres. *slink* — Past. *slinked, slunked, slinkt* — Pass. Part. —.
Pres. *speak* — Past. *speaked, spoked, spoken, -ed* — Pass. Part. —.
Pres. *spin* — Past. *spinned, spint, spunt* — Pass. Part. —.
Pres. *spring* — Past. *springed, springt, sprungt* — Pass. Part. —.
Pres. *stan'* — Past. *stan'* — Pass. Part. *stan'.*
Pres. *steal* — Past. *stealed, stealt, stoled, stolened* — Pass. Part. —.
Pres. *sting* — Past. *stinged, stingt, stunged, stungt* — Pass. Part. —.
Pres. *stink* — Past. *stinked, stinkt, stunkt* — Pass. Part. —.
Pres. *strike* 'strucken' — Past. *striked, strukt, strucked, struckened* —
         Pass. Part. —.
Pres. *strive* — Past. *struv', striv', stroved* — Pass. Part. —.
Pres. *swear* — Past. *swo', swa'* = *swah, swo'd* (*he swo'd he would*) —
         Pass. Part. —.
Pres. *swell* — Past. *swull, swolned* — Pass. Part. —.
Pres. *swim* — Past. *swimmed, swimt, swumt* — Pass. Part. —.
Pres. *swing* — Past. *swinged, swingt, swungt* — Pass. Part. —.
Pres. *take* — Past. *tuck, tucked, taken, -ed* — Pass. Part. —.
Pres. *tear* — Past. *tored, teared, to'ne* (*he to'ne it up*) — Pass. Part. —.

Pres. *th'ow* (throw) — Past. *th'owed, th'own, th'ewed* — Pass. Part. —.

Pres. *tread* — Past. *treat, trodden, -ed* — Pass. Part. —.

Pres. *weave, weef* — Past. *weaved, woved, weefed* — Pass. Part. —.

Pres. *win* — Past. *winned, wint, wunt* — Pass. Part. —.

Pres. *wine* 'wind' — Past. *wined, woun'* — Pass. Part. —.

Pres. *wring* — Past. *wringed, wringt, wrungt* — Pass. Part. —.

Pres. *write* — Past. *writ* (cf. Keats, Addison etc.) *written, writtened* — Pass. Part. —.

Observations:

1. It will be observed that the participial forms are continually used as past tenses, and that, as with children, there is a strong tendency to regularize all forms by adding *-ed* to form the past tense and past participle.

2. The irregular participial forms in *-en* are taken as a basis of departure for new participial forms, which, again, are converted readily into past tenses; *I writtened er letter* etc. Cf. existing double participial forms like *excepted* etc.

3. Such forms as *cutted, putted, cotched, luff* 'laughed', *wep', slep', crep'* (cf. O.E.), *told* (as an infinitive; *to tole him*), *heerd* (cf. Dr. S. Johnson's pronunciation), *teached, larn* 'to teach', (cf. Shakespere and the Prayer Book), *sayed, wukked* 'worked', *sticked, weared* (cf. Chaucer), *het* 'heated', *pled* ('pleaded'; a Scotticism), *gniawed* 'gnawed' etc. are of constant occurrence in the dialects.

ADVERBS

Almost any adjective may be used adverbially; *she singed beau'ful*; *he talk' splendid.*

1. Place: *here (yer), dar, whar, nigh by, yonner, 'bove, b'low, unner, down yonner, 'way, 'way down yonner, thoo* 'through', *in (een), out, widout (bidout), 'roun', fort', forf* 'forth'.
   Compounds: *yer by, yer'pun* 'here upon', *darbouts, dararter, derepon, dar-on, wharby, wharfo', ennywhar, -whars, sumers, somewhars, wharsumever.*

2. Time: *Ever, of'n, berfo', yit, ter dis day, sence.*
   (a) Time present: *now, ter-day, present'y, still, fortwid* 'forthwith', *dis minnit* etc.
   (b) Time past: *Berfo', yerterfo'* 'heretofore', *a'reddy, oncet, yistiddy* etc.
   (c) Time future: *Yerarter* 'hereafter', *arterwuds, soon, 'mejiately, termorrer, no mo'* etc.

3. Duration and Repetition: *Ever, never (nuvver), a'ways, of'n, rar'ly, erg'in, agin, oncet, twicet, hou'ly, montly, anyerly* 'annually'.

J. A. Harrison

4. Degree and Measure: *much, little* (*leetle*, when VERY little is intended), *ve'y, fur, 'ceedin'ly, ve'y little, skacely, putty* 'pretty', *'nuff, ve'y much, ginerly* 'generally', *tu'ibly* 'terribly', *'mos', a'mos', leas', mo', bes', wuss', 'zackly, puffickly* 'perfectly', *jes', jus', des* 'just', *also, lakwise, bersides, too.*
5. Belief, disbelief, certainty etc.: *Sho'ly, surtunly* 'certainly', *not, 'haps* 'perhaps', *ve'ily* 'verily', *'zackly, 'deed, yas, yeh* 'yes', *co'se* 'of course', *in trufe* 'truth', *Yea, Lawd,* even so, *Lawd, jes' so, des' so, toobysho* 'to be sure', *notterbit* 'not a bit', *nottertall* 'not at all', *mebbe* 'maybe', *likely.*
6. Cause and Effect: *Derefo', thuffo'* 'therefore', *wharfo', wuffo', why, dus* etc.
7. Manner, Quality: *Well* 'wall', *sof'ly, quick, easy* 'easily' etc.
8. Phrases: *in de skiyes, ev'y two year, oncet on er time, day 'fo' yistiddy, nex' year, in my born days, tell Cris'mus, ter tell de trufe, in fack, ef my life 'pen on it* etc.
9. Different parts of speech used adverbially: *Home, er straw, er bit, er h'ar* (as completing negations), *dead drunk; skin deep* etc.; *nudder* (*won't do it, nudder* = 'neither'), *de gun went bang, she went spang inter de w'arf* etc.

Prepositions
(Alphabetically arranged)

Abode: all abode! abode ship 'aboard' — *'bout, erbout* — *'bove, erbove* — *'cross, 'crosst, ercrosst* — *atter, arter* — *'ginst, erginst, 'gin* (cf. Scotch use in time-phrases) — *erlong, er long er* (*ur, of*), *'long* — *in de 'midster* — *'mungs', mungst* — *'loun'* 'around' — at.

Befo', berfo', 'fo' — *behine, behime, berhine* — *b'low, berlow* — *b'neath, b'neat'* — *b'side, 'sider* (*of*), *berside* — *b'sides, 'sides* — *'tween, b'tween, bertween* — *'twix', betwix* — *beyand* — *but* — *by.*

Down.

Fur, fer — *fum* 'from'.

In, een — *intów, eentów, ínter.*

Uv, er, ur, a (*of*) — *on, orn* — *ónter, ontow* — *ovur, ova.*

Pas', pars (Virginia).

Roun'.

Sence.

Thoo, troo 'through' — *thoo'out, troo-out* — *tell, twel* — *toe, ter* 'to' — *todes, tords, toe-wards.*

Und', unda 'under' — *un'neath, un'neat'* — *ontell, ontwell* — *onto* 'unto' *unter* — *up* — *upon, 'pun.*

Wid, wif, wi' — *widin* — *widout, bidout.*

Participial Prepositions: *'batin', consarnin', 'ceppin', 'cep'n, 'pen'in', notwidstan'in', regyardin', 'speck'n, tetchin'*.

Prepositional Phrases

Abode ur, er 'of'; *'cordin' ter, 'long wid, ez ter* 'as to', *fer ter* (with infinitive), *'kase of, ur, er; from 'mungs, 'mungst, fum twix' fum und, unda, stidder* 'stead of', *instidder* 'instead of', *outer, out'n* 'of', *ovar 'ginst, 'roun' bout, des 'bout, longer* 'along' *(of =* 'by'), *in 'sponse ter, 'longsider, endurin' er, off'n* 'off of', *in de intruss er, erlonger, on accounter, by meanser* 'of', *by he'p er, fur de saker* 'of', *widder eye ter, as fur, aster* 'to', *on de matter er, on de p'inter* 'of', *in 'specker* 'of', *in caser* 'of', *settin' side, lettin' 'lone, fur fum, in spiter* 'of', *in roomer* 'of' etc.

Obs.: 1. *Dan* 'than' has a prepositional force in Negro: *blacker dan me* (cf. Proverbs XXVII: "*A fool's wrath is heavier than them both*").
2. Prepositions are often omitted especially in quantitative designations: *plenty beef, er fine chance goobers* etc.

CONJUNCTIONS

Co-ordinate

1. Copulatives: *An', en', bofe-an', en'; ez well ez; 'cordin'ly, bisides, furdermo', mo'over, now, so, den, derefo' (thuffo')*.
   Examples: *En' I sez, sez I; bofe you en me 'ull go; ez sho ez I live! 'cordin'ly, he go; bisides, he gwine blab; furdermo' I never sot yes on 'm; mo'over, who kin tell? now he tu'n 'roun en run; so he jes' laff; den de hot wedder come; thuffo'* (a preacher's word), *bredren, foller de gospel!* etc.
2. Adversatives: *But, howuver (-uvver), howsumuver, nebberdeless, notwidstan'in', on de contrairy, still, yit*.
   Examples: *But w'at I say? Well, but, de goodnis en de gracious! However, de goos' kis' de gander; howsumuvver, we kilt 'im; notwidstan'in', dat happen so; on de contrairy, de fack uv de matter muz dis; still, he come crost 'im arter er w'ile; yit de Lawd pervail!*
3. Alternatives: *Needer, nuther, nair, nary, ne'er, -nor, ner; eeder; ee'er, air, ary, -or, ur, er; else, udderwise, yutherwise, u'erwise*.
   Examples: *Nary de wun ner de yuther; needer you ner me is ter blame; eeder 'Tildy er 'Ria got de brekkus, air one* 'either one'; *else I wouldn't seh so; yutherwise, its de Lawd's trufe*.

Subordinate

Adverbial

1. Time: *Atter, arter* 'after', *sence, 'ginst, 'gin, 'gin he come, tell (twel), ontell, ontwel, w'en, w'enuver, w'ile, w'iles.*
2. Place: *whar, wharuver.*
3. Degree: *ez, dan* 'than', *dat, de* (with comparative).
4. Manner: *ez.*
5. Cause: *ez, 'kase, berkase, fur (fer), sence, dat, wharez.*
6. Condition: *'cep, 'ceppin'* 'excepting', *ef, purvided dat, so, onles', les', less'n, widout.*
7. Concession: *aldo, do* 'though', *ef* 'even, if', *notwidstan'in'.*
8. Comparison: *like, lak, same-like.*
9. Substantival: *ef, les, dat, whedder, wuther, how, w'en, whar, why.*

INTERJECTIONS

The Negro dialects are peculiarly rich in interjections, interjectional phrases etc., specimens of which follow:

Aing-got no time, chile! Wot er wopper! Wot I done tole you! I boun' you! I say de word! Well, ef dat don't beat! Fur missy sake! Fo' God! My sakes! Sakes erlive! Er nice muss! I 'clar ter gracious or goodnis! I declar! I 'clar! Well, ef dat doan' bete de Jews! Dis bless d minnit! Stop yo' jawin'! My Jesus! G'long gal! De Gawd's trufe! Dunno' bout dat! Lord a' mercy! Po' white trash! Dern fool! Er sin en er shame! Bless yo' soul! Goodnis knows! Yea, Fader in hebben! Yea Lord! Now mine you! Dont fool wid' me! Glory! Ten' ter yo' biznis! No siree! Dar now! Gone, gal! Fer de worl'! O gee! Dog gorne it! Slambang! Go, nigger! Lo and beholes! I be bless! Bless Gracious! Oh Lordy! Nebber you min'! Low-live' cuss! My goodniss! Whoa ... da! Git up! What er muss! Phew! Kingdom come! By gum! Lissen at him! Youer a goner, sho! Shoo! (to fowls) De gracious en de goodness! Oh ... yi! Sh-sh-sh! (to children) Oh shucks! De name er goodness! Well, well, well; Cowfoun' it! Golly! Great golly! De great gollies! Geewhullikins! None er yo' biznis! Go it, ole hoss! I buss yo' blame' head! By Jinks! Comin'! Yas, marm! Black ape! Go long, boss! Don't bodder me! Hear dat! Great gums! Don't talk, honey! No use talk'n', boss! G'long chile! Farwell! Be good ter yo'self! Youer talkin' now! Dat 's me! Hole on dar! G' way, honey! You better b'leeve! Lor'! A mighty likely tale! Do please don't! Jes' lissen at him! W'y, cose he did! Don't you bet! Comin', Lord Jesus! Blame my buttons! Oh my! Dat 's cool! Ef dis don't! Dribe away! Gred Jerichoes! Big doin's! Plag'id imp! Jes' lemme tell yer! Heish! Ans'er me dis! Better min' w'at yo' bout! Min' yo' eye! Well, den, you better! Doggone my cats! W'at I tell you? Now you talkin', honey! I won't never do so no mo'! 'Deed, en dat he d dn't! Squot down! Now den, ladies en' gents! Dat 's sinful! Dat 's de p'int! Youer nice feller, you is! Cla'r de track! Gosh! De mischief you say! Gimme room! Hole on dar honey! Tell yo' mammy, den! Thunderashun!

Obs.: 1. The dialect is very rich in pious ejaculations, scriptural reminiscences in interjectional form, indignant or contemptuous exclamations etc. *Bless* (or *bress*) *de Lord! Hallyloo! Hallylooyah! Lord-er-mighty! Fer de Lord sake! Bless yer! In de name er goodness!*

     2. The negro dialect is full of onomatopoeias derived from the imitation of animal cries, many of them exceedingly felicitous.

     3. The oaths of the low whites of East Tennessee are very picturesque: *Durn, durnation, infurnel cuss, cursed fool, I durned ef ... durned fool, dorg my cats, I'll be bad-dratted, darn please* (*darn* is thrown in as a modifier: *ez they darn please* etc.), *durned ole fool, infurnel ignurunt cuss, durn my skin, by jimny, durn his ole soul to thunder, great golly grampus, durn my everlastin' picter, by the livin' jingo, durn um, durn his alligater hide, a durn site faster, ketch thunder* etc.

     4. *Durn* is an euphemism for *damn.* Cf. the word *devil* (*deil*) as a negation in the Scotch dialects.

Modes of Address:

Massa, Mister Gemman, Cap'n, Kurnel, Gin'l, Doctah, 'Fesser, Honey (to children), Missis, Marstar, Marm, Sah, Yassah, Ole Miss, Mistiss, Unc', Uncle, Aunt, Awnt, Aunty, Mammy, Brudder, Brer, Bredren (of a religious community), Sistren, Granny, De ole man, De Gub'ner, Son, Sonny, Daddy, Pap, Paps, Popper, Dad, Ole boy, Heyo, Fokes, Hello, Smarty, Sis', Boss, Ole Hoss, Chile, Sis (in religion), Jedge, Ole 'coon.

Answers:

Middlin', tollerbul, thankee! Dat 's so! Dat I is! Dat I don't! Yessum! Yes marm! Tooby sho! Dat 's who! Dat I aint! I is dat! Sho' you bawn! Ketch thunder! Mawnin' boss! You is, dat' s who! Mighty shacklin'! Much obleege!

Obs.: 1. *Uncle, aunt, aunty* are titles of respect exacted by Negro etiquette of strangers, children etc. (cf. the Sicilian *tio, tia*).

     2. *Ole Marstar, Ole Miss,* are titles given to the elder heads of families. *Miss* here does not imply maidenhood.

     3. *Boss, Cap'n* are the usual titles given to strangers.

     4. *Mammy* is the title of the white children's nurse.

     5. *Granny* is the title usually given to the *Hebamme.*

     6. Married people are called by their christian, never by their family, names: *Miss Sidney, Mars John* (cf. a certain French usage).

Intensives

There are many peculiar intensives in the Negro dialect designed to give emphasis to an assertion:

Plum': *he fell plum ter de bottom.*
Rott'n: *er rott'n lazy nigger.*
Heap: *er heap better.*
Gred 'great': *er gred big buster.*
Lots: *'twuz lots better'n dat.*
Spang: *he done come spang down!*
Clean: *he clean gone; to git clean erway* (cf. O.E. and Mod.E.).
Fool: *er fool nigger!* (cf. Spenser's etc. usage).
Blessid: *I tole yo' ma dis blessid night.*
Dat: *I foute tell I waz dat tired, dat* etc.
Blame': *he wuz er blame' fool fer doin' it!*
Durn: *er durn site mo' nicer'n you!*
Buck: *er gred big buck nigger.*
Sho' nuff: *so 'twuz, sho' nuff.*
Plag-gone: *to be er plag gone ape* 'plague-so-on'.
Away: *Dey kyarve en dey slash away; 'way out dar.*
Thunder: *to lam like thunder!*
Dorggone: *I be dorggone ef ...*
Cownfown'ed: *er cownfown'ed jackass!*

Expletives

1. *Dough, nudder, sezee, nohow, sorter, kinder, maybe, he say, tu'n me loose, sezee* etc. Examples *Sez Brer Fox, sezee* etc.; *sorter tollerbul, sorter so-so; I done bin sorter bleach out.*
2. Pronouns are constantly used expletively: *Marster he did; Ole Miss, she say* etc.
3. The double negative is a favorite Negro locution: *'twan't no use; won't give' um no milk* etc.; *na'er one never drap; he warn't gwine nowhar skacely.*
4. *Done* is often pleonastically used: *aint done been dar; she done run pas her shadder* etc.
5. So, *have*: *ef I had er seed him!* 'have'.
6. So, *en', an'* are thrust in between verbs: *she up'n say; he tuck'n jine, tuck'n 'low* etc.
7. So, *des'*: *hits des like I tell yer* etc.
8. So, *dat* and *wa't*: *dey will dat; I tell you wa't.*
9. Two present verb forms are used, as: *he aint sayin' nuthin* 'he says nothing'; *I aint keerin'* 'care not'.
10. *Fer* is thrust in before *ter* and an infinitive: *I got sumfin' fer ter tell you* (cf. O.E. and M.E.).

11. *It* accompanies a certain class of verbs pleonastically: *to play it sharp on somebody.*
12. Object pronouns are often interjected redundantly: *I'm agitten 'me out er ros'n-piece* 'roasting-piece'.
13. Phrases are often repeated in reverse order, for rhetorical effect: *Dey cut en' dey kyarved en' dey kyarved en' dey cut.*
14. *W'at* is sometimes thrust in pleanastically: *Mars Jeems wuz heavier sot dan w'at you is.*

Agglutinations

Sheshee 'says she', *sezee, 'twan't, ain't, yuther, I'se, gimme, lemme, 'tain't, dasn't, dar's, hatter, dunner* 'dont know' *dunno, gwines on, bimeby, on accounter, useter, mouffle* 'mouthful', *'twon't, wanter, sump'n, tuck'n fix* 'took and fixed', *'twuzn't, wuzen't, wunner* 'one of', *youer* 'you are', *soze* 'so as', *w'a daer* 'what do you', *ferter* 'for to', *mo'n* 'more than', *oughter, youk'n* 'you can', *lightered* 'light-wood', *tuck'n say, up'n low, outer, kinder, I k'n* 'I can', *gotter* 'got a, or got to', *off'n* 'off of', *couldn't er bin, gwine-on* 'of age', *mout-a-had, watch-yer-mer-callums, w'atzisname, dere'll* 'there will' *howdy, datswats* 'that is what is', *neenter* 'needn't to', *you'der bin* 'you would have been', *passeler* 'parcel of', *w'atter* 'who do you', *mighter, lookee-here, thankymam, tudder, nosicherthing, arterwhile, dey'd, yesser* 'yes sir', *widder* 'with a', *nuther* 'another' etc.

Archaisms

Negro speech contains many archaisms, archaistic pronunciations, obsolescent usages of words etc., many of which are traceable to the Elizabethan usage of the early settlers in the Atlantic States. Some of these words have dropped out of cultivated American usage, while they are still used in England.

Miscellaneous examples:

To fetch (cf. English and American usage); *to ax* 'ask' (cf. A.S.).

To l'arn a man a thing (cf. Bible and Prayer-book usage).

Kyarvin, kyar, gyardin (cf. A.S. geard), *Kyarpinter* (cf. English provincial pronunciation kynd etc.).

Chany, 'bleedzd 'china', 'obleege' (last century pronunciations).

Pail, palin's 'bucket', 'pence'.

Heap (in numbers: *heap er men*).

The archaic plurals, *sistren, doghtren.*

'Most for *almost.*

Laying stress on final syllables: *wondermént, jedgmént* (as in Chaucer) etc. (last century Huguenot and Creole influence).

Using *kep', crep', wep'* as past tenses.

Whiles for *whilst*; *gang* for *company*.

Insertion of *dat* after relatives: *de man w'ich dat wuz dar*.

Yard 'garden'; *afeared* 'afraid'.

To ail 'to be unwell'; *mout* = 'might'.

Dreckly 'directly', 'as soon as' *dreckly he wuz outer sight*.

The Virginia broad a (*harp, parst*) and the pronunciation *skiy, giide* 'guide', *kyind* etc. (last century pronunciation).

The use of *mighty* and *right* as intensives: cf. *"Er mighty empty head is er mighty loud gong"* (cf. Elizabethan usage).

The use of *fer* (for) before *ter* (to) to express the infinitive of purpose: *I gwine fer ter say* etc.

The substitution of *d* for *th*, so common in the Negro dialect, is as in Old English; cf. *moder, fader* etc. (so Modern Scotch).

The Negro use of the *s* throughout the verb (*I duz, you duz, he duz, we duz* etc.) may be partly paralleled by the old Northumbrian and the Modern Scotch (Anglian) usage.

The principle of forming past tenses by vowel-change is still active among the Negroes: *brung, thunk, whul* 'wheeled', *crop* 'crept', *driv, skunt* 'skinned', *hilt on, kotch, riz, drug* 'dragged', *drap, retch* 'reached', *chomp* 'champed', *dove* 'dived', *hope* 'holp', *klum, wrop, lip up* 'leap up', *totch* etc.

The dropping of the *g* in present participles may be an unconscious reversion to the simpler O.E. forms in *nde*, with final letters slightly sounded.

The use of double negatives: *he dunno nuthin' bout no fishes*.

The survival of *h* before *it*: *hit* etc.

The use of *fool* (cf. *fool-hardy*, Spenser's *fool-happie*, Chaucer's *fool-large* etc.) as an intensive.

The reversion to the forms *'twix, w'iles, 'mungs'* (without *t*) and to the forms *lam', lim'* (without *b*).

The use of the reflexive dative: *we sot us er trap*.

The putting of *s* before existing verbs, to intensify: *to squench, to sqush* 'crush' (cf. kratzen and scratch).

Use of *'gin, 'ginst* in expressions of time or as conjunctions, *'gin I come* etc.

The survival of *'em, 'um* (O.e. him hem) = *them*.

The use of double comparatives and superlatives.

The constant prefixing of *a* before present part. in verbal forms.

The use of *mo'* for *more*.

The survival of many archaic words like *poke* 'bag', *poly, sick* (in 17th century sense) *spancel*, in Negro speech; so French words *piroot* 'pirouetter' etc.

Use of the singular for the plural with *mile, pound* etc.

Use of *no* for *not* in: wuther times is hard er no.

SPECIMEN NEGROISMS[1]

I reckin 'I suppose, think, or fancy'.
To have er mighty young nater 'to have youthful feelings'.[2]
To feel mighty gay an' limbersome 'to be glad'.
Er heap ur times; lots ur fokes 'often; many people'.
Quick ez you kin 'instantly'.
To run agin sump'n' 'to run against something'.
To be in er mighty bad way 'to be ill, to fare badly'.
To try yo' bes' 'to do as well as you can'.
By de tim' you ketch me! 'indefinitely'.
To feel good 'to feel well'.
To git bustid 'to fail'.
To know whar ter put yo' foot nex' time 'to learn by experience'.
No matter which een' go fo'mos' 'a matter of indifference'.
Dat jes' beats my time! 'that is too improbable'.
To clam up arter sump'n' 'to seek for something by climbing'.
To stir up lazy fokes 'to rouse the lazy'.
To git 'ligiun 'to become religious'.
To be 'some punkins' 'to be of some value'.
To git kilt 'to be killed'.
To git ur holt 'to catch hold of'.
To make yo'se'f skace 'to run away'.
Not ter complain too fas' 'to repress one's feelings'.
Ur fus' class thing 'an excellent thing'.
To be 'cordin' ter human nater 'to be natural'.
To fool wid 'to be officious, to tamper with'.
To bump agin 'to knock against'.
To bus orf or off 'to run away quickly'.
De same lick, de same pop 'at the same time'.
To cuss a bile orf (or *off*) *yo' laig* 'to fly into a passion'.
To keep mopin' an' gronin' 'to be in poor spirits'.
To sling sassy words at 'to be impertinent to'.
To have mis'ry somers (*head, stummuck* etc.) 'to be in pain'.
Not ter put nuthin' in yo' head 'to eat nothing'.
To git 'long wid 'to get along with'.
To make-bleeve ter sorter like 'to pretend to like a little'.
To bile de juce out ur brick-bat 'to attempt the impossible'.
To boss er thing 'to be at the head of something'.
To be mighty well loaded 'to be "top-heavy"'.

[1]   *er* and *ur* both represent *a*; *orf* and *off*; *en'* and *an'*; *outer* and *outen.*
[2]   The English equivalents are far from conveying the pungent meaning of the Negro expressions.

To be heap better'n 'to be much better than'.
To tote ur lucky-bone in yo' pocket 'to carry a luck-penny'.
To git all yo' kin 'to be grasping'.
To keep 'way fum 'to keep aloof'.
To cackerlate 'to calculate'.
To study 'to meditate'.
To cos' mo' an it cum ter 'not to be worth the trouble'.
To knew when ter set out 'tater-slips 'to possess good judgment'.
To rudder have 'to prefer'.
To stick ter ur thing 'to persist in'.
To clam up de knollige-tree 'to acquire knowledge'.
To ax sump'n' hard 'to ask a hard question'.
To 'dunno' 'bout sump'n' 'not to know about something'.
Dar's no tellin' 'perhaps, it may be'.
To count on gittin' 'to expect to get'.
To 'ten ter 'to mind, attend to'.
Er mighty keerless somebody 'a very careless person'.
Not ter like de fus' looks er 'not to be prepossessed at first with'.
To be er long ways fum home 'to be much mistaken'.
To boss er chune at er night-meetin' 'to brow-beat one's colleague at a night-meeting'.
Rank ez anybody 'as well as' etc.
To come out short medjer 'to get less than one expects'.
To be 'speckful ter ole fokes 'to respect the old'.
De soones' nigger on the plantashun 'the cleverest' etc.
Fo' sun-up 'early in the morning'.
Er little chunk er midnight 'a coal-black negro'.
Er big buck nigger 'a large negro'.
To slam loose on or at 'to inveigh against, censure'.
To projick wid 'to experiment with'.
To let in on 'to begin with'.
Er fool nigger 'a foolish negro'.
Er bran-new sooter Sunday-go-ter-meetins 'a new Sunday suit'.
To look shiny en' sassy in de sun 'to deceive'.
To cave in en' play plum out 'to be utterly ruined'.
To larn so fas' you mos' buss de school-house open 'to learn with great rapidity'.
Right smart 'a good deal'.
To run plum orf de track 'to be entirely wrong'.
To keep things gwine 'to keep up one's courage'.
To need bilin' down 'to need correction or rebuke'.
To be in er fa'r way ter git ruint 'to be on the road to ruin'.
To need skimmin' bad 'to need a taking down'.

To weed yo' own row 'to mind your own business'.
Not ter holler fo' you git hit 'not to be in a hurry, not to be over-appre-
    hensive'.
To take'n skip off 'to escape'.
To look cool 'not to be afraid'.
No wusser skeered beas' 'no worse frightened creature'.
He jes' lay dar en shuck en shiver 'he just lay and shivered'.
To punch his water-million 'to knock him on the head'.
Some projick er nudder 'an undertaking'.
Not ter make no head ner tails er 'to be unable to understand'.
Ef dis don't bang my times! 'to pass belief'.
To year no fuss 'to hear nothing, no noise'.
To be skeered outen his skin 'to be panic-stricken'.
To spill er man out 'to upset'.
To be er goner 'to be dead or caught'.
To be natally or natchully live wid 'to swarm'.
To have er spell er dry grins 'to be greatly embarrassed'.
Fum up Norf 'from the North'.
To say ez how 'to say how'.
Er reg'ler collidge nigger 'an educated negro'.
Er hifalutin' nigger 'a negro that talks big'.
To b'leeve in ha'nts 'to believe in ghosts'.
To browse 'roun' er hen-'ouse 'to try to steal hens'.
Sho's you bawn (asserverative) 'unmistakably'.
To be in er nice fix, sho' nuff 'to be badly off'.
To jerk outer 'to relieve of'.
Er outlandish sorter creetur 'a curious creature'.
To chassay 'roun' 'to dance around, to be polite'.
To be done plum thoo or froo 'to have finished entirely'.
To dreen outer or outen 'to escape, get away'.
To be pow'ful spry 'to be very lively'.
To knock 'roun' de gals 'to visit the girls'.
To bin done gone down ter 'to have gone down to'.
To done bin had ter scratch 'roun' 'to have been obliged to work'.
To slip bodiaciously inter de callerboose 'to get into jail'.
To be 'live en' kickin' 'to be well'.
To make er raid on 'to visit, to surprise, to steal'.
To tate 'to carry'.
To tell de ole 'oman 'to confess'.
To keep pow'ful warm 'to keep very warm'.
To drap 'roun' 'to visit informally'.
To year sho' 'nuff cussin' 'to hear passionate words'.
To strike up wid 'to meet accidentally'.

To know wharbouts 'to know where'.

Right den an' dar 'on the spot'.

To be as fon' as de nex' man 'to like as much as any one'.

To be bustid up 'to be bankrupt, to fail'.

To boss 'roun' 'to domineer'.

To tell up an' down 'to tell plainly'.

To maul 'to beat'.

To bresh up agin 'to meet, to insult'.

I lay an' fetch you! 'I'll catch you!'

To look mighty spin'lin' en' puny 'to look delicate'.

To git de Affikin up 'to evoke the African nature'.

To be proned inter 'to be well established in'.

To be ketched up late 'to be caught up late'.

To let de sun er salvashun shine sqar' in yo' face 'to be truly religious'.

To kick up shines 'to be proud, to put on airs'.

To put er game on 'to get the better of'.

To come a-lopin' 'to come running'.

To look sassy 'to look saucy'.

To wanter have some confab wid 'to want to talk with'.

To be monst'ous full er 'to be very full of'.

To be dat hongry 'to be extremely hungry'.

To take up conterbutions 'to borrow'.

To git sorter seasoned like 'to become used to'.

To come foolin' 'longer 'to bother or molest'.

To flipp yo' sass at 'to be saucy to'.

To sling yo' jaw at 'to be saucy to'.

To git yo' hide greased 'to get flogged'.

To be a-hoopin' en' a-hollerin' at 'to call some one'.

To fling sense inter er nigger wider bar'l stave 'to flog a Negro severely, for purpose of improvement'.

To f'arly fly 'to run fast'.

To be de ruinashun er 'to be the ruin of'.

To dassent hardly ax 'hardly to dare ask'.

To git beyant yo' biznis 'to be above yourself'.

No use talkin' 'that is enough!'

To done had de spe'unce 'to have had experience'.

To tu'n nuthin' loose on 'to waste'.

To keep de bref in yo' body 'to keep alive'.

To put yo' hand ter reckommends 'to write a recommendation'.

To be feared fer ter 'to be afraid to'.

To be gwine 'roun flatterin' up 'to be a persistent flatterer'.

To stan up mighty squar' 'to be open about, not to be afraid'.

Not to stan' de racket wuf er durn 'not to be able to endure'.

No longer'n yistiddy 'only yesterday'.

Be good ter yo'se'f! 'Farewell! Goodbye!'

To be er gittin' too ole fer 'not to be able to catch one in a thing'.

To get ter scuffle fer 'to be obliged to fight for'.

To go 'roun' a-puttin' up an' a-pullin' down 'to be undecided'.

To fix um better'n dat 'to treat them better than that'.

To take yo'ne hot 'to take yours hot'.

To look lonesome 'to be depressed'.

To be mighty right 'to be quite right'.

To be bleedzd ter 'to be obliged to'.

To be right whar de mink had de goslin' 'to be in a tight place'.

To git de shudders 'to have chills; to be afraid'.

To set on de mo'ner's bench 'to repent of one's sins'.

Not to be wuff shucks 'to be entirely worthless'.

To fraile out 'to whip well'.

To lay er man out flat 'to knock a man down'.

To watch ef 'to see if'.

To cut up capers 'to behave badly'.

To lan' in de middle er nex' week 'to send a man to "Jericho"'.

Let 'lone doin sump'n 'to leave off doing'.

To git mixed up wid 'to get embroiled with'.

Leas' ways ter do er thing 'at least to do a thing'.

De whole blessid chunk 'the whole piece'.

To git at sump'n 'to get to the point'.

To done bin an' swallered er thing 'to have swallowed' etc.

To keep up er racket 'to continue making a noise'.

To be a Seekin' 'to seek "religion"'.

To 'pen upon 'to depend upon'.

To done jine de chu'ch 'to have joined the church'.

Stidder dat 'instead of that'.

What er nigger's gwinter lan'? 'where is a negro going to stop?'

To be done quit so'shiatin' wid 'to have ceased to associate with'.

To go back on 'to lie or deceive'.

Tell de las' day in de mornin' 'till Judgment Day'.

To kyar roun' wid 'to carry around with'.

To stan' up like you oughter 'to be a man'.

To swing on 'to attach oneself to, to get in' (a vehicle).

To put yo' money on dat 'to wager'.

To be fixed 'to have things set to rights'.

Dat beats me! 'that is beyond my comprehension'.

To sop graby wid er 'coon skin 'to act ridiculously'.

To beat sassengers wid er pile-driver 'to act ridiculously'.

Take keer! 'look out!'

To fool folks 'to deceive people'.
To be up ter 'to be cunning enough for'.
Ur sho' 'nuff 'oman 'a real woman'.
To claw de stuffin' outer 'to reduce to one's senses; to injure severely'.
To be plum crazy 'to be entirely insane'.
To be boun' ter 'to be obliged to'.
I boun' 'I'll warrant'.
To pick de banjer 'to play on the "banjo"'.
His mushmillion 'his head'.
Outlandish 'strange'.
Jinin' on 'next to'.
Chune up 'begin; go on!'
To guv out 'to give out; to be exhausted'.
He jes' oughter 'he just ought to'.
A mess 'a dish' (of strawberries, fish etc.).
You nebber did see 'you never saw!'
To git ter squabblin' 'to squabble'.
To rush 'to run'.
Doins, gwines-on 'events, happenings'.
Deze diggins 'this place'.
Tain't no harm er sin 'it is quite innocent'.
To git er mistookin 'to mistake'.
To sorter alter 'to alter somewhat'.
To shet down on 'to bite'.
To have a big job fo' yer 'to have much work ahead'.
To git de wuss sorter bode 'to get very poor fare' (board).
To tree er 'possum 'to run an opossum up a tree'.
To be gwinter ketch somebody sayin' or doin' sump'n' 'to surprise some
    one in the act of'.
To say zakly how it all gwinter tu'n out 'to predict the end'.
To see fur ahead 'to be provident'.
To swap souls wid 'to exchange souls'.
To gib one er noshun 'to give one an idea'.
To be drivin' at 'to mean, to intend'.
To op'n de do' ter 'to explain clearly'.
Anyway you fix er thing 'no matter how' etc.
To hang the right feller 'not to make a mistake'.
To work 'long tergidder 'to work along together'.
To be up en' doin' 'not to be idle'.
To be lierbul ter 'to be apt to'.
To pester fokes 'to molest people'.
To 'have yo'se'f 'to behave yourself'.
To look like you oughter 'to be *comme il faut*'.

To tu'n er nigger right loose 'to give a man free play'.
I 'spect' 'I expect' (also, of the past).
To take ter 'to like, be prepossessed with'.
He tuck'n done 'he did'.
I lay 'I wager'.
I 'low 'I maintain'.
To put in de groun' 'to bury'.
To git er big 'lowance er 'to get a large portion of'.
Dat sorter rackit 'such noise as that'.
Biznis (in *dis tombstone biznis*) 'matter, affair'.
To scrape wid er tinpinny nail 'to make great efforts to'.
De big Herearter '*le Grand Peut-Être*'.
Deeds done in de meat 'deeds done in the body'.
You kin jes' bet! 'Depend upon it'.
To stan' er red-hot cross-'zamination 'to be "tried and true"'.
To fling plum out 'to cast one out'.
To be all right 'to be in good condition'.
To fling 'way de money 'to be extravagant'.
To do mighty well by 'to treat one very well'.
To sail away (of the soul) 'to die'.
'Taint no use er 'there is no use in'.
Fokes all ded en' gone 'dead people'.
To sack de plow inter 'to begin business'.
Dats 'bout de way 'that is about the way'.
To have nuffin' mean 'bout yer 'to be generous'.
You neenter penter yo' mine 'don't trouble yourself'.
Ur right smart chance er 'a good deal of'.
Hifalutin' fokes '"toploftical" people'.
'Taint no sicher thing! 'it is untrue'.
Neighborhood 'place'.
Light 'ood, kindlin' wood 'pieces of pitch-pine for lighting fires'.
To see de pen'tenchery 'to be put in jail'.
To be closte er 'nuff to melt er paper coller 'to be very close'.
To run no resk ef you kin he'p it 'to be very careful'.
To dribe fer 'to make for'.
Right now, right away 'immediately'.
To be no wuss orf'n 'to be no worse off than'.
To git lef' de wuss sort 'to be very much mistaken'.
To jump de eberlastin' draw-bars 'to die'.
To kick de bucket 'to die'.
To git m'on you bargin fur 'to get over-much; to get a flogging'.
To sorter rake over de coals 'to "blow up", to scold'.
To make friends 'to become reconciled'.

To up en' say 'to say'.
To have great doins 'to entertain handsomely'.
To git up sump'n' 'to originate, to make preparations'.
To raid on 'to intrude, to come on suddenly'.
To sorter dally roun' 'to idle'.
To be 'gree'ble 'to permit'.
Aint gwinter 'am not going to'.
To come mighty nigh 'to approach closely'.
To see w'at de news is gwinter be 'to see what will happen'.
To be ez sassy ez er jay-bird 'to be extremely saucy'.
To fetch up on 'to stop'.
How duz yo' sym'tums segashuate? 'how are you?'
How you come on den? 'how are you?'
To be stuck up 'to take on airs'.
To larnur pusson 'to teach a person'.
To tell one howdy 'to greet'.
To bus' one wide open 'to kill'.
To keep on sayin' nuffin' 'to be silent; to talk trifles'.
To take one sider de head 'to strike one on the head'.
Lemme loose! 'let me go'.
To fetch er wipe wid 'to strike with'.
To kick de natchul stuffin' outen 'to kick severely'.
To squall out 'to cry out'.
Dats all de fur 'no farther'.
He mout en' den agin he mouten't 'he might and he might not'.
To run 'long 'to go away'.
To call by fer 'to call by engagement, to stop casually'.
To gobble up 'to eat voraciously'.
De balance er de settlement 'the rest of the village'.
A natchul pacer 'a swift runner'.
To sorter laugh 'roun' de cornders er de mouf 'to laugh slyly'.
To come a-zoonin' 'to come running' (imitation of a bee's buzzing).
Not ter wait fer ter say howdy 'to begin at once'.
To des sail inter 'to attack vigorously'.
To fetch a grin fum year to year 'to grin broadly'.
To keel over like 'to fall down suddenly'.
To be cut out fer 'to be well adapted for'.
To go skaddlin' thoo 'to run through'.
To rack off 'to run off'.
To fine de co's' cle'r 'to find no obstacles'.
To hole yo' head high 'to be proud'.
To git mighty mad 'to become very angry'.
To 'soshiate wid 'to visit or associate with'.

Er free fight goin' on 'a general row'.
To larf fit ter kill 'to laught immoderately'.
I aint no mo' fear'd dan 'I am no more afraid than'.
To be skeered on 'to be afraid of'.
To put in w'en do time come 'to begin at the right time'.
I aint mo'n tech you, 'fo 'I had hardly touched you when'.
To fix fer ter 'to get ready to'.
Er little mo'n 'almost' (a little more, and ...).
Gwinter be smashed fer 'going to be called to account'.
To dis'member yo' own name 'to forget your own name'.
Er soon beas' 'a clever creature'.
To lay out fer ter 'to intend to'.
To fetch up at 'to stop'.
Needer yer ner dar 'indifferent'.
To git ur man dis time 'to catch in the act'.
To done come ter de een' er de row 'to die'.
To bounce 'roun' 'to be energetic'.
De boss er de hole gang 'the head of the business'.
An invite; a reckommend 'an invitation, recommendation'.
To fire her up 'to light a fire under'.
To bobbycue 'to roast'.
To talk mighty 'umble 'to show great humility'.
Not to keer w'at you duz 'to be careless what you do'.
To snatch out 'to pull out'.
Mushmillion-patch 'a musk-melon garden'.
To done bin swop off mighty bad 'to have been grossly deceived'.
To skip out 'to run away' (also a common Westernism).
'Way back yonder 'a long time ago'.
To 'lecshuneer 'mungs 'to seek votes'.
To have lots mo' 'to have an abundance (more)'.
To sorter straighten out marters 'to smooth out matters'.
Plum down ter 'as far as, quite to'.
To begin fer ter commence 'to commence'.
To fling de langwidge 'roun 'to talk excitedly'.
'Longer wunner nudder 'with one another'.
To tromp on 'to advance'.
To sqush 'to crush'.
To be pow'ful lackin' 'to be very deficient'.
To done bin tooken sick 'to have fallen sick'.
Er fussavul 'a church festival or fair'.
Not to know w'at minnit gwinter be de nex' 'to be very uncertain'.
To let on 'to pretend'.
Not to pester wid 'to let alone'.

Not to bodder longer 'not to trouble oneself with'.
To put er thing down 'to understand'.
To tackle some one 'bout 'to attack about'.
To set up er monst'ous gigglement 'to giggle immoderately'.
Like hit wer' guv 'as it was given'.
To pay one's 'specks 'to pay one's respects'.
To look mighty dumby 'to look "glum"'.
To shake de jew off de tail 'to be in a great hurry'.
To make er straight shoot fer 'to go straight'.
To git 'way wid 'to kill'.
'Ceppin' I fotch' you 'unless I fetched you'.
To have it up en' down 'to quarrel'.
To ride mos' up ter 'to ride almost up to'.
To sorter rig up 'to dress oneself moderately'.
To look peart 'to be well'.
Same like sho' 'nuff hoss 'like a genuine horse'.
To git over groun' 'to travel fast'.
To smack one's jaws 'to box one's ears'.
To santer inter 'to go into'.
To squar' back 'to draw back' (with hostile intent).
To fetch one all right 'to cause one to recover'.
To praise up 'to flatter'.
To chunk de chickens 'to throw at the chickens'.
To sick de dogs on 'to urge on the dog'.
To fling rocks 'to cast stones'.
To drap spang 'to let fall suddenly'.
Not ter go ter do 'not to intend'.
To 'spishun 'to suspect'.
He done done 'he has done'.
Wid proudness 'with pride'.
Dan I mos' ever see 'than I ever saw'.
To settle one's hash 'to chastise, to defeat'.
To give er heat start 'to give one a head's start'.
To gib it to 'um good 'to chastise them well'.
Deze days 'at present'.
'Twix er bauk en' er break-down 'so-so' (of health).
How yo' fokes? 'how are your people'?
To march upter 'to walk up to'.
To sorter back off 'to retreat'.
To cut de pidgin-wing 'to dance' (a negro dance).
To cut out fer home 'to run home'.
My ole man or 'oman 'husband' (cf. German *Mann*) 'or wife'.
De las' wunner 'the last one of'.

I 'lowed bein's how dat 'I thought inasmuch as ...'.
To git hurtid 'to get hurt'.
To jestify de stummack 'to appease hunger'.
W'at dish yer gwine on now? 'what is this going on now?'
To reckin' may be 'to think perhaps'.
Er puny man 'a delicate man'.
To be po'ly 'to be in poor health'.
To take atter 'to resemble'.
Er hunk or chunk er bread 'a piece of bread'.
To primp up 'to make a careful toilet'.
To run up wid 'to meet'.
To ax one howdy an' spon' howdy 'to exchange salutations'.
I don't keer ef I do 'certainly'.
Time fer confabbin' 'a time to talk'.
To come mighty handy 'to be just the thing'.
To make er great 'miration 'bout 'to wonder at'.
Biznis cookin' 'trouble brewing'.
To feel monst'ous skittish 'to be very timid'.
To rip en' r'ar 'to move excitedly'.
To cavort or go cavortin' 'to prance'.
Wrassle wid yo' shadder 'to attempt the impossible'.
Mighty nigh 'almost'.
To light out atter 'to pursue'.
To giedder yo' mine tergyudder 'to collect your thoughts'.
To come floppin' long 'to come along unexpectedly'.
To view de premusses 'to look around'.
No, I ain't ded nuther 'I am not dead, either'.
To have one pent up 'to keep one penned up'.
To git er man 'to catch'.
Tell Cris'mus 'indefinite time'.
To lope off 'to run off'.
I ain't a-keerin' 'I don't care'.
To kick up er racket 'to make a row'.
To rush 'roun' 'to become excited'.
To bounce in on 'to surprise'.
To holler 'Cris'mus gif'' 'to cry "Christmas gift"'.
To be des in time 'to be just in time'.
I done heered 'I have heard'.
To lam away at 'to make an attempt to'.
To maul rails 'to make oneself ridiculous'.
Right den en' dar 'instantly'.
To make like 'to pretend'.
Lemme 'lone! 'let me alone!'

De lowdonest cuss 'the lowest creature'.
To done bin tampered with 'to have been deceived'.
To fetch up de re'r 'to whip'.
To be whimplin' 'roun' 'to whimper'.
Bad ez de chilluns 'bout dem tales 'as eager as the children' etc.
To lay low 'to be on the watch'.
De big road 'the highway or turnpike'.
De big house 'the family dwelling' (on the plantations).
To be fa'rly kivvered wid 'to be covered with'.
To take er big chaw terbacker 'to bite off a large piece of tobacco'.
To tu'n de mine over 'to deliberate'.
To chunk up de fier 'to make the fire burn'.
To sif' thoo 'to leak (out)'.
To do de bisznis 'to end the matter'.
To hole er reg'ler juberlee 'to have a fine time'.
To break one up 'to interrupt'.
To talk back at 'to be impertinent to'.
To be brash 'to be rash or quick-tempered'.
To 'gin ter git kinder familious wid 'to begin to get on familiar terms with'.
To try yo' han' ennyhow 'to make an attempt at least'.
To have er monst'ous streke er luck 'to be very fortunate'.
To bag er sight er game 'to kill much game'.
To sing like er nigger at er frolic 'to sing vociferously'.
To be salvashun sho' 'to be absolutely sure'.
To sorter study 'to mediate over'.
Gwinter was'e 'going to ruin'.
Ef I'd a knowed 'if I had known'.
He did had some peace 'he had some peace'.
I'll des 'bout git in 'I'll just get there in time'.
To prank en' pester 'roun' 'to be troublesome'.
Er hole let uv um 'a good many of them'.
Er gaily ridin'-hoss 'a spirited riding-horse'.
To drap er bow 'to bow'.
Whatter you reckin'? 'what do you think?'
To make great wonderment 'to winder greatly'.
To be er caution 'to be wonderful'.
Yo' all's chu'ch 'your church'.
Done gone en' lef' 'he has left'.
To make er break fer 'to run to'.
Er branch 'a creek or small stream'.
Dem eyelids er yone 'your eyelids'.
To lay 'roun' loose 'to be a vagabond'.
To rope in 'long wid 'to carry along with'.

Bimeby 'after a while'; *kyar'ns-on* 'carryings on'.
To come up wid 'to overtake'.
To sorter palaver on 'to go on talking'.
To git de drap on 'to get the better of'.
Wo' ter er frazzle 'worn out'.
To lam aloose 'to knock hard'.
W'ich un 's dis? 'which one is this?'
Gwine arter 'going after'; *to tear* 'to run fast'.
To set up wid 'to keep a lych-wake'.
To hole yo' breff'n wait 'to wait anxiously'.
Dis long-come-short 'this long time'.
W'at ail you? 'what is the matter?'
To gwinter out er man 'to get him out, to baffle'.
To be in wid 'to conspire with'.
Done useter 'to be used to'.
Stidder mindin' uv his biznis 'instead of minding his business'.
To git kotch up wid 'to get "tit for tat"'.
To gallop 'roun' 'to get the better of, to surpass'.
To sen' ter 'struckshun 'to send to perdition'.
To go on 'to behave badly'.
W'en Ole Miss was livin' 'a long time ago'.
To happen 'long 'to come along accidentally'.
To stan' to it dat 'to persist in it that ...'.
To hate mighty bad fer ter 'to object strongly that ...'.
To bin tuck up 'to have been arrested'.
He want mo'n gone 'he had hardly gone'.
He gone en' done it 'he did it'.
To come er scootin' 'to come rapidly'.
To wink de off eye 'to wink secretly'.
To go inter fahmin' 'to farm'.
To keep sto' 'to keep a shop'.
To squinch yo' eyeballs 'to close the eyes'.
To sorter go snacks 'to go into partnership'.
To be in er wuss fix'n 'to be worse off than'.
To sell er man out 'to deceive'.
To keep up er monst'ous thinkin' 'to think profoundly'.
To be high up fer 'to be inclined to'.
To squod down 'to cower'.
Bein's you so good 'seeing that you are so good'.
To 'vide fa'r en' squar' 'to divide fairly'.
To 'scoot en' scat' 'to say "Shoot" and "s-s-cat"!'
To 'ten on er quiltin' 'to attend a "quilting-party"'.
To cle'r up the th'oat 'to clear the throat'.

To talk biggity 'to talk big, to order'.
Er sweetnin'-tree 'a sugar cane'; *long-sweetnin'* 'molasses'.
To rassle wid 'to throw hard'.
To dob 'to daub'; *to lif'* *at er thing* 'to try to lift'.
To 'spute over 'to have a dispute about'.
To make tracks 'to run away'.
To drap off ter sleep 'to fall asleep gradually'.
To 'ny er thing ter de las' 'to deny absolutely'.
En' mo'n dat 'and furthermore'.
To git one jammed up in de cornder 'to have in a tight place, to refute'.
To wirl in 'to go to work'.
Mo' samer dan 'quicker than'.
To take er runnin' start 'to start running'.
To santer 'roun' same like 'to go about like'.
Er biggity fice 'a wretched fice' (dog).
Er rumpus 'a row'.
To des vow dat 'to insist that …'.
To pass de time er day with 'to exchange compliments with'.
De ve'y spi't en' immijer 'the image of'.
To gib yo' wud en' nonner 'to give your word and honor'.
To make fer 'to direct oneself to a place'.
To come a-bulgin' or *a-b'ilin'* 'to hurry, to be wrought up'.
To skaddle off 'to "scatter" off, run away'.
To finger er thing 'to appropriate, to handle'.
To be mighty ketchin' 'to be contagious'.
Not ter be fitten fer 'not to be fitted for'.
To be projickin' *'longer* 'to undertake'.
To stripe one's jacket 'to whip'.
To tell on 'to disclose something against'.
To be mixin' up wid fokes 'to associate with'.
To be livin' clean tell yit 'to be alive now'.
Uppity 'pert'; *to git even wid* 'to repay a grudge'.
To cuss en' r'ar 'roun' considerbul 'to be excited'.
To weed yo' inguns 'onions' 'to be industrious'.
De fus' Babtis', Methodis' 'the first Baptist etc. Church'.
To play 'possum 'to pretend illness'.
To toll fokes 'way fum 'to keep people away'.
To have sho' 'nuff pains 'to be really in pain'.
To be no 'count 'to be worthless'.
Er sixteen-shillin' lawyer (Va. expression for 'pettifogger').
Er little cross-roads villidge 'a small town'.
To hab nuffin ter brag on 'to be very poor or ignorant indeed'.
To git yo' head tu'n slam 'roun' 'to all wrong about'.

Ain't got no manners! 'an indecent creature' ("manners" plays a great rôle in the Negro vocabulary. Negroes are naturally polite and resent with indignation any violations of their code).

To los' his politeness 'to lose' etc.

Mighty curisome noshuns 'bout 'to have curious ideas about …'.

To stir up er bobbykew 'to get up a pic-nic'.

To heep rudder be 'to prefer greatly'.

To hab eb'rything de matter 'to be very low-spirited'.

De whole enju'in' time 'the whole time'.

To tech on er mighty sof' spot 'to approach a delicate subject'.

To be putty tollerbul sartin 'to be pretty certain'.

To slam out de State 'to leave the State'.

Lots en' cords er things 'a great many things'.

All by it lone se'f 'entirely alone'.

To be ez strong ez er lame horse-fly 'to be very weak'.

To scratch de wrong place 'to be mistaken'.

To lay sump'n' on somebody 'to accuse some one'.

To go hankerin' atter or arter 'to desire much'.

Er slouch uv er musicioner 'a poor musician'.

To cuss out 'to drive away by cursing'.

To sw'ar ter grashus 'to declare emphatically'.

To be right sharp 'to be "smart"'.

To start er grabe-yard 'to kill or get killed'.

To be slab-sided 'to be awkward'.

To beat 'to whip or punish'.

To go 'bout tellin' stories 'to lie'.

To gib or give er lammin' 'to chastise'.

To slam in de mud 'to throw' etc.

To git right jam up'mungs' de feelin's er 'to be loved by …'.

To scrape in er right good slice er eddication 'to learn pretty thoroughly'.

To take up mighty quick fer 'to take sides for'.

De succumj'inin' neighborhood 'the country around'.

To be jes' spilin' fer 'to be very anxious to'.

To bus' er scantlin' on 'to break a board over'.

De quarters 'the Negro living-houses' (on the plantations).

To have mighty quar' noshuns 'to be eccentric'.

'Twan't long fo' 'in a little while'.

To lump de vittles in one pile 'to put the food together'.

To be done gone en' tuck mighty sick 'to be very ill'.

Er right smart w'ile 'a good while'.

By now 'by this time'.

To feel sorter splimmy 'to feel "bright"'.

To russle 'roun 'to bustle'.

190   *J. A. Harrison*

To try ter walk off wid 'to try to overcome, to steal'.
Des ez natchul ez de nex' one 'quite natural'.
To have de purchis on 'to have the advantage of'.
Never ter go back on nobody 'to adhere to a statement, promise'.
To hang up de fiddle en' de bow 'to cease from, to die'.
Er born blessin' 'a real blessing'.
To lay down de law ter 'to give one's orders about a thing'.
Sech er come off ez dis 'such behavior'.
To lay de case 'fo' 'to show or explain'.
To be no 'count fo' de wah 'war' 'to be "poor white trash"'.
To have one's head hot 'to be excited'.
De riff-raff er creashun 'poor white people' (for whom the Negro has great contempt).
House-niggers (a term of contempt).
Not ter let nuthin' pass 'to appropriate everything'.
To go 'long wid han' en' mouf open 'to be prepared to take anything'.
Er mess er anything 'a portion, quantity' etc.
To have de stummuck growl en' holler 'to be very hungry'.
To be hail-fellers 'to be on good terms with'.
To be mos' pe'ish out 'to be almost dead'.
To git er bait er 'to get a bite of'.
To see some fun 'to have some fun'.
To hustle off fer ter 'to hurry off to'.
De same ole chune 'always the same thing'.
To light out fer 'to run for'.
To git strankle 'to get strangled'.
To fine out who's w'ich 'to discriminate'.
You better whirl in 'better go to work'.
To grabble 'mungs 'to dig among'.
To kiver yo' tracks 'cute 'to deceive by cunning'.
To fix up er tale fer 'to prepare a lie'.
Up dar in de eleménts 'in the air'.
Jump up! 'get up!'
'Taint bin proued inter 'it has not been given'.
To talk at 'to talk to'; *to lissen at* 'to listen to'.
To have sum biznis wid 'to have to answer to'.
To done gone on by 'to have passed by'.
To be drivin' at 'to intend, to mean'.
To sqench 'to crush'; *to raise up* 'to rise'.
To boo-hoo 'to cry'.
I 'speck 'I suspect and I expect'.
To feel scrumpshus 'to be pleased'.
To fergit off'n de mine 'to forget, to lose from memory'.

To be gwine amblin' 'long 'to go along quietly'.
To open up de confab 'to begin the conversation'.
De baptizin' crick 'a stream for open air baptism'.
To drap yo' water-million 'to make a mistake'.
De outnes' man 'the cleverest man'.
To guv er candy-pullin' 'to give an entertainment' (where "candy" is "pulled").
To men' de fier 'to see after the fire'.
To be cuttin' up didos 'to behave badly'.
To done put de foot down 'to take a stand against'.
To kyar outer projick 'to carry out a project'.
To git good en' gone 'to have gone'.
To gin er big juk 'to give a big jerk'.
To come p'radin' 'long 'to walk ostentatiously'.
To fine one in er fix 'to find one in a bad plight'.
To be mighty low wid 'to be very ill'.
To be in fer dem kinder pranks 'to take part in, to understand'.
Wa'nt mo'n outer sight 'fo' 'was hardly out of sight when ...'.
W'at kin'er W'atzyname is you, ennyhow? 'who are you, pray?'
To play rap-jacket 'to thrash soundly'.
To git frozzle out 'to wear out'.
To show up 'to appear'.
To lissen at de racket 'to hear the noise'.
To open up at 'to abuse'.
I thank you fer ter 'please!'
To look sorter stove up 'to look used up'.
To have no onfrennelness 'not to be unfriendly'.
To be w'isserlin' up de dogs 'to whistle up the dogs'.
To go co'tin' en sparkin' 'roun' 'to visit the young ladies'.
To roach de ha'r 'to arrange the hair of children in a particular fashion'.
To be dat flirtashus 'to be extremely fond of "flirting"'.
To have chicken-fixins fer dinner 'to have chicken for dinner'.
To pop in 'to enter suddenly'.
To be dad-blame ef (an oath) 'to be determined not to'.
To gin um er game 'to "show" them something'.
To have somebody pesterin' 'roun' 'to have some one in the way'.
De whole caboodle on um 'the entire company'.
To git de pick er anything 'the best of' etc.
To wuk yo' mine 'to think hard'.
To put yo' 'pennunce in 'to depend on'.
To chunk at 'to throw at'.
To strop 'to chastise'.
'Taint so mighty fur 'not so far'.

To git de swell-hededniss 'to put on airs'.
To happin up wid 'to meet by accident'.
To wanter save yo' manners 'to be anxious to be polite'.
Ain't seed you iner 'coon's age 'haven't seen you for a long time'.
How all down to yo' house? 'how are all at your house?'
To be one's gal 'to be one's daughter or sweetheart'.
To amble 'long sorter familious like 'to go along easily'.
To keep one eye on 'to be on the look-out'.
To have some biznis cut out fer 'to have something for somebody to do'.
To drap yo' 'joyments 'to give up one's enjoyments'.
Tell de middle er nex' munt' 'an indefinite future'.
To kick one inter de middle er nex' week 'to kick severely'.
To b'leeve one'll go 'long 'to think' etc.
Wid dat 'there upon'; *to tote off* 'to carry off'.
To do de rushin' 'roun' 'to do the real work'.
Dat's sinful 'a shame'; *to settle wid* 'to punish'.
To go trollopin 'roun' 'to idle around'.
To traipse 'to saunter'.
To keep de news mighty close 'to keep a secret'.
Dat's w'at make I say 'that is what makes me say'.
Ain't been handid 'roun' ter 'has not come down to'.
To hunt 'roun' yo' 'membunce 'to try to recollect'.
Mister what you may callum 'Mr. "Thingumbob"'.
Less des call him 'let's just call him'.
To walk right spang inter 'to walk blindly'.
To put yo' foot in it 'to blunder'.
Same ez t'er (tother) one 'like the other one'.
Munt' in en munt' out 'for months'.
To roll in dram 'to be a drunkard'.
Er passle er fokes 'a "parcel" of people'.
Er fote er July bobbycue 'a fourth of July picnic'.
Musser bin hongry 'must have been hungry'.
To have bin er right good long time in de worl' 'to have lived long'.
Hight-l'arnt talk 'learned talk'.
In all my bawn days 'since I was born'.
To ax pard'n 'to ask pardon'.
To plank down de money 'to put down' etc.
To jes' slam loose right en' lef' 'to speak one's mind'.
Dat annimule 'that animal'.
To lay off er straight-shoot 'to run off instantly'.
Not ter stop ter fool on de way 'to go without delay'.
'Taint no use callin' names 'no use to indulge in personal abuse'.
'Pens on succumstances 'depends on circumstances'.

Er sway-back lie 'a poor lie'.
To w'ar one ter frazzle 'to whip severely'.
'Taint no gittin' 'roun' 'it cannot be avoided'.
To stagnate 'to stop, to prevent'.
To fling er shadder 'to cast', etc.
To shoot quicker 'to strike'; *sto'-closze* 'store-clothes'.
To do de plum squar' thing 'to do the right thing'.
To stick up ter er thing 'to adhere to a statement'.
To git jolted 'to get the worst of it'.
To keep er good holt on de tongue 'to restrain the tongue'.
To see er man 'way off yonder 'to see a man at a distance'.
To he'p yo' long pow'ful 'to be of great assistance to you'.
To git at de pint of er fack 'to ascertain the gist of a matter'.
To shuffle up kinder late 'to come somewhat late'.
To up'n do 'to begin to do'; *up'n koff* 'to cough'.
Leetle mo'n 'a little more, and ...'.
To have er crick in de neck 'to be incapacitated'.
To grab holt er 'to take hold of'.
To let it go at dat 'to be content with that'.
To be de ball-headest creetur 'to be the biggest fool'.
'Twix dis an' nex' Jinawerry 'indefinite period'.
De lot 'the back-yard'; *to cunjer fokes* 'to bewitch'.
Wunner dem dat 'one of those'.
To be broozin' 'roun' 'to wander around'.
To take'n kyo' 'to cure'.
To lam sider de head 'to strike on the side of the head'.
De koam er de house 'the gable of the house'.
Fixin' fer ter 'getting ready for'.
To steer cle'r er 'to avoid'.
De Bad Man 'the Devil'; *de Bad Place* 'hell'.
To come dress up like w'ite fokes 'to come well dressed'.
To make er trade wid 'to exchange with'.
To sail in fer ter have fun 'to "go in" for fun'.
Ain't got no time fer ter tarry 'am in a hurry'.
To poke fun at 'to make fun of'.
'Twan't doin' no good 'it was of no use'.
To give er ne'er ('another') *showin'* 'to give another opportunity'.
To lay er progance 'to lay out a program'.
To perlaver 'to argue or talk'.
To know de gran'daddy er a luckyman 'to know a luckyman's grand-
     father'.
To warrant er pa'r er shoes 'to guarantee a pair of shoes'.
To have de picter took 'to have one's picture taken'.

To git 'nuff ter las' er long time 'to be amply satisfied'.
Right sharp happiness 'a good deal of happiness'.
To let in en' 'to go to work to'.
To worry ter de bottom er 'to carry through a matter', 'to understand well'.
I gwinter de meetin' 'I am going to church'.
To lif' de song 'to start the chorus'.
To look mighty sharp 'to be on the alert'.
To cla'r de track 'to get out of the way'.
To hitch up de team 'to get the team ready, to begin'.
Piny woods niggers (term of contempt) 'pine-woods negroes'.
Nuthin' or nuffin' comes up ter 'nothing is equal to'.
Up Norf 'at the North'.
To call de figgers (in a dance) 'to call out the figures'.
Chassay forrard! 'move forward'.
To string out behine 'to get in a line'.
To knock de splinters 'to work hard'.
To do yo' lebbel bes' 'to do your very best'.
To show er man er thing or two 'to initiate', 'to explain'.
To tech de fancy fling (in dancing) 'to try to put on airs'.
To han'le sich er pile er feet 'to dance so well'.
To kick de dus' plum out de planks 'to dance admirably'.
Mighty slicky 'very slippery'.
To hill up de corn 'to put the finishing touches to'.
To luv like de mischuf 'to love exceedingly'.
To pick up er libbin' 'to make a living'.
Er one-horse scrub 'a worthless creature'.
Gwinter ter be fus' in de fam'ly sho' 'certainly going to take the lead'.
To butt agin 'to come in contact with'.
Er critter 'a horse or mule'.
Er milerterry nigger-chap 'a negro soldier'.
To chap de cotton-rows 'to hoe the rows of cotton'.
'Way back yander 'a long time ago'.
To onkink de ha'r 'to uncurl the hair'.
To put up mighty po' mouf 'to make a sad tale of it'.
To s'ply widder chunk er fier 'to furnish with fire'.
To slasherway 'to cut or carve'.
To be gone, sho' 'to be certainly lost'.
To set up er howl 'to weep bitterly'.
Er stupe-head 'a stupid dunce'.
To be gwinter lash 'to intend to whip'.
To lam, ef it's de las' ack 'to flog if it costs one's life'.
To keep on quollin' 'to continue quarrelling'.

To git a thing straight 'to get the authentic version'.
To be 'ginst de rules 'to be unlawful'.

Obs.: The humorous and proverbial character of many of these expressions shows a distinct feature of the Negro mind. The talk of the African abounds in metaphors, figures, similes, imaginative flights, humorous delineations and designations, saws and sayings. These have so interwoven themselves with his daily speech as to have become an unconscious and essential part of it.

The author is much indebted to the writings of J. C. Harris, J. A. Macon, Sherwood Bonner, and others, for help in forming this collection.

Lexington, Va., U.S.A.

L. W. PAYNE, Jr.

A WORD-LIST FROM EAST ALABAMA (EXCERPTS)

In addition to the usual difficulties confronting the student and collector of dialect and colloquial expressions, there is in the South the vexing problem of the influence and range of the distinct negro dialects common in the various sections. The ordinary southerner would scoff at the idea that it is the negro dialect of his section that has largely molded his own speech. For my own part, after a somewhat careful study of east Alabama dialect, I am convinced that the speech of the white people, the dialect I have spoken all my life and the one I have tried to record here, is more largely colored by the language of the negroes than by any other single influence. In fact, the coalescing of the negro dialect with that of the illiterate white people has so far progressed that for all practical purposes we may consider the two dialects as one. Still, knowing as we do the peculiar ear-marks of the negro dialect, and often having a more or less distinct consciousness of the pure negroisms, we may be justified in the attempt to exclude all such from this list. To differentiate here has often been very difficult, of course, and there are no doubt numerous errors in my work just at this point. For instance, I have excluded the familiar negro change of *th* sonant (ð) to *d*, and of *th* surd (þ) to *f*, as for example in *dis*, *dæt*, *dem*, *udder*, etc., *fru*, *toof*, etc. Occasionally a word rather common among the white people, as *furder*, or *mouf* (particularly in *moufful*), has been admitted.

The exact locality studied falls in east Alabama and west Georgia, centering around the town of Auburn in Lee county, Alabama, and extending south to include Macon and Russell counties, west to include

Reprinted from *Dialect Notes* 3 (1908):279-285, by permission of the University of Alabama Press and The American Dialect Society.

Tallapoosa county, north to include Chambers and a small part of Randolph, and east to include the counties of Troupe, Harris, and Muscogee in Georgia. The first twenty-one years of my life were spent in the college town of Auburn, which is practically in the center of this territory. The small amount of college slang included in the list appertains to the Alabama Polytechnic Institute, which is located here. Later I spent six years in Conecuh county in south Alabama, where, as teacher in a State Agricultural School, I came in intimate touch with crude country boys and girls from this and the surrounding counties, and I have included in my list a few expressions peculiar to this section.

I have had to depend largely on my own ear in gathering material, but I have verified every point on which I had any doubt, or, where verification was impossible, discarded the entry. The work of collecting has covered a period of four years of intermittent effort. Numerous local newspapers and advertising sheets, personal letters, and dialect stories have been read for new material. In admitting quotations from such writers as Longstreet, Harris, W. P. Thompson (*Major Jones's Courtship*) etc., I have been very careful to avoid the ready-made or humorous dialecticisms of the author, and have used the material more as a source of suggestion than as authoritative records. From Harris I have admitted only such speeches as were put into the mouths of white characters.

Much of the originality of the article has been forestalled by the appearance of Professor Carr's articles on northwest Arkansas dialect in recent numbers of the *Dialect Notes*. Many of the finds which I flattered myself would be new material have appeared in his articles. I am largely indebted to his lists, however, for many suggestions, as well as for additions to my own collection. The dialects of all the southern states, when fully collected, will, I am convinced, show marked similarities in the general vocabularies and in the minuter details of phonological and philological values. The general tendencies noted by Professor Carr (*D.N.* iii: 101) are applicable to Alabama as well as to Arkansas speech. For the sake of certain divergencies, however, I shall add a few notes below.

NOTES

1. RECESSIVE ACCENT is noticeable in foreign or Latin words of two syllables; as *rˈî-ses, ˈî-vent, dˈî-têlz, hˈô-tel, ˈai-dîə* or *ˈai-dî, bˈô-kê* etc.

2. PROCESSIVE ACCENT is quite as frequent in similar words of more than two syllables; as *pîˈê-tə, ekskwˈi-sit, dî-fˈi-sit, contrˈê-ri, mû-ni-sˈip-əl, mis-tfˈî-vus, mauntˈê-ni-us* etc.

3. STRONG FINAL ACCENT is heard in many words of two or more syllables

particularly those ending in -*ine* and -*ment*: *gen-û-a·in, fê-vo-r·ait, govərm·ent, presid·ent, Birminh·æm* etc.

4. Many OBSOLESCENT or OLD PRONUNCIATIONS are preserved; as in *bail, spail, appaint, paisn* etc. This pronunciation of *oi* is very common in closed syllables. Also *pæm, bæm, sæm* etc.; *tʃêni* 'China' in *tʃê-ni ber-i* etc. See *D.N.* iii:101.

5. Other VOWEL CHANGES may be noted as follows:

(1) *e* becomes *i* in *kittl, tʃist, klivis, git, stid, stiddi* (sometimes *studdy*); also in many plurals, as *houziz*, etc. *e* becomes *ê* in *êg, lêg* etc.: chiefly a negroism. *e* becomes *æ* in *kæg, kærôsîn* etc.; *e* for older *a* becomes *i* in *mini, ini* 'many', 'any' etc. *e* becomes *î* in *flîm* 'phlegm', *dîf* etc.

(2) *a* becomes *æ* in closed syllables almost universally; as in *ænt, gæp, cæf, pæs, mæm, læf, dæns* etc. *æ* becomes *e* in *geðə, ketʃ, keë, skeë* etc. *æ* becomes *o* in *pompə, job, stob, wrop* etc.

(3) *î* becomes *i* in *krittə, slik* 'sleek', *brim* 'bream', *tit* 'teat'. *i* becomes *î* in *mistʃ·î-vus, dî-strik(t), îtʃ, zînia* 'zinnia'. *i* becomes *e* in *hendə, ef, peþ* etc.

(4) *a* becomes *û* in *sûp-l* 'supple'.

(5) *o* becomes *ɒ* in *kɒklbë(r)*. *o* becomes *æ* in *dræp, cræp* etc. *o* becomes *ɔ* in *tʃomp, tromp, trompl, stomp, tosl, wote(r), hog, dog* etc. Also in many words in *un-*: *onsîn* etc. Final *ô* (-ow) usually becomes obscure *ə, fellə, yallə* etc.

(6) *ɔ* becomes *o* in *dob, dirt-dobber* etc. *ɔ* become *æ* in *dʒændərz* 'jaundice', *dʒænt* 'jaunt', *hænt* etc.

(7) *û* becomes *ô* in *kæn-ta-lôp*.

(8) *iu* is usually *û*; as in *blû, Sû, revôlûʃon* etc., but *niu, nius* (never *nûs*). *oi* becomes *ai* in closed syllables. The intrusive *y* in *gyarden, gyirl, kyar* is only heard sporadically.

6. CONSONANT CHANGES:

(1) *Semi-vowels.* *w* initial disappears in *(w)oman*, and is retained in *swoard*. *w* medial is often lost in words compounded with -*wards*, as *tô(w)a(r)ds, awk(w)ard, back(w)ards* etc. *y* is lost in *yeast* (pronounced *îst*).

(2) *Liquids.* *l* in *flail* becomes *r* by dissimilation; *frail* is a very common word in the South. *l* medial disappears in *amost, aready, sef, hep* etc. *r* is widely lost in medial and final positions, as in *kuss, bust, hoss, passel, pusli* etc.; *dô, flô, ʃô; wo* 'war', *fâ* etc. Whole syllables containing *r* disappear, as *comʃtabl, tolabl, difənt, seval, considabl, Sædi, slâvi taim*. On the other hand, intrusive *r* frequently occurs as a consonant bridge between two open sounds, as *kæppar ælfa, ði aidîərov it* 'the idea of it', *yûrænd ai* 'you and I' etc.

(3) *Nasals.* m is often vocalized or made into a full syllable by prefixing a vowel sound, as in *ell(u)m, hel(u)m* etc. m final is lost in *rû-mi-tiz.* n has become vocalic m after *p* or *b*, as in *cap-m, somp-m, hap-m, ôp-m, heb-m, seb-m, leb-m.* n is usually lost in *an* before vowels; if preserved it is usually attached to the noun, as *ə-naul* 'an owl'. See also *spread-nadder.* has become n in unstressed syllables, particularly in final -*ing*; medial in *Birmin-hæm.* *Anything* retains ŋ, but *nothing* and *something* become *nuþin, somþin* (or *somp-m*).

(4) *Labials.* p has become vocalized in *Babtis* etc. p is lost in *wɔs* (never *waps*). p occurs for þ in *somp-m*; and for t in *dremp.* b is vocalized in *marvlz* etc. b is inserted in *fæmbli,* and by analogy *bl* is substituted for n in *tʃimbli.* v becomes b in *lib, lubly, nâbl, lebm, sebm, hebm, culbert, ribet* etc. Sometimes *vbm* 'oven' is heard. v becomes f in expressions like *hæf tə* 'have to', and disappears in expressions like *gi'mi* 'give me'. ʃ medial is sometimes lost in *after* (pronounced *ætə* or *âtə*). f occurs universally in *nefiu.*

(5) *Dentals.* Medial t becomes tʃ in *oistʃə.* Final t disappears after voiceless consonants, *kep, bænkrup, sɔf, lɔf, mus, dʒes* 'just', *ês* 'haste', *gris-mil, wɔs-nes* etc. Occasionally also after voiced consonants, as in *fac.* Initial t becomes þ in *þribl.* Medial t is lost in *les* 'let's'. Excrescent t is common among the illiterate in *(a)krost, twaist, wunst, klôst, dôst, wiʃt* (present), *klift, skift, sermont, sudənt* etc. Final t becomes k in *projeck.* d medial is lost in -*ndl* combinations, as in *bunl, cænl, dwinl* etc. Also after l in *tʃil-en* 'children'. Final d often becomes t as in *æst, kilt, helt, secont* etc. Excrescent d is sometimes heard in *draund, gaund.* Final d is usually lost after l and n and in -*ldz* and -*ndz* plural forms, as *wil(d), ol(d), col(d), fin(d), han(d), bran(d)* etc.

ð is lost in *wher* 'whether' among careless speakers. ð in all positions has, under negro influence, largely become d, as in *udder, furder, wid, dî* 'they' or 'the', *dis, dæt* etc. ð becomes þ in *wiþ, bûþ, bi-nîþ. With* often becomes *wi.* þ becomes ð in many plurals, as in *trûðz.* þ in all positions has become f under negro influence, as in *trûf, tûf* 'tooth', *frû* etc. þ rarely becomes t. The old forms *drauþ* and *haitþ* are very common among good speakers.

(6) *Sibilants.* s initial is added in *skrûtʃ* 'crouch', and it occurs final, alone or with t, in *unbeknowns(t).* s becomes f in *likôriʃ* and sometimes in *hërʃ* 'hearse'. s becomes tʃ in *pintʃərs.* ʃ before r becomes s in *srink* (pret. *srunk* or *swunk*). z becomes voiceless s in *belus* (cf. the v. *bellows*).

(7) *Gutturals.* The changes in gutturals are not frequent or noteworthy. Through negro influence dʒ in *dʒes* 'just' becomes d among the illiterate.

(8) *Metathesis.* Pre- and per- often interchanged, as preform, perserv. per- for pro-, *perfesə.* inter for intro-, *interdûs.* Also *tʃildern, hunderd, skaunderl, apern,* and perhaps in *crany-crow* (see *carion-crow*). *Aks* for *ask*

is chiefly a negroism, but widely used among the white people.

(9) *Svarabhakti*, as in *ellum, umberell(a)*. An inserted syllable occurs in *blæsfî-mi-us, trîmend-i-us* or *trî-men-dʒu-us, maun-tê-ni-us, mistʃi-vi-us* etc.

7. VERBS. Abnormal preterits:

(1) *brung, crope, driv, et, fit* or *faut, frez* or *friz, gin, maut, riz, sot* etc.

(2) *blowed, choosed, drawed, growed, knowed, shined, throwed* etc.

(3) *clum* (*clam* has *clammed*), *dôv, drug, fotch(t), found* (*fine*), *hearn, het, ketcht, kotch(t), skunt, skwez, skwoz, sont, teacht* etc.

(4) *Attackted, busted* (also *bursted*), *costed, drownded, galded, stalded, stold, spreaded, underminded* etc.

(5) Participles as preterits, *done, drunk, seen, taken* etc.

(6) Almost any preterit may be used as a past participle, as *wrote, took, broke, went* etc.

(7) Presents are occasionally used as participles, as "I would have *give* him one".

(8) Presents are often used as preterits, as *wisht, come, give* etc.

(9) Transitives for intransitives, as *lay, raise, set.*

(10) *Will* and *would* are used in almost all locutions where *shall* and *should* are demanded by literary usage.

(11) *Lack to* and *like to.*

(12) *Use to could.*

(13) Singular forms are constantly used for plurals, particularly with plural pronouns as subjects.

(14) Abnormal forms in third singular, *do* and *don't, does* (pronounced *dûz*), *costes, tastes* etc.

(15) Reduplications, as in *I'm am, done done it, had of had* 'had (have) had' etc.

(16) Frequent abnormal contractions, as *whyn't* 'why don't, didn't' etc.

8. NOUNS. Abnormal plurals: *bretherin, brutherin, sisterin, nestes, postes, beastes, beasteses, galluses, locusses* 'locusts', *oxens* (*oxen* is often sing.), *tomatuses, louses, mouses, mices, gooses, geeses*; singulars used as plurals: *cheese, license* (sometimes *licenses* for *license*), *(mo)lasses, measles* etc.; nouns of collective sense, singular and plural alike, *mile, pound, foot, biscuit* etc.

9. PRONOUNS:

(1) *You all, yall* (with regular possessive *yalls*).

(2) Disjunctive possessives, *hisn, hern, ourn, the(i)rn, yourn.*

(3) Reflexives, *hisself, theyselves, the(i)rselves*; also *his fool self, my fool self* etc. The *l* is usually lost in pronunciation of *self.*

(4) *Hit* occurs in emphatic and even in unemphatic position.

(5) *Thisn, thatn, this here, that there,* emphatic demonstratives.
(6) *As* for rel. frequent; *whom* not used at all by uneducated.
(7) Nom. for obj. and obj. for nom. frequent.
(8) *airn* and *nairn, tother, yuther,* occur frequently.

10. PREPOSITIONS. *a* for *on,* in *a purpose, a fire* etc.; *for to* still used by old-fashioned people; *off on, out on,* for *off of, out of; wait on* for *wait for; listen at* for *listen to; different to* (or *than*) for *different from; nothing to* for *nothing in.* Redundant prepositions are frequent, and omission of needed prepositions is also common. *In* is usually used for *into* in all locutions. *Onto* is common.

11. ADJECTIVES AND ADVERBS. *A* is used for *an* before vowels. Adjectival forms are constantly used for adverbial forms. Double comparatives and superlatives are frequent, as in *beterer, mô beterer, mô worser, mô puttier, leastest, mostest* etc. Abnormal comparisons, *badder, baddest, littler, littlest, farer, farest* etc. *Real* (pronounced *rêl*) is used for the absolute superlative with comparatives. Adverbial *-s* survives in *anywheres, leastways, nowheres* etc.; also probably in *a long ways, a little ways* etc. *All the* is used with adverbs to express degree. "That's *all the far* I can jump" etc. *Yonder* is used for *there*: "In *yonder* you will find it". *That* is frequently used for *so*: "It was *that* late we never could a got there".

12. FOLK ETYMOLOGIES. *Cowcumber, cramberry, Johniequil, mushmelon, redish, pussley, satisfac, shoemake, treadsalve, crapgrass, animule, pullikins, fice dog* 'faust dog, faist dog', *camphire, Christian flycatcher, spitin image, coverlid, niggerly, dry grins* (prob. from *chagrin*), *tumble sets, croker sack, noxvomit* etc.

13. INVERTED COMPOUNDS. *Peckerwood, hoppergrass, rightdown, everwhich* etc.

PAUL CHRISTOPHERSEN

SOME SPECIAL WEST AFRICAN ENGLISH WORDS[1]

Isolated parts of a language area tend to develop peculiarities of their own, especially in vocabulary, and West Africa is no exception. Different European languages, English, French, Dutch, Danish and Portuguese, are or have been spoken there, and they all use or have used special West African words. The purpose of this paper is to point to the lexicographical interest of West African English. A number of special West African words are in fact shared by several European languages, but none of the standard dictionaries of these languages devote much attention to West Africa. English is probably better served in this respect than any other language, but even the Oxford Dictionary has many omissions, and the words that it does record are not always satisfactorily treated. A cursory reading of a series of early accounts of travels in West Africa[2]

Reprinted with permission from *English Studies* 34 (1953), 282-91.
[1] I am obliged to Dr. K. O. Dike, of University College, Ibadan, and to Professor H. Sten, of the University of Copenhagen, for advice on various points in this paper.
[2] The works to which I shall have occasion to refer below are:

J. Atkins, *A Voyage to Guinea, Brasil, and the West-Indies* (London, 1735).
W. B. Baikie, *Narrative of an Exploring Voyage up the Rivers Kwora and Binue* (London, 1856).
C. Behrens, *Da Guinea var Dansk* (Copenhagen, 1917).
W. Bosman, *Nauwkeurige Beschryving van de Guinese Goud-, Tand, en Slave-Kust* (Utrecht, 1704).
R. F. Burton, *Abeokuta and the Camaroons Mountains*, vol. II (London, 1863).
A. & J. Churchill, *A Collection of Voyages and Travels* (London, 1732).
J. Duncan, *Travels in Western Africa in* 1845 & 1846, vol. I (London, 1847).
R. Hakluyt, *The Principal Navigations, Voiages*, etc., vol. II (London, 1599).
J. Houstoun, *Some New and Accurate Observations on the Coast of Guinea* (London, 1725).

has convinced me that there is a great deal of material to be collected here, and I shall give examples below of the sort of discoveries that one can make in these early travel-books. But first I must say a few words about West African English in general.

There are several distinct kinds, or layers, of English spoken in the British territories on the west coast of Africa. There is a kind of Pidgin, used chiefly in intercourse between Europeans and illiterate Africans, and sometimes among the Africans themselves if they belong to different tribes. Pidgin is a language consisting mostly of English words, but with a grammatical structure all its own. Secondly there is educated African English. This is characterized by an accent which is very different from any other English accent, owing to influence from African languages, and by occasional though fairly systematic deviations from Standard English in vocabulary and phraseology. Finally there is the English spoken by those Europeans on the west coast who have English as their mother tongue. Since they have learnt their English in different parts of the English-speaking world, they do not share a common accent; but new-comers gradually adopt certain words and uses of words which are peculiar to West Africa, and which are handed down traditionally from generation to generation of "old coasters". It is with these peculiarities of "old coasters" English (let us call it Coast English) that this paper will be concerned.

To talk of only three kinds of English in West Africa to-day is perhaps to simplify matters unduly; the three kinds shade into one another. More-over, there are minor variations between the different territories, and the so-called Patois or Creole spoken by some Sierra Leonians is in a class by itself, though akin to Pidgin. My remarks in this paper are based on observations made in Nigeria and relate, as I said, to the English used by Europeans among themselves. Educated African English is in inten-tion Standard English, and is in fact an approximation to it. Pidgin English is boldly independent; but despite its independence it shares some of its peculiarities in vocabulary with Coast English.

What are these peculiarities of Coast English? They are fewer now

J. B. Labat, *Voyage du Chevalier Des Marchais en Guinée*, etc., vol. II (Paris, 1730).

H. C. Monrad, *Bidrag til en Skildring af Guinea-Kysten* (Copenhagen, 1822).

F. Moore, *Travels into the Inland Parts of Africa* (London, n.d. 1740?).

W. J. Müller, *Die Africanische auf der Guineischen Gold-Cust gelegene Landschaft Fetu* (Hamburg, 1676).

W. F. W. Owen, *Narrative of Voyages to Explore the Shores of Africa*, etc., vol. II (London, 1833).

S. Purchas, *Pvrchas His Pilgrimes*, vol. II (London, 1625).

L. F. Römer, *Tilforladelig Efterretning om Kysten Guinea* (Copenhagen, 1760).

W. Smith, *A New Voyage to Guinea* (London, 1744).

Villaut de Bellefond, *Relation des Costes d'Afrique, appelées Guinée* (Paris, 1669).

than in former centuries. Many of the special words used by early travellers and traders have been replaced by the corresponding standard terms; thus *assagai* has become 'spear', *caboceer* has become 'chief' or 'headman', and *pitto* is often just 'native beer' (or some similar phrase). The reality covered by *panyar* 'to seize' or 'kidnap' has largely vanished, and the word is no longer used. The word *fetish*, with the phrases *to make fetish* and *fetish-men* or *fetisheer*, is seldom heard nowadays in West Africa, its original home. Since its appropriation by anthropologists for more general use, the word has been largely replaced in British West Africa (but not, I believe, in the French territories) by the phrase *ju-ju*, about which I shall have more to say presently. The following are some of the words and phrases still commonly used in Coast English, but not generally known in Standard English, or not known in the particular West African sense: *chop, Dane gun, dash, ju-ju, palaver* and *watchnight*. To these one might add such words as *calabash, pawpaw* and *pickin*, which are shared by several regions within the English-speaking world.

Before I comment on some of these words I should like briefly to sketch in the historical background. The first European nation to build permanent establishments, in the form of forts and trading-stations, on the Guinea coast were the Portuguese. For about a hundred years, i.e. roughly from 1475 to 1575, they enjoyed a virtual monopoly of the trade to West Africa. During this period many of the negroes learnt Portuguese, of a sort, and it seems that they came to regard this as the language of the white man of whatever country. The result was that when other nations, notably the Dutch and the English, shortly before 1600 began to challenge the supremacy of the Portuguese in this part of the world, they had to teach themselves Portuguese for the purpose of communicating with the Africans. For a long time the medium of communication between Europeans and Africans remained Portuguese; and even after the negroes living near the trading-stations of other nations, Dutch, English, or Danish, had learnt a little of the languages of these nations, a large number of Portuguese words survived in their speech and were adopted by the Europeans also. The interesting thing is that early travellers sometimes naïvely assumed that the names for various objects quoted to them by the Africans were those of the local African language and not, as so often happened, the equivalent Portuguese words in a corrupt form. Thus in *Pvrchas His Pilgrimes* (p. 941) we find: "They haue also a Priest, who in their speech they call a *Fetissero*". Francis Moore (p. 85) includes *mercador* in a list of Mandingo words and gives "factor" as its English equivalent. Many similar mistakes could be quoted.

When I talk of the Portuguese used in West Africa in former centuries, I mean so-called Negro-Portuguese, a kind of Pidgin Portuguese. This is not the place to discuss the characteristics of this *lingua franca*, as it was sometimes called, but it is important to realize that it was a "bastard" language, as Moore says (p. 27), "scarce understood in Lisbon". It showed certain archaic or Spanish features.[3] It is also important to realize that it was used in intercourse between Englishmen and Africans from the earliest times until well into the eighteenth century.[4]

Portuguese influence on African speech may have been strengthened in later times through Brazil. In the second half of the nineteenth century freed slaves returned in large numbers from Brazil. Their influence is noticeable in southern Nigerian architecture, which sometimes looks strikingly Portuguese. There are many Portuguese surnames in Nigeria, and to this day there are negroes in West Africa who can speak a little Portuguese, learnt either in Brazil or from parents who had learnt it there. Nevertheless, it is doubtful whether this Brazilian influence has affected the English spoken on the Guinea coast. The Portuguese words that one finds in Coast English to-day are centuries old, and no new ones have been adopted in recent times.

By the end of the nineteenth century, of the European nations which had had possessions on the Guinea coast only the British remained, and the other nations' languages died out with their departure. In the meantime the French had acquired a small foothold in the colony of Dahomey; up till then their interests had been chiefly confined to the Senegal and later also to equatorial Africa, but not to the Guinea coast proper.

Such then is the background against which we must view the problem of Coast English. Speakers of Coast English come from all parts of the English-speaking world, but on their arrival in West Africa they step into a tradition with its roots deep in West African history. And yet that tradition is not so strong now as it was; a great many words of Portuguese origin have died out. Let us look a little more closely at some of these words.

Officers of state in the West African kingdoms of former times were

---

[3] As in the following phrase, which according to Müller (p. 193) was used by a negro when warning him not to open a fetish-basket: "O Senor, no abrid; pretto diabol sta adentro." i.e. 'O, Sir, do not open it; there is a black devil inside.'

[4] Thus, about the visit of one Nicholas Lambert and other merchants to the king of Benin in 1553 we read: "And now to speake somewhat of the communication that was between the king and our men, you shall first vnderstand that he himselfe could speake the *Portugall* tongue, which he had learned of a child [= as a child]" (Hakluyt, p. 12). John Barbot, a Frenchman who was on the coast in the 1670's and 1680's, makes it clear (*Churchill*, vol. V, p. 360) that the Europeans, and he specially mentions the English and the Dutch, used Portuguese in their trade with the people of Benin. On the Gambia, says Moore (p. 27) in the eighteenth century, next to the local language the commonest medium was Negro-Portuguese. In the course of the eighteenth century Pidgin English seems to have become the common medium between Englishmen and negroes, and in the nineteenth century it supplanted Negro-Portuguese as the *lingua franca* on the coast.

often given Portuguese titles. Among those that occur in English writings
are: *caboceer* 'headman', *fidalgo* 'governor', *mercador* 'Government-ap-
pointed trade agent' and *viador* 'overseer'. These have all been recorded
in the O.E.D., though *mercador* is stated to be a rare word of Spanish
origin, and no West African examples are quoted. A title which is not
recorded in the O.E.D. is *braffo* (used e.g., by Smith, p. 219, and Barbot,
Churchill's Collection, vol. V, p. 290), which is from Portuguese *bravo*
'brave'. In West Africa it meant 'standard-bearer' or 'general'.

Two other Portuguese words which are no longer in common use in
British West Africa are *fetish* and *panyar*. They are both satisfactorily
dealt with in the O.E.D. Among Portuguese words one might also list
assagai, which despite its Arabic origin came into English from the
Portuguese in Africa. Under the word *custom* the O.E.D. records a
special West African use, namely, to signify the periodical massacres in
the former kingdom of Dahomey. This definition is too narrow; the
word meant 'holiday' or 'festival'. Thus, Duncan (p. 31) writes: 'The yam
custom, or holiday, is another annual ceremony.' Since this special
meaning of the word is found also in Coast Danish, there is reason to
think that it goes back to Negro-Portuguese.

A rather surprising omission in the O.E.D. is the term for a type of
small shell which for centuries was used in West Africa as currency and
especially as small change.[5] Nowadays these shells are referred to as
cowries, an Indian word, but in former times they were known by the
Portuguese word *buzio* (< Latin *bucina*). All the other European languages spoken on the coast adopted this Portuguese word, and each
shaped it differently according to its sound system, but no dictionary
known to me has recorded any of these borrowings. In English a variety
of forms were used (e.g. by Atkins, Houstoun, Barbot and Phillips; the
latter two in *Churchill's Collection*, vols. V & VI); the word appeared
most often as *booge*, a form probably influenced by Coast French *bouge*[6]
(used e.g., by Labat, p. 40); other forms were *buji* and *bousie*. From about
1700 the word *cowrie* began to take the place of *booge*.

Let us now turn to some of the special words which are still used in
West Africa to-day. One of them, *palaver*, is clearly of Portuguese origin.
From West Africa the word was brought to England by travellers, and

---

[5]   Thus, James Welsh after his visit to Benin in 1588 reported: "Their money is pretie
white shels, for golde and siluer we saw none" (Hakluyt, p. 129). And Leo Africanus,
in John Pory's translation, says: "The Coine of *Tombuto* is of Gold without any stampe
or superscription: but in matters of small value they vse certaine shels brought hither
out of the Kingdome of *Persia*, foure hundred of which shels are woorth a Duckat"
(*Pvrchas His Pilgrimes*, p. 828).
[6]   The Portuguese retracted [s] and [z] were heard by Frenchmen, with their dental
s-sounds, as [] and [ʒ]. Hence *feitiço* became *fétiche*, and *buzio* became *bouge*. The
English forms of these words in their later stages were influenced by French.

it is now part of Standard English in the sense of 'talk' or 'parley'. But in West Africa this meaning is obsolete. In Pidgin and very largely in Coast English the word has come to mean 'business' or 'trouble' (e.g. "That's your palaver", "That has caused a lot of palaver" and "He had some tummy palaver last week"). From the original meaning 'talk' the word had already in the eighteenth century come to mean 'dispute' or 'law-suit' (see Moore, p. 221, and Smith, p. 32), occasions on which there is invariably in West Africa a great deal of loud talk. It seems that the further extension to mean 'fuss' and 'trouble' took place in the nine-teenth century; the frequent use of the word in Pidgin was probably instrumental.

Another word which really belongs to Pidgin and which has hardly as yet become acclimatized in Coast English is *watchnight* in the sense of 'night-watchman'. It appeals to the ordinary English-speaker by its quaintness and simplicity.

I come now to three problem words, *chop*, *dash* and *ju-ju*, and I shall deal with them one by one. They belong to both Pidgin and Coast English.

Chop is both a noun 'food' (e.g. "They live on native chop", "I gave him some money to buy chop with" and "Chop is ready", i.e. dinner is served) and a verb (e.g. "The white ants have chopped it"); but the verb is more common in Pidgin than in Coast English. The O.E.D. Supplement records the noun from 1870 and the verb from 1896; but the noun is found in Burton (p. 145) and the verb in Owen (p. 327). Weekley suggests that the word may either be from the obsolete verb *chop* 'to devour' or may have been suggested by *chopsticks*. The former is the more likely suggestion. We may have a corroboration of this etymology in the occurrence of a word *chap-chap* 'to eat' in a list of words of the 'Old Calabar' language given by Barbot (*Churchill*, vol. V, p. 383), whose last visit to West Africa was in 1682. The language spoken in Old Calabar at the present day is Efik, but *chap-chap* is not an Efik word. What language is it then? English influence on the language of West Africans at that early date would be something very unusual, but I have no better ex-planation to offer than to suggest that *chap-chap* is the obsolete English verb *chap* or *chop* 'to take into the chops and eat' with the usual African reduplication for emphasis.

Dash is one of the first words that a European learns on his arrival in West Africa. Pidgin phrases like "Massa give me dash" and "Massa no dash me enough" illustrate its meaning and use. It means 'tip' or 'present', and it is both a noun and a verb. It is extremely common both in Pidgin and in Coast English. How far back does it go, and what is its origin? The earliest example quoted in the O.E.D. is from 1788, but a theory is propounded there that the word is a corruption of *dashee*, a hypothetical Negro word, through taking the plural *dashees* as *dashes*. The authority for the form *dashee* is Atkins (pp. 60, 64, 100, 102 *et al.*), who calls it a "Negrish" word; but Atkins was a surgeon and not a philologist, and his pronouncements on language should be taken with a pinch of salt. His list of "Negrish" words (p. 60) is in fact open to doubt; it contains a word *cockracoo* meaning 'fowl' or 'chicken', which can be no other than Portuguese *cocoroco* 'cock-a-doodle-do'. The same word for 'fowl' or 'chicken' is included by Barbot in his Old Calabar vocabulary, and it is used by Thomas Phillips (*Churchill*, vol. VI, p.191). It was obviously a common Negro-Portuguese word used all along the Guinea coast. Even the ending *-ee* is not above suspicion, since Atkins uses it regularly in his attempts to render Pidgin English: "after Death the honest goodee Man go to Godee, livee very well, have a goodee Wife, goodee Victuals, &c." (p.105).

Having now thrown suspicion on the O.E.D.'s theory, can we suggest anything better? First of all it should be realized that the word is older than the eighteenth century, and that it occurs also in Coast French, Dutch and Danish. Barbot (*Churchill*, vol. V, p.416) quotes a Gold Coast phrase *mame-dasche* 'give me something', and Villaut de Bellefond (p. 322) talks of the negro habit of clamouring for "quelque présent (qu'ils appellent *Daché*)". In an account translated from a Dutch original, which is apparently no longer extant, and included in *Pvrchas His Pilgrimes*, a noun *Dache* meaning 'present' is used (pp. 937-38), and the same noun, spelt *Dasje*, occurs in a later Dutch writer, Bosman (part II, p.274). In Coast Danish a verb *dadse* (covering a pronunciation [dasə]) was used in the nineteenth century (Monrad, p.215, and Behrens, pp. 86, 89-90).

Can we on the basis of these further occurrences propose a more probable etymology? The wide use of the word in different European languages on the coast speaks in favour of a Portuguese origin, since the common element in the various "coast" forms of European languages is mostly Portuguese. But there is no obvious Portuguese word that one can think of in this connexion; the verb *deixar* 'to bequeathe' or 'leave behind' is a possibility, but no more. A particular use of West African *dash(ee)* may, however, afford a clue; the word is often in practice synonymous with 'enforced tribute', 'fee' or 'commission'. Thus, Atkins (p. 64) writes: "there is a *Dashee* expected before Ships can wood or water here"; and (p.198): "each [tribe] has a Captain or Leader, who always craves or claims some *Dashee*, before you strike a Bargain with any of the other *Negroes*". The same meaning is clearly implied by Villaut de Bellefond and some of the other authors who have used the word. Now there exists in some Romance languages a word meaning 'toll' or 'tribute' with a form not very different from West African *dash*. There was at one time a French word *dace* or *dache* (see von Wartburg's etymological dictionary); Italian has *dazio* and Spanish *dacio*, and medieval Latin (according to Du Cange) had *data, datio, datia* and *datium* all meaning 'tribute'. The word has not been recorded in Portuguese, but that does not mean that it never existed; moreover, Negro-Portuguese had some Spanish admixture. As regards the ending, the word may have existed in two parallel forms, corresponding to the vacillation between *booge* and *buji*.

Ju-ju, the word that has now replaced *fetish*, is recorded in the O.E.D. from 1894; but it is much older, and the O.E.D.'s etymology, from French *joujou* 'toy' or 'plaything', is almost certainly wrong. Baikie, after his expedition up the river Niger in 1854, described a palaver with some Africans, which began by "drinking a glass of wine ... a few drops of which they, before tasting it, poured on the deck as dju-dju, or sacred" (p. 42). This custom is centuries old. In the previously mentioned Dutch account included in *Pvrchas His Pilgrimes* a drinking ceremony on the Gold Coast in about the year 1600 is described as follows: "at the first draught, they drinke not the Cabas full out, but leaue a little in it, which they throw vpon the ground, saying *Iou*, as giving their *Fetisso* that to drinke" (p. 936).[7] It is no doubt also our word that James Barbot, John Barbot's brother, heard in 1699, when he visited the king of Dony, east of Calabar in the present-day Camaroons. He says (*Churchill*, vol. V, p. 462): "I lay that night in the king's house, near his idol-house, which they call *Jou-Jou*." It is worth noting that, although this account was first published in English, the author was a Frenchman. Nevertheless, Barbot does not seem to have recognized *jou-jou* as a French word, and it is clear that he and the king spoke Portuguese together, for Barbot says (ib.): "The king ... is a very good-natur'd civil man, speaks *Portuguese*, and seems to have been instructed by *Romish* priests ... from *St. Tome* and *Brazil*." In view of the wide geographical distribution along the coast of Guinea, the word is more likely to be Portuguese than African. The best explanation I can offer is that it is a corruption of Portuguese *Deus* 'God', in its later forms with reduplication.

Finally I should like to comment on a phrase composed of ordinary English words, but with a special meaning in West Africa, namely, the term *Dane gun*. This term is sometimes used even outside West Africa when referring to events and conditions on the coast. Thus a *Times* leader of 19 May 1953 on the recent disturbances in Kano reported that "the rioters have been using Dane guns". To my knowledge, the only dictionary that records the phrase is the O.E.D. Supplement, which defines its meaning as "a gun used in the Guinea Coast area of West Africa" and gives three quotations, the earliest from the year 1900. In 1847, how-

---

[7] Purchas prints the word as I. OV, but that is undoubtedly a mistake. The German translation included in De Bry, *Orientalische Indien*, part VI (Frankfurt, 1603) has: "das schüttet er aus auff die Erden vnd saget: *Iou*" (p. 26).

ever, Duncan (p. 240) referred to "the long Danish musket"; but the term is still older, as is the gun itself.

That the Dane gun as a type of gun is of considerable antiquity is clear from its antiquated appearance. It is a long-barrelled, smoothbore, muzzle-loading flint-lock gun, rather like an old-fashioned military musket. But although the type as such is old, most of the representatives that one comes across nowadays are of quite recent origin. In fact the life of each individual gun is probably quite short, judging by the number of accidents that occur every year from exploding Dane guns.

Despite the name these guns are produced locally. Throughout the West African territories Dane guns are manufactured to this day by village blacksmiths. And they are obviously made in large quantities, for they are extremely common. Wherever the African peasant and hunter has abandoned the bow and arrow, he has taken to the Dane gun instead. The interesting thing is that the African nowadays looks upon the Dane gun as an indigenous weapon. To his mind, the Dane gun is *his* gun as distinct from guns imported from Europe. He does not of course call it a "Dane gun", which is a term used by the Europeans on the coast. The various African languages have different names for this gun, but they all seem to mean or imply "a native gun". How does it come about that this gun of African manufacture is known to the English on the coast as a "Dane gun"?

The Danes had trade relations with the west coast of Africa for several centuries. They also at one time had possessions on the coast, the last of which were sold to Britain in 1850. It is natural, therefore, to seek the origin of the term *Dane gun* in some article of trade which the Danes in former times sold to the Africans. This theory is confirmed by a search through various accounts written by early Danish travellers.

The fullest information is given by Römer, who was on the coast between 1739 and 1749. Talking of events in the 1730's he says (pp. 164-65):

Our Danish flint-lock guns were highly prized by the Akim, and they would pay 32 rix dollars or 2 ounces of gold for 7 pieces, although they could get 10 Dutch or 12 English guns for the same money. Our gunbarrels had all been proved with a double charge and could be trusted not to burst, whereas of the Dutch and English flint-locks almost half would burst in pieces, and the buyer would thus suffer injury not only in respect of his gun; but he who fired the gun usually became so injured that they sometimes had to amputate his hand.

A little further on (p. 171) we read that "the clever Dutchmen on the coast tried to cut us out by telling many tales to the Akim which were not to our advantage, and in particular this, that there was a fetish on our flint-locks, so that those who used them against their enemies would lose."

Finally we are told (p. 213) that after an inter-tribal battle in 1742 the surviving Akim put the blame for their defeat on our Danish flint-lock guns; they began to think that the Dutch had not lied when they told their forefathers that there was a fetish on them. We on the coast hastened to inform the Directorate [in Copenhagen] that our flint-locks had gone out of fashion in that part of the country, advising them to alter the guns a little, and above all to make them 1½ hands higher [*sic*; longer?], which restored the situation, and henceforth our flint-locks were just as salable as before.

It is clear from the above quotations that there was a brisk trade on the west coast in guns of Danish manufacture — or pretending to be of Danish manufacture, for according to Römer (pp. 213-14) the British imitated the Danish guns and sold their imitations as "Danish guns". Even the French ordered such guns from England for re-sale on the coast.

It was not the British and French alone who resorted to doubtful practices. Some Danish supplier cheated and imported guns from Celle in Hanover for re-exportation to the coast as Danish guns. And so, says Römer (p. 214), "we Danes got a bad reputation over the so-called Danish guns". It is worth noting that Römer says "the so-called Danish guns". It seems that already in his day the term *Danish gun* was beginning to mean a particular type of gun not necessarily made by the Danes.

The same impression emerges still more clearly from the account of a later writer, H. C. Monrad, who was on the coast from 1805 to 1809. He says (pp. 284-85): "The commonest things which are traded with the negroes are: guns (among which the so-called *Danish* ones, which are manufactured near Hamburg and which the British have imitated so cleverly and sell as 'Danish guns', are the most easily salable) ..." Evidently by Monrad's time the association between Danes and "Dane guns" had become rather loose. The guns were in fact no longer made in Denmark.

A search through Danish archives would doubtless reveal further details, but would scarcely alter the general picture. The only link that is now missing is the transition from the importation of Dane guns, of whatever origin, into West Africa to the local manufacture of these guns and the cessation of the import. On this point I have no documentary evidence, though no doubt it could be found. But that would be a task for the economic historian rather than the philologist.

Ibadan, Nigeria.

PAUL CHRISTOPHERSEN

A NOTE ON THE WORDS *dash* AND *ju-ju* IN WEST AFRICAN
ENGLISH

In a paper on the vocabulary of West African English[1] a few years ago,
I pointed out that *dash* 'gift' and *ju-ju* 'idol, fetish' can be traced back
to a description of the coast of Guinea printed by Samuel Purchas in
vol. II of his *Pilgrimes* (London, 1625); but I was unable to trace the
account to its ultimate source, which I was inclined to think had been
lost. The English account purports to have been "Translated out of
Dutch, conferred also with the *Latine* Edition", and in a note we are
told that the Latin version had been "Translated out of Dutch by *G. Artus
Dantisc*". It is not certain whether *Dutch* in these statements means
German or Dutch in our sense, but from the German and Latin editions
it is clear that the account appeared originally in Dutch (= Netherlandish)
and was translated by Gothard Arthus (sometimes named Dantiscanus
from his native city of Danzig) first into High German and published by
the brothers de Bry in their *Orientalische Indien*, part VI (Frankfurt, 1603),
and afterwards into Latin and published in de Bry, *India Orientalis*, part
VI (Frankfurt, 1604).[2]

Since my earlier paper appeared I have discovered that not only is the
Dutch original still extant, but it has been reissued in a modern edition
by S. P. L'Honoré Naber in *Werken uitgegeven door de Linschoten-
Vereeniging*, 5 (The Hague, 1912). The title is *Beschryvinghe ende His-*

Reprinted with permission from *English Studies* (1959), 115-18.
[1] "Some Special West African English Words", *English Studies* XXXIV (1953):
282-91. [This volume, pp. 206-11.]
[2] Another German translation, by L. Hulsius, published in 1603, has not been
available to me. An anonymous French translation, *Description et recit historial du
riche royaume d'or de Gunea*, appeared at Amsterdam in 1605.

torische Verhael van het Gout Koninckrijck van Gunea, and the original
edition was printed at Amsterdam in 1602 by Cornelis Claesz.[3] Of the
author very little is known: he hides himself under the initials P. D. M.
and says that he had at various times visited the coast of Guinea. We
are able to expand the initials into Pieter de Marees, and there seems
every reason to believe his statement about his own travels. Beyond that
hardly anything is known.

It is in this work, then, that we have the first known occurrences of
the words *dash* and *ju-ju,* and it is important to bear this in mind in
considering the possible origins of these words. De Marees states ex-
pressly that they are words he has heard the Africans use; he quotes them
as foreign words.[4] But de Marees frequently makes the mistake, made
also by other travellers in West Africa, of assuming that the names for
various objects quoted to him by the Africans were those of the local
African language and not, as so often happened, the equivalent Portuguese words in a more or less corrupt form. For the Portuguese were
the first European nation to build permanent establishments on the coast
of Guinea, and the Portuguese language came apparently to be looked
upon by the Africans as the language of the white man of whatever
country. Negro-Portuguese, a kind of Pidgin Portuguese with some slight
admixture from other Romance languages, continued in use as a lingua
franca in West Africa for centuries. As an example of the fallacy to
which de Marees was prone I may quote "sy hebben mede eenen Man
die sy houden als Predicant, op hunne tael ghenoemt Fetissero" (p.68)
or, in the translation printed by Samuel Purchas, "They haue also a
Priest, who in their speech they call a *Fetissero*" (p.941).

When, therefore, we find de Marees saying "so moetmen hunlins
schenckasie geven, d'welck sy noemen Dache" (p.47) (Purchas p.937:
"then we must giue them some-what to boot, which they call *Dache*"),
there is good reason to think that he has made the usual mistake of regarding a Negro-Portuguese word, quoted by the Africans for his benefit,
as a genuine African word. As pointed out in my earlier paper, the original meaning of *dache* seems to have been 'toll' or 'tribute', and several
of the Romance languages offer close parallels in form and meaning, for
example earlier French *dache,*[5] Spanish *dacio,* and Italian *dazio,* all meaning 'tribute'.[6]

[3]   The references in the following pages are to L'Honoré Naber's reprint.
[4]   As L'Honoré Naber points out (p. 48 footnote), a dutchified form *dasje* occurs in an
official document of 1642, and the same spelling is used by W. Bosman, *Nauwkeurige
Beschryving van de Guinese Goud- Tand- en Slave-Kust,* vol. II (Utrecht, 1704): 274.
Dutch can probably claim the honour of being the first European language to naturalize
this word.
[5]   See Godefroy, *Dictionnaire de l'ancienne langue française,* vol. IX.
[6]   Since the above was written, a still earlier occurrence of our word has come to my

The word *ju-ju* presents greater difficulties, chiefly because it is not immediately recognizable in the form in which de Marees quotes it. He uses the word twice. First, in describing a drinking habit of the negroes: they do not empty their cup at the first draught, he says, but leave a little in it, which they pour on the ground saying "Jou" as if they were giving it to their fetish to drink. His spelling, however, is peculiar: "segghende I.O.V. als ghevende hunne Fetissos dat te drincken" (p.43). Gothard Arthus's German and Latin versions have *"Iou"* (pp.26 and 24 respectively), while Purchas has "saying, *I. OV*, as giuing their *Fetissos* that to drinke" (p.936). The second instance of our word in de Marees is in a description of a religious ceremony: after delivering an oration the fetish priest drinks from a pot of some liquid, while the congregation clap their hands together and cry "Jou, Jou". This time de Marees uses a somewhat different spelling, "roepende I. Ou. I. Ou" (p.69); Gothard Arthus's German and Latin versions have "I, ou, I, ou" and "Iou, Iou" respectively (pp.43 and 39), while Purchas has "cry *I. ou, I. ou*" (p.942). The case for identifying de Marees's word with modern *ju-ju* is in the first instance the similarity or identity of meaning, for obviously I.O.V. (or I. OV; I. Ou; I. ou; I, ou; or Iou) must be associated or identified with the meaning "fetish". Secondly, and this is the strongest argument, we find the same drinking habit mentioned by later travellers, who use the word *ju-ju* in describing it. Thus Oldfield[7] says, "When they take rum, they pour a little on the deck or in the river for the Ju-ju", and Baikie[8] describes a palaver with some Africans, which began by "drinking a glass of wine ... a few drops of which they, before tasting it, poured on the deck as dju-dju, or sacred".[9]

---

notice. G. B. Ramusio, in his *Navigationi et viaggi*, vol. III (Venice, 1565: pp. 423-32, prints a description of the coast of Guinea written about 1540 by an anonymous Frenchman from Dieppe. Of the Portuguese on the coast the author says that if they want any merchandise they must buy it from the local inhabitants, and they must pay dues (*datii*, modern *dazii*) to the king and princes of the country: "bisogna che le comprino da quelli del paese, & che ne paghino datij alli Re, & principi del paese" (p. 429). Here, at last, we seem to have traced the word back to its natural habitat, a Romance language.

[7] M. Laird & R. A. K. Oldfield, *Narrative of an Expedition into the Interior of Africa*, etc., vol. I (London, 1837): 323.

[8] W. K. Baikie, *Narrative of an Exploring Voyage up the Rivers Kwora and Binue* (London, 1856): 42.

[9] In a description of the coast of Guinea by B. Paludanus, published as part III of Linschoten's *Iterario* (1596; reissued by the Linschoten Society, The Hague, 1934), we find what is perhaps only an accidental likeness to our word. We are told that the natives on the banks of the river Gabon in present-day French Equatorial Africa greeted a party of white visitors with cries of "Io, Io, ende andere woorden" (p. 9). An anonymous French translation (3rd edition, Amsterdam, 1638) spells the phrase "Jo Jo" (p. 190).

The present English pronunciation of *ju-ju* is ['dʒu:dʒu:]. The relative antiquity of this pronunciation seems vouched for by spellings such as *Jew-Jew* (Crow, 1791)[10] and *Dju Dju* (R. & J. Lander, 1830).[11] One may wonder what pronunciation de Marees was aiming at representing when he wrote *Iou* (assuming that to be the right interpretation of his spelling). He obviously treated this word as well as *Dache* as foreign, and since it is clear from his African vocabulary (pp. 254-9) that he consistently rendered the vowel [u] in African words by *ou*, *Iou* appears to stand for [ʒu] or [dʒu] or more probably, as pronounced by Africans, [ɟu] with a dorso-palatal plosive instead of the affricate.

The next occurrence of our word that I have noted is in James Barbot's account of his visit in 1699 to Dony,[12] where he saw the king's "idol-house, which they call *Jou-Jou*" (p. 462). From the late eighteenth century onwards instances become fairly common in the literature of travel.

All occurrences of the word other than the first one in de Marees show reduplication, but since this is a common feature in many West African languages, we need not assume that it was an original part of the word: it could easily have been added later. Despite the widespread use of *ju-ju* in West Africa, the word seems to this day to be regarded by many Africans as the white people's term for a venerated object. Like *dash*, the word is probably European, and most likely Portuguese, in origin. A possible source would be the Portuguese word *Deus* 'God' with loss of the final consonant and change of [dĕu] to [dju] and [dʒu]. This etymology would form an interesting parallel to the development of *joss* "idol" from Portuguese *Deos* (a by-form of *Deus*) in Chinese Pidgin English.

The line of inquiry here pursued would seem a more satisfactory approach than the acceptance of the surgeon John Atkins's view of *dash* as a "Negrish" word and the repetition of the conjecture (originated by Mary Kingsley?) that *ju-ju* is derived from French *jou-jou* 'toy'. Both the latter explanations are to be found in the Oxford English Dictionary and are repeated, regrettably, in the revised third edition of the *Shorter Oxford English Dictionary* published in 1955.

Oslo.

---

[10] *Memoirs of the late Captain Hugh Crow of Liverpool* (London, 1830): 37.

[11] *Journal of an Expedition to Explore ... the Niger*, vol. III (London, 1832): 266.

[12] Near New Calabar and not, as erroneously stated in my earlier paper, in the Cameroons. The account is printed in A. & J. Churchill, *A Collection of Voyages and Travels*, vol. V (London, 1732).

C. M. WISE

NEGRO DIALECT

It is a principle discoverable by observation that small details of dialectal
difference tend to lose themselves in the surrounding language, so that
where the following outline does not appear to cover a given case, the
reader is safe to fall back upon the language of the section in which the
dialect is found. This is interestingly noticeable in the case of the two
French-American dialects, French-Canadian and Creole, where in the one
case that part of the sound system used which is not French, is English
of the general American type (usually), and in the other case of the
southern type.

But the principle is even more noticeable in Negro speech. Off-hand,
one would say that the Negro speech is of all dialects the most strikingly
different from cultivated English. In a sense this is true, but very many
of the differences are not articulatory or enunciatory, and are therefore
not easily reducible to phonetic terms. These differences are, instead,
somewhat as follows:

a.   Those of vocabulary, covering many, many word-substitutions, such
as *sont* for *sent* and *hope* for *help*.

b.   Of conjugation, as

ah	*has*	*we*		
you ⎫		*we's*	⎫	
yo' ⎬ *has*		*we-all*	⎬ *has*	
y'all ⎭		*us*	⎭	
		y'all	*has*	
he	*has*	*dey*	*has*	

(elegant) *have*

Reprinted with permission from the *Quarterly Journal of Speech* (1933).

c. Of declension, as

	Nom.	man	mens
	Gen.	man's	mens's

and

	Nom.	ah	we / we's / we-all / us
	Gen.	mah / mine	ouah, ouahs / we-all's / us's
	Acc.	me	we-all / us

d. Of intonation, (which is baffling to record on paper, despite excellent work on it by noted phoneticians), but which is really one of the outstanding characteristics of Negro speech.

e. Of placement, which is closely related to intonation and almost equally baffling to record phonetically — or rather to interpret, even when recorded — but which, nevertheless, is almost the characterizing element of Negro speech. (As between ignorant southern white speech and slightly literate Negro speech it often is THE characterizing element.)

It is more than ever necessary, then, for him who would reproduce the dialectal speech, to hear it, and to catch its intonations and placements at first hand. Having done this, he can, by observing the spellings of a given author and the sound system suggested herein, make a satisfactory approach to his task, for the Negro intonation patterns and placements are among the easiest in all languages to imitate successfully, perhaps for the very reason of their great differences from those of educated white speech.

A word is in order about dialect spelling, not merely of Negro dialect, but of all dialects. Authors cannot be expected to be phoneticians, and consequently their spellings are often inescapably imperfect. Moreover, writers must follow conventional spellings to a considerable degree, in order not to be annoying and unintelligible to the average reader. These spellings have to be interpreted by the reader or actor in the light of the probable intention of the authors. Southern authors, particularly, are careless about the handling of *r*'s. They will very likely indicate a silent *r* in *dah*, because that pronunciation is so radically different from their own *there* (ðɛə) that they feel as if something ought to be done about it; but since the Negro's pronunciation of *butter* is not likely to be different from the writer's own [bʌtə], it does not occur that to write it b-u-t-t-e-r will be misleading to every reader of the general American speech area. The reader simply has to understand that all the r's he encounters are to be treated as southern r's are customarily treated in the given contexts. Of course, if the southern writers desired to indicate a strikingly aberrant pronunciation, like [bʌtɐ] they might indicate it with b-u-t-t-a-h.

Despite the disclaimer of ability to put on paper anything of much help as to placement, the temptation remains to state thus much: the characteristic Negro vocal quality seems to result from a tongue position which may possibly be a heritage from the original African speech. This quality surely cannot result from any peculiar physical formation of Negro resonance cavities, for northern Negroes, reared among a majority of whites, have nothing of this Negro voice quality. When in relatively complete isolation from large numbers of their race who are either fresh from the South or who have preserved their southern voices by reason of social segregation and forced association with their own kind, these northern Negroes cannot be distinguished from white people through any voice characteristic. The test of the telephone in northern cities repeatedly proves this.

This southern Negro quality appears to come from a consistent elevation of the blade of the tongue in the direction of the hard palate — or of the juncture between the hard and soft palates. All vowels are consequently something less than open and free. The front vowels tend to take on a kind of [e]-resonance — [æ] and [ɛ] do so especially.

Negro enunciation tends to be lax and careless. Sometimes consonants seem actually to be omitted almost entirely. A certain Negro bricklayer, in saying NO, SIR, uses no pure consonant whatever — only a vowel and some vowel-like nasal continuants. In Evangeline Parish in Louisiana, it is often necessary to move very close to a group of Negro conversationalists to make sure whether the burbling stream of their vocables is intended for English or French — or a mixture of the two.

The speech of the Virginia Negroes is considerably different, and of the Carolina Negroes somewhat different, from that of Negroes in the rest of the South. Not that the rest of the South has homogeneous Negro speech; but in the rest of the South Negro speech is sufficiently homogeneous for general treatment. The data below apply to the South at large.

[ɑ] is used where customarily used in the South. That is, it is not used in "broad-a" positions, with the notable frequent exception of master [mɑːstə]. (Dialect writers of southern nativity often spell this word marster, using the supernumerary r as a lengthening sign, not realizing that general American speakers will pronounce the word [mɑrstər]. Other analogous variants, like strap [strɑp], stamp [stɑmp], will always be indicated in the spelling of the dialect writer. As a matter of fact, [ɑ] is by no means so frequently a pronunciation of an *a*-spelling as of "short *o*", as will appear. [ɑ] becomes [æ], however, in *drop* [dræp], *crop* [kræp].

[j] is inserted before vowels in words like *garden* [gja:dn], *kind* [kjaind] in some sections, principally Virginia and the Carolinas.

it is frequently [hɪt] in accented positions.

l is omitted from *self* [sɛf], *shelf* [ʃɛf], etc.

t is dropped from *next* [nɛks], *best* [bɛs], *soft* [sɔf], etc.

ts is dropped from *posts* [povs], *ghosts* [govs:], etc.

d is dropped from *sand* [sæn], *land* [læn], etc.

[ð] is changed to [d] in *this* [dɪs], *that* [dæt], *these* [diz], *them* [dɛm], *they* [deɪ], *with* [wɪd] and occasional other words. This substitution is practically universal for these particular words, but very scattering in other words. The Negro can say [θ] and [ð] perfectly well. It is only that he does not understand them to belong with the definite article, the demonstratives, the third personal plural pronoun and the preposition *with*. (Regretful to admit, neither do numbers of white people. However, in Louisiana, the substitution by whites very frequently originates in French accent.) [ð-θ] in *with* [wɪð, wɪθ] sometimes becomes [f] — [wɪf].

[b] is traditionally said to be substituted for [v]. Sometimes it really is, as in *culvert* [kʌlbət], *rivet* [rɪbət] etc., where the same substitution is common among illiterate whites even in the North. *River* may be heard as [rɪbə], but more often in sentimental pseudo-Negro song than in the speech of Negroes. Where the phonetic context sets the stage for [b] as in *does ye lub me* [dʌz ji lʌb mɪ], the [b] appears readily enough, but not in *leabe home* [lib hovm], as would-be consistent writers seem to believe.

Nasalization is found in Negro speech, but not to so great an extent as in white speech.

Hyper-urbanizing is known, as in [kitʃiŋ] for *kitchen*, [tʃikiŋ] for *chicken* etc.

Of idiosyncratic words there are hundreds. The spelling may be depended upon to suggest the pronunciation, if the suggestions above are remembered. Once more, intonation and vocal organ placement are the *sine qua non* of reproducing Negro speech.

The following tentative statement of hypothesis[1] concerning the persistence of Negro dialect and the reciprocal action of white and Negro speech upon each other in the South may help to clarify the relationship of white and Negro speech.

In the beginning, Negroes arriving from Africa learned their speech from their white owners, male and female; that is to say, the adult Negroes did. The children, prohibited from any great freedom of the white houses,

---

[1] This hypothesis is ventured without dogmatism. The writer is anxious to improve it and invites correspondence on the subject.

and to some extent prohibited from playing with white children, had to learn from their elders, who, of course, spoke a very broken English with their own characteristic placement and intonation. The children of these children learned from their own parents, and so on even to the present time, so that the faulty Afro-English of the first slaves has repeated itself generation after generation with only such modifications as the following may suggest.

It is true, as is often said, that the upper social class has a strong influence on the speech of the lower class. The operation of this principle in the South is considerably interfered with by the fact that on a plantation there may be only one white family and anywhere from ten to fifty Negro families, so that the numerical preponderance of speakers of broken English is very great. Then too, only a few so-called house Negroes have much opportunity to hear white people speak. Male Negroes hear white speech very little indeed, except from the overseers, who, through enforced continual association with field or industrial workers, often grow to speak considerably like Negroes themselves.

The result is not so much an improvement of the lower class speech in respect to pronunciation as a borrowing of high sounding words after the well known Negro fashion. The improvement might by this time have been much greater if the Negroes had been in the least degree literate, or if, like the lower classes of England, they might have realized that there was such a thing as a speech problem and become sensitized to differences between their own speech and that of white people. But the average southern Negro is entirely unconscious of his variant speech, and does not know that improving it would improve his social standing — up to a point where his pigmentation would effectually block further advancement.

There is the added fact that a very large majority of southern Negroes have always, both before the war and after, been quite content in their subordinate positions, conditioned to them from childhood. They have no idea of how affairs could be different. Now that Negroes are becoming slightly educated, some of the principles just explained will gradually cease to operate.

It may be interesting to consider for the moment how white speech has been influenced by Negro speech. In infancy, nearly every white person is cared for by a Negro servant and first learns to talk partly from her. The social scorn which he will later feel for Negroes and Negro speech is not yet operative and his neuro-muscular patterns are rapidly becoming fixed. If allowed to play with Negro children at all, the white child will be further conditioned to Negro speech, for it is well known that children learn their speech from playmates much more than from their busy, preoccupied parents. After the child leaves the nurse's hands, impacts of Negro speech on his own lessen in frequency very greatly except perhaps in the case of some women who converse more or less freely with their Negro house servants. In the adult life of males, the influence returns, as we have seen, in isolated cases where a single white man will be overseeing large groups of Negro workers. One may in rare cases hear such speakers whose speech not merely has the intonation of Negroes, but which has taken over the Negro verb-forms, as in *You is*, *is ye*, and *Ah gin it up*.

In general, one may say that white speech affects Negro speech very little indeed, and that Negro speech affects white speech very little after the childhood of the white speaker.

Louisiana State University

WILLIAM A. STEWART

SOCIOLINGUISTIC FACTORS IN THE HISTORY OF AMERICAN NEGRO DIALECTS

Within the last few years, the increased national commitment to bettering the lot of socially and economically underprivileged groups of Americans — the so-called "disadvantaged" — has caused educators to consider ways in which the schools may involve themselves in this task. Of the many possibilities, certainly one of the most obvious is to deal with the chronic language problems associated with many of the disadvantaged. Yet, although there is a general awareness that certain of the disadvantaged do have language problems, there is at the same time a lack of agreement as to what these problems entail, and therefore what to do about them. Some investigators (often educational psychologists) have maintained that the disadvantaged characteristically do not use verbal communication to the extent that members of the middle class do, and are thus impoverished in "communicative skills". To alleviate this situation, they have recommended programs aimed at encouraging the use of verbal communication of a variety of kinds by disadvantaged pupils. A few investigators have theorized that members of disadvantaged groups may even engage less in abstract thinking than do middle-class persons. For this there have been suggested programs designed to teach more perception and conceptualization on the part of the disadvantaged pupils.

On the other hand, linguists have tended to emphasize one other type of language problem which some disadvantaged groups often have, and for which evidence is quite accessible — being encountered every day in the nation's classrooms. This is the purely structural conflict between on

Reprinted with the permission of the *Florida FL Reporter* and the author from vol. 5, No. 2 (Spring 1967): 11, 22, 24, 26, 30, Alfred C. Aarons, ed.

the one hand the patterns of a non-standard dialect which an individual may have learned at home or in peer-group interaction, and on the other hand the equivalent patterns of standard English — the language of modern technology and of the middle class. This is one kind of problem which many of the nation's schools ought to be ready and willing to cope with. One indication of the readiness of the schools is the fact that traditional English teachers are rapidly abandoning the older "sloppy speech" and "lazy tongue" views of non-standard speech in favor of a realization that it usually represents the speaker's use of some language system which, though it may differ from standard English in form and sometimes even in function, is nevertheless logical, coherent, and (in its own way) grammatical. Another indication of the readiness of schools to cope with the problem of dialect differences is the growth of a cadre of specialists in the teaching of English to speakers of other languages. With them, there has come into being a set of new techniques for teaching English to persons coming from a different language background.

Just as they are ready, America's schools certainly ought to be willing to deal with dialect-based problems, since there are a number of ways in which, by themselves, they can render a non-standard speaker dysfunctional in exchanges with standard-English-speaking members of the middle class. One way is for minor pronunciation differences between a non-standard dialect and standard English — each one perhaps trivial by itself — to pile up in an utterance to such an extent that the non-standard version becomes unintelligible to a middle-class listener, even though in grammar and vocabulary it may be quite similar to its standard equivalent. Thus, a non-standard version of 'I don't know where they live' might, in one dialect, become cryptic to the standard-speaking listener, merely because of its being pronounced something like *Ah 'own know wey 'ey lib*. Or, a standard English speaker may misunderstand a non-standard utterance, even though he thinks he has deciphered it correctly, because it contains non-standard grammatical constructions which are unknown to him. For example, a middle-class listener may take a non-standard sentence *Dey ain't like dat* to mean 'they aren't like that', when it really means 'They didn't like that'. The standard-English speaker is simply unaware that *ain't* is this particular dialect's way of negating verbs in the past tense, as he is unaware that the usual equivalent in the same dialect of 'They aren't like that' would be either *Dey not like dat* or *Dey don't be like dat* (the two variants indicating a difference in meaning which is not easily expressed in standard English). Of course, similar breakdowns in intelligibility may also occur in the other direction, when the non-standard speaker tries to understand standard English. Finally, even when he does succeed in making himself understood by his middle-class listeners, the non-standard speaker may still fall victim to the difference in social prestige between his dialect and standard English. In other words, although middle-class persons may understand what he is saying, they may still consider him uncouth for saying it the way he does.

Professionally able though the schools may now be to embark on programs which would deal effectively with this kind of problem, the likelihood of their actually doing so in the near future is certainly not increased by the unwillingness of many educators and even some applied linguists to approach the problem in any but the most general terms. For, unfortunately, the technical know-how necessary to teach standard English to speakers of non-standard dialects is simply not embodied in an awareness of the problem at the level of "Some children should probably be taught standard English as a second dialect" — no matter how true such statements may be. The necessary know-how will begin to be adequate when and only when applied linguists can give, and educators will take seriously, details of the type "The verb system of such-and-such a nonstandard dialect operates in such-and-such a way, and the verb system of standard English operates in such-and-such a way, so that structural interference is most likely to occur at points *a*, *b*, and *c*. Therefore, the following lessons and drills in the standard English verb system are what children who speak this non-standard dialect will need."[1]

One reason why there is little remedial English now being taught based upon a systematic comparison of the differences between non-standard dialects and standard English is that information about one of the pedagogically most important features of non-standard dialects — their grammatical systems — is still largely lacking. This lack is due in great part to the fact that American dialect studies have traditionally emphasized differences in pronunciation and vocabulary, at the expense of information on systematic grammatical differences.

Now that linguists have begun to fill this information gap, however, they are finding their observations on language variation among the disadvantaged received with uneasiness and even hostility by many teachers, administrators, and community leaders. The reason for this is undoubtedly that the accurate description of dialect variation in American communities — particularly in urban centers — is turning out to show a disturbing correlation between language behavior on the one hand and socio-economic and ethnic stratification on the other.[2] The correlation

[1] See William A. Stewart, editor, *Non-Standard Speech and the Teaching of English* (Washington, D.C., Center for Applied Linguistics, 1964).
[2] The American Dream notwithstanding, it is well known to social scientists that American society is stratified into a number of social classes and ethnic groups, and that each of these exhibits a "characteristic" configuration of customs, attitudes, roles, life-ways and, as it turns out, speech patterns. The literature on social and ethnic stratification is extensive, but good introductions are Egon Ernest Bergel, *Social Stratification* (New York, McGraw-Hill Book Co., 1962), and Tamotsu Shibutani and Kian

is particularly controversial insofar as it involves the speech of large numbers of American Negroes, since at the present time Negro leadership (and this includes most Negro educators) is probably more achievement-oriented than any other. Because of this orientation, Negro elites tend not to welcome any evidence of uniform or stable behavioral differences between members of their own group (even lower-class ones) and those of the white-dominated middle class. Yet the fact is that Negroes account for most of the most pedagogically problematic non-standard dialect speakers in the larger cities, and also include within their group speakers of the most radically non-standard dialects of natively-spoken English in the entire country.[3] Furthermore, because *de facto* segregation in housing has caused non-standard-dialect-speaking Negroes to predominate in many schools and because these Negroes appear in many cases to have different kinds of problems with standard English than non-standard-dialect-speaking whites have (even in the same area), the sweeping, for political purposes, of Negro dialect descriptions under the white-oriented geographic dialect rug would probably be more detrimental to disadvantaged Negro children than it would be advantageous to Negro elites.[4]

On the other hand, linguists should realize that the fears and anxieties of Negro leaders about public discussion of ethnically correlated behavioral differences may have some foundation. It is possible, for example, that quite objective and innocently-made statements about dialect differences between whites and Negroes might be interpreted by white racists as evidence of Negro cultural backwardness or mental inferiority, or even seized upon by black racists as evidence of some sort of mythical Negro "soul". Linguists should not censor their data, but they should make sure that their statements about Negro-white differences are not divorced from an awareness of the historical, social, and linguistic reasons why such differences may have come into existence and been maintained. Perhaps it would serve that end to point out here some of the socio-

---

M. Kwan, *Ethnic Stratification* (New York, The MacMillan Co., 1965). For an exhaustively documented study of the correlation between language variation and social class, ethnicity, and age in an American metropolis, see William Labov, *The Social Stratification of English in New York City* (Washington, D.C., The Center for Applied Linguistics, 1966).

[3] These two facts may not be entirely unrelated. For a graphic indication of the relatively more non-standard grammatical norms of Negro children over white children in a single city, see Figure 18 (page 53) in Walter Loban, *Problems in Oral English: Kindergarten Through Grade Nine* (Champaign, Ill. National Council of Teachers of English, 1966).

[4] For a discussion of Negro dialect in one urban community, see William A. Stewart, "Urban Negro Speech: Sociolinguistic Factors Affecting English Teaching", in Roger W. Shuy, editor, *Social Dialects and Language Learning* (Champaign, Ill., National Council of Teachers of English, 1965). The non-standard dialect patterns cited earlier in the present article are also Negro dialect.

linguistic factors involved in the evolution of American Negro dialects, factors which explain why certain kinds of American Negro dialects are both different from the non-standard dialects of American whites, and more radically deviant from standard English.

Although the linguistic history of the Negro in the United States can be reconstructed from the numerous literary attestations of the English of New World Negroes over the last two and a half centuries, and by comparing these with the English of Negroes in the United States, the Caribbean, and West Africa today, this has never been done for the English teaching profession. In presenting a historical sketch of this type, I realize that both the facts presented and my interpretations of them may embarrass or even infuriate those who would like to white-wash American Negro dialects by claiming that they do not exist — that (in spite of all sorts of observable evidence to the contrary) they are nothing but Southern white dialects, derived directly from Great Britain. I will simply make no apologies to those who regard human behavior as legitimate only if observed in the white man, since I feel that this constitutes a negation of the cultural and ethnic plurality which is one of America's greatest heritages. On the other hand, I do regret that such a historical survey, although linguistically interesting, may at times conjure up out of the past memories of the Negro-as-slave to haunt the aspirations of the Negro-as-equal.

Of those Africans who fell victim to the Atlantic slave trade and were brought to the New World, many found it necessary to learn some kind of English. With very few exceptions, the form of English which they acquired was a pidginized one, and this kind of English became so well established as the principal medium of communication between Negro slaves in the British colonies that it was passed on as a creole language to succeeding generations of the New World Negroes, for whom it was their native tongue.[5] Some idea of what New World Negro English may

---

[5] In referring to types of languages, linguists use the terms PIDGIN and CREOLE in a technical sense which has none of the derogatory or racial connotations of popular uses of these terms. When a linguist says that a variety of language is pidginized, he merely means that it has a markedly simplified grammatical structure compared with the "normal" (i.e. unpidginized) source-language. This simplification may be one way in which speakers of different languages can make a new language easier to learn and use — particularly if they have neither the opportunity nor the motivation to learn to speak it the way its primary users do. In addition, some of the unique characteristics of a pidgin language may be due, not to simplification, but to influences on it from the native languages of its users. What is important to realize, however, is that pidginized languages do have grammatical structure and regularity, even though their specific patterns may be different from those of the related unpidginized source-language of higher prestige. Thus, the fact that the sentence *Dem no get-am* in present-day West African Pidgin English is obviously different from its standard English equivalent 'They don't have it' does not necessarily indicate that the Pidgin English speaker "talks

have been like in its early stages can be obtained from a well-known example of the speech of a fourteen-year-old Negro lad given by Daniel Defoe in *The Family Instructor* (London, 1715). It is significant that the Negro, Toby, speaks a pidginized kind of English to his boy master, even though he states that he was born in the New World.

A sample of his speech is:[6]

Toby. Me be born at Barbadoes.
Boy. Who lives there, Toby?
Toby. There lives white mans, white womans, negree mans, negree womans, just so as live here.
Boy. What and not know God?
Toby. Yes, the white mans say God prayers, — no much know God.
Boy. And what do the black mans do?
Toby. They much work, much work, — no say God prayers, not at all.
Boy. What work do they do, Toby?
Toby. Makee the sugar, makee the ginger, — much great work, weary work, all day, all night.

Even though the boy master's English is slightly non-standard (e.g. *black mans*), it is still quite different from the speech of the Negro.

An idea of how widespread a pidginized form of English had become among the Negro population of the New World by the end of the Seventeenth Century can be gathered from the fact that it had even become the language of the coastal plantations in the Dutch colony of Surinam (i.e. Dutch Guiana), in South America. In an early description of that colony, the chapter on the Negro ends with a sample conversation in the local Negro English dialect. The dialogue includes such sentences as *Me bella well* 'I am very well', *You wantee siddown pinkininne?* 'Do you want to sit down for a bit?', and *You wantee go walka longa me?* 'Do you want to take a walk with me?'[7] In these sentences, the use of the enclitic vowel

---

without grammar". In producing such a sentence, he is unconsciously obeying the grammatical rules of West African Pidgin English, and these determine that *Dem no get-am* is the "right" construction, as opposed to such ungrammatical or "wrong" combinations as *No dem get-am, No get dem-am, Get-am dem no* etc. If a pidgin finally becomes the native language of a speech community (and thereby becomes by definition a creole language), it may expand in grammatical complexity to the level of "normal" or unpidginized languages. Of course, the resulting creole language may still exhibit structural differences from the original source-language, because the creole has gone through a pidginized stage. For more details, see Robert A. Hall, Jr., *Pidgin and Creole Languages* (Ithaca, N.Y., Cornell U. Press, 1966).
[6]   The same citation is given in a fuller form, along with a number of other attestations of early New World Negro speech, in George Philip Krapp, *The English Language in America*, vol. I (New York, The Century Co., 1925): 255-65. Other attestations are cited in Tremaine McDowell, "Notes on Negro Dialect in the American Novel to 1821", *American Speech* V (1930): 291-96.
[7]   J. D. Herlein, *Beschryvinge van de volksplantinge Zuriname* (Leeuwarden, 1718):

in *wantee* recalls the same in Defoe's example *makee*. Also, the speaker, like Toby, uses *me* as a subject pronoun. In the first Surinam sentence, we see an early example of a construction without any equivalent of the standard English verb *to be*. Toby also would probably have said *Me weary*, since the *be* in his first sentence was in all likelihood a past-tense marker (as it is in present-day West African Pidgin English) — the sentence therefore meaning 'I was born in Barbadoes'. In the last Surinam sentence, a reflex of English *along* is used with the meaning of standard English 'with'. It may or may not be accidental that in the Gullah dialect, spoken by the Negroes along the South Carolina coastal plain, the same phenomenon occurs e.g. *Enty you wantuh walk long me?* 'Do you want to take a walk with me?' Some Gullah speakers even still use *me* as a subject pronoun e.g. *Me kyaan bruk-um* 'I can't break it', and enclitic final vowels seem to have survived in such Gullah forms as *yerry, yeddy* 'to hear'.

Early examples of Negro dialect as spoken in the American colonies show it to be strikingly similar to that given by Defoe for the West Indies and by Herlein for Surinam. In John Leacock's play, *The Fall of British Tyranny* (Philadelphia, 1776), part of the conversation between a certain "Kidnapper" and Cudjo, one of a group of Virginia Negroes, goes as follows:[8]

Kidnapper. ... what part did you come from
Cudjo. Disse brack man, disse one, disse one, disse one, come from Hamton, disse one, disse one, come from Nawfok, me come from Nawfok too.
Kidnapper. Very well, what was your master's name?
Cudjo. Me massa name Cunney Tomsee.
Kidnapper. Colonel Thompson — eigh?
Cudjo. Eas, massa, Cunney Tomsee.
Kidnapper. Well then I'll make you a major — and what's your name?
Cudjo. Me massa cawra me Cudjo.

Again, the enclitic vowels (e.g. *disse*) and the subject pronoun *me* are prominent features of the Negro dialect. In the sentence *Me massa name Cunney Tomsee* 'My master's name is Colonel Thompson', both the verb *to be* and the standard English possessive suffix *-s* are absent. Incidentally,

121-23. Herlein gives the Negro English dialogues in Dutch orthography. I have retranscribed these sentences in the kind of spelling which his English contemporaries would have used in order to show better the relationship between the Surinam dialect and the other examples. In the Dutch spelling, these sentences appear as *My belle wel, Jou wantje sie don pinkinine?*, and *Jo wantje gaeu wakke lange mie?*
[8] This citation also occurs in Krapp, and with others in Richard Walser, "Negro Dialect in Eighteenth-Century American Drama", *American Speech* XXX (1955): 269-76.

Cudjo's construction is strikingly similar to sentences like *My sister name Mary* which are used by many American Negroes today.

One possible explanation why this kind of pidginized English was so widespread in the New World, with widely separated varieties resembling each other in so many ways, is that it did not originate in the New World as isolated and accidentally similar instances of random pidginization, but rather originated as a *lingua franca* in the trade centers and slave factories on the West African coast.[9] It is likely that at least some Africans already knew this pidgin English when they came to the New World, and that the common colonial policy of mixing slaves of various tribal origins forced its rapid adoption as a plantation *lingua franca*.

In the course of the Eighteenth Century, some significant changes took place in the New World Negro population, and these had their effect on language behavior. For one thing, the number of Negroes born in the New World came to exceed the number of those brought over from Africa. In the process, pidgin English became the creole mother-tongue of the new generations, and in some areas it has remained so to the present day.[10]

In the British colonies, the creole English of the uneducated Negroes and the English dialects of both the educated and uneducated whites were close enough to each other (at least in vocabulary) to allow the speakers of each to communicate, although they were still different enough so that the whites could consider creole English to be "broken" or "corrupt" English and evidence, so many thought, of the mental limitations of the Negro. But in Surinam, where the European settlers spoke Dutch, creole English was regarded more objectively. In fact, no less than two language courses specifically designed to teach creole English to Dutch immigrants were published before the close of the Eighteenth Century.[11]

Another change which took place in the New World Negro population primarily during the course of the Eighteenth Century was the social cleavage of the New World-born generations into underprivileged field-hands (a continuation of the older, almost universal lot of the Negro slave) and privileged domestic servant. The difference in privilege usually meant, not freedom instead of bondage, but rather freedom from degrading kinds of labor, access to the "big house" with its comforts and

[9] See, for example, Basil Davidson, *Black Mother; The Years of the African Slave Trade* (Boston, Little, Brown and Co., 1961), particularly p. 218.

[10] In the West Indies, creole English is usually called PATOIS, while in Surinam it is called TAKI-TAKI. In the United States, the only fairly "pure" creole English left today is Gullah, spoken along the coast of South Carolina.

[11] These were Pieter van Dijk, *Nieuwe en nooit bevoorens geziende onderwijzinge in het Bastert Engels, of Neeger Engels* (Amsterdam, undated, but probably 1780), and G. C. Weygandt, *Gemeenzame leerwijze om het Basterd of Neger-Engels op een gemakkelijke wijze te leeren verstaan en spreeken* (Paramaribo, 1798).

"civilization", and proximity to the prestigious "quality" whites, with the opportunity to imitate their behavior (including their speech) and to wear their clothes. In some cases, privilege included the chance to get an education and, in a very few, access to wealth and freedom. In both the British colonies and the United States, Negroes belonging to the privileged group were soon able to acquire a more standard variety of English than the creole of the field-hands, and those who managed to get a decent education became speakers of fully standard and often elegant English. This seems to have become the usual situation by the early 1800's, and remained so through the Civil War. In Caroline Gilman's *Recollections of a Southern Matron* (New York, 1838), the difference between field-hand creole (in this case, Gullah) and domestic servant dialect is evident in a comparison of the gardener's "He tief one sheep — he run away las week, cause de overseer gwine for flog him" with Dina's "'Scuse me, missis, I is gitting hard o' hearing, and yes is more politer dan no" (page 254). A more striking contrast between the speech of educated and uneducated Negroes occurs in a novel written in the 1850's by an American Negro who had traveled extensively through the slave states. In chapter XVII, part of the exchange between Henry, an educated Negro traveler, and an old "aunty" goes as follows:[12]

"Who was that old man who ran behind your master's horse?"
"Dat Nathan, my husban'."
"Do they treat him well, aunty?"
"No, chile, wus an' any dog, da beat 'im foh little an nothin'."
"Is uncle Nathan religious?"
"Yes, chile, ole man an' I's been sahvin' God dis many day, fo yeh baun! Wen any on 'em in de house git sick, den da sen foh 'uncle Nathan' come pray foh dem; 'uncle Nathan' mighty good den!"

After the Civil War, with the abolition of slavery, the breakdown of the plantation system, and the steady increase in education for poor as well as affluent Negroes, the older field-hand creole English began to lose many of its creole characteristics, and take on more and more of the features of the local white dialects and of the written language. Yet, this process has not been just one way. For if it is true that the speech of American Negroes has been strongly influenced by the speech of whites with whom they came into contact, it is probably also true that the speech of many whites has been influenced in some ways by the speech of Negroes.[13]

[12] Martin R. Delany, "Blake; or the Huts of America", published serially in *The Anglo-African Magazine* (1859). The quotation is from vol. 1, no. 6, June (1859): 163.
[13] See Raven I. McDavid, Jr. and Virginia Glenn McDavid, "The Relationship of the Speech of American Negroes to the Speech of Whites", *American Speech* XXVI (1951): 3-17.

Over the last two centuries, the proportion of American Negroes who speak a perfectly standard variety of English has risen from a small group of privileged house slaves and free Negroes to persons numbering in the hundreds of thousands, and perhaps even millions. Yet there is still a sizeable number of American Negroes — undoubtedly larger than the number of standard-speaking Negroes — whose speech may be radically non-standard. The non-standard features in the speech of such persons may be due in part to the influence of the non-standard dialects of whites with whom they or their ancestors have come in contact, but they also may be due to the survival of creolisms from the older Negro field-hand speech of the plantations. To insure their social mobility in modern American society, these non-standard speakers must undoubtedly be given a command of standard English; that point was made in the early part of this paper. In studying non-standard Negro dialects and teaching standard English in terms of them, however, both the applied linguist and the language teacher must come to appreciate the fact that even if certain non-standard Negro dialect patterns do not resemble the dialect usage of American whites, or even those of the speakers of remote British dialects, they may nevertheless be as old as African and European settlement in the New World, and therefore quite widespread and well-established. On various occasions, I have pointed out that many speakers of non-standard American Negro dialects make a grammatical and semantic distinction by means of *be*, illustrated by such constructions as *he busy* 'He is busy (momentarily)' or *he workin'* 'he is working (right now)' as opposed to *he be busy* 'he is (habitually) busy' or *he be workin'* 'he is working (steadily)', which the grammar of standard English is unable to make.[14] Even this distinction goes back well over a century. One observer in the 1830's noted a request by a slave for a permanent supply of soap as "(If) Missis only give we, we be so clean forever", while *be* is absent in a subsequent report of someone's temporary illness with "She jist sick for a little while".[15]

Once educators who are concerned with the language problems of the disadvantaged come to realize that non-standard Negro dialects represent a historical tradition of this type, it is to be hoped that they will become less embarrassed by evidence that these dialects are very much alike throughout the country while different in many ways from the non-standard dialects of whites, less frustrated by failure to turn non-standard Negro dialect speakers into standard English speakers overnight, less impatient with the stubborn survival of Negro dialect features in the speech of even educated persons, and less zealous on proclaiming what is "right" and what is "wrong". If this happens, then applied linguists

---

[14] See, for example, *The Florida FL Reporter*, vol. 4, no. 2, Winter (1965-66): 25.
[15] Frances Anne Kemble, *Journal of a Residence on a Georgian Plantation in 1838-39* (New York, 1862). The first quotation is from page 52, and the second is from page 118.

and educators will be able to communicate with each other, and both will be able to communicate with the non-standard-speaking Negro child. The problem will then be well on its way toward a solution.

Center for Applied Linguistics

WILLIAM A. STEWART

CONTINUITY AND CHANGE IN AMERICAN
NEGRO DIALECTS

In a previous article on the history of American Negro dialects[1] I cited
examples of the kind of literary and comparative evidence which exists
for determining earlier stages of these dialects, and which practically
forces the conclusion that the linguistic assimilation of the Afro-American
population to the speech patterns of English-speaking American whites
was neither as rapid nor as complete as some scholars have supposed.[2]

Reprinted with the permission of *The Florida FL Reporter* and the author from
vol. 6, no. 1 (Spring 1968): 3-4, 14-16, 18, Alfred C. Aarons, ed.
[1] William A. Stewart, "Sociolinguistic Factors in the History of American Negro Dialects", *The Florida FL Reporter*, vol. 5, no. 2, Spring (1967). [This volume, pp. 222-32.]
[2] E.g. "The Negroes born in this country invariably used, according to these records,
good English." Allen Walker Read, "The Speech of Negroes in Colonial America",
The Journal of Negro History, vol. 24, no. 3 (the quote is from page 258). The records
which Read refers to are for the most part runaway slave advertisements published
before the American Revolution. Of course, the evidence which they supply on slave
speech is indirect (i.e. they give impressions of the particular slave's competence in
English, but no examples of that English), since the information was merely intended to
help identify the runaway. If these indirect records say what Read interprets them as
saying, then they are certainly at variance with what direct evidence (quotations in
slave dialect) is available from the same period. Furthermore, the far larger number of
attestations of slave speech during the nineteenth century which show wide-spread use
of non-standard dialect, together with a similar situation observable today, would
mean that American Negro speech generally became less standard after that first generation of American-born slaves. Needless to say, such a process would be difficult to explain
either structurally or historically. The trouble with Read's conclusion seems to be that,
in interpreting such advertisements, he did not consider the possibility that in the parlance
of slave owners a term like "good English" might have meant something very different
when applied to Negroes than it would have if applied to whites. Indications that this
was probably the case seem to exist in the advertisements quoted on pp. 252-53.

Of the Negro slaves who constituted the field labor force on North
American plantations up to the mid-nineteenth century, even many who
were born in the New World spoke a variety of English which was in
fact a true creole language — differing markedly in grammatical structure
from those English dialects which were brought directly from Great
Britain, as well as from New World modifications of these in the mouths
of descendants of the original white colonists.³ And, although this creole
English subsequently underwent modification in the direction of the more
prestigious British-derived dialects, the merging process was neither in-
stantaneous nor uniform. Indeed, the non-standard speech of present-
day American Negroes still seems to exhibit structural traces of a creole
predecessor, and this is probably a reason why it is in some ways more
deviant from standard English than is the non-standard speech of even
the most uneducated American whites.

For the teacher, this means that such "Negro" patterns as the "zero
copula",⁴ the "zero possessive"⁵ or "undifferentiated pronouns"⁶ should
not be ascribed to greater carelessness, laziness or stupidity on the part
of Negroes, but rather should be treated as what they really are —
language patterns which have been in existence for generations and which
their present users have acquired, from parent and peer, through a perfectly normal kind of language-learning process.⁷

³ The Gullah (or Geechee) dialect, spoken by many Negroes along the South Atlantic
coast, appears to be a fairly direct descendant of the older kind of plantation creole.
⁴ The term "zero copula" refers to the absence of an explicit predicating verb in
certain dialect constructions, where standard English has such a verb (usually in the
present tense). Compare non-standard Negro dialect *He old, Dey runnin'*, and *She a
teacher* with standard English 'He is old', 'they are running' and 'She is a teacher'.
⁵ The term "zero possessive" refers to the absence of an explicit suffix in noun-
noun constructions, where standard English has such a suffix. Compare non-standard
Negro dialect *My fahver frien'* with standard English 'My father's friend'.
⁶ The term "undifferentiated pronoun" refers to the use of the same pronoun form for
both subject and object, and sometimes for possession as well. The pronominal form
used may be derived from either the standard English object form, or the subject form.
Compare such non-standard forms as *Him know we, Him know us* (beside *He know us*)
with the standard English 'He knows us' to which they are equivalent. Or compare
He fahver (beside *His fahver*) and *We house* (beside *Our house*) with standard English
'His father' and 'Our house'.
⁷ If the term "Negro dialect" is understood to refer to non-standard varieties of
American English whose more unique (i.e., non-white and non-British) structural
features are simply due to the historical influence of an earlier plantation creole, then
it should be clear that such a term does not imply any direct genetic determination of
speech patterns, in spite of its ethnic reference. The "Negro" in "Negro dialect" is
merely a recognition of the fact that the creole predecessor for such structural features
was itself the result of African migration to and acculturation in Anglo-Saxon America,
and that those present-day dialects which show the greatest influence from such a
creole are precisely those which are used by the descendants of the Negro field hands
who originally spoke it. In addition, the speech of American Negroes is often charac-

Since the main purpose of the earlier article was to document the use of creole English by native-born American Negroes during the colonial and ante-bellum periods, almost nothing was said about the course of Negro dialects since Emancipation. But, as anyone can see who compares written samples of Negro dialect from around the Civil War with Negro dialect today, there have been changes. And, equally interesting, one can also see that there are still many similarities between the two. An overview of the interacting processes of continuity and change in American Negro dialects as they relate to one important aspect of language variation — grammatical structure — will help educators to put the classroom language problems of today's disadvantaged Negro children into a clearer perspective.

One of the more important changes which have occurred in American Negro dialects during the past century has been the almost complete decreolization of both their functional and lexical vocabulary. Although this process actually began long before the Civil War (particularly in areas with a low proportion of Negroes to whites), the breakdown of the plantation system apparently accelerated it considerably, even in the coastal areas of South Carolina and Georgia. In the process, overt creolisms which were so common in early attestations of slave speech, such as *been* for marking past action (with no basic distinction between preterite and perfect), undifferentiated pronouns for subject and object (e.g., *me*, *him*, and *dem* also as subject pronouns and *we* also as an object pronoun), a single subject pronoun form (usually *him* or *he*) for masculine, feminine and neuter in the third person singular, *-um* (or *-am*) as a general third person (all genders and numbers) object suffix, *no* as a verbal negator, and *for* as an infinitive marker became quite rare in even the more non-standard speech of Negroes born after Emancipation.[8]

---

terized by special kinds of syllable and breath dynamics, as well as unique uses of pitch, stress and volume. But even these language habits are always socially learned and transmitted ones, although it is difficult to tell whether they represent survivals of African speech habits, creole speech habits, or are more recent innovations. That they are not the product of any special Negro vocal physiology should be obvious from the fact that some whites can mimic such features quite well, while there are some Negroes in whose speech the same features are not normally present.

[8] Judging from the literary treatment of Negro dialect, these features were characteristic of the non-standard speech of even New England Negroes up to the close of the eighteenth century. Within the first decades of the nineteenth century, however, the northern limit of their common occurrence in adult speech appears to have receded to the Delaware region, and to somewhere in the Carolinas by the middle of the same century. Of course, most of these creolisms still occur in Gullah — at least sporadically. And it is likely that the *for to* infinitives of some Deep South Negro dialects are the result of incomplete de-creolization (the adding of non-creole *to*, without giving up the creole *for*), rather than the borrowing of a white non-standard dialect pattern, as some might suppose. In the first place, such white dialects (Appalachia, Georgia, etc.) usually

However, the speed and thoroughness with which the plantation field-hand dialects were thus made more "proper" varied both according to the region and according to the social characteristics of the speakers themselves. Because people learn most of their language forms from others, the change took place more rapidly and completely in areas where speakers (white or Negro) of more-or-less standard varieties of English were present in numbers than it did in areas with a high concentration of field laborers. On the other hand, because children generally are more affected by the language usage of other children than by that of grown-ups, and because lower-class child peer groups tend to remain rather isolated from the stylistic innovations of adult discourse, the change took place more slowly and less thoroughly in the speech of young children than it did in that of adolescents and adults.

The result of this uneven "correction" of the older plantation dialects was that, while they seemed to have died out by the end of the nineteenth century (particularly outside the South Atlantic coastal area and the Mississippi Basin), juvenile versions of them actually continued to survive in many Negro speech communities as "baby talk" or "small-boy talk".[9]

---

have a contrast between *to* and *for to* e.g. *I come to see it* (i.e. 'It dawned on me') vs. *I come for to see it* ('I came in order to see it') while many Negro dialects in which *for to* occurs do not make such a distinction. In the second place, there is piecemeal evidence of the addition of *to* after *for* along the South Atlantic coast, where the change has been relatively recent. For example, in *Drums and Shadows: Survival Studies Among the Georgia Coastal Negroes* (Athens, Ga., 1940:144) a team of the Georgia Writers' Project interviewed an old lady (then approximately one hundred years old) who, speaking of an African-born slave whom she knew in her youth, recalled "I membuh he say 'Lemme cook sumpm fuh nyam.' He mean sumpm fuh to eat." Notice also the de-creolization of the Gullah and Caribbean Creole English verb *nyam* 'to eat'. In some areas, the changeover was not so complete, cf. a literary reflection of a Gullah Negro's alternation between the same two verbs in Ambrose E. Gonzales, *The Captain: Stories of the Black Border* (Columbia, S.C.: The State Co., 1924:149), "You hab mout' fuh nyam da' haa'd hoecake you juntlemun gi' you fuh eat."

[9] The impression that the rustic and creole features of the older plantation dialects died out entirely during this period is easy to get, considering that the speech of children hardly appears at all in the records of folklorists or dialectologists, or even in the fictional use of dialect, since the main concern of the social scientist and the novelist alike has been the adult. Evidence that the older dialects have in fact survived in the speech of children is only now coming to light through recent studies of present-day Negro speech communities. See William A. Stewart "Urban Negro Speech: Sociolinguistic Factors Affecting English Teaching", in Roger W. Shuy, editor, *Social Dialects and Language Learning* (Champaign, Ill.: National Council of Teachers of English, 1965), particularly pp. 16-18, and J. L. Dillard, "Negro Children's Dialect in the Inner City", *The Florida FL Reporter*, vol. 5, no. 3, Fall (1967). It would seem that the preservation of a more conservative dialect by young children in communities where the older language forms are being encroached upon by imported ones is not limited to Negro communities. During a recent sociolinguistic survey of the Appalachian region, I found full-fledged mountain dialect still being used by pre-school-age white children in communities where it had been abandoned by all but the oldest adults.

That is, the older non-standard (and sometimes even creole-like) dialect features remained in use principally by younger children in Negro speech-communities — being learned from other young children, to be given up later in life when "small-boy talk" was no longer appropriate to a more mature status.[10] And even though the adult dialects which these child dialects were ontogenetically given up for were also structurally non-standard and indentifiably Negro in most cases, they were still more standard — enough, at least, so that conspicuous retentions of child-dialect forms in the speech of an adult could sometimes result in the accusation that he or she was "talking like a child" or simply "talking bad".[11]

Interestingly enough, the use of an older, more conservative form of Negro dialect as child speech was not always limited to Negroes. In the Old South, many upper-class whites went through a similar linguistic metamorphosis from the non-standard dialect of their Negro playmates to the relatively standard English of their adult station in life. As John Bennet described the situation for the Charlestonian aristocracy of his day:

It is true that, up to the age of four, approximately, the children of the best families, even in town, are apt to speak an almost unmodified *Gullah*, caught

[10]   Like Dillard, I feel that this constitutes the most plausible explanation of the sporadic but not infrequent occurrence in the speech of lower-class Negro children of such "mistakes" as *been* as a general past-time marker (e.g. *He been hit me*), pronominal forms which are undifferentiated for case or gender (e.g. *Me gonna try* and *He out p'ayin'* — the latter said in reference to a girl) etc., since these same features were quite normal in older forms of Negro dialect (and still are in Gullah) and since there is, after all, an uninterrupted chain of language transmission from those earlier speakers to Negro children of the present day. Because some of the features are similar (at least superficially) to ones which are characteristic of certain stages of language development in virtually all English-speaking children, most specialists have attributed the Negro child patterns to developmental causes. However, since the Negro patterns are sometimes used by children who are well beyond the developmental stage (which normally ends at age 3.6 or 4 for whites), this would imply that Negroes develop linguistically more slowly than do whites. And, since there are even Negro octogenarians who use these forms, one would be forced to the absurd conclusion that some Negroes must not have completed the developmental process at all.
[11]   In Washington, D.C., I know of an adolescent Negro who for some reason had retained many child-dialect features in his speech. His peers characterized his speech by saying that "He talk just like a small boy". And in her *Folk-Lore of the Sea Islands, South Carolina* (Cambridge, Mass.: American Folklore Society, 1923), Elsie Clews Parson gives a Negro folk-tale (no. 148, The Girl Who learned to Talk Proper) in which the speech of a young lady who was said to "talk very bad" is marked by the use of creole pronominal forms (e.g. "Me ain' col', suh!"). It is interesting that the conclusion of this tale also shows popular recognition of the effect of out-migration on speech habits, since the same girl did finally "learn to talk proper" when an outsider married her and "kyarried her to his country".

from brown playmates and country bred nurses; but at that age the refinement of cultivation begins, and "the flowers o' the forest are a' weed awa!"[12]

It was undoubtedly in this manner that such white southern writers as Joel C. Harris and Ambrose E. Gonzales first acquired their knowledge of the Negro dialects which they immortalized in print.[13]

Today, genteel southern whites no longer learn non-standard Negro dialects as children, since the social conditions which once prompted them to do so have now become part of history. In their pre-school childhood, however, many Negroes still learn and use such dialects, and although they may modify these in later life, few ever attain anything like the elegant standard English which was the familial and social heritage of the older white aristocrats. Yet, when they enter the standard English milieu of the school, Negro children from this kind of language background are expected to compete linguistically with children (usually white) who have known and used standard English all their lives. Of course, a few of these Negro children do succeed, not because of good teaching, but because of their own exceptional abilities. But a far greater proportion of these children — the average ones, as well as the few who are truly below average — fail conspicuously. And, because there is

[12] John Bennett, "Gullah: A Negro Patois", *The South Atlantic Quarterly*, vol. 7, Oct (1908) and vol. 8, Jan (1909), quote from vol. 7:339. This same process had evidently been going on for at least a century and a half before Bennett's time. It was noted during the first half of the eighteenth century by G. L. Campbell, a British traveler to the American colonies. "One Thing they are very faulty in, with regard to their Children", he wrote of the white planters in the July 1746 number of *The London Magazine*, "which is, that when young, they suffer them too much to prowl amongst the young Negroes, which insensibly causes them to imbibe their Manners and broken Speech." Quoted in Allen Walker Read, "British Recognition of American Speech in the Eighteenth Century", *Dialect Notes*, vol. 6, part 6, July (1933): 329. Since even the most aristocratic British children undoubtedly picked up non-standard English or Scottish dialects from children of the servant class, it must have been the "broken" (i.e., creolized) character of colonial Negro speech which Campbell found so disagreeable in the North American situation.

[13] Elsewhere (Stewart, "Urban Negro Speech...", p. 13, fn. 7), I have taken Ambrose E. Gonzales to task for his racistic explanation of some of the structural characteristics of the Gullah dialect. At the same time, one can see how he would come to such a point of view, since he was obviously unaware of pidginization as a linguistic phenomenon, and therefore unable to account scientifically for its operation in the speech of the Gullah Negroes. In addition, a genetic explanation of language differences fitted quite comfortably into the rhetoric of the caste-cloven society of which Gonzales was so much a product. This theoretical weakness notwithstanding, Gonzales' literary rendition of Gullah was superb. Considering the accuracy of his dialect phonology and syntax, and the ease with which he handled subtle dialect differences and even individual switching behavior, he can certainly qualify as America's greatest dialect writer. For a similar opinion of Gonzales, see Ann Sullivan Haskell "The Representation of Gullah-Influenced Dialect in Twentieth Century South Carolina Prose: 1922-30" (University of Pennsylvania Ph.D. dissertation, 1964):238-41.

obviously some sort of ethnic correlation between pupil success and failure in newly-integrated school situations, the embarrassed educational
establishment and the frustrated public enter into a crisis relationship.
Some whites charge (privately, at least) that the schools are being given
the impossible task of teaching unteachable Negroes. And some Negroes
charge (not so privately) that white educators are involved in a conspiracy
to deliberately keep Negro children from learning. Parents protest blindly, and school administrators run helter-skelter, holding councils of de-
spair with colleagues who understand the problem no better.

A basic reason why so many Negro children fail in school is not that
they are unteachable, but that they are not being taught efficiently or
fairly. And this fact may have little or nothing to do with a white conspiracy against integrated schools. Rather, it may be the result of a far
less deliberate yet equally devastating insensitivity of the educational process to the social and cultural characteristics of the school population.
This is probably nowhere more striking than in the area of language
since, as speakers largely of non-standard dialects which are among the
most deviant from standard English now being used in America, many
Negro children are burdened at every turn with achievement barriers in
the form of extra (and uncompensated for) language learning requirements. For example, all children are expected to learn how to read in
school. But, for many Negro pupils, the problem is made more difficult
by the fact that they are unfamiliar, not only with the sound-spelling-
meaning correspondences of many of the words, but even with the grammatical patterns which these words make up in their reading lessons.
Consequently, the reading achievement of these children becomes dependent upon their own success in deciphering standard English sentence
structure. And the same type of problem is reflected in other subject
areas in the schools. The irony, here, is that the traditional educational
system is itself creating much of the pedagogical disadvantagement of its
linguistically-different pupils by requiring them to accomplish, on their
own, as much again as middle-class pupils from a standard English background are expected to accomplish with expert help.

In many ways, the plight of the Negro child who enters school speaking
a non-standard dialect is similar to that of a foreign-language-speaking
child entering an American school. And, while it can be argued that no
Negro dialect is as different from standard English as is, say, Spanish,
this does not necessarily mean that the linguistically-different Negro's
task is that much easier. For, while the boundaries between a full-fledged
foreign language and English are usually clear-cut (the Spanish-speaking
child, for example, will usually know at any given point whether Spanish
or English is being used, and so will the teacher), the many similarities
between any Negro dialect and standard English make it difficult to tell

exactly where one leaves off and the other begins.[14] Thus, even the linguistic similarities between a non-standard dialect and standard English can be pedagogically and psychologically disadvantageous, since they can camouflage functional differences between the two linguistic systems. Furthermore, while a wealth of linguistic knowledge and pedagogical know-how is currently brought to bear on the language problems of the child who speaks a foreign language such as Spanish, no similar competences have yet been developed to help the child who speaks a non-standard dialect, although his needs are just as great — and his numbers greater. Considering his educational prospects as they stand at present, the linguistically-different Negro child might well say "I look down de road an' de road so lonesome."

Although English teachers, speech therapists and other language-oriented educators are now dedicating themselves more than ever to the task of helping disadvantaged children — and especially disadvantaged Negro children — acquire proficiency in standard English, very few of these dedicated professionals have demonstrated any real understanding of the language characteristics of the communities from which these children come. For their part, teachers of English to Spanish-speaking Mexican, Puerto Rican or Cuban children know that an understanding of the structure of Spanish will give insights into the problem which such children have with English, and these teachers would be shocked by any suggestion that a comparative approach to the language of the school and the language of the child is unnecessary. In contrast, teachers of English to disadvantaged Negro children have generally remained aloof from the serious study of non-standard Negro dialect.

This lack of interest on the part of many English teachers in the non-standard language of Negro children is in large part the product of a normative view of language which has long been the mainstay of traditional teacher training. Either overtly or by implication, the teacher-to-be is taught that the kind of usage which is indicated in grammar books, dictionaries and style manuals (and which is presumably followed by educated speakers and writers) represents a maximum of structural neatness, communicative efficiency, esthetic taste and logical clarity. Once this normative view has been inculcated in the prospective teacher (and it must be admitted that popular beliefs about "correct" and "incorrect" language practically guarantee this) then the teacher will quite naturally

[14] Because the structural relationships which hold between the two "dialects" in such a case are in part like those between completely foreign languages and in part like those between two style levels of a single language, I have coined the term "quasi-foreign language situation" to describe it. See my "Foreign Language Teaching Methods in Quasi-Foreign Language Situations" in William A. Stewart, editor, *Non-Standard Speech and the Teaching of English* (Washington, D.C.: Center for Applied Linguistics, 1964).

regard departures from the norms of standard English as departures from structure, clarity, taste, and even logic itself.[15]

Of course, there have always been exceptional teachers who have seen that chronic deviations from standard English usage on the part of their pupils may indicate simply their normal use of some other variety of English, with its own structure and logic. William Francis Allen was an early example of a teacher who not only discovered this, but came to realize that even apparent "ignorance" in coping with logical or experiential problems could sometimes be traced to mere difficulty with the language in which the problems were posed. He recorded the following incident, which occurred while he was teaching Gullah Negro children on Port Royal Island, South Carolina, during the Civil War.

I asked a group of boys one day the color of the sky. Nobody could tell me. Presently the father of one of them came by, and I told him their ignorance, repeating my question with the same result as before. He grinned: "Tom, how sky stan'?" "Blue," promptly shouted Tom. [16]

But in attempting to teach standard English to children who speak a non-standard dialect, even those teachers who understand that there is a language conflict involved, and who would accordingly like to borrow techniques from foreign-language teaching methodology, are likely to find their efforts hampered by too limited a knowledge of the structural characteristics of whatever non-standard dialect the children speak. For, in all too many cases, the best pedagogical grasp of the structural features of a particular non-standard dialect will consist of little more than a list of certain "folk" pronunciations and an awareness of the use of such grammatical shibboleths as *ain't* and the double negative. Unfortunately, this kind of superficial knowledge of the structural details of the speech of disadvantaged children will not only prevent the teacher or therapist from understanding the reasons for many of these children's "mistakes" in standard English, but it is also likely to lead to an inadvertent lumping together of children who speak different dialects (and therefore who have different kinds of problems with standard English) under a generalized remedial English approach which would not take these differences into account. In the likely event that both Negroes and whites make up the disadvantaged student population of a school system, this egalitarian

[15] Linguistic and cultural relativists will be pleased to learn that the dialect tables have been turned on the normativists at least once. In his essay, John Bennett ("Gullah: A Negro Patois", vol. 7:340) reports that Gullah-speaking Negroes passed judgment on visiting Yankees with "Dey use dem mout' so funny!".

[16] William Francis Allen, Charles Pickard Ware, and Lucy McKim Garrison, *Slave Songs of the United States* (New York, 1867): xxvii. What the father of the boy knew was that, in Gullah, observable characteristics are usually indicated by means of the verb *stan'* (or *'tan'*) which can be translated roughly as 'look', 'seem' or 'appear'.

approach to their language problems may prove almost irresistible in the face of a particularly unsophisticated kind of social liberalism, currently in vogue among educators, which regards it as a manifestation of racism to entertain even the most well-qualified hypothesis that differences in ethnicity (such as being "white" or "Negro" in America) might possibly correlate with differences in behavior (in language usage, for example). In fact, so strong is the hold upon today's educators of this sociologically simplistic philosophy, with its "all children are the same" credo, that many educators and teachers even find uncomfortable the anthropologist's contention that correlations between ethnicity and behavior are not only possible but probable, when one considers that ethnicity is more of a social phenomenon than a physiological one, and that so much of human behavior is socially conditioned rather than genetically determined. And instead of seeing the chronic failure of disadvantaged Negroes in integrated school situations as a strong indication that this "sameness" credo is inadequate and counter-productive in terms of the real goals of education, many educators let such unpleasant realities force them into clinging all the more blindly and tenaciously to their simplistic views of the matter.

But the failure to perceive structural differences between the nonstandard dialects of American Negroes and those of American whites has not been unique to English teachers and speech therapists. Some prominent dialectologists also have claimed that Negro dialects represent, at the most, a minor statistical skewing of white dialect features.[17] And

---

[17]   As one dialect geographer expressed his view of the matter, "the range of variants is the same in Negro and in white speech, though the statistical distribution of variants has been skewed by the American caste system". Raven I. McDavid, Jr., "American Social Dialects", *College English*, vol. 26, no. 4, January (1965): 258, fn. 7. In an even more recent article, McDavid rejects the idea of a pidgin or creole background for American Negro dialects, saying "To a naive social scientist, what is generally known about the operations of the domestic slave trade should be sufficient to refute such an argument." Raven I. McDavid, Jr., "Needed Research in Southern Dialects", in Edgar T. Thompson, editor, *Perspectives on the South: Agenda for Research* (Durham, N.C.: Duke University Press, 1967): 122. In view of the numerous attestations of the actual use of pidgin and creole forms of English by American Negro slaves in the contemporary literature (see my "Sociolinguistic Factors in the History of American Negro Dialects", for a few references), it is difficult to imagine any historical basis for McDavid's statements. Since he must have seen at least the reprintings of some of these in scholarly books and articles, it can only be that he has not considered the linguistic implications of their rather non-European grammatical structure. Furthermore, if there is anything in what is known about the slave trade, slave life, or plantation social stratification in America which would call into question these early attestations of pidgin and creole English, it is strange that it has never been articulated in such standard works on American Negro slavery as Philip Alexander Bruce, *Economic History of Virginia in the Seventeenth Century* (New York: The MacMillan Co., 1895); Ulrich B. Phillips, *American Negro Slavery* (New York: D. Appleton and Co.,

still others have passed over the subject altogether.[18]

One further reason why both language teachers and dialectologists have failed to appreciate the extent to which non-standard Negro dialects may differ from non-standard white dialects (even in the Deep South) may simply be that such differences now remain mostly in syntax (i.e. grammatical patterns and categories) rather than in vocabulary or lexico-phonology (i.e. word forms), and are thus not normally uncovered by the word-comparison techniques which dialectologists and non-linguists rely on so heavily. Yet, a comparison of the grammatical details of white and Negro non-standard dialects suggests a very different kind of historical relationship than is evident from a comparison of words alone. This can be illustrated by the comparison of a standard English (STE) conjunctive sentence like "We were eating — and drinking, too" together with its equivalents in representative varieties of southern white non-standard basilect (WNS), Negro non-standard basilect (NNS), and Gullah Basilect (GUL):[19]

STE: We were eating — and drinking, too.
WNS: We was eatin' — an' drinkin', too.
NNS: We was eatin' — an' we drinkin', too.
GUL: We bin duh nyam — en' we duh drink, too.

If one compares only the forms of the equivalent words in these sentences, NNS (Negro non-standard) appears to be virtually identical to WNS (white non-standard), with both of them about equally different from

1918) and his *Life and Labor in the Old South* (Boston: Little, Brown and Co., 1929); Marcus William Jernegan, *Laboring and Dependent Classes in Colonial America: 1607-1783* (University of Chicago Press, 1931); Frederick Bancroft, *Slave-Trading in the Old South* (Baltimore: J. H. Furst Co., 1931): Kenneth M. Stampp, *The Peculiar Institution: Slavery in the Ante-Bellum South* (New York: Alfred A. Knopf, Inc., 1956); Herbert S. Klein, *Slavery in the Americas: A Comparative Study of Virginia and Cuba* (University of Chicago Press, 1967).

[18] None of the four recent publications on American dialects which have been written for the use of English teachers contain any substantive reference to Negro dialect — not even a simple statement of the historical and definitional issues involved in the concept. This omission is probably due to the tacit acceptance on the part of the various authors of the theory that most Negro speech is identical to southern varieties of white speech, and therefore that the description of the latter in their manuals takes care of Negro speech as well. These four publications are: Jean Malmstrom and Annabel Ashley, *Dialects-USA* (Champaign, Ill.: National Council of Teachers of English, 1963); Jean Malmstrom, *Language in Society* (New York: The Hayden Book Co., 1965); Carroll E. Reed, *Dialects of American English* (Cleveland: World Publishing Co., 1967); Roger W. Shuy, *Discovering American Dialects* (Champaign, Ill.: National Council of Teachers of English, 1967).

[19] The term BASILECT refers to that variety of a particular dialect which is structurally the most deviant from standard English. See William A. Stewart, "Urban Negro Speech: Sociolinguistic Factors Affecting English Teaching", particularly pp. 15-17.

STE (standard English).[20] Judged by the same criteria, GUL (Gullah) appears to be radically different from all the others, including NNS.

Because of such word-form similarities and differences, many dialectologists have concluded that, while Gullah itself may be a creolized form of English (rather than a direct descendant of any British dialect or dialects), there is no evidence that other kinds of American Negro speech are related to it in any direct way.[21] For, according to the same kind of word-form comparisons, these represent little more than the use by Negroes of dialect patterns which are also used by (and presumably borrowed from) whites in the Deep South.

However, a comparison of the sentence structure of these dialects shows a somewhat different kind of relationship. In the foregoing equivalent sentences, this is evident in the treatment of the subject pronoun and the tense-marking auxiliary (or copula). For, although STE, WNS, NNS, and GUL can all repeat the subject pronoun and auxiliary in a conjunctive clause (e.g. STE "We were eating — and we were drinking, too"), this is not generally done in any of them. Instead, one or both will usually be omitted (provided, of course, that the subject and temporal referents remain the same). But in terms of what they omit, these dialects split along lines which are different from those indicated by word-form similarities and differences. Both STE and WNS normally omit both the subject pronoun and the auxiliary in a conjunctive clause, although the tense-marking auxiliary must be present if the subject is not omitted. But NNS, like GUL, often repeats the subject pronoun in a conjunctive clause while omitting the auxiliary — even when this indicates past tense.[22]

[20] The literary dialect spellings which I have used in these examples may well make the individual words in WNS and NNS seem more alike than they actually are when pronounced. But, for the sake of argument, I would just as soon allow for the possibility that some words might have identical phonological forms in the different dialects.

[21] This concession as to the creole nature of Gullah was largely forced upon an intensely Anglo-centric American dialect-studies tradition by Lorenzo Dow Turner's *Africanisms in the Gullah Dialect* (University of Chicago Press, 1949) which, though it concentrated more on African survivals than on creole influences and dealt more with naming practices than with linguistic structure, did at least make the point rather strongly that Gullah is a creolized form of English.

[22] Those who have had enough contact with Negro non-standard dialects to know that constructions like *We tryin'* usually indicate the present tense (i.e. STE 'We are trying') might assume that the superficially similar construction *we drinkin'* in the NNS sentence *We was eatin' — en we drinkin', too* also indicates the present tense — the whole thereby meaning 'We were eating — and we are drinking, too' with an erroneous lack of tense agreement between the two clauses. Although it is true that *we drinkin'* does mean 'we are drinking' in most circumstances (cf. NNS *We drinkin' right now*), in the sentence cited the phrase really represents we *was drinkin'* with the past tense marker *was* omitted. By the same token, GUL *we duh drink*, can mean 'we are drinking' as well, but represents *we bin duh drink*, with the past tense marker *bin* omitted, in the sentence cited.

An example of the same phenomenon in American Negro speech at the beginning of the nineteenth century is to be found in A. B. Lindsley's play *Love and Friendship* (New York, 1807). A Negro says: "I tink dey bin like sich a man de bess, for dey like for be tumel 'bout." Side by side with *dey bin like* in the first clause is *dey like* in the second one, even though the context makes it reasonably clear that both mean 'they liked'.[23]

If, in such features as the omission of a redundant auxiliary (while retaining the redundant subject pronoun), Gullah and other non-standard Negro dialects part company with standard English and non-standard white dialects (of both America and Great Britain), they do have counterparts in a number of pidgin and creole forms of English which, though used far from the shores of the United States and in widely separated places, are all the legacy of the African slave trade. To illustrate how much these forms of English resemble Gullah and other non-standard Negro dialects with respect to auxiliary omission, the same equivalent sentences are given in Jamaican Creole (JMC), Sranan (SRA), the creole English of Surinam in South America, and West African Pidgin English (WAP):[24]

JMC: We ben a nyam — an' we a drink, too.
SRA: We ben de nyang — en' we de dringie, too.
WAP: We bin de eat — an' we de dring, too.

In addition to the grammatical correspondences, the word-form similarities of these languages with Gullah will be apparent.[25]

[23] Quoted in George Philip Krapp, *The English Language in America*, vol. I (New York: The Century Co., 1925): 258-59.
[24] For comparative purposes, I have written these languages in a spelling which is as close to that of standard English as the literary dialect spellings used in the preceding set of equivalent sentences. Scientific (phonemic) orthographies have been devised for these languages, however, and in them the same sentences would appear as: JMC *We ben a nyam — an we a dringk, tu*; SRA *we ben njan — en we de dringi, toe*; WAP *Wi bin de it — an we de dring, tu*. See Frederic G. Cassidy, *Jamaica Talk* (London: Macmillan Co., Ltd., 1961); Beryl L. Bailey, *Jamaican Creole Syntax* (Cambridge University Press, 1966); A. Donice, *De Creolentaal van Suriname* (Paramaribo: Radhakishun and Co., 1959); Gouvernement van Suriname, Bureau Volkslectuur, *Woordenlijst van het Sranan-Tongo* (Paramaribo: N.V. *Varekamp & Co.*, 1961); Gilbert D. Schneider, "West African Pidgin English" (Ph. D. Thesis, Hartford Seminary Foundation, 1966); David Dwyer, *An Introduction to West African Pidgin English* (African Studies Center, Michigan State University, 1967).
[25] The past tense markers in this series are *ben* (JMC, SRA) and *bin* (WAP), the latter having a common variant — *be*. The preverbal *a* in JMC is a modern reduction of an older *da*, obviously related historically to GUL *duh*, as well as to SRA and WAP *de*. In fact, the preverbal *a-* in some southern Negro dialects (e.g. *he a-workin'*) may well derive from just such a source, rather than from the verbal prefix *a-* of many white dialects. This seems likely in view of the fact that, in those white dialects in which such a

These correspondences are much too neat to be dismissed as mere accident. Rather, they seem to indicate that at least some of the particular syntactic features of American Negro dialects are neither skewings nor extensions of white dialect patterns, but are in fact structural vestiges of an earlier plantation creole, and ultimately of the original slave-trade pidgin English which gave rise to it.

This kind of evidence — existing in abundance for those who will admit it — calls for a complete reassessment of the relationships between British dialects, white American dialects, Negro American dialects (including Gullah), and the pidgin and creole English of Africa and the Caribbean. In particular, a new and more careful look at the question of American Negro dialects needs to be taken by those working within orthodox American dialectology — most of all by those who have made an almost exclusive use of American Dialect Atlas materials and techniques. High on the list of priorities for determining Negro and white dialect relationships should be: (1) the relationship between Gullah and other Negro dialects, and (2) the relationship between Negro dialects (other than Gullah) and white dialects. In such a reassessment, many new insights into the history of these relationships will be gained from studies of the syntax, not only of present-day dialects, but also of literary attestations of early Negro and white non-standard dialect, and by comparative studies of European, pidgin, and creole dialects of English.

All-in-all, it looks very much like the word-form similarities between non-standard Negro dialects and non-standard white dialects are the result of a relatively superficial merging process, in which creole-speaking Negroes tried to make their "broken" (i.e. creole) English become more like that of the whites by means of minor pronunciation changes and vocabulary substitutions. But the creole grammatical patterns of these Negroes' speech, being less amenable to conscious manipulation, remained more resistant to this substitution process.[26] In an earlier article

---

prefix is used functionally, there is usually a contrast between its presence and its absence (e.g. *he's workin'* 'he is working within view' vs. *he's a-workin* 'he is off working somewhere'), while Negro dialects with preverbal *a-* use it like Gullah uses preverbal *duh* — for the simple durative. Finally, Gullah actually has *a* (or *uh*) as a variant of *duh*, especially after *bin*.

[26] Even persons who are quite familiar with American Negro dialects may be led, by dissimilarities in word-forms, to overestimate the difference between them. For example, as keen an observer of dialect as E. C. L. Adams stated in *Nigger to Nigger* (New York: Charles Scribner's Sons, 1928): viii, that the speech of the Congaree Negroes of inland South Carolina was "absolutely distinct" from the coastal Gullah. Actually, the many striking syntactic similarities between the two dialects would suggest that the former is only a slightly de-creolized form of the latter. Observers of Gullah, from John Bennett on, have all remarked on how the older "pure" form of the language has been undergoing modification (i.e. de-creolization), particularly in the

on urban Negro dialect in Washington, D.C., I pointed out how Negro children who reach school age speaking a radically non-standard dialect often modify it in the direction of standard English in a similarly superficial fashion as they grow older.[27] It is interesting to consider that, in the language-socialization process of their individual lifetimes, many American Negroes may actually repeat something of the larger process of Negro dialect history.

Now, the pedagogical implications of a historical relationship of this kind between Negro and white non-standard dialects and, more particularly, between non-standard Negro dialects and standard English ought to be clear. For, if American Negro dialects have evolved in such a way that structural similarities with other dialects of American English (including standard English) are greatest at the superficial word-form level, then it is possible for these similarities to mask any number of grammatical differences between them. And the teacher, concentrating on the more obvious word-form differences, is quite likely to miss the grammatical differences in the process — thereby leaving them to persist as apparent malapropisms, awkward turns of phrase, and random "mistakes" in speech and composition through grade school, high school, and frequently even through higher education.

As the grammatical study of non-standard Negro dialect progresses, it is quite probable that many more differences will be found between Negro and white speech patterns, and it may well turn out that at least some of these will also be traceable to a creole English, pidgin English, or even African language source. Of course, such discoveries are bound to cause embarrassment to those superficially liberal whites who will accept the Negro for what he is only if his behavioral patterns prove to be as European as their own, and they will be disquieting to those racial image-conscious Negroes who are so often preoccupied with the question "What will the white folks think?" But quite apart from whether he thinks they are a help or a hindrance in integration, good or bad for the Negro's racial image, the dedicated educator should welcome the discovery and formulation of such ethnically correlated dialect differences as do exist. For, only when they are taken into account in the teaching process will the linguistic cards cease to be stacked against the disadvantaged Negro pupil in the nation's classrooms.

Center for Applied Linguistics

---

cities and towns. Seeing this "modified Gullah" always as a new phenomenon, they never expressed any awareness of the possibility that they might have been watching a continuation of the same process which earlier gave rise to the contemporary forms of other American Negro dialects.

[27] William A. Stewart, "Urban Negro Speech: Sociolinguistic Factors Affecting English Teaching", p. 17.

IAN F. HANCOCK

SOME ASPECTS OF ENGLISH IN LIBERIA*

Whether to publish original but incomplete material quickly, or to spend
time — even years — amassing more complete data before presentation,
is a familiar problem to those engaged upon linguistic research.

In the case of the volume under review this question is again brought
to mind, the more so since it is itself an elaboration of an earlier work
prepared in 1962 for the first Peace Corps project in Liberia.[1] During
the eight intervening years the word list has been expanded from fifty
to five hundred items although, as the compiler makes clear (p.i), the
glossary is still "far from comprehensive".

The book is certainly useful as an introduction to the life and speech
of urban Liberians, and is all that its title claims it to be; but as the first
and only full-length study of the subject to have appeared to date, one
regrets that it did not include more historical and sociolinguistic material.
No distinction is made, for example, amongst the at least four varieties
of English[2] spoken in Liberia, and while pages 65-74 are devoted to the
phonology of the items dealt with, no attempt has been made to describe
the structure of any variety of the language. These appear to comprise
Standard Liberian English (SLE), Merico, Liberian Pidgin English (LPE)
and Kru Pidgin English (KPE), each spoken by different groups within

Reprinted with permission from *Liberian Studies Journal* III, 2 (1970-71).
* Review/Discussion of Warren d'Azevedo, *Some Terms from Liberian Speech*,
(United States Peace Corps in Liberia: Monrovia, 1970: iii, 76).
[1] W. Welmers and W. d'Azevedo, *Some Liberian English Usages*, mentioned on p. ii.
[2] This includes all varieties spoken in Liberia, including pidginized and creolized
English. Not discussed here are expatriate forms of English such as British or American,
or the Krio spoken by many Sierra Leonean residents in the country.

the country, and each exerting varying degrees of influence upon the other.

STANDARD LIBERIAN ENGLISH

Standard Liberian English is employed in broadcasting and in other official capacities, and represents the only prestige form of English discussed here. It differs little from other varieties of Standard English spoken elsewhere in West Africa but has a distinctive phonology demonstrating considerable influence from American English. This has been briefly described by Smalley.[3]

MERICO

MERICO, or — less popularly — AMERICO-LIBERIAN, is also known as Brokes, Kwasai, Waterside or Water Street English. This is the first language of most Liberians of Settler[4] ancestry, although its use is largely restricted to home and informal situations. Many parents discourage their children from speaking Merico, regarding it as "bad" English and an obstacle to SLE acquisition. It represents in its modern form a partially decreolized offshoot of mid-nineteenth century southern U.S. Black English, and as such is of considerable importance *vis-à-vis* the study of Gullah, with which it is most closely identified.[5]

While no more than a cursory examination has been made of the structure of this speech, the following grammatical characteristics have been noted:

a. Unmarked nominal plural: *rak* 'rock, rocks', or marked with postnominal *-dẽ: rak-dẽ* 'rocks'. This latter is possibly a feature from LPE or KPE.
b. Adjectivals occurring with or without copula link: *hi big* 'he is big', *dæs gud* 'that's good', *ai sʌ tayə sitĩ hyʌ* 'I am tired of sitting here'.

[3] W. A. Smalley, *Manual of Articulatory Phonetics* II (phonology of SLE) (Tarrytown, New York, 1962): 401-404.
[4] The Settlers or Americo-Liberians came to Liberia from the southern states of America from the time the colony was established, in 1816, until the late 1860's. At this time they numbered nearly 19,000. The earliest colonists were settled for some time in Freetown, Sierra Leone, while the American Colonization Society negotiated for land at Cape Mesurado, in Liberia, where Monrovia is now located.
[5] On more than one occasion in the writer's experience, Krio-speaking Sierra Leoneans have thought that a recording of Gullah which was played to them was in fact Liberian English.

c. Verbal stem without markers to indicate past action: *ai si dɛ mɛ̃* 'I saw the man'. Forms closer to SLE may also occur in Merico, *hi gɔ̃* 'he's gone'.

d. Use of the aspect marker *də* or *lɛ*[6] indicating action in progress: *hi də spiish* 'he's talking at length', *shi lɛ kræ* 'she is crying'. This appears to be a variant form of the construction incorporating the suffix *-i* or *-ĩ*[7] e.g. *ai kʌmĩ* 'I am coming', *yo jææbĩ mi* 'you're teasing me'.

e. The future tense marker is usually *wu*[8] as in *wi wu kʌ̃* 'we will come', although constructions with *guæ* have been noted, regularly with *bi: dæs guæ bi ɛ big jab* 'that's going to be a big job', *yo guæ kʌ̃ tumɔro?* 'are you going to come tomorrow?'

f. Use of the completive aspect marker *dɔ̃* or *nɔ̃*[9] e.g. *de dɔ̃ go dædəwe* 'they've gone that way', *lilpiis nɔ̃ lɛf* 'there's a small piece left'.

g. The copula verb *sʌ*,[10] as in *hi sʌ mɛ̃* 'he is a man', *shi sʌ smo* 'she is small'. This may be optionally deleted in prenominal position as well as pre-adjectivally: *dis mʌ hou* (alongside *dis sʌ mʌ hou*) 'this is my house', *shi smo* 'she is small'.

h. The widespread creole locating verb *de* also occurs in Merico, although in more anglicized varieties of the language it seems to be replaceable by *sʌ*: *di gɛɛ de hyʌ, di gɛɛ sʌ hyʌ*.

---

[6]   The form *lɛ* seems to be restricted to Liberia, although the similar *li* occurs in at least one variety of East Cameroun Pidgin English. If this derives from the English 'live', it is paralleled by the Jamaican Creole form of the same item, viz. *da* for which the *Dictionary of Jamaican English* suggests as a possible source Twi *da* '... live, remain, rest'. In Gullah and Krio, *lib* occurs as a locating verb, even with inanimates, e.g. Gullah *di chiə bin ə lib iin di kɔɔndə* 'the chair was in the corner'. Grade gives *me live for go* for 'I am going', and fairly consistently represents this aspect of the verb with *live for* throughout the article. P. Grade, "Bemerkungen über das Neger-Englisch an der Westküste von Afrika", *Archiv für das Studium der neueren Sprachen*, LXXXIII (1889): 267. Conversation with a Kru, 271-72.

[7]   Stewart makes a distinction between the verb with *lɛ*, which he regards as the simple present, and the verb with suffixed *-ĩ*, which he treats as continuative; W. A. Stewart, "Foreign language teaching methods in quasi-foreign language situations", in, *Non-standard Speech and the Teaching of English* (Washington, 1964):1-15. Discussion of LPE and/or Merico: 5.

[8]   Cf. Jamaican Creole *wi* as future-marker. Both are from English 'will'.

[9]   Probably from English 'done', although convergence with Wolof (Senegal and The Gambia) *dɔɔn*, as past habitual tense marker, is possible. Cf. also Wolof *di*, as marker of present habitual action, with Liberian and Gullah *də*, Krio and Cameroon *di/de*.

[10] Probably from *is* + the verbal auxiliary *a-* as in 'he's a-coming'. Ottley, in his *Trinibagianese* (Port-of-Spain, 1965-67) records the use of a similar word in Trinidad: *you suh nuh fuh talk* 'you shouldn't talk', *she suh ain today story* 'she's not today's story' (i.e. 'she's old'). Note also Pitcairnese *yu han sə blʌd; ai sə dan* 'your hand is bloody', 'I am finished', and Norfolkese *wi sə glad; dɛm sə slai* 'we're glad', 'they're unwilling (lit. 'sly')', as recorded in A. S. C. Ross and A. W. Moverley, *The Pitcairnese Language* (London, 1964).

i. The negating particle is *ẽ* or *ɛ̃*,[11] as in: *ai ɛ̃ æs di chææ* 'I didn't ask the child', *tẽ so* 'it isn't so'.

j. The following pronominal forms have been recorded: subject pronouns *ai* or *a, yu, yɔ* or *yo, hi* or *i, shi, wi,* and *de* or *dɛ̃*. Object pronouns include *mi, yu, hi* or *hĩ, hɔ, wi* or *ɔs,* and *dɛ̃*. Possessive pronouns include *mʌ* or *mi, yu, yo, hi* or *i, shi* or *hɔ, ou,* and *dɛ*. No separate second person plural pronoun has been noted (Cf. Gullah *unə,* Krio *una*). For 'myself', both the pronunciations *misɛf* and *mʌsɛuf* have been recorded. The former corresponds with the Krio form of the word, and may reflect LPE influence.

LIBERIAN PIDGIN ENGLISH

Liberian Pidgin English is mainly spoken in the interior by tribal Liberians of different linguistic backgrounds in their dealings with each other, and with Africans and Europeans from the coast. While having absorbed a great many Merico and SLE features, especially phonologically, LPE represents a separate branch of Atlantic Pidgin[12] being a variety of West African Pidgin English immediately related to other coastal dialects. It differs from Merico in its lack of gender distinction, use of *no* as negator, *bi* as copula verb, and *fɔ* (instead of Merico *to*) as preverbal 'to'. LPE has been inadequately described both by Wilson and Büttikofer.[13]

KRU PIDGIN ENGLISH

Kru Pidgin English, similar in many respects to Sierra Leone Krio, is employed as a second language by Kru fishermen, who seem to have been instrumental in carrying Pidgin features along the entire Guinea coast. KPE, while employed as a second language appears to be structurally a creole rather than a pidgin, and may well have been acquired as a discrete language from native speakers in Sierra Leone.[14] Short texts in

[11] From 'ain't'. Also Gullah and Caribbean.
[12] See I. F. Hancock, "A Provisional Comparison of the English-based Atlantic Creoles", *African Language Review* VIII (1969): 7-72 for a discussion of this. Reference to Merico, with some examples, on page 23.
[13] J. Büttikofer, *Reisebilder aus Liberia* 2 vols (Leiden, 1890). On LPE see, II:237-240; C. M. Wilson, *Liberia* (New York, 1947). LPE, 59-63.
[14] This reflects the inadequacy of present terminology in creole linguistics. While a pidgin is by definition a second language, not every second language is a pidgin, even if that second language is a creole. In other words it is possible for a creole to be re-pidginized, but just as possible for non-native speakers to speak a creole perfectly. While there is some justification for retaining the term "pidgin", use of the term "creole"

Kru Pidgin English may be found in Crocker, Grade, and Zöller.[15]

It would be wrong to compartmentalize these varieties of Liberian English too rigidly; there is considerable inter-influence amongst them, especially from LSE and among Merico, LPE and KPE, and with the exception of LSE, there is marked social pressure against the use of each variety in the wrong context.

Despite the fact that we are still awaiting a comprehensive description of Liberian English, a start, at least, has been made, and for this we must thank Professor d'Azevedo. SOME TERMS FROM LIBERIAN SPEECH, apart from being of considerable practical use to Peace Corps members and other expatriates in Liberia, also provides a useful source of lexical material for researchers into the field of Atlantic creole studies. If criticism has to be levelled in any particular direction, it should be at the creolists themselves, for having ignored a linguistic situation which may well prove more than any other to unravel much of the mystery still surrounding the internal relationships of the Atlantic creoles. It has taken an anthropologist to take the initial step in this direction, a step which one hopes, particularly, will stimulate further research into this fascinating and complex area of Black English studies.

The following comments apply to d'Azevedo's terms; those followed by (A) are from the *addenda* to the second edition.

Again [Still, yet, already]. Paralleled in all Caribbean and West African English creoles in this sense.

Ba [Namesake, friend]. Also occurs in Krio, Jamaican, Sranan, Gullah and Cameroon Pidgin. Cf. Vai *bɔ* 'friend, fellow companion' (Koelle), and Mandinka *ba* 'term of address to either sex'.

Barbered [Hair cut]. The back-formation *barb* also occurs in Merico, as a verb.

Beard-beard [Reference to someone with a beard or moustache]. This appears to be Krio/Cameroon *biabia* 'beard'.

Beat [Bested, failed]. Also Krio.

Belly [Pregnant]. The verb phrase *get belly* is a widespread creole calque on both sides of the Atlantic.

Benniseed [Sesame seed]. Ultimately from Wolof *bɛne*, or Mandinka *bene*.

Bite-and blow [Reference to rats gnawing the soles of the feet]. 'Blow'

---

would appear to be unnecessary. Ideally each creole should have its own name, and be regarded no differently from other languages.

[15] W. R. Crocker, *Nigeria, a Critique of British Colonial Administration* (London, 1936). On pages 167-68 there is a story in KPE; Grade, "Bemerkungen über das Neger-Englische", 271-72; Hugo Zöller, *Das Togoland und die Sklavenküste* (Berlin, 1885). Kru English, 242-43.

here probably means 'take a rest', its Krio/Caribbean meaning, rather than 'blow' or 'puff'.

Book [*To know book*, literate]. A LPE usage.

Bugabug [termite sp.]. This item was first recorded in Moore's *Travels* (1738). The word has the Liberian form and meaning in the Gambia, but the pronunciation is unknown in Sierra Leone where it is pronounced *bɔgbɔg* or *gbɔgbɔg*. Mandinka has *bagabaga*, and Susu *boghbokhi* 'termite', probably also the source of English 'bug'.

Buku [Plenty, much]. Also Krio and Cameroon/Nigerian Pidgin *bɔku*.

Carry [Take, convey]. In the sense of 'accompany' this verb is widespread in West Africa, the Caribbean and the southeastern United States. Wright, in his *English Dialect Dictionary* (London, 1905), lists *carry* or *kerrie* (Cf. Krio *kɛri*) as occurring in Irish and Scottish dialects with the meaning 'take, convey'.

Chokla [Mixed up]. The same word as Krio *chakra*, Cameroon *chakara* or *chakala*, and Jamaican *chakra* or *chakachaka*. Probably ultimately Ewe *tsaka* 'mix, be mixed'.

Chuck [Throw]. Common in many U.S. dialects.

Civilized [Reference to knowledge of western religion and education]. This also means 'duped' in Merico (and Krio).

Cold Water [Gift to soothe ruffled feelings]. Probably via Krio where *kol-wata* has the same meaning, and may even be extended to mean simply kind words. Cf. Krio *kol-wata* also meaning gin or rum, a calque from Yoruba *omi-tutu*. This is used to appease certain society spirits or totems such as the Hunting Society's *Egun*.

Come [I'm coming, I'm going]. This could have been better glossed as 'I'm coming back', said on the point of departure. Liberian 'I'm coming to go' means 'I am about to leave' (Cf. Krio *a de kam go*), and is paralleled in several West African languages.

Company, komping [Informal mutual aid society]. Krio *kɔmpin* and Cameroon *kɔmbi* (as well as Sranan/Saramaccan *kompe*) mean 'peer, companion'. Mutual aid societies have various names in the creoles, e.g. Krio *esusu* (ex Yoruba), although nineteenth century sources list Freetown "compins" as being benefit and welfare organizations.

Corn row (A) [Hair style for women]. Krio has *kɔn-rol* 'corn roll', with the same meaning.

Dash [Tip, gift]. This item is probably African rather than Portuguese; Ewe has *dase* 'thank you' (Cf. China Coast Pidgin 'cumshaw', a tip or gift, from Hokkien *kʌm chia* 'thank you'). However various other etyma are possible: Africans may have been rewarded with a "dash" of rum for services rendered. "Dash" has the meaning 'make a show or display' in Scottish dialects, and 'throw' or 'fling' (*e.g.* coins) in Jamaican Creole.

Dear [Expensive]. British English. Cf. use of 'cheap' for 'inexpensive', in Liberia and other parts of West Africa.

Dollbaby [Figurine, stickdoll]. This term for 'doll' is found in some U.S. dialects, and occurs in Krio.

Dumboy [Boiled cassava dough]. The word is found in Mende and Vai, with the same meaning. English (Yorkshire dialect) has *dumboy* as a kind of syrup-covered bread (Wright, *EDD*).

Ene [Is that so? Well!]. Merico term, cognate with Gullah and Krio *ɛnti* 'really?', 'indeed?' from Cornish dialect *enti* 'indeed' (Wright, EDD). Cf. also Twi *enti* 'that's why', and Cockney *inniP* 'isn't it?'

Fresh cold [a cold]. Widespread in the Caribbean, and in Krio.

Gbo ye [Boiled egg]. Kra has *nyɛ* 'egg'.

Grona [urchin]. From Krio *grona, gronatrit* i.e. 'grew up in the street', a prostitute.

Ground pea [Peanut]. Krio has *grampi, graumpi*, probably Liberianisms. The more usual Krio name is *granat*.

Gwana (A) [Monitor lizard]. *Gwana* is the usual pronunciation of *iguana* in Krio, the Caribbean and Australia.

Helluva [Big, bad, mighty]. Krio has *ɛlɛba* with the same meaning.

Help [Do something specific]. This may also mean 'do something on my behalf', thus "help me go shopping" will mean 'go shopping for me'.

Hobo Jo [Prostitute]. d'Azevedo's etymology implied in his spelling is unlikely, although no satisfactory alternative has yet been found. Krio has *obójó* 'prostitute'.

Humbug [Tease, bother, annoy]. In Krio, the Caribbean, Neo-Melanesian and Hawaiian Pidgin, *humbug* has the same meaning, suggesting the retention of an older English meaning of the word. Cf. U.S. Black English "humbug", meaning 'fight'.

I Say! [Listen!]. British equivalent of American "Say!".

Jale [Kitchen]. Cf. Krio *gyali* 'kitchen' from "galley". The author notes that this word is used mainly by the Kru.

Jam [Press, force beset]. This has the meaning 'be stalemated' in Krio. Cf. English "in a jam".

Jina [Spirits]. This is the indefinite Vai and Mende form. Krio *jinai* is probably via English "genii" rather than Mende, the definite form of which is *jinɛi*, not *jinai.

Judas [Dummy dragged through the streets at Easter]. This custom is also observed on Good Friday in Freetown, accompanied by the refrain "Judas die done tiday, we go bur' am tumarra" (*judas dai dɔn tide, wi go bɛr am tumara*).

Ko beya! [Cold beer]. This is the Merico pronunciation, *ko biɛ*.

Ko breya [Corn bread]. This is the Merico pronunciation, more correctly *kõ breə*.

Ko wa! [Cold water]. This is the Merico pronunciation, *ko wɔɔ*.

Lappa [Cloth garment]. From English "wrapper".

Lasmo [Fetish or medicine packet]. From Susu *lasmami* "greegree", ult. Arabic *la simam*, "there is no poison". Krio has *lasmami-wata*, water which has been used to wash sacred Koranic writings, and which therefore has magical properties.

Mami Water [Water woman]. Compare Krio *mami-wata*, Sranan *mama-watra*, Caribbean French Creole *mama-dlo*, and Brazilian Negro Portuguese *mãe de água*, all meaning 'mermaid, water spirit'. An African calque, cf. Yoruba *iya-olodo* (mother of the water) 'mermaid'.

Moli [Mohammedan, esp. a diviner]. Cf. Krio *more-man*, a Muslim diviner. Also English *Moor*, Manding *moli*, a Muslim.

N'mind ya [Don't worry]. Cf. Krio *nɔ mɛn ya* 'don't worry' (no + mind + y'hear).

No-way [impasse]. This expression is enjoying current vogue in the U.S.A.

Popo [Excrement] Cf. Krio *pupu*.

Portugee [Portuguese]. Cf. Krio *Podogi*, Portuguese.

Roundneck [T-shirt]. Also Krio.

Runny-stomach [Diarrhoea]. Cf. Krio *rɔn-bɛlɛ*, diarrhoea, Trinidad *Running-belly*, dysentery.

So-so [sort of, rather]. This would have been better glossed as "nothing but", Cf. Sranan, Caribbean, Krio *soso* 'just, nothing but'. English *so-so*, Portuguese *só* 'only'.

Sumangama [Incest]. Also occurs with this pronunciation in Krio. Cf. Mende *simɔŋgama* 'incest'.

Torch [Flashlight]. British English. Cf. Krio *torchlight*.

Tote [Carry a burden]. There are at least three possible origins for this item: Old English *totian* 'lift, elevate', which may have given rise to later "tote" in Piers Ploughman *then toted I into a tavern* (Crede, Ed. 1553, BIII) or the name *tote* applied to the handle of a carpenter's plane; French *tauter*, to ease the moving of a large object by placing rollers beneath it — Cf. U.S. *tote sled* in particular; and Kikongo *tota* 'pick up'. This also occurs in Gullah, Trinidad, Cameroon Pidgin and Krio.

Upstairs [Drink, drunk]. Cf. Krio *(a)kpɛtɛsi*, meaning (a) 'upstairs' or a storey-house, and (b) illicitly distilled spirit. From Yoruba, although ultimately English 'upstairs'. (Both Gã and Bini also have *kpɛtɛsi*, *patɛsi*, 'upstairs; gin'.)

Wayo Baby (A) [Prostitute]. From a popular highlife song. *Wayo* is via Krio, ultimately from Hausa *wààyó* 'trickery, deception, ingenuity'.

IAN F. HANCOCK
PIAYON E. KOBBAH

APPENDIX: LIBERIAN ENGLISH OF CAPE PALMAS

Since writing the preceding, it has been possible to examine one variety
of Liberian English in rather more detail. This dialect, briefly (and still
inadequately) described below, belongs to none of those listed in the
foregoing article; it represents the local speech of the Cape Palmas area,
in eastern coastal Liberia, West Africa, situated a few miles from the
border with Ivory Coast. It is referred to here as "Kepama" i.e. "Cape
Palmas", as locally pronounced, for lack of an existing designation.

The Kepama described here is that of my colleague Mr. Piayon
Emmanuel Kobbah, who was born in 1949 and who is from Behwan, a
township of ca. 6,000 people located on the Lower Kru Coast. Mr.
Kobbah attended junior high school at nearby Grand Cess, and senior
high school at Cape Palmas, about 50 miles up the coast. Most of his
life has been spent in Liberia's Eastern Province, although he has lived
for some time in Ghana and is currently resident in Austin, Texas, where
he is a student of chemistry at the local state university. He is Grebo
by birth, and speaks both Grebo and Kru, but regards Kepama as his
first language and the one in which he exhibits greatest fluency. His
command of standard (U.S.) English is exceptionally good, a fact which
has affected his Kepama to some degree; e.g. for the entry "burn" in the
following word-lists the form [br̃] was initially elicited, and later corrected
to [bɔ̃ɪ] as being more typical of the dialect. Similarly the phrase "breeze
...agree sun was strong past him" in the text (below) was chosen over
earlier "breeze surrender" since the latter was felt by Mr. Kobbah to be
representative only of the speech of an educated minority.

The exact relationship of this dialect to Black English dialects in the

U.S.A. has still to be ascertained. That it is less like Gullah than other Liberian varieties may be due to the fact that the area was originally founded in 1837 as a colony for liberated Afro-Americans called Maryland in Liberia, separate from Liberia and developed and peopled under the direction of the Maryland State Colonization Society in the U.S.A. It did not join with Liberia until Independence in 1857.

Not only does Kepama differ from Gullah in its suprasegmental phonological features, which resemble much more closely other forms of U.S. Black English, but one would expect to find a far higher proportion of shared lexical items of non-English origin — including the presumed Africanisms occurring in Black English outside of the Gullah area such as "dig", "jazz", "honkey", "goober", etc. A few do occur, e.g. "jibe" and "tote", but the Merico of Monrovia appears to have more in common with specifically Southern forms of U.S. Black English than does Kepama.

Kepama differs from Liberian Pidgin English in having Standard features such as a complete pronominal system and gender distinction, while lacking many of those associated with the Atlantic creoles, such as the occurrence of the pluralizing morpheme *dɛm* or a particle indicating progressive or habitual action. It also differs from Merico in that it has no copula or locative verbs, nor the *lɛ/də* marker, which aspect is indicated by the bound morpheme [-ɪ̯n] (<"-ing"), suffixed to the verb. Like the Atlantic creoles, however, Kepama indicates adjectival comparison with [pas], shows possession by syntactic ordering alone, and lacks distinction of number. It also shows considerable influence in vocabulary, idiom and phonology from non-Liberian forms of West African Pidgin. The principal linguistic features of the dialect are outlined here.

*Phonology**

Kepama phonology is far more complex than other varieties of English in West Africa. No attempt has yet been made to compile a phonemic inventory of this idiolect; all transcriptions are very broadly phonetic and certainly in need of revision and correction. There appear to be at least three variants for some items, depending upon whether they stand before a following initial consonant, an initial vowel, or prepausally. Rapidity of speech also seems to have some bearing upon consonantal realization, but this has not been investigated.

Most final syllables are open: *ga:* 'got', *bri* 'breeze', *lɪto* 'little' etc., but this is not invariable, cf. *šus* 'shoe', *waɪf* 'wife', *dæš* 'dash' (i.e. 'tip') etc. Where such an unrealized consonant occurs before a following initial vowel, it is sounded — as voiced [d] in the case of historic *t*:

* Because of a lack of a suitable sign to indicate the open vowel *a*, we will use *ä:* for this.

a ga ma pepə   'I've got my paper'
a ga‿d e   'I've got it'

Consonants which appear only under these environmental conditions are indicated with the link-sign (‿). Prepausally, the historic consonant may occur, but is unreleased, indicated by (ʔ) in the word-lists:

a n:no hwæ yu ga‿tʔ   'I don't know what you've got'

Items containing final vocalized [l] show some difference in overall form prevocalically e.g.:

dɛ pvə hɛvɛ   'the pole's heavy'
dɛ pol ĭsaɪ   'the pole's inside'

Final nasals are realized historically before a following initial vowel, and homorganically with following initial corresponding plosives. Plosives themselves are usually strongly aspirated initially and medially, as is the historic combination "*wh-*".

Verbs

Verbs derive from various English verb-forms e.g. *tɪklĭš* 'tickle' *fu* 'fill' (both also Krio), *ga* 'get, have' (also Guyanese) etc. These are uninflected for number but take the ending *-ĭ* for the present continuous or immediate future:

a goĭ wɪa yu o!   'I (am/will be) going without you!'
sta tɪklĭšĭ mĭ   'Stop tickling me'
hudæ kǎmĭ‿n dǎu dɛ ro? 'Who is coming down the road?'
hudæ kǎmĭ‿n tənãɪ‿tʔ? 'Who is coming tonight?'

The verb without suffix indicates past/non-past tense; auxiliary *bin* as found in Krio, Gullah, etc., does not occur. Examples of past time reference include:

hi hʌmbə ɔ: dɛ pipo   'He annoyed all the people'
dæ dɔ bwʌɪ mĭ fɔ tšru   'That dog really bit me'
a si hɔ dɛ: 'I saw her there'

And non-past:

yv fvl‿ə tšrɪkʔ   'You're full of tricks'
a m:bɪliv yv   'I don't believe you'
a gä wã hɪɛ   'I have one here'
ši lv džala mĭ   'She looks just like me'
ma waɪf grõmbo te: 'My wife grumbles so much'

It also occurs without affix in the imperative:

we̲d ɛ mĭ:	'Wait a minute'
pʋ dɛ̃ o:wɔ dɛ reə	'Put them over the rail'
liv e lõ̲n	'Leave it alone'

Completive aspect is indicated by *nǎ̃* (< "done"), less frequently by *fĭni* (< E. "finish" or Fr. "fini" from neighboring Ivory Coast?):

a nǎ̃ ri̲d e	'I have read it'
a fĭni ri̲d e	'I have (finished) read(ing) it'
yʋ nǎ̃ ple kɛlɛ tʋmɔš	'You've played the hypocrite too much'

The future tense is indicated by auxiliary *wɪ* (< "will"):

bʌ yʋ wɪ gɛ wǎ̲̃n tumɔrə	'But you will have one tomorrow'
wi wɪ dʋ e sũ	'We'll do it soon'

For "have/possess" the future and infinitive is *gɛ̲tʔ/d*, and the past/present is *gä̲tʔ/d*:

a gädä gɛ ma hæ̲tʔ	'I have to get my hat'
a wɪ gɛ ma hæ̲tʔ	'I will get my hat'
a gä ma hæ̲tʔ	'I have my hat'

The copula verb is lacking in the present tense:

hi ma frɛ̃	'He is my friend'
hi ɛ hafɔdu pɔɪsõ	'He's an effete person'
dɛ pä fu̲l ə wɔ:	'The pot is full of water'
a n:no hudæ tšra̲ĭ	'I don't know who's trying'
õ:nɛ mɛ̃: sɔpo to gɛ gusɛpaɪ̲pʔ	'Only men are supposed to have adam's apples'
e̲d ɛ bǎdo	'It's a bottle'

As is also the locative verb:

ʔe ʔǎ̲n dɛ tebo	'It's on the table'
a no hwɛ: e ɛʔ	'I know where it is' (lit. 'at')
fritǎv fawe põ:	'Freetown is very far away'
hya yɔ dæš	'Here's your tip/lagniappe'

For zero copula/locative, the future tense is *wɪ bi*, the past is *wɔ* and the completive *nǎ̃ bi*:

ši wɪ bi dɛ wǎ̃	'She'll be the one'
ʔe wɔ ʔĭ̲n dæ bɛ:̲gʔ	'It was in that bag'
yʋnǎ̲̃m bi ma nebə tʋ lõ	'You've been my neighbor for too long'

The complimentizer *se* seems to occur only after *tɛə* 'tell', and not after "hear", "know", etc. as in other Atlantic creoles:

    hi tɛə mĩ se hi sɪ‿kʔ   'He told me that he was ill'

Negation

Verbs are negated by *ɛ̃ ~ ẽ*, except for *kɛ̀* 'can, be able' which has the separate negative form *kɛ́*. The zero copula/locative is also negated with *ɛ̃ ~ẽ*:

    a ẽ gä nɔtĩ   'I have nothing'
    e Pẽ so!   'It isn't so!'
    e Pẽ dɛ: 'It isn't there'
    a kɛ̀ fãɪ‿n dɛ̃   'I can find them'
    a kɛ́ fãɪ‿n dɛ̃   'I cannot find them'

In rapid speech, the negator may be realized as nasal lengthening before nasals or stops, with accompanying raised voice pitch:

    a ɲ́:kɛ: 'I don't care'
    a ḿ:bɪliv yv   'I don't believe you'
    a ń:no   'I don't know'

"Won't" and "don't" appear to have coalesced in some interrogative constructions to become *õ*:

    hwæ yv õ sɪ‿dãv?   'Why don't / won't you sit down?'
    hwæ yv õ laɪ‿k e?   'Why don't you like it?'
    hwæ ši õ du e?   'Why won't she do it?'

This *õ*, however, is only employed with present/continuous tense or aspect; past tense constructions take *ẽ ~ ɛ̃*:

    hwæ ši ẽ du e?   'Why didn't she do it?'

The negative imperative *dõ* is better treated as a separate morpheme in the dialect rather than as *du* + neg., which is *ẽ‿n du*:

    dõ hala mĩ, mɛ̃:!   'Don't shout at me, man!'
    dõ sta‿d e nãv   'Don't start it now'
    wi ẽ du e yɛ‿tʔ   'We haven't done it yet'

Nominal negation is indicated by *nã̆* (< "not"), which is also used as the negating particle with the verbal auxiliaries *wɔ* and *wɪ*:

    yv nã̆ ma frɛ̃ nomo   'You're not my friend any more'
    maɪko nã̆ dɛ lidə   'Michael isn't the leader'
    a wɔ nã̆ dɛ: 'I wasn't there'
    wi wɪ nã̆ du e   'We won't do it'

Nouns

These are uninflected for number or possession, the latter being indicated
by apposition of the possessor before the possessed thus:

dɛ lɪto bɔɛ sɪsə	'The little boy's sister(s)'
ma pa fiə	'My father's field(s)'

Object pronominals such as "mine", "hers", etc. are translated by "my
own", "her own", etc.:

dɪ wã ma õ	'This one's mine'
dæ wã hɔ õ	'That one's hers'

Adjectives

Unlike the more conservative creoles such as Krio, Sranan or Saramaccan,
adjectives in Kepama must follow *bi* in future-tense constructions (thus
following the pattern of Gullah, English, etc.):

dɛ lif grĩ	'The leaf is green'
dɛ lif wɔ grĩ	'The leaf was green'
de lif wɪ bi grĩ	'The leaf will be green'
	(cf. Jamaican Creole *di liif wi griin*)

Like the Atlantic (especially African) creoles on the other hand, adjectives
are compared regularly with *pa(s)*. Older forms of Gullah also employ this:

ma sɪsə to pas yʊɔ	'My sister is taller than you (pl.)'
	(Cf. Gullah *ma šíšə tɔl pas hə́nə*)

Absolutes are similarly indicated, as in Krio:

hwɪš pä smo?	'Which pot is smallest?'

Adverbs

Regular adverbs are indicated syntactically, having the same form as the
corresponding adjectives:

dɛ gʊ gɛ: ku kP	'The good girl cooked'
dɛ gɛ: kʊ gʊ dP	'The girl cooked well'

Adverbs of interrogation do not alter subject-verb word order:

hwæ yʊ kɛ̃ kã?	'Why can't you come?'
hwɛ̃tãɪ de wɪ si ɔ?	'When will they see us?'

Vocabularies

The following lists are based upon the comparative creole vocabularies
found in Ian F. Hancock, "A provisional comparison of the English-based
Atlantic creoles", *African Language Review* VIII, 7-72 (1969): 36-67.
Each entry is followed by a parenthesized number corresponding to the
entries in the *ALR* lists.

The following abbreviations occur: [+ V], before following initial
vowel; (—), not in the *ALR* lists; n., noun; v., verb.

A. VERBS

1. Abuse (1) *kɔs.*
2. Agree (2) *gri.*
3. Annoy (3) *bádə, hʌmbə‿g.*
4. Ask (4) *äks.*
5. Attend, wait (5) *we‿d.*
6. Awaken (6) *wékɔp.*
7. Bang (—) *bæɪŋk.*
8. Be [equating] (7) *Ø.*
9. Be [locating] (8) *Ø.*
10. Beg (10) *be‿g, bæ‿g,
    ho fv‿tʔ/d.*
11. Begin (11) *stä‿d, bɪgȋ‿n.*
12. Believe (12) *bɪlív.*
13. Bend down (13) *bɛ̃ dãv‿n.*
14. Bite (14) *bwʌɪ‿tʔ/d.*
15. Blow, puff (—) *blo.*
16. Boil (16) *bɔɪ‿l.*
17. Bore, drill (17) *bo.*
18. Borrow (18) *lɛ̃‿n.*
19. Break (19) *bre‿kʔ.*
20. Breathe (—) *briv.*
21. Brush (20) *brəš.*
22. Burn (21) *bɜ̃ɪ‿n, bɔ̃‿n, br̃.*
23. Burst (22) *bɔs.*
24. Buy (23) *baɪ.*
25. Call (—) *ko‿l.*
26. Can, be able (24) *kɛ̃‿n, kɛ̃‿n.*
27. Cannot (—) *kɛ̃‿n, kɛ̃‿n.*
28. Care (25) *kɛ:.*
29. Carry; accompany (26) *kɛ:.*

30. Carry on the head
    (27) *to‿tʔ/d.*
31. Catch (28) *kɛš, kætš.*
32. Chew (29) *tšu.*
33. Choke (30) *tšukʔ.*
34. Climb (32) *klæɪ‿m.*
35. Cohabit, copulate (34) *yus, du,
    pãvs, fɔ‿k.*
36. Come (35) *kä‿m.*
37. Cook (36) *kv‿kʔ.*
38. Count (—) *kãv‿n.*
39. Cover (37) *kɔ́bə.*
40. Crush (38) *mæš.*
41. Dare (40) *dɛ:.*
42. Dip (41) *dɪ‿pʔ.*
43. Do (42) *du.*
44. Dream (43) *džrȋ‿m.*
45. Drink (44) *džrȋ‿ŋkʔ.*
46. Drive (45) *džraɪ‿v.*
47. Drop (46) *džrap.*
48. Eat (47) *i‿tʔ/d.*
49. Exchange (49) *tšɛ̃ndž.*
50. Fall (50) *fɔ́dãv‿n.*
51. Fasten (51) *stɪ‿kʔ.*
52. Fight (52) *fɔɪ‿tʔ/d.*
53. Fill (53) *fv‿l.*
54. Find (54) *fäɪ‿n.*
55. Flatter (55) *swi-mɔf.*
56. Flog, whip (56) *bi‿tʔ/d, hwip.*
57. Fly (57) *flaɪ.*

58. Force (—) *fósɪ.*
59. Forget (58) *fɔgé͜ tʔ/d.*
60. Forgive (59) *fɔgí.*
61. Give (60) *gi.*
62. Go (61) *go.*
63. Gossip (62) *bækʔbaɪ͜ tʔ/d, kɔ̃ŋk, me stĩŋkmɔf.*
64. Grow (63) *groə, groəd.*
65. Hang (64) *hæ̃ŋg.*
66. Have (65) *gä͜ tʔ/d; gɛ͜ tʔ/d* [infin./fut.].
67. Hear, understand (66) *híɛ.*
68. Help (67) *hɛp.*
69. Hit (—) *hɪ͜ tʔ/d.*
70. Hold (68) *ho͜ l.*
71. Hunt (69) *hɔ̃nt.*
72. Hurry (70) *meké.*
73. Hurt (71) *həɪ͜ tʔ/d.*
74. Jump (72) *džəmp.*
75. Keep (73) *kip, ho͜ l.*
76. Kill (74) *kɪv; kɪl* [+V].
77. Kiss (75) *kɪs.*
78. Knock (76) *näk.*
79. Know (77) *no.*
80. Laugh at (78) *láfä͜ tʔ/d.*
81. Leave, go out (79) *go av͜ tʔ/d.*
82. Leave, let alone (80) *liv.*
83. Lie down (81) *lédãv͜ n.*
84. Lift (82) *lɪf.*
85. Live (82) *lɪv; ste.*
86. Look at (84) *lúkä͜ tʔ/d.*
87. Look after (85) *mãɪ͜ n.*
88. Make (86) *me͜ kʔ.*
89. Marry (87) *mǽri.*
90. Menstruate (88) *si mũ͜ n, õ͜ n tãɪ͜ m.*
91. Move (89) *muv.*
92. Must (90) *gǎdə.*
93. Nag (91) *grɔ̃mbo͜ l, pikʔ fɔs, lʋkʔ fɔ plǽbə.*
94. [be] Named (92) *nẽ.*
95. Need (93) *nid, wǎ͜ n.*
96. Open (94) *ópĩ͜ n.*

97. Push (96) *puš, džukʔ.*
98. Put (98) *pʋ͜ tʔ/d.*
99. Release, free (—) *lúsn.*
100. Remember (99) *rəmẽ́mbə.*
101. Resemble (100) *févə, lʋ dža la:.*
102. Rest (101) *rɛs.*
103. Ride (102) *raɪ͜ d.*
104. Rub (—) *rɔb.*
105. Scratch (103) *skraš.*
106. See (104) *si.*
107. Seek, look for (—) *fãɪ͜ n, lʋ fɔ.*
108. Sell (—) *síɛ; sɛl* [+V].
109. Shake (105) *še͜ kʔ.*
110. Shout, Shout at (106) *hǎlä.*
111. Shut (107) *šɛ͜ tʔ/d, klo͜ z.*
112. Singe (108) *bɔ̃ɪ.*
113. Sit (109) *sídãv͜ n.*
114. Slap (110) *slæpʔ.*
115. Sleep (111) *slipʔ.*
116. Slip (112) *slɪpʔ, fɔ:͜ l, fɔ́dãv͜ n.*
117. Spill (113) *wes.*
118. Spit (—) *spɪ͜ tʔ/d.*
119. Split (114) *splɪ͜ tʔ/d.*
120. Spoil (115) *spɔ́ɛ; spɔ:l* [+V].
121. Squat (116) *skwä͜ tʔ/d.*
122. Squeeze (117) *skwis.*
123. Stab (118) *džukʔ.*
124. Stand (119) *stã͜ n, stãnɔ́p.*
125. Stay (120) *ste.*
126. Steal (121) *sti͜ l, tif.*
127. Stop (122) *stäpʔ.*
128. Stutter (123) *stámə.*
129. Swallow (124) *swǎlə.*
130. Take (125) *te͜ kʔ.*
131. Take off (—) *tek ɔ́͜ f.*
132. Talk (127) *tɔ:͜ kʔ.*
133. Talk at length (—) *spiš.*
134. Teach (—) *titš, lɔ̃ɪ͜ n.*
135. Tease (—) *džæ:b.*
136. Thank (128) *tæŋkʔ, tǽŋkɪ.*
137. Think (129) *tĩ͜ ŋk.*
138. Throw (—) *tšɔ̃ŋk, tro.*
139. Tickle (130) *tíklɪš.*

264 | Ian F. Hancock and Piayon E. Kobbah

140. Tie up (131) *ta:ɪ, táɛɔpʔ*.
141. Tilt (132) *lĭ‿n*.
142. Tremble (133) *tšrĭmbo‿l*.
143. Try (—) *tšra:ɪ*.
144. Vomit (—) *tro ɔpʔ, vămɪ*.
145. Walk (134) *wɔ:‿kʔ*.
146. Want (135) *wã̆‿n*.

147. Wash (136) *waš*.
148. Wear (137) *wɛ:*.
149. Wipe (138) *wɛpʔ*.
150. Work (139) *wɔ:kʔ, wɔ:kʔ*.
151. Write (140) *rɛɪ‿tʔ/d*.
152. Yawn (141) *gyapʔ*.

B. ADJECTIVES

153. Able (—) *ébo‿l*.
154. Abundant (142) *bʊkú, plɛ̃ntɛ*.
155. Afraid (143) *fíɛ, skɛ:‿d*.
156. All (144) *ɔ:‿l*.
157. Angry (145) *vɛ:*.
158. Bad (146) *ba:‿d*.
159. *Better* (147) *bédə*.
160. Big (148) *bɪ‿g*.
161. Black (149) *blæ‿kʔ*.
162. Blind (150) *blã‿n*.
163. Blue (151) *blu*.
164. Bogus, fake (152) *nã̆ río*.
165. Bold (153) *bo‿l, brev, džraɪáɪ*.
166. Broken (154) *bre‿kʔ*.
167. Casual (155) *ẽ kyɛ:, ẽ gä no šẽ, ízɪ*.
168. Chockful (156) *fʊ to dɛ brĭ*.
169. Clean (157) *klĭ‿n*.
170. Close (—) *klo‿s*.
171. Cold (158) *ko‿l*.
172. Crooked (159) *krúkɛ, bẽ‿n*.
173. Cunning (160) *fʊ‿l ə tšrɪkʔ, sæbi, fɪásko, tšríkɪ, rásko‿l*.
174. Dark (161) *däkʔ*.
175. Dead (162) *de:, de: ɔ̃ bérɪ*.
176. Deaf (163) *kɛ̆ hɪɛ*.
177. Deep (164) *dipʔ*.
178. Drunk (165) *džrɔ̃‿ŋkʔ, haɪ, búz*.
179. Dry (166) *džraɪ*.
180. Dumb (167) *kɛ̆ tɔ:kʔ*.
181. Every (168) *ɛvrɛ*.
182. Expensive (—) *díɛ*.

183. Far (169) *fa:, fáwe, fáwe pŏ:*.
184. Fat, plump (—) *fæ‿tʔ/d, bɪ‿g*.
185. Fine (170) *fãɪ‿n*.
186. First (171) *fɔ̃ɪs*.
187. Foolish (172) *fúlɪs*.
188. Glad (173) *glæ:‿d*.
189. Good (174) *gʊ‿d*.
190. Greedy (175) *grídɪ, bo‿l, gä bɪ ha:‿tʔ/d*.
191. Green (176) *grĭ‿n*.
192. Hard (—) *hä‿d, stšrã̆‿ŋg*.
193. Heavy (177) *hévɛ*.
194. High (178) *haʔɔ̃p, tɔ:‿l*.
195. Hot (180) *hä‿tʔ/d*.
196. Impudent (181) *sæsɪ, fɪtɪáɪ*.
197. Insolvent (182) *bʌ́stɛ, bro‿kʔ, džraɪ*.
198. Jealous (183) *džǽlə‿s*.
199. Lazy (184) *lézɛ*.
200. Long (185) *lɔ̃‿ŋg*.
201. Many (186) *plɛ̃tɪ, lådə, bʊkú*.
202. Mean (187) *grídɛ, mĭ‿n, lɔ̃ŋ-aɪ*.
203. Mediocre (188) *nyamanyámá*.
204. Middle (189) *mídə*.
205. Naked (190) *nékɛd*.
206. Near (—) *nɪɛ*.
207. New (191) *nyũ*.
208. Occasional (192) *wãwã̆‿n, sɔ̃ntãɪ*.
209. Old (193) *oə, o‿l, [+V] rɔ́stɪ*.
210. Old-fashioned (194) *o tãɪ*.
211. Only (195) *ɔ̃́lɛ, sóso*.

212. Other (196) ɔ́də.
213. Own (197) õ‿n.
214. Painful (198) so, həɪtɪ̆.
215. Poor (199) po.
216. Pretty (200) fãɪ‿n, gv lŏkĭ.
217. Red (201) re‿d.
218. Rich (202) rítš.
219. Ripe (203) re‿d, raɪ‿pʔ.
220. Rotten (204) rătĭ‿n.
221. Round (—) răv‿n.
222. Second (205) sékə̃‿n.
223. Short (207) šɔ:‿tʔ/d.
224. Small (208) smo‿l, lĭto‿l.
225. Soft (209) sɔf.
226. Softly (210) sɔ́flɪ.
227. Sour (211) sǎwə.

228. Square (212) skwɛ:.
229. Straight (—) stšre‿tʔ/d.
230. Strong (213) stšrã‿ŋg.
231. Tasty (214) swi‿tʔ/d.
232. Thin (215) džraɪ [person]; wɔtəwɔ́tə [liquid].
233. Third (216) təɪd.
234. Tired (217) táɪə.
235. Tough (218) tɔf.
236. Ugly (219) wɔwɔ́.
237. Untidy (220) tšäklă.
238. Warm (221) wɔ̃‿m.
239. Wet (222) wɛ‿tʔ/d.
240. White (223) hwaɪ‿tʔ/d.
241. Wide (—) waɪ‿d.
242. Yellow (224) yélə.

C. ANIMALS

243. Alligator (225) æligétə.
244. Animal (226) mit.
245. Ant (227) æs.
246. Ape (228) babŭ‿n.
247. Bee (229) bĭ.
248. Bird (230) bəɪ‿d.
249. Boa constrictor (231) bokɔ̃stšrʌ́ktə.
250. Cat (232) kyætʔ.
251. Centipede (233) tavznlég.
252. Cow (234) kav.
253. Crab (—) krɛ:b.
254. Deer (—) díɛ.
255. Dog (235) dɔg.
256. Duck (236) dəkʔ.
257. Elephant (237) éləfɔ̃‿n.
258. Frog (—) frä‿g.
259. Goat (239) go‿tʔ/d.
260. Grasshopper (—) grahápə.
261. Hawk (240) hʌ:kʔ.
262. Hen (241) hɛ̃‿n.

263. Iguana (242) gwǎnə.
264. Louse (243) laɪs.
265. Monkey (244) mɔ́ŋkɛ.
266. Mosquito (245) mäskíto.
267. Mouse (246) ræ‿tʔ/d.
268. Parrot (247) pɔ́lɛ.
269. Pig (248) pig, häg.
270. Porcupine (—) pɔ́kyʊpãɪ‿n.
271. Rabbit (249) ræbɪ‿tʔ/d.
272. Rat (250) ræ‿tʔ/d.
273. Rooster (251) rústə.
274. Sand-flea (252) džígə.
275. Scorpion (253) skɔ́:pyə̃‿n.
276. Snail (—) snéə‿l.
277. Snake (254) sne:kʔ.
278. Spider (255) spáɪdə.
279. Tadpole (—) frǎ-bébɪ.
280. Tortoise (256) tɔ́tɔ.
281. Wasp (258) bĭ.
282. Wing (—) wĭ‿ŋ.
283. Worm (259) wɔ́rə̃‿m.

D. PLANTS AND FOODSTUFF

284. Bark (—) skǐ͜n.
285. Bean (260) bǐs.
286. Bread (262) bre͜d, bréə͜d.
287. Burnt food (263) krəs,
    bɔ̃ɪ-fu͜d.
288. Bushland (264) bvš.
289. Calabash, gourd (265, 278)
    kæləbǽs.
290. Cashew (266) kɔ́šu.
291. Cassava (267) kæsá:lə.
292. Coconut (268) kokónʌ͜tʔ/d.
293. Dried fish (269) draɪ-fíš.
294. Egg (270) e͜gʔ.
295. Fat, grease (—) ɔ:ɪ͜l.
296. Flour, flower (271) fla:v.
297. Food (272) fu͜dʔ, grʌbʔ.
298. Fruit (273) frutʔ.
299. Fufu (274) fúfu.
300. Ginger (277) džǐndžə.
301. Grass (—) gra͜s.
302. Lagniappe (279) dæš.
303. Mango (280) plɔ̃͜m.
304. Meat (282) mitʔ.

305. Mushroom, fungus (275)
    mʌ́šrũ͜m.
306. Nut (283) nətʔ.
307. Ochra (284) ókrə.
308. Onion (285) ɔ̃́yɔ̃͜n.
309. Papaw (—) pɔ́pɔ.
310. Peanut (286) grãvmpí.
311. Pepper (287) pépɛ.
312. Pineapple (288) panápv͜l.
313. Potato (289) potéto.
314. Pumpkin (290) pɔ̃́ŋkǐ͜n.
315. Rice (291) raɪ͜s.
316. Rind (292) pílǐ͜n.
317. Root (293) ru:͜tʔ/d.
318. Salt (294) sɔ:͜l.
319. Thorn (295) tɔ̃:͜n.
320. Tobacco (296) tobǽko.
321. Tomato (297) tɔméto.
322. Tree (298) tšri.
323. Water (300) wɔ:, wɔ́tə, wɔ́ɾə.
324. Wood (301) wv͜dʔ.
325. Yam (302) yǽ͜m.

E. NATURAL PHENOMENA

326. Ash (303) ǽšɪ.
327. Bank (—) wɔ́ɾəsaɪ.
328. Beach (—) biš.
329. Coast (304) kos.
330. Copper (305) kɔ́pə.
331. Country (306) kɔ̃́ntrɛ.
332. Dawn (307) sũ mɔ̃́nǐ͜n.
333. Day (308) de.
334. Day after tomorrow (309)
    de ǽftə tvmɔ́rə.
335. Ditch (310) gwɔ́tə.
336. Earth (311) dəɪ͜tʔ/d.
337. Fire (312) fáɪə.
338. Gold (313) go͜l.
339. Ground (314) grãv͜n.

340. Iron (315) áɪɔ̃͜n.
341. Midday (316) twɛ ǐ dɛ de.
342. Midnight (317) twɛ ǐ dɛ
    naɪ͜tʔ/d.
343. Moon (318) mũ͜n.
344. Morning (319) mɔ̃́nǐ͜n.
345. Mud (320) mədʔ, pɔtɔpɔ́tɔ.
346. Night (321) naɪ͜tʔ/d.
347. Powder (322) pǎdə.
348. Rain (323) rɛ̃͜n.
349. Rainbow (324) rɛ̃́mbo.
350. River (325) rívə.
351. Rock (326) rä͜kʔ.
352. Sand (327) sɛ̃͜n.
353. Smoke (328) smo͜kʔ.

354. Star (329) *sta.*
355. Sun (330) *sɔ̃‿n.*
356. Swamp (331) *swã‿m.*
357. Thunder (332) *tɔ̃ndə.*
358. Time (333) *taɪ‿m.*
359. Today (334) *tvdé.*

360. Tomorrow (335) *tvmɔ́rə.*
361. Wind (336) *brɪ‿s.*
362. World (337) *wɔɪ‿l, wɔɪ‿l.*
363. Year (—) *yíɛ.*
364. Yesterday (338) *yésəde.*

F. HOUSEHOLD, ETC.

365. Backyard (339) *bækyá:‿dʔ.*
366. Bed (340) *be‿dʔ.*
367. Bell (—) *bíɛ; bɛl* [+V].
368. Boat (341) *bo‿tʔ/d.*
369. Book (342) *bv‿kʔ.*
370. Bottle (—) *bǎdo‿l.*
371. Bowl (—) *bóə; bol* [+V].
372. Bucket (343) *bɔ́kɪ‿tʔ/d.*
373. Candle (345) *kǽndə.*
374. Church (346) *tšɔtš.*
375. Co-operative society (—) *súsu, ku, kɔ̃mpǐ‿n.*
376. Court (347) *ko‿tʔ/d.*
377. Doorway (349) *dómav.*
378. Drum (—) *džrɔ̃‿m, sãŋgbá.*
379. Fence (350) *fɛ̃s.*
380. Fishhook (—) *fíšĭ-hvkʔ.*
381. Fork (351) *fɔ‿kʔ.*
382. Funeral (352) *fɔ́nərə‿l.*
383. Hammock (354) *hǽmɔ‿kʔ.*
384. House (355) *häv‿s.*
385. Hut (—) *həɪ‿tʔ/d.*
386. Job (356) *wɔkʔ.*
387. Kettle (357) *tíkɪtv‿l.*
388. Kitchen (—) *kítšǐ‿n, džǽlɛ.*
389. Knife (358) *naɪ‿f.*
390. Mat (359) *mæ‿tʔ/d.*
391. Mortar (360) *mǎtə.*

392. Mortuary (361) *fɔ́nərə hõ‿m.*
393. Net (—) *nɛ̃‿ntʔ.*
394. Oven (362) *békə.*
395. Paddle (363) *pǽdə‿l.*
396. Pestle (363) *pɛ̃́nsə‿l.*
397. Pigsty (364) *hǎgpɛ̃‿n.*
398. Place (365) *ple.*
399. Pole (—) *pvə; pol* [+V].
400. Pot (366) *pä‿tʔ/d.*
401. Proverb (367) *pǽrəbə‿l.*
402. Portion (368) *pi‿s, plɔgʔ* [of e.g. orange].
403. Public-transport vehicle (—) *hólehóle.*
404. Rope (—) *ro‿pʔ.*
405. School (369) *sku‿l.*
406. Scissors (370) *sízə.*
407. Song (371) *sɔ̃ŋ.*
408. Spear (—) *spíɛ.*
409. Spoon (372) *spǔ‿n.*
410. Story (373) *stɔ́rɛ, te‿l.*
411. Street (374) *stšri‿tʔ/d.*
412. String (—) *stšrɛ̃‿ŋg.*
413. Town (375) *tãv‿n.*
414. Verandah (376) *pɪǽzə, bǽnɪstə, potš.*
415. Window (—) *wĩndə.*
416. Word (377) *wɔɪ‿dʔ.*

G. CLOTHING

417. Bag (—) *bɛ:‿g.*
418. Clothes (378) *klo‿s.*
419. Comb (—) *kõ‿m.*

420. Earring (379) *íerĭ‿n.*
421. Fan (—) *fɛ̃‿n.*
422. Handkerchief (380) *hǽŋkɛtšɛ.*

423. Hat (381) hætʔ.
424. Headpad (382) kɔ́tə.
425. Headscarf (383) hétaɪ.
426. Loincloth, wrapper (384) lapá.
427. Maraccas (385) sása.

428. Pipe (386) paɪ‿pʔ.
429. Sandal (387) slípəs.
430. Shoe (388) šus.
431. Trousers (389) trávzɛ.
432. Walking-stick (391) wɔkɪ̃-stɪ‿k

H. PEOPLE

433. Afro-American (—) kɔ́lɔ.
434. Bastard (392) avsáɪ-tšaɪ‿l, bástə.
435. Boy (393) bɔ́ɛ.
436. Brother (394) brɛ́də.
437. Child (395) tšaɪ‿l.
438. Children (—) tšívrɔ̃‿n.
439. Co-wife (396) sɛkɔ̃ waɪf.
440. Creole (397) krió, frítāv‿m-bɔbɔ́ [Sierra Leonean; see 450 below].
441. Devil (398) dévə‿l.
442. Family (400) fǎmlɛ.
443. Father (401) pa.
444. Girl (402) gɛ:.
445. Girlfriend (403) gɛ́:frɛ̃‿n.
446. God (404) gɔ:‿dʔ.
447. Guest (—) stšrɛ̃́ndžə, džɛs.
448. Hunter (405) hʌ́ntə.
449. Liar (406) láɪə.
450. Liberian of Settler ancestry (—) kɔ́ŋgɔ.
451. Man (407) mɛ̃:‿n.
452. Master (408) mǎsə.

453. Mermaid (409) mamɪ-wɔ́tə.
454. Mother (410) ma:.
455. Mulatto (411) mɔlǽto.
456. Mute (—) bobó.
457. Negro (412) nígro.
458. Overseer (413) hé: mɛ̃:‿n; obəsí [vb.].
459. People (415) pípo‿l.
460. Person (416) pɔ́ɪsɔ̃‿n.
461. Portuguese (417) potogí.
462. Preacher (—) pá:stə, révrɔ̃‿n.
463. Priest (—) fádə.
464. Sister (418) sísə.
465. Spirit (419) spírɪ‿tʔ/d.
466. Terms of address (420) ba, bra, mɛ̃:.
467. White man (421) wáɪmɛ̃‿n, kwɪ.
468. Wife (422) waɪf.
469. Woman (423) wúmǽ‿n.
470. Workman (424) lébrə.
471. Yoruba, Ibo, Ashanti and other coastal peoples (425) kóstə.

I. ANATOMICAL

472. Arm (426) ã‿m.
473. Armpit (427) ɔ́nə dɛ ʔã‿m.
474. Back (428) bæ‿kʔ.
475. Beard (429) bíɛ, bíɛbɪɛ.
476. Birthmark (430) báʔmäkʔ.
477. Blood (431) blʌ.
478. Body (432) bǎdɛ.

479. Bone (433) bõ‿n.
480. Brain (434) brɛ̃‿n.
481. Breast (435) bɔbí.
482. Buttocks (436) bɔtʔ, as.
483. Bump, callus (437) bɔ̃m‿pʔ.
484. Chin (—) tšĩ‿n.
485. Cold, catarrh (—) freškó‿l.

486. Ear (438) *fɛ*.
487. Excreta (439) *púpu; dʌbəsí*
[also Latrine].
488. Eye (440) *aɪ*.
489. Finger (441) *fĩŋgə*.
490. Hair (444) *hɛ:*.
491. Hand (426) *hæ͜n*.
492. Head (445) *he:͜dʔ*.
493. Heart (446) *hä:͜tʔ/d*.
494. Hunger (447) *hɔ̃ŋgrɪ*.
495. Knee (448) *nĩ*.
496. Larynx (—) *gúsɛ-paɪ͜pʔ*.
497. Leg/foot (449) *fʊ͜tʔ/d*.
498. Leprosy (450) *lépɔsɪ*.
499. Liver (451) *lívə*.
500. Mouth (453) *mɔ͜f*.

501. Navel (—) *nébə*.
502. Nipple (454) *nípo͜l*.
503. Nose (455) *nos*.
504. Nostril (456) *ho ʔĩ dɛ nos*.
505. Penis (457) *nɔtʔ/d*.
506. Pus (460) *pɔs*.
507. Side, trunk (—) *saɪ͜dʔ*.
508. Skin (461) *skĩ͜n*.
509. Stomach (462) *bélɛ, stɔmækʔ*.
510. Thigh (463) *taɪ*.
511. Thirst (464) *tɔ́ɪstɪ*.
512. Tongue (465) *tɔ̃ŋg*.
513. Tooth (466) *titʔ*.
514. Vulva (467) *púsɛ, tĩ͜ŋ*.
515. Yaws (468) *yɔ:*.

J. PRONOUNS AND VERBAL MARKERS

516. I (469) *a*.
517. Me (—) *mĩ*.
518. My (—) *ma*.
519. You [sg.] (470) *yʊ*.
520. Your [sg. + pl.] *yɔ:*.
521. He (471) *hi*.
522. His (—) *hɪ*.
523. Him (—) *hĩ͜m*.
524. She (472) *ši*.
525. Her (—) *hɔ*.
526. It (471) *ʔe*.
527. We (473) *wi*.
528. Us (—) *ɔ*.
529. Our (—) *ʔäv*.
530. You [pl.] (474) *yʊ́ɔ*.

531. They (475) *de*.
532. Their (—) *dɛ:*.
533. Them *dɛ̃͜m*.
534. Durative marker (476) V+ -*ĩ͜n*.
535. Future marker (477) *wɪ*.
536. Past marker (478) *Ø*.
537. Completive marker (479) *nǎ, fĩnɪ*.
538. Negator [preverbal] (480) *ɛ̃͜n, ẽ͜n*.
539. Negator [prenominal] (480) *nã*.
540. Negator [imperative] (480) *dõ͜n*.

K. NUMERALS

541. One (481) *wǎ͜n*.
542. Two (482) *tu*.
543. Three (483) *ʈri*.
544. Four (484) *fo*.
545. Five (485) *fa:*.
546. Six (486) *sɪ*.

547. Seven (487) *sévɛ̃͜n*.
548. Eight (588) *ʔe͜tʔ/d*.
549. Nine (489) *nã:͜n*.
550. Ten (490) *tẽ͜n*.
551. Eleven (491) *lévɛ̃͜n*.
552. Twelve (492) *twɛ:*.

270   Ian F. Hancock and Piayon E. Kobbah

553. Twenty (493) twḗnɛ.   556. Thousand (496) távzɛ̃‿n.
554. Thirty (494) tɔ́ɪdɛ.   557. Dozen (497) dɔ́zɛ̃‿n.
555. Hundred (495) hɔ̃ndrɛ.

L. GRAMMATICAL AND MISCELLANEOUS

558. Again (499) (e)gḗ‿n.   592. Never (532) névə.
559. Against (500) gɛ̃s.   593. News (533) nyũ.
560. All right (501) ɔ́raɪ‿tʔ/d.   594. Nothing (534) nɔ́tĭ‿ŋ.
561. Always (502) ɔ́we.   595. Now (535) nãv.
562. And (503) æ‿n.   596. On top [of] (536) ắntắp(ɔ).
563. Any (504) ḗnɛ.   597. Only (537) ɔ́:nɛ.
564. As (505) ʔɛs.   598. Outside (538) avsáɪ.
565. At (—) ʔɛ‿tʔ/d.   599. Over (539) ó:wə.
566. Because (506) bɪkɔ́.   600. Own (540) õ‿n.
567. Before (507) bɪfó.   601. Perhaps (542) mébɪ.
568. Behind (508) bəhãɪ‿n.   602. Recently (543) dɛ ʔədə de.
569. But (509) bʌ‿tʔ/d.   603. Someone (544) sắmbädɪ.
570. Even (511) ivĭ‿n, sɛf.   604. Soon (545) dʒʌ́snãv, sũ‿n.
571. Ever (—) évə.   605. Speed (546) spi‿dʔ.
572. Everywhere (512) évɪhwɛ.   606. That (547) dæ.
573. For (513) fɔ.   607. Then (548-9) dɛ̃‿n.
574. Formerly (514) fɔɪs tãɪ‿m.   608. There (550) dɛ:.
575. Hello (515) hádv.   609. These (551) di.
576. Here (516) ya, hɪ́ɛ.   610. This (552) dɪ.
577. How (517) hav.   611. Those (—) do.
578. How many (518) hámɔ̌š.   612. To [preverbal + locative]
579. If (519) ɪf.   (553-4) to.
580. In (520) ɪ̃‿n.   613. Too (555) tv.
581. Inside (521) ɪ́saɪ.   614. Too much (556) túmɔ̌š.
582. Intensifier [verbal] (522) te:.   615. Under (557) ɔ̃nə.
583. Interjection of incredulity   616. Underneath (—) ɔ̃nənɪ́‿tʔ/d.
     (524) šɔ:.   617. Until (558) téə; tel [+V].
584. Interjection of pain (525) ʔía:.   618. Up (—) ɔ‿pʔ.
585. Interjection of surprise (526)   619. Very (—) hélɔvə, tv, plḗntɛ.
     ʔɛ́ʔɛ̃̀, dǽmɛ.   620. What (560) hwä, hwätĭ‿ŋ.
586. Just (527) dʒɔs.   621. When (561) hwɛ̃, hwɛ̃ntắɪ‿m.
587. Like (505) lɛkʔ.   622. Where (562) hwɛ:, hwɛplɛ́.
588. Magic (528) dʒudʒú, nyãntɔ́nɔ,   623. Which, that (563) dæ.
     vákwɛ, wɪš.   624. Who (564) hu, húdæ, húzdæ.
589. Manner, way (529) fǽšɔ̃‿n, we.   625. Why (565) hwæ:.
590. Mercy (530) másɛ.   626. With (566) wɪ.
591. More than (531) pa‿s.   627. Without (567) wɪáv.

628. Yes (568) *yɛ.*   630. Yonder (570) *yånda.*

629. Yet (569) *yɛ‿tʔ/d.*

Text (I.P.A. standard passage)

The North Wind and the Sun

dɛ bri frå dɛ nɔ: æ‿n dɛ sɔ̃‿m pɪkʔ fɔs əbav hwɪš wå stšrå‿m pas dɛ ɔdə wå. hwa de wɔ tɔkĭ wå mɛ̃: kå‿m baɪ wɛ:ĭ wɔ:‿ŋ ko‿tʔ. de gri dæ hu kʋ me dæ mɛ̃:‿n te‿k äf hɪ ko wɪ bi stšrå‿m pas dɛ ɔdə wå.

fɔɪs dɛ bri blo ha: bʌ dɛ mo hi blo dɛ mo dɛ mɛ̃‿m pu hɪ ko råv hĭ sɛf. dɛ̃‿n dɛ bri stä tšra‿ĭ. sɔ̃ šaĭ hä‿d å‿n dɛ mɛ̃‿n teə hi te hɪ ko‿d äf. bri frå‿n dɛ nɔ: gri sɔ̃ wɔ stšrå‿m pas hĭ.

'The Breeze from the North and the Sun pick fuss about which one strong past the other one. While they were talking, one man come by wearing warm coat. They agree that who could make that man take off his coat will be strong past the other one.

First the Breeze blow hard, but the more he blow, the more the man pull his coat around him self. Then the Breeze stop trying. Sun shine hot on the man till he take his coat off.

Breeze from the North agree Sun was strong past him.'

University of Texas at Austin

Section III: Black English and the Acculturation Process

INTRODUCTION TO SECTION III

One of the most bizarre facets of the relationship of Black and white in the New World has been the failure, especially where the continental United States is concerned, to consider the possibility of persisting cultural differences which might have served as the matrix for language differences between the two groups. It has regularly been assumed, *a priori*, that assimilation was rapid and relatively complete, in spite of the known inhibiting factors of slavery and caste distinction. Of course, acculturation was relatively facilitated for one group of slaves, the house servants (Frazier 1957), and perhaps to an even greater degree for other groups like the artisans, who often worked away from the plantation, and the freedmen. But, at the time of Emancipation (nearly two and a half centuries after slaves were brought to the continental colonies), striking cultural differences had been maintained by the race-caste system and were regularly recorded by observers like the plantation novelists. It is no radical hypothesis that the group which is today less acculturated (the "disadvantaged" in much recent educationist terminology) is composed primarily of the descendants of the plantation field hands.[1] The reason for failure, in the academic community, to acknowledge the cultural

---

[1] Goveia (1964:242) says very explicitly of the West Indies
"However, they [the slave owners] did not consider it part of their business to 'civilise' the slaves, and, in any case, the lack of social contact made it impossible for them to assimilate the field slaves culturally. Those slaves therefore remained the most isolated and the most 'African' group in a society where the words Negro and slave were almost synonymous and everything African was held to be, by definition, inferior."

differences which have persisted to the present are detailed by Stewart (forthcoming).[2]

In spite of the difficulty which such cultural differences have posed for New World historiography, which by and large has wanted to consider those features which cannot be explained in terms of the spread of European patterns as spontaneous innovations, the most cursory survey of events reveals how great the differences were and how drastic their consequences have been. Accounts of slave revolts were very early accompanied by wondering comments on their language and naming patterns, and on other elements of their life style (Horsmanden 1744). Events as prominent in American history as the Salem witch trials were occasioned by inability of groups like the Puritans to comprehend African cultural patterns like the religion of Tituba (Drake 1866). An occasional early observer like Cotton Mather (*The Angel of Bethesda*, 1721) perceived that the West African-derived slaves possessed techniques (in this case, a form of inoculation against smallpox) not known by the European colonists in the Americas. But the history of cultural differences has remained largely obscure, darkened by American *naiveté* regarding cultural diversity and by guilt feelings about slavery.

Where cultural differences have been dealt with at all, they have tended to center around the Sea Islands, where isolation offered an ecological pseudo-cause which enabled Americans to forget survivals from the native West Africa of the original slaves. That such survivals were also found on a somewhat less isolated island, Long Island, was known (Furman 1875) but conveniently forgotten. And, to fit the Gullah islands into the pattern, it was necessary to develop the fiction that the Gullah were not acculturating at all, because of their allegedly complete isolation, but perhaps even continuing to diverge from mainstream American culture.

To a few scholars, like Melville J. Herskovits, William R. Bascom, and Lorenzo Dow Turner, this was obvious nonsense. One of the outstanding points of Turner (1949) was that he established Africanisms, especially in naming practices, which could only be survivals and could not be New World innovations. Others, like Puckett (1937; see also Dillard 1968) actually established that naming patterns like the day names (DeCamp 1967; Cassidy 1961; Dillard 1971, 1972) actually extended far beyond the Gullah islands. But the tradition was able, through a kind of intellectual contortionism, to ignore such evidence and to maintain that specifically Afro-American culture was and had always been limited to the Sea Islands.

The amount of evidence to the contrary is of course immense, when

---

[2] As will be noted below, the work of certain musicologists (Courlander 1963:4-5) is a major exception.

folklore, music, the dance,[3] and other such factors are taken into account. It will be impossible to give, here, even a sketchy account of work in those fields. Jazz and Negro folk music alone (Courlander 1963, Ramsey and Smith 1939, Stearns 1956, Stearns 1968, Jones 1963, Lomax 1950, Jackson 1967, Keil 1966, among many others) offer an embarrassment of riches insofar as evidence is concerned.[4] Unfortunately, attempts to link jazz and its technical vocabulary ("slang") directly to the creole language tradition (Oliver 1963, Gold 1964) were so crude as to make their well-wishers cringe for them.

In folklore, especially, there is a vast amount of the kind of evidence which can be fairly easily evaluated. Fauset (1927), Lomax (1968), Abrahams (1962, 1964, 1968, *inter alia*), and many others documented the unique character of Black folklore and speculated with more or less success on its probable African origins. Complications arose from such obstructions as the prominent obtuseness of Dorson (1959), who believed that Brer Rabbit stories and Anansi stories could not be related because Brer Rabbit was a rabbit and Anansi a spider! The most elementary feature analysis would reveal that each (like Ti Malis in the Haitian stories) was a small, tricky, marginally malicious and even felonious character who depended upon intelligence rather than strength — and that each had a dupe who was the opposite in all respects except perhaps malice and felony.[5] That there is a depth of West African religious survival which is not hinted at in popularly known collections like those of Joel Chandler Harris is indicated even by the title *Old Rabbit the Voodoo* (Owen 1893). Herskovits saw the connections, but his insights were only sporadically followed up (Whitten and Szwed 1970).

Although there are materials in Turner (1949) which show acculturation

[3] Courlander (1963:190) reports "Only three-quarters of a century ago, a number of dances were known in Louisiana which have disappeared almost entirely." For descriptions of surviving dances, which may be of the same type, see Herskovits and Herskovits (1936).
[4] On musical acculturation, see especially Merriam, "African Music", in Bascom and Herskovits (1962).
[5] On the artificial Europeanization of West Indian folklore, see Dillard "How Not to Classify the Folktales of the Antilles", *Caribbean Studies* 3 (1964): 39-44. In the motif treated in some detail there, the equivalence of Ti Malis:Bouqui::Anansi:Tiger::Lapin :Tigre::Rabbit:Tiger is treated in some detail. Although most of these comparisons are restricted to West Indian tales, some comparison is presented in one Louisiana tales. Courlander (1963:173) reports Boukee [sic] and Rabbit together in one Louisiana tale. The manner in which Negro "English" folklore and Negro "French" folklore interact and even merge in Louisiana has been overlooked by more conventional folklorists, just as the Black dialects have been overlooked by dialect geographers. Spider and Cunnie [Cunning] Rabbit both occur in the West African Pidgin English tales presented in Florence M. Cronise and Henry W. Ward, *Cunnie Rabbit, Mr. Spider, and the Other Beef* (1903).

of the Gullah,[6] the area was apparently abandoned after *Africanisms in the Gullah Dialect*. Earlier observers, like Crum (1940), were forgotten or even condemned because of their amateurism or because they occasionally used the racist terminology which they found in their climate of opinion. Crum, for example, wrote

On the islands near Charleston the dialect is less intense, probably because of the proximity of these areas to the city and to the outside currents that flow into urban centers (p. 103).

and also

This dialect, commonly known as Gullah, is spoken also by many whites in a more or less modified form (p. 101).

On the latter statement, see McDavid and McDavid (1951) and Dillard (1972:chapter V).[7]

Failure of groups like the *Linguistic Atlas of the United States and Canada* to discover those styles and varieties which represented the "African" end of the acculturation continuum is partly traceable to its concentration upon adult, often even elderly, informants. As Stewart (1965) established for the United States (hinted at in Dillard 1964, reprinted here), the more "deviant" features of the variety Black English are characteristic of the speech of young children rather than of adults. DeCamp (1971:351) stresses the same condition in Jamaica:

The degree of acculturation varies with such factors as age, poverty, and isolation from urban centers.

But such insights have rarely been applied to the continental United States. It is no accident that Stewart (1965) was produced by a well-known creolist (Stewart 1962a and b).

In the great American desert of studies, Bascom (1941, reprinted in this section) stands out like an oasis. That acculturation was an ongoing process, even among the allegedly isolated Gullah, would not have sur-

---

[6] As Stewart (f.c.) emphasizes, Turner makes a great deal of African language survivals like the use of Fula *ðego* (*ðe* 'five' plus *go* 'one') 'six' without directly calling attention to forms like [faɪw n wʌn sɛnt] 'five and one cent' (1949:260, 261). Although Turner was undoubtedly aware of the point, it seems worth emphasizing (particularly in the context of institutionalized obtuseness all too often found in the United States) that *five and one* is only slightly less "African" than *ðego*.

[7] For Black-to-white linguistic influence in the West Indies, see Goveia (1964:248-49) and Dillard, "White Through Black: The Neglected Side of New World Communication Patterns", in Craig (ed.), *Creole Languages and Educational Development* (f.c.).

McDavid and McDavid present (1951) what is, in my opinion, an unnecessarily restricted set of conditions under which it may be accepted that white speech has been influenced by that of Negroes. Criticisms of the limitations of this presentation are to be found in Dillard (1972: chapter V).

prised Thomas Wentworth Higginson (*Army Life in a Black Regiment,* 1870) or any of the host of post-Civil War visitors to the Sea Islands (Stewart f.c.). But Bascom put the whole matter into the framework of professional anthropology.

Since they are perhaps even more completely outside awareness than language structure, gestural systems offer much promise for the study of an acculturation process which is still far from complete. (There are, of course, problems in tracing such patterns to West Africa, particularly given the paucity of study of West African systems.) A bicultural and bigestural investigator, Kenneth Johnson, has combined his concern about Black educational problems with an interest in non-linguistic communication systems. His article (reprinted in this section) is a pioneering effort in the field. By the very nature of the data, Johnson's descriptions are hardly comparable to the forms of motor behavior concerned with planting seed which Bascom describes (p. 285). But it seems significant that both refer to differences between Black and white motor behavior.[8]

Linguistic acculturation is primarily treated in Stewart (1967 and 1968, reprinted in section II). My own article, immodestly offered, can have little but historical value at this point. Although this essay antedated Bailey (1965) and Stewart (1965), only the accidents of publication give

---

[8] There are very interesting respects in which postural and kinesic features of Black culture are linked to dancing:

"A superstition in respect to posture is by some rigorously observed. It is, that religious people must never sit with their legs crossed. The only reason given —though we cannot help suspecting that there must be another kept in concealment — is that *crossing the legs is the same as dancing, and dancing is a sin*" (William Owens, *Lippincott's Magazine* XX (1877): 748-55, reprinted in Jackson 1967:146).

We can compare Courlander (1963:195)

"The tension generated in the course of the shout has certain approved outlets, such as ecstatic seizures or possessions, but the feet are required to be kept under control. A person who violates this commonly understood proscription by 'crossing his feet' — that is to say, by 'dancing' — is admonished or evicted from the service," and "He was often turned out of church for crossing his feet or singing a 'fiddle sing'" (1963:329).

When the African cultures, in which dancing quite obviously had a functional part, came into contact with certain fundamentalistic Southern (white) religious cults in which dancing was held to be sinful, adjustment was not easy. (I can testify, from childhood experience, to the difficulty of Southern whites in reconciling the obviously intense religion of Blacks with the love for "sinful" activities like dancing.) To follow the Southern white revivalist sects so far as to eliminate dancing completely, even in church, was obviously too much of an acculturative demand on the transplanted West African (Jones 1963:36-39).

For the influence of such religious dancing on minstrel show dancing and "into the outer world through the frontiersman" (Nathan 1962:82-83), there is more evidence than has usually been taken into account. Nathan (1962) is more direct and, in my opinion, more accurate than the usual historian in ascribing direct influence on white dancing to Black dancing.

it any kind of priority. All three of us were — and are — fiercely independent. And other creolists, like Mervyn Alleyne and Richard Allsopp, who have come relatively late to the study of Black American English in the United States, have not depended upon us for insights. Any creolist who is exposed to the speech of poor Black Americans over a reasonable length of time, whether in the North or in the South, sees what we were and are driving at.

The aim of this republication is rather that of its original publication: to honor Melville J. Herskovits, one of the few innovators in Afro-American studies. Unfortunately, Herskovits — like his sometime associate Lorenzo Dow Turner — is not easy to represent through excerpts. To present the pages entitled "Linguistic Notes" from *Suriname Folk-Lore* (1936:117-135) would be fair to Herskovits only if every reader would promise to make an industrious effort to place that section within the totality of Herskovits's contribution.

All living authors within this collection have been allowed to revise their original contributions, and I have allowed myself the same privilege. The original article was part of an "In Memoriam" issue of *Caribbean Studies* — for which, as it happened, only Sidney Mintz and I submitted copy — and contains a great deal which was definitely "in-house". The comparison of "zero copula" in Haitian Creole and in Black American English, in the center of the article as now reprinted, is actually from "Toward a Bibliography of Works Dealing with the Creole Languages of the Caribbean Area, Louisiana, and the Guianas" (*Caribbean Studies* 1962:84-95). But these two works have been mixed in the Creolist-Black English tradition; Stewart's reference (1969) seems to be more directly to the bibliographical sketch than to the Herskovits article.

Revisions are, however, totally in the interest of intelligibility and completeness. They do not involve any backing down from positions expressed either in 1962 or in 1964. Some of the positions are sketchily presented: the marveling at the anti-relativism of some academic liberals seems particularly anemic in view of Stewart's "Sociopolitical Issues in the Treatment of Negro Dialect" (1969). The "zero copula" has been given extensive — but, to my mind, not convincing — treatment in terms of extension of the process of contraction and deletion in Standard English (Labov 1969b). The 1962 treatment could hardly be expected to refute such a later expression of a different viewpoint. But I stand by the position that both Haitian (along with some other creoles) and Black English have

(1) Zero copula in non-exposed, non-emphatic environments—where it does not, however, represent underlying present (or non-past) tense.
(2) Hypercorrect forms, resembling Standard French and Standard

English forms, respectively, in those same linguistic environments but in formal conditions and/or to unfamiliar interlocutors.

(3) Fillers (Haitian *yé*, BAE *is, are, am*) in exposed position and in emphatic position.

Insofar as I can now see, the issue is essentially the same as it was in 1964 — and much earlier, when Herskovits raised it. A population, marked as African in descent by its very features and skin color (and, more importantly, in kinesics and in other cultural features),[9] which has linguistic structures strongly resembling those acknowledged to be typical of the creole languages, may itself have used a creole variety of English in the past. The conditions favoring the use of a pidgin contact variety can hardly have cancelled themselves simply because a portion of the West African-derived slave population came into what was later to become the province of the American Dialect Society, with its isoglosses and its preconceptions of British "folk" origin for all features of American English dialects.[10] The theory implicit in Herskovits and explicitly (although briefly) expressed by Bloomfield (1933:474) of

(1) The use of a pidgin in the linguistically mixed slave groups.
(2) Creolization of that pidgin.
(3) Partial decreolization (or "merger" — in effect, linguistic acculturation — with European-derived dialects).

seems to be the only historical theory capable of accounting rationally for the existence of Black American English today. It is also abundantly supported by historical documentation. If, as the contributors to this section attempt to demonstrate, it also fits into a general pattern of still ongoing acculturation by Black citizens of the United States, there seems to be no rational reason to continue to deny the validity of the theory.

[9] In most of the United States, except for the Sea Islands, the West African woman's sitting position (legs spread wide apart, with the European-style dress tucked between them like a loin cloth) has almost completely disappeared. In Puerto Rico, it can be observed in rural districts, although the women are extremely self-conscious about exhibiting such behavior before outsiders. The specifically West African way of carrying the baby on the mother's back is not generally found in the New World.

[10] See section II, "The History of Black English". Historically speaking, the acculturative process probably offers the best explanation of the attitude of prominent Black organizations like the National Association for the Advancement of Colored People toward treatments of Black English. An acculturative organization by its very nature, the NAACP has tended to resist efforts at legitimization of Black dialect, actually preferring the explanation that economically disadvantaged Negro children use language more poorly than middle-class groups, Black or white. (In linguistic terms, this would mean that such Black children were consistently the producers of a much greater number of "performance errors" than other population groups!) Some of these problems are treated in *Ford Foundation Letter*, "Which English?" volume 2, no. 7 (October 15, 1971): 2.

WILLIAM R. BASCOM

ACCULTURATION AMONG THE GULLAH NEGROES

The analysis of the accommodation of African and European customs in the New World presents a particularly difficult problem in the United States because the processes of acculturation have gone much farther here than in other regions. In dealing with the Negro cultures in South America and the West Indies, the African traits that have been retained are specific enough and numerous enough to make possible the identification of the tribes whose cultures have been involved. But even among the Gullah in the coastal regions of South Carolina and Georgia,[1] where the Negroes have been as isolated as anywhere in the United States, resemblances to specific African tribes are very rare. For the most part the similarities are to those elements which are common to West Africa as a whole — to the common denominators of West African culture — and not to those aspects of culture which are distinctive of the tribes within that area. It is therefore extremely difficult to determine what particular West African cultures have contributed to the present situation.

It is now recognized that the differences in the general pattern of the cultures of Africa and Europe were not great; in fact their fundamental similarity justifies the concept of an Old World Area which includes both Europe and Africa. There were a number of institutions common to both regions, including a complex economic system based on money,

Read before the Central Section, American Anthropological Association, Indianapolis, April 26, 1940. Reprinted by permission of the American Anthropological Association from *American Anthropologist* 43:1 (1941): 43-50.
[1] Field work in Georgia and South Carolina during the summer of 1939 was made possible by a grant-in-aid from the Social Science Research Council of Northwestern University.

markets, and middle-men, as well as a large number of crafts among which iron-working was important; a well developed system of government based on kings, and courts of law in which cases were tried by specialists (lawyers) and in which ordeals were employed to decide certain cases; a religious system with a complex hierarchy of priests and deities; a common stock of folklore and a common emphasis on moralizing elements and proverbs. Aside from writing, the wheel, the plow, and Christianity, most of the distinctive traits of Western civilization seem to have followed the industrial revolution.

This similarity between the fundamental patterns of Europe and Africa has further complicated the problem of assessing the relative influences of these areas in the culture of the Gullahs. Since most African traits of a specific nature have disappeared, what is to be found is, for the most part, a series of institutions which differ from the European forms only in their African flavor. To a person who is not familiar with West African cultures, it might seem possible to explain Gullah customs entirely in terms of European influence. The resemblances that are to be found might well be rejected as too general and too indefinite to prove diffusion from Africa to the Sea Islands, if taken by themselves. But we have the historical record of contact with Africa through the importation of African slaves into this region, so that the problem becomes not one of proving that there has been contact, but of assessing the importance of a known factor.

The result of the contact of the Negroes with the whites, both in slavery and in the period of freedom, seems to have been that in those cases where there was a difference or a conflict between African and European customs, the African customs have for the most part disappeared. But those institutions which were present in similar forms in both Africa and Europe, while manifesting a great many specifically European details, have retained an African stamp and have had a place in Gullah life the importance of which cannot be explained in terms of European forms alone. In these cases the two streams of tradition have reinforced one another.

An excellent example of the operation of this process is to be found in the institution of cooperative work among the Gullahs. In West Africa, cooperative work is a widespread and important institution, which among the Yoruba,[2] for example, takes two forms. There is first of all the *aro* which is a simple labor exchange between two or three farmers who have small families and are too poor to own slaves or "pawns". Such men work a certain amount of time on the farm of one, and then the same

---

[2] Discussion of Yoruba material is based on field work in Nigeria, carried on during 1937-38 under terms of a fellowship grant from the Social Science Research Council of New York City.

amount on the farms of the second and third. The other form of cooperative work is the more spectacular social event, *ɔwe*, in which a man calls
upon his friends, relatives, or society members to help him with the work
he is required to do for his father-in-law: hoe the fields, thatch the house,
build its mud walls, or whatever may be required. On such occasions a
large number of men work together while the host directs the activities.
Meanwhile the wife, who has called her friends and society together to
help her, prepares a large feast for the men with palmwine or gin, if her
husband can afford it. In this case there is no attempt to keep track of
the amount of work accomplished or time spent, as is done for *aro*.

In Dahomey,[3] besides the cooperative work done by members of the
same guild, there is the *dokpwe* which is the equivalent of the Yoruba *ɔwɛ*
or working bee. The *dokpwe* is apparently even more closely associated
with the society, however, and it differs in that the host hires a drummer
to set the pace for the men working in the field, so that all the workers
keep step and finish their rows at the same time. The Yoruba work in
a line, so that each man hoes his own row, but they do not work in
unison to music, although they are familiar with this procedure from
contact with the Hausa. This Dahomean form of cooperative work,
complete with hoeing in unison to a drummer, is a pattern which has
been retained among other New World Negro cultures. It has been observed by Herskovits in Haiti,[4] by J. C. Trevor in the Virgin Islands, and
by Miss Katherine Dunham in Jamaica.[5]

Cooperative work, on the other hand, is not foreign to the European
pattern. Certainly it played an important part in American colonial life
in the form of house-raisings, quilting bees, log-rollings, husking bees,
and the general pattern of neighborliness. According to informants, the
white masters frequently loaned their slaves to one another for occasions
of this sort, so that the Gullah had first hand contact with the European
forms. Memories of the house-raisings, log-rollings, quilting bees, and
even the associated candy pulls which the Negroes held on their own
accord after freedom are still vivid in the minds of the older individuals.
But at the same time certain forms of cooperative work show a closer
correspondence to the West African pattern, especially with regard to
hoeing side by side, hoeing in unison to music, and the association between cooperative work and the societies.

On Sapeloe Island in Georgia informants remember large groups, apparently of between 30 and 50 persons, hoeing side by side in the fields.
This in itself is significant, since, during the period of slavery, work was
assigned by the task in this region so that each slave worked out a

[3] M. J. Herskovits, *Dahomey* (Augustin, New York, 1938): vol. I, 63-77.
[4] M. J. Herskovits, *Life in a Haitian Valley* (Knopf, New York, 1937): 70-76.
[5] From unpublished field notes.

separate area by himself. Furthermore, after freedom when a man got behind in his work, he would call on his neighbors or his society for help; and even today, on Sapeloe, people will still "jump right into the field and help you out". In the old days the man would give a big dinner on a long table under a tree, but nowadays people are invited into the house. In hoeing each person takes his own row, and while the host did not hire a drum for use in the fields, the people frequently sang church songs and worked in unison, finishing their rows at the same time. When they worked without singing, couples talked and fell behind so that they did not all finish together. As in Africa, working together is said to make the work more pleasant and to make it go faster; as one informant put it, "You're really cuttin' grass then".

Similarly, if a man needed help, he might call upon a neighbor, and this favor would be returned when requested. This resembles the Yoruba *aro* except that no strict account was kept of the amount of work done. The person called upon might be a relative, or a good friend, or just a neighbor. Significantly, these arrangements were more or less permanent, so that a man would always call upon the same person to help him out. Usually the host gave the helper a meal; but if he were alone and ill, this was omitted.

On the island of Hilton Head, South Carolina, cooperative work has disappeared, but shortly after slavery it existed in two forms. In the first place neighbors might help each other even when they were not ill, working first in the fields of one family and then in the fields of the other. In the second place, the societies such as Mutual Friendly Aid would come without being asked to help a member who fell behind in his work. In this case they did not take note of the amount of work done, but just went in and "hoed him out", while the host provided a dinner for his helpers, serving whatever he could afford. When several people hoed the fields together, each took his own row, and when they sang their hoeing was in unison and was said to go faster and with less effort. In recent times the Hilton Head societies have been primarily "policy clubs" of the type so common in the South, and the function of working in the fields has been abandoned.

African elements are not so evident in other parts of the coastal regions as they are in Hilton Head and Sapeloe. On St. Simons Island, Georgia, neither neighbors nor societies helped in the fields; and while several members of the same family might hoe side by side, each taking his own row, even when they did sing they did not work in unison. On St. Helena, South Carolina, it is said that neighbors never worked each other's fields, but on this island the society called Knights of Wise helped members who were not well and fined those who did not show up to work. Members of the Sisters of Zion were likewise expected, but not forced, to turn out to work the fields of a sick member; if the man proved to be lazy instead of ill, he was given a mock whipping. There was no singing while farming on St. Helena, where they say they had to "sing with the hoe". About Darien and on Harris Neck, on the Georgia mainland, the pattern of cooperative work was once strong, but the forms it took were mainly European, with log-rollings, quiltings, and the like. People would come to hoe the fields of a neighbor who was not well, but the work was not done in unison to music, and while societies were important shortly after slavery, they did not help their members with their work.

It is difficult to explain these local variations in terms of the information at hand, but explanations are probably to be sought in differentials in isolation, the rules laid down by individual slave owners, and perhaps the African sources of the slaves and the dates at which slaves were last imported directly from Africa. While cooperative work persisted in these localities for a long time, it has disappeared in all of them except Sapeloe Island. In all these places except St. Simons, informants respond with conviction to the suggestion that people were more neighborly in the old days than they are now.

Friendship is another institution which is common to both the European and African tradition, but in West Africa it takes a slightly different form and is considerably more formalized than it is in our society. Among the Yoruba there is a distinct emphasis on the best friend (*korikosun*) with whom every contemplated undertaking is discussed, and whose advice in financial matters, or affairs with women, or any matter whatsoever is very seldom disregarded. The best friend is told how a man wants his property to be divided and is called in by the family to see that these wishes are carried out when his partner dies. There are folktales which show that a man's best friend is more to be trusted than his own mother; and the best friend is told things which a man does not confide to his wife. A man's wife or members of his family would attempt — supposedly always without success — to find out a man's plans by "pumping" his best friend.

This affection between best friends is legendary. A man speaks of loving his best friend "like a woman", and there are stories of men dying of grief at the passing of their friends. The Yoruba belief is that women's mouths are "too big" to keep a secret; they do not remain faithful to any friend, but go through life with a series of them. In Dahomey[6] the same general pattern holds but the institution is itself more elaborate in form. Each man has a first best friend in whom he confides everything; a second best friend to whom he tells slightly less; and a third best friend who receives only a part of his confidence.

---

[6]   M. J. Herskovits, *Dahomey* (Augustin, New York, 1938): vol. I, 239-42.

In the Sea Islands the European practice of writing wills has been accepted completely so that an important and distinctively African function of friendship has disappeared. At most a man asks his friend's advice about the way his property should be divided. A few informants in their discussion of friendship, did, however, give an emphasis to the institution which seems characteristically African.

On Hilton Head men used to have one or two "sworn friends" upon whom they could depend and to whom they told all their secrets. These friends interpreted each other's dreams, gave advice on financial ventures, and criticized each other's behavior, for instance, in such matters as having "affairs" with women. A man's wife or even his parents might go to his sworn friend in an attempt to find out what plans he had in mind, and in some cases a wife's persistence in this led to a gradual breaking up of the friendship, since the man would stay away from the house rather than be forced to betray his confidence.

Such friendship had a special importance in the time of slavery when slaves banded together against the master. They continued for a time after slavery, but in succeeding generations people came to confide in too many individuals — having too many sworn friends — so that secrets soon spread. The inability of women to keep a secret was blamed in part for the disappearance of the institution, for "as soon as you tell a girl, your secret is gone".

An African influence can be seen in the present form of a number of other institutions which will simply be enumerated. It is apparent in the functions of the local clubs or societies such as the Mutual Friendly Aid, the Jolly Boys, the Golden Link, the Seaside Branch, and the Union Gospel Travellers on Hilton Head. In most other regions these local societies were followed by the well-known, national, chartered lodges, which in turn have almost disappeared. In the structure of the Gullah family there seems to be a certain matrilineal emphasis for which there are counterparts in West Africa. For example, there is the feeling that an individual is somehow more closely related to his mother than to his father. There are several rationalizations for this, but one is the same as that offered in Africa, namely that a person is fed on his mother's milk.

The emphasis on special circumstances of birth is characteristically African. Parsons[7] has already pointed out how children born with a caul, children born "foot fo'mos'", twins, and the seventh child are all believed to have special qualities or abilities. The Gullah, like the West Africans, bury the navel cord in the yard, and frequently nursed their children for one, two, or three years in the old days. One woman was said to have nursed her child after it was old enough to help her in the fields.

[7] E. C. Parsons, *Folk-Lore of the Sea Islands, South Carolina* (*Memoirs of the American*

286   *William R. Bascom*

And people today remember women who carried their children on their backs, in some cases when working the fields. Certain Gullah beliefs are obviously comparable to the taboos of the West Africans; for example, the idea that a nursing mother should not eat beans, green corn, crabs, prawns, or net fish (channel fish caught with hook and line are all right), because it is not good for the baby's stomach.

The interpretation of dreams in order to predict the future is important in West Africa as well as in European tradition and it is wide-spread in the Sea Islands. Magic likewise is not foreign to the European tradition, but certain details of the practice are specifically African; the importance of "grave-yard dirt", of "foot track dust", and of hair and nails in working conjure; and the importance of "frizzled chickens" as a means of detecting charms buried in the earth.[8]

The belief in multiple souls, the very vivid belief in ghosts, the special burial rites for persons who die by drowning, lightning, small-pox, and suicide, all resemble African beliefs more closely than they do European. A baby that is taken to a funeral must be passed across the coffin so that its soul will not accompany that of the deceased.[9] When a mother starts home after a visit she takes her baby in her arms, and then calls its name so that its soul will not be left behind.[10] As in Africa, a distinction is made between ghosts and witches, who take off their skins and can be caught either by sprinkling pepper and salt about the room in good African tradition,[11] or by the distinctly European method of putting a Bible under the pillow.

Turning once more to agriculture, we find that a specifically West African form of motor behavior has been retained widely in this region. In the planting of several crops, and especially of rice in the old days, the hole into which the seed was dropped was first made with the heel and then covered over with the foot. Moving pictures taken in West Africa and in Haiti by Herskovits[12] show very plainly this West African procedure which, as far as can be ascertained, was entirely foreign to European tradition.

Gullah speech, which has long been recognized as distinctive among

---

Folk-Lore Society, vol. XVI) (Cambridge and New York, 1923): 197-98.

[8] Cf. *Drums and Shadows* by the Savannah Unit of the Georgia Writers' Project (University of Georgia Press, Athens, 1940).

[9] Cf. Parsons, *Folk-Lore of the Sea Islands*, p. 213; G. B. Johnson, *Folk Culture on St. Helena Island, South Carolina* (Chapel Hill, The University of North Carolina Press, 1930), 172.

[10] Cf. Parsons, *Folk-Lore of the Sea Islands*, 199; Johnson, *Folk Culture on St. Helena Island*, 172.

[11] Cf. J. Peterkin, *Black April* (Grosset & Dunlap, 1927): 100.

[12] See M. J. Herskovits, *Life in a Haitian Valley* (Knopf, New York, 1937), illustrations facing p. 100.

Negro dialects in the United States, has a number of African idioms and grammatical peculiarities. A detailed analysis may show African influences in the phonetic system as well. Dr. Turner of Fisk University has listed several thousand words which he believes to be of West African origin.[13] These are mainly in the form of nicknames and words for plants and animals, and are used only within the family circle so that they would not be noticed unless someone set out to look for them. Lastly there are the very specific correspondences between the animal tales of the Gullah and those of West Africa, the first aspects of Gullah culture to be recognized as having an African origin.

In conclusion then, while it is impossible in the case of the Sea Island Negroes to assign African influences to particular tribes, and while we are dealing with the problem of the relative influence of European and African culture on institutions common to both traditions, rather than with African origins of non-European institutions, these influences can be recognized in many aspects of present-day Gullah life. It would thus seem historically incorrect as well as methodologically unsound to explain Gullah customs by reference only to European culture. It is quite true that, as elsewhere in the United States, the European elements outnumber by far the African elements which have been retained, yet that Africanisms can be traced indicates the importance of the study of this society as an aid in the analysis of acculturation.

Northwestern University
Evanston, Illinois

[13] By personal communication.

J. L. DILLARD

THE WRITINGS OF HERSKOVITS AND THE STUDY OF THE LANGUAGE OF THE NEGRO IN THE NEW WORLD

It seems reasonably safe to say that a complete re-evaluation of the Negro's use of languages, largely European in origin, which he encountered in the New World has come about. Where it has not come about, it is certainly long overdue. A part of the delay may have been caused by an effort at liberalism, laudable in itself, which has been misplaced — or perhaps has rather outlived its function. One of the cruelest and stupidest of the racist fallacies was the "thick lips" interpretation of the Negro's speech habits, and linguists have been properly eager to disprove that popular error. But the error has been disproved *ad infinitum*, and laboring the point — except in publications at the newspaper level or so — seems useless. More important for language study is the consideration that the school of linguists, once dominant, who wanted to explain language through a phonemics based essentially on articulation patterns has suffered a crushing defeat; the approach is dead, although occasionally a new result comes forth from it, doomed to be fossilized before born. Even if "thick lips" could determine phonetic patterns and a phonemic inventory, that phonemic inventory could not possibly determine what syntactic and morphological patterns would occur. Nothing about "awkwardness" of pronunciation, even if that awkwardness did exist, could cause the "loss", for example, of suffix morphemes which Jourdain (1956) postulated for Martiniquan Creole. The broader ("higher level") approach, which allows even for cultural and contextual factors, is obviously called for again in linguistics.¹ It is perhaps fitting to make an attempt to point out how much of what is really known about the language of the Negro in the New World was discovered by a student of Negro culture, Melville J. Herskovits.

Among the many works which are concerned with re-evaluation of the role of African languages in forming the speech of Negroes, and not even impossibly of whites, in the New World, sections from two books by Herskovits have a kind of elder statesman dignity which looms larger than ever now. These are *The Myth of the Negro Past* (1941) and *Suriname Folk-Lore* (1936). Despite the snowballing number of such works today, it is not too long since these works and Turner's *Africanisms in the Gullah Dialect* (1949) stood almost alone against blanket denials that the Negro had anything peculiar to his language except the scraps of borrowings from lower-class whites and retentions of archaic forms which, in American dialectology, rather closely paralleled what writers like Jules Faine were saying about Haitian Creole.

In this context, it is remarkable how well Herskovits's statements, considered in their general tenor, stand up against the works of specialists in linguistics. Indeed, since many of the works on languages like Sranan Tongo are dressed in the frayed straitjacket of Structuralism, a book like *Suriname Folk-Lore* probably gives more real information on that language than any methodologically complex re-statement work. The Caribbean, particularly, has been unfortunate in having little to bridge the gap between near-racist works and those tied to Structuralism. And the North American continent still has virtually nothing more than the intuitions and parallels drawn from anthropology by Herskovits to go with the solid research of Turner, although the position has recently been strengthened by a weakening of the strongest rival position — a doctrinaire belief in the traceability to a multiplicity of British dialects.²

When Herskovits's first works on the subject appeared, it was fashionable to find the same sort of historical vacuum for the Negro's language as for his culture. Sophisticated scholars, when they noticed the subject at all, mainly exerted themselves in debunking the attitude of the naive

¹ For linguistics, which will eventually have to deal with discourse patterns, there may be some instructive insights in Herskovits's "Some Next Steps in the Study of Negro Folklore" (Herskovits 1943).
² Atwood (1963:42) observes: "Our knowledge of the present-day distribution of dialect features in England is far from complete, and our knowledge of Early Modern English dialects is extremely limited. To argue from present-day distribution that a certain form must have been brought to the American colonies from a certain area of England is risky." Francis (1961) repeats Atwood's caution, with specific application to verb forms. McDavid and McDavid (1951) admit that British dialect forms in such sources as Wright's *Grammar* and *Dictionary* were "collected by amateurs with uneven training and without any systematic procedure" (p. 7).

layman, who was rather too willing to share Charles Dickens's notion
(letter to Forster, April 15, 1842) that the people who "have been bred
in the slave states speak more or less like Negroes, from having been
constantly in their childhood with black nurses".[3] Said naive layman, who
heard differences in the Negro's speech and knew that he heard them, in
his own crudely naive way assumed that those differences must have
something to do with other languages (although he could not have called
that something interference); and since a German immigrant's English
sounded like English mixed with German it seemed reasonable that an
African immigrant's language should sound like a mixture of English
and some African language. The scholars who set out to correct them won
all the academic battles; but, as often happens, a lot of learning was a
dangerous thing (particularly when the learning was most usually limited
to the Germanic philological tradition) and the intuitions of the unskilled
matched the discoveries of brilliant investigators to come rather better
than did the erudition of the merely learned. The last were confident;
Leyburn,[4] for example, used comparisons between Antillean Negroes'
speech and that of Negroes in the United States as proof that the former
showed no influence from African languages, it being considered beyond
doubt that the latter were uninfluenced from Africa. So two assumptions,
neither of which could stand alone, held each other up in a manner which
would be the envy of Hindu rope tricksters.

The books which develop these two assumptions are legion; perhaps
I may be forgiven for working on that of Cleanth Brooks,[5] which is more
easily available at the moment. It is, morever, symptomatic in its way:
A writer working outside the professional field in which he was to
achieve prominence felt that he could deal confidently with so pat a
matter in spite of unimpressive professional training. Consider a typical
statement:

The first conclusion to be drawn from the variants given above is that the
speech of the negro and of the white is essentially the same, the characteristically
negro forms turning out to be survivals of earlier native English forms (p. 63).

There were many others who said the same thing, and at later dates. Even
such an outstanding contributor to the study of New World Africanism as

---

[3] There were, of course, many such statements in the eighteenth and nineteenth
centuries. Some of them are discussed in Read (1933) and (1935).
[4] *The Haitian People* (New Haven, 1941).
[5] Brooks (1935). Although conveniently close to Herskovits and Herskovits (1936)
in time of publication, this book is not singled out as the worst in its tradition. It is,
rather, an indication of the nature of the tradition itself. In view of Brooks's later
career, outside dialectology and linguistics, it seems unlikely that he was personally
very deeply involved in the point of view expressed. More extreme examples could be
cited; e.g. G. P. Krapp, "The English of the Negro", *American Mercury*, June (1924).
It is notable, however, that Brooks cites this article with approval.

Manuel Álvarez Nazario wrote *El Arcaísmo Vulgar en el Español de Puerto Rico* (1957) several years before *El Elemento Afronegroïde en el Español de Puerto Rico* (1961). But only a year after Brooks's work Herskovits was already beginning to show that the problem required more than a corpus of New World Negro forms and a (drastically incomplete) Atlas of the European language. Balance this statement from *Suriname Folk-Lore* against the quotation from Brooks (1935):

It soon became apparent that the characteristics which could be singled out in the Negro-English of Paramaribo were also manifested in other regions of the New World where Negroes speak English (p. 119).

Although the casual listener to Paramaribo Negroes can hear forms like *more furder*, there are things in Sranan Tongo which cannot conceivably come from British "folk" dialects or from "earlier native English forms".

Insofar as his linguistic comments go, Herskovits did not make an exception of the United States, although of course he did not emphasize that area:

Many of the idioms and phonetic shifts of Suriname speech, the West Indies, and the United States appear in these excerpts [from a Dahomey-born Nigerian who learned English "only by ear"] (p. 124).

Why — except that it has become traditional to do so — do we say that "Creole" forms belong in one linguistic world and general American Negro forms in another? Why is Haitian *yo ché* Creole in syntax when Negro *They high* is not? Ralph Ellison, to use the most obvious of literary examples, frequently characterizes Negro-American speech by forms like *He a fool man*, and many of us can add forms from our own observation. Why is the "loss" of /r/ in certain positions a Creole characteristic in Haiti and a survival from British dialects in the United States, where it is observably much more frequent (even in the South) from Negroes than from whites? Why has no linguist yet made any comparison of West African English as spoken in Sierra Leone, Liberia, Nigeria, the West Cameroon, Fernando Poo, etc., and that of the United States on any scale to compare with the (necessarily somewhat informal) data assembled by the anthropologist Herskovits?[6]

For some rather special reasons, the broad-scale comparison made by Herskovits in *Suriname Folk-Lore* was the only approach which was likely to yield valid results in the days before intensive work like that of Turner on Gullah. The most traditional way of tracing linguistic origins,

[6] All of this paragraph, except the first sentence (with its inset quotation) is from the 1962 bibliography in *Caribbean Studies*. It might also be noted that this bibliography specifically called attention to Bloomfield's tracing of U.S. Negro dialect to "the last stages of levelling" (or "decreolization").

word etymology, yields embarrassingly scanty results even when applied
to the recognized Creoles. However much Africanism might complicate
the problems of etymology through reinforcement, almost all the forms
which a researcher who does not saturate himself in the language and its
people is likely to encounter have a possible European history. If you
WANT to believe that Papiamentu *tabata* is from a kind of stutterer's
way of saying Spanish *estaba*, you will find plenty of quasi-authoritative
company. Even the speakers of Papiamentu are likely to prefer that
interpretation, skipping such intermediate "nonsense" as trade pidgins
and slave *koinés*.

If the non-Africanists were willing to accept even performance errors
in explaining the origins of New World Negro forms, not all of them were
unwilling to edit the speech they examined. Brooks wrote:

I have omitted from consideration, of course, malapropisms and forms resulting from confusion with other words or analogy (p. 5).

This is defensible procedure in more formal grammatical terms. The
brilliant new school of linguists headed by Chomsky has established beyond
doubt that a grammar of a language must focus first upon the rules by
which sentences are produced which the native speakers recognize as
well-formed. Hockett[7] had something like the same idea before it became
widely known as a generativist principle, and Long[8] quoted Hockett
with approval before acceptance of the transformationalists became a
factor in such approval. But Creolists know that speakers of Creole
languages are often reluctant to transmit their true perceptions as to
whether sentences are well-formed to outsiders.

In many cases, further, the judgment "malapropism" may be the surest
indicator of the relationship of the Creole lexicon to that of the "standard"
language. The investigator frequently hears, from Antiguans, sentences
like *We don't have much likeness for him* (said of a local get-rich-quick
type). It is a pity that Brooks and others could not put down in writing
all the slips and malapropisms they encountered, but we can't have everything.[9]

---

[7] *A Course in Modern Linguistics* (1958:142).
[8] "Review of Dwight L. Bolinger, *Interrogative Structures of American English*",
American Speech.
[9] Negro malapropism is certainly a basic feature of (white) folk beliefs about Negro
speech, having been carried to absurd lengths in Minstrel Shows, Blackface comedies
etc. Large numbers of informants, mainly from the Texas area, have furnished me many
examples of such "malapropisms" on the part of Negroes; and many of them seem,
upon inspection and comparison, to be accurate as data, in spite of the objectionable
racism of the readily proferred explanations. (An example: *Dem folks in West Texas
show a lot of comanderation* [consideration?] *for dem pine trees*.) Virtually everyone
cites *funeralize*, in an area where the white population would say *conduct the funeral*

But if even malapropism is culturally conditioned, the necessity is re-emphasized for an interpretation of language forms in a cultural context. Such studies are not lacking, but they can achieve an incredible superficiality where the Negro is concerned. Operating on the pre-Herskovits theory that the Negro has no cultural traditions, writers were often tempted to investigate solely the past of the whites who served first as slave owners and then as the upper caste. An extreme example is Arthur A. Norton's tracing of Gullah to a French Canadian accent, lost by the more progressive owners and their descendants, but retained by the ever-archaic offspring of slaves![10] This is worse than anything ever done by the immediate followers of Krapp and Brooks, but it is embarrassingly like their method of operation. If Norton had been aware of similar developments in the French Creoles, he might have looked for French Canadian migration to Haiti.

Awareness of these parallel developments which in many respects rivals that of Herskovits is a distinguishing feature of the work of Lorenzo D. Turner.[11] Unlike certain more recent writers, neither Herskovits nor Turner was inclined to treat the Creoles as something set apart. Herskovits's work on Bahia Negroes is paralleled by Turner's repeated inclusion of the Negro-Portuguese of Brazil[12] along with Haitian Creole etc. in his comparisons of the other Creoles with Gullah. It is of course fitting that the most explicit statement where language is concerned should come from Turner:

All of my African informants who have recently learned to speak English use the substitutes, and it is reasonable to suppose that their ancestors who came to South Carolina and Georgia direct from Africa as slaves reacted similarly ... (p. 245).

"These substitutes" refers to phonetic patterns almost identical to some which Brooks had confidently traced to British dialects. It seems perfectly clear that one's view of the overall cultural pattern of the Negro in the

---

or just *bury*. Many examples of such "malapropisms" are contained in the writings of Negro folklorist J. Mason Brewer (e.g. *The Word on the Brazos*, Austin, 1953). The writings of Brewer are themselves marvelous, far from thoroughly explored, sources of Black English.

[10] "Linguistic Persistence", *American Speech* VI (1931): 140.

[11] *The Myth of the Negro Past* (1941) refers to material from Turner's studies. Turner's important onomastic section (pp. 31-32) quotes Herskovits on secret names; and Turner elsewhere calls Herskovits, Frances Herskovits, and Elsie Clews Parsons chief among writers on the similarities between New World Negro and African cultures. Turner's "Some Contacts of Brazilian Ex-Slaves with Nigeria, West Africa", *Journal of Negro History* (1942), and his references to Brazilian Negro speech in Turner (1949) parallels to some extent Herskovits's Bahian studies ("Afro-Bahian Religious Songs", Album XIII of *Folk Music of Brazil, Library of Congress Archive of Folk Song*).

[12] Turner (1949): chapter I.

New World is crucial to his acceptance of either Turner-Herskovits or
Brooks-Krapp.

By this time, a great deal of detailed research has been done in most
of the areas which Herskovits's early work — which was, of course, not
without its linguistic precedents — had singled out. This is particularly
true of those languages which everyone is willing to call Creoles, and of
Jamaican English, no matter what one calls it. Hall[13] has pointed up the
need for such work even within the United States, but little has come of it.
In places where the teacher finds that integration is only the first step in
solving educational problems rather than the automatic solution to
them, some understanding of the Negro's linguistic backgrounds will be
indispensable. There are some James Baldwins and Richard Wrights, but
the composition teacher who finds his freshman class made up of mixed
"white Anglo-Saxon" youths, those of Mexican descent, and Negroes is
going to find that the first group manages the shibboleths of "good"
English much more easily than do the latter two. Liberal or not, he may
have to fail most of the last two groups if he follows departmental
requirements. If he has any intuition about language, he may be tempted
to think that the troubles of the two groups come from similar sources,
linguistic backgrounds within the groups of their strongest cultural ties
which differ from that of the textbook writer and teacher. This would be
the linguistic reflex of the statement that

He is set apart by his color in a culture in which the predominant traditions
are not his, and the members of the predominant population group, both in
numbers and in influence, are different from himself ... he will, by and large,
succeed only insofar as he adapts himself to the patterns of the dominant
culture.[14]

This may not seem so idealistically liberal as the determination to ignore
the differences. But it would seem that a greater chance of success would
come from observing the differences, understanding where they come
from, and being prepared to cope with them. In the Caribbean, the
problem is more nearly that the islanders tend to adopt a model which
is exterior to their group, even outside their area of contact. This tends
to be true of culture or of language, particularly when the language is
English (including Creolese). But surely an obscuring of the sources can
be of no advantage here.

If the current trend in the direction of bringing discourse into linguistic
analysis continues, and especially if my hunch that language interacts
with culture most perfectly at the discourse level proves tenable, then a

13   Hall (1950).
14   Herskovits, *The American Negro, A Study in Racial Crossing* (New York 1930):
54.

section of *Suriname Folk-Lore* may prove to be the most valuable thing ever written on the languages of the Caribbean.[15] This will, however, be only one of the many important contributions which the broad perspective of Herskovits has given to the study of New World Negro language.

REFERENCES

Atwood, E. B.
   1963   "The methods of American dialectology", *Zeitschrift für Mundartforschung* 30:1-30.
Brooks, Cleanth
   1935   *The Relation of the Alabama-Georgia Dialect to the Provincial Dialects of Great Britain* (Baton Rouge, Louisiana).
Francis, W. Nelson
   1961   "Some dialectal verbs forms in England", *Orbis* X:1-14.
Hall, Robert A., Jr.
   1950   "The African substratum in Negro English", *American Speech* 25:51-54.
Herskovits, Melville J.
   1943   "Some next steps in the study of Negro folklore", *Journal of American Folklore*, vol. 56.
Herskovits, Melville J. and Frances S. Herskovits
   1936   *Suriname Folk-Lore* (Columbia University Press).
Jourdain, Elodie
   1956   *Du Français aux Parlers Créoles* (Paris).
McDavid, Raven I., Jr. and Virginia Glenn McDavid
   1951   "The relationship of the speech of American Negroes to the speech of whites", *American Speech* xxvi: 3-16.
Read, Allen Walker
   1933   "British recognition of American Speech in the eighteenth century", *Dialect Notes* VI: 313-34.
   1935   "Amphi-Atlantic English", *English Studies* 17: 161-78.
Turner, Lorenzo Dow
   1949   *Africanisms in the Gullah Dialect* (Chicago).

[15]   Herskovits and Herskovits (1936): 145-46.

KENNETH R. JOHNSON

BLACK KINESICS — SOME NON-VERBAL
COMMUNICATION PATTERNS IN THE BLACK CULTURE

Although much research has been written on VERBAL communication
patterns of Black people, little research has been directed toward their
non-verbal communication patterns. The research of Bailey, Baratz,
Dillard, Fasold, Kochman, Labov, Shuy, Stewart, Wolfram and others
on the verbal communication patterns of Black people has demonstrated
that many Black people speak a variety — or dialect — of English that
differs from other varieties of English. The existence of Black dialect or
Black English or Nonstandard Negro dialect (it has been given these
labels) has been conclusively demonstrated; thus, it can be expected that
non-verbal communication patterns in the Black culture, too, differ from
those in the dominant culture or other American sub-cultures. Indeed,
many of those who have researched verbal patterns (particularly Kochman and Stewart) have commented on this difference. The purpose of
this paper is to describe some of these non-verbal communication patterns
of Black people and the meanings these patterns convey.

Bailey, Dillard and Stewart have suggested that Black dialect did not
evolve from a British or American variety of English, but that it evolved
through a pidginization-creolization process. Further, they suggest that
its evolution has been influenced by the African languages Black people
originally spoke. Turner's monumental study of the dialect of the Gullahs,
or Geechies, demonstrated the survival of "Africanism" in the Gullah
dialect. (The Gullahs — or Geechies, as most Black people call them —
are a group of Black people who live mainly on the islands off the coast of

Reprinted with the permission of *The Florida FL Reporter* and the author from vol. 9,
nos. 1 and 2 (Spring/Fall 1971): 17-20, 57, Alfred C. Aarons, ed.

South Carolina and along the coasts of South Carolina and Northern Georgia and who speak what is clearly a creolized variety of English which, most likely, is the prototype of Black dialect.) Black dialect, however, is much more like standard English (and other varieties of English) than the Gullah dialect. Still, its evolution — according to some researchers — has been influenced by the former African languages Black people originally spoke.

The hypothesis that Black dialect has a different base of development from other varieties of American English (even though it is similar to other varieties of American English and it shares many common features) can be extended to non-verbal communication patterns. That is, non-verbal communication patterns in the Black culture that are not commonly exhibited by other Americans possibly have their origins in African non-verbal communication patterns. This does not mean that all non-verbal communication patterns of Black people differ from those of other Americans. As with language patterns, Black people share many non-verbal patterns with other Americans. On the other hand, those unique non-verbal patterns of Black Americans don't necessarily have to be identical to African non-verbal communication patterns in order for them to have an African origin. Years and years of separation of Black Americans from their original African cultures could have produced alterations in these original non-verbal patterns, and separation could have produced entirely new patterns unrelated to African patterns.

Some support for the hypothesis that Black non-verbal communication patterns have an African base can be gained through observing Africans. For example, the non-verbal patterns — specifically, body movement — of a touring dance troupe from a West African country which visits the United States periodically are remarkably similar to those of Black Americans. This dance troupe includes a street scene in its repertoire and except for the props and, to a lesser extent, the costumes, the spirited talk ("lollygagging", "jiving", "signifying" and "sounding") accompanied by body movements (especially walking) and gestures is not very different from what can be seen on any busy ghetto street during a hot summer evening. The similarity is too great to be due to chance.

Much research to support this hypothesis needs to be done. The purpose of this paper is not to establish the link between African non-verbal communication patterns and those of Black Americans. Instead, the hypothesis is suggested to provide a possible theoretical base to explain the differences between Black non-verbal communication patterns described here and the non-verbal communication patterns of other Americans.

A second hypothesis is that the isolation of the Black population from other Americans produced some differences in non-verbal communication patterns within the Black culture. Perhaps research will establish the validity of both hypotheses — that is, non-verbal communication patterns in the Black Culture could be a result of former African patterns and also a result of patterns that have evolved out of the indigenous conditions of Black Americans.

The focus of this paper will be on those non-verbal patterns that have been labeled KINESICS by Birdwhistell. Specifically, kinesics refers to how people send messages with their bodies through movement, expressions, gestures etc. Birdwhistell has pointed out that these non-verbal patterns are a learned form of communication which are patterned within a culture, and that they convey a particular message. Some of these patterns that are unique to the Black population and the messages they convey are described below.

Not every Black person exhibits every feature in his non-verbal behavior. However, these features occur with such great frequency in the Black population that they can be considered patterned behavior. (The same is true of Black dialect features. Not every Black person who speaks Black dialect will have all the features of this dialect in his speech.)

In stress or conflict situations, particularly when one of the participants is in a subordinate position (for example, a conflict situation involving a parent and child or a teacher and student). Black people can express with their eyes an insolent, hostile disapproval of the person who is in the authority role. The movement of the eyes is called "rolling the eyes" in the Black culture.

"Rolling the eyes" is a non-verbal way of expressing impudence and disapproval of the person who is in the authority role and of communicating every negative label that can be applied to the dominant person. The movement of the eyes communicates all or parts of the message. The main message is hostility. The movement of the eyes — rolling the eyes — is performed in the following way. First, the eyes are moved from one side of the eye-socket to the other, in a low arc (usually, the movement of the eyes — that is, the rolling — is preceded by a stare at the other person, but not an eye-to-eye stare). The lids of the eyes are slightly lowered when the eye balls are moved in the low arc. The eye balls always move AWAY from the other person. The movement is very quick, and it is often unnoticed by the other person, particularly if the other person is not Black. Sometimes, the eye movement is accompanied by a slight lifting of the head, or a twitching of the nose, or both. Rolling the eyes is more common among Black females than it is among Black males.

This movement of the eyes is different from the movement of the eyes which is called "cutting the eyes" in the dominant culture. In "cutting the eyes", the movement of the eyes is always TOWARD another person. Furthermore, after the eyes are focused on the other person (following the cutting) they usually remain focused in a stare. In other words, the stare follows the cutting action.

Black people (particularly females) will often roll their eyes when being reprimanded or "lectured to" about some infraction of a rule. After the person who is in the authority role has continued the lecture for a while, the Black person in the subordinate role (the "receiver" of the lecture) will roll the eyes. Rolling the eyes can also be used to express a kind of general disapproval. For example, if two Black women are together and a third woman enters their social sphere wearing a dress that the other two Black women know costs $5.95 and obviously giving the impression that she not only looks good but that the dress is much more expensive, then one of the two Black women will roll her eyes. In this situation the message communicated is "She sure think she cute but she don't look like nothing, 'cause that dress cost $5.95."

Rolling the eyes is probably partly responsible for the saying used by many Black people: "Don't look at me in that tone of voice." In fact, one of the indications that rolling the eyes is a hostile impudent non-verbal message is that when it is done the Black person in the authority role will stop lecturing and say, "Don't you roll your eyes at me!" (The implied meaning of this command is, "I know what you're thinking and I know the names you're calling me.") Sometimes, this command is punctuated by a slap "up-side the head".

Often, white teachers (who are in an authority role and who have contact with Black children) will miss the message communicated by Black children when they roll their eyes. It's just as well, because rolling the eyes gives the Black child an opportunity to non-verbally release his hostility and endure the reprimand with a minimum amount of conflict. Black teachers, on the other hand, usually recognize the action and properly interpret the message. As mentioned before, this sometimes causes them to punish the child, thus escalating the conflict and worsening the situation.

It is not known whether or not rolling the eyes is a non-verbal pattern in Western African cultures. It would be interesting and also a test of the hypothesis presented above if this could be determined.

Another eye behavior used by many Black Americans is found in many West African cultures. I am referring to the "reluctance" of Black Americans to look another person (particularly, another person in an authority role) directly in the eye.

Thus, the stereotyped view of many whites (particularly in the South) has some truth. That is, many Blacks (especially Black males) don't look another person in the eye, if the other person is in an authority role. To look another person in the eye (in the context of the dominant culture) is a non-verbal way of communicating trustworthiness, forthrightness, masculinity, truthfulness, sincerity etc. In the Black cultural context, avoiding eye contact is a non-verbal way of communicating a recognition of the authority-subordinate relationship of the participants in a social situation.

Many Black children are taught not to look another person (particularly an older person) in the eye when the older person is talking to the younger person. To do so is to communicate disrespect.

In the South Black males were taught — either overtly or covertly — not to look a white male in the eye because this communicated equality. Thus, not to look white males in the eye was really a survival pattern in the South.

Note how "culture clash" can occur because of the avoidance of eye contact: in the dominant culture, eye contact is interpreted one way, while it is interpreted in another way within the Black culture. Avoidance of eye contact by a Black person communicates, "I am in a subordinate role and I respect your authority over me", while the dominant cultural member may interpret avoidance of eye contact as, "Here is a shifty unreliable person I'm dealing with."

Avoiding eye contact to communicate respect and acknowledgement of one's being in a subordinate role is a common pattern in Western Africa. (This pattern is also found in other cultures, for example, in the Japanese culture.) It could well be that this particular pattern within the Black culture has its origins in former African cultures of Black Americans.

Reinforcing the avoidance of eye contact is a stance that young Blacks take in a conflict situation (this stance sometimes is taken by adult Blacks, too). Often, in a conflict situation Black youngsters (particularly, males) will slowly begin to take a limp stance as the reprimand from the person in the authority role goes on and on. The stance is as follows: the head is lowered, the body becomes extremely relaxed and the Black person stands almost as if he is in a trance. The stance is not taken immediately, but slowly evolves as the reprimand proceeds.

Young white males usually stand very rigid with their legs spread and their arms extended stiffly down the sides of their bodies (fists balled up) as the reprimand is delivered.

The limp stance is a defense mechanism which non-verbally communicates: "I am no longer a person receiving your message of reprimand; I am only an object." Or, it communicates: "My body is present, but my mind is completely removed from the present encounter." In any case, when a Black person adopts this stance in a conflict situation, the best thing to do is to terminate the reprimand — the Black person is not receiving the message. The person in the authority role — the person delivering the reprimand — can be sure whether or not this is the non-verbal message if he notices the way the Black person walks away from him after the reprimand.

Before describing the walk away from a conflict situation, it is necessary to describe the "Black walk". It communicates non-verbal messages in other situations besides conflicts.

Young Black males have their own way of walking. Observing young Black males walking down ghetto streets, one can't help noticing that they are, indeed, in Thoreau's words "marching to the tune of a different drummer". The "different drummer" is a different culture; the non-verbal message of their walk is SIMILAR to the non-verbal message of young white males, but not quite the same.

The young white males' walk is usually brisk, and they walk on the balls of their feet with strides of presumed authority. Both arms swing while they walk. The non-verbal message is: "I am a strong man, possessing all the qualities of masculinity, and I stride through the world with masculine authority."

The young Black males' walk is different. First of all, it's much slower — it's more of a stroll. The head is sometimes slightly elevated and casually tipped to the side. Only one arm swings at the side with the hand slightly cupped. The other arm hangs limply to the side or it is tucked in the pocket. The gait is slow, casual and rhythmic. The gait is almost like a walking dance, with all parts of the body moving in rhythmic harmony. This walk is called a "pimp strut", or it is referred to as "walking that walk".

The walk of young Black males communicates the same non-verbal message as that of young white males. In addition, the Black walk communicates that the young Black male is beautiful, and it beckons female attention to the sexual prowess possessed by the walker. Finally, the Black walk communicates that the walker is "cool"; in other words, he is not upset or bothered by the cares of the world and is, in fact, somewhat disdainful and insolent towards the world.

The young Black male walk must be learned, and it is usually learned at quite a young age. Black males of elementary school age can often be seen practicing the walk. By the time they reach junior high school age, the Black walk has been mastered.

The description of the walk is a general description, and it includes all the components that can be present in the walk. All the components are not always present in each individual's walk, because each individual must impose a certain amount of originality onto the general pattern. Thus, some young Black males will vary the speed or swing of the head or effect a slight limp or alter any one or a number of the components of the Black walk to achieve originality. The general "plan" of the walk, however, is recognizable even with the imposed originality. This imposed originality also communicates the individualism of each young Black male.

The Black walk is used for mobility (as any walk is) and to arrive at a destination. Sometimes, however, one gets the feeling that WHERE the young Black male is going is not as important as HOW he gets there. There is a great deal of "styling" in the walk. The means are more important than the end.

The walk is also used as a hostile rejection of another person in a conflict situation. For example, after a person in an authority role has reprimanded a young Black male, the person with authority can tell whether his reprimand has had positive effects (e.g. the young Black male follows the dictates of the reprimand, he is sorry for the offense etc.) by the way the young Black male walks away from the authority figure. If the young Black male walks away in a "natural" manner, then the reprimand was received positively; if he walks away with a "pimp strut" it means that the young Black male has rejected the reprimand and in fact is non-verbally telling the authority person to "go to hell".

Young Black females communicate the same non-verbal message when walking away from a person in an authority role after a conflict situation by pivoting quickly on both feet (something like the military "about face") and then walking briskly away. Sometimes the pivot is accompanied by a raising of the head and a twitching of the nose.

When either the young Black male or the young Black female walks away from the authority person in the above manners, the knowledgeable authority person (particularly if he or she is Black) will angrily tell the young Black person to "come back here and walk away right". To walk away "right" means to walk away without communicating the negative, disrespectful, insolent message. This is proof that these walks are sending a message.

The Black walk is reflected in the stance young Black males take while talking in a group. For example, when talking in a group, the participants (say, four or five young Black males) will often adopt a kind of stationary "pimp strut". This means that while the young Black males are talking, they stand with their hands halfway in their pockets, and they move in the rhythmic, fluid dance-type way (without actually walking) to punctuate their remarks. The arm that is free will swing, point, turn and gesture as conversation proceeds. It's almost as if they are walking "in place". This kind of behavior always accompanies a light or humorous conversation, or a conversation about masculine exploits. It never accompanies a serious discussion about more general topics (planning something, difficulties with parents, political issues, etc.). However, if these kinds of topics are discussed in terms of the young Blacks' masculinity or if they are "styling" while discussing these topics, the stationary "pimp strut" stance WILL be taken.

Often, when this stance is taken HOW one says something — the style — is more important than WHAT one says.

Another interesting thing that happens when a group of young Black males talk in a group is that the periphery of the group continually fluctuates. That is, the group moves in and out toward and from the center. (Young white males, when they are talking in a group, usually maintain a tight circle during the discussion.) When something particularly interesting or funny is said (if the statement reflects a use of language that is unique, creative and "styled") one or more of the participants will turn his back to the center of the group and walk away — almost dance away — with great animation to non-verbally communicate his confirmation of what has been said and his recognition of the creative way in which it was said. In other words, when young Black males are discussing a "light" or humorous topic, the observer can expect a great deal of movement and fluctuation in the periphery of the circle of discussants.

Another non-verbal behavioral pattern easily noticed in Black male group discussion is the way males punctuate laughter. Often, when something especially funny is said by a Black, the audience (either one or more other Blacks who are in the audience or group) will raise a cupped hand to the mouth and laugh. The hand is not actually placed over the mouth; instead, it is held about six inches away from the mouth as if to muffle the laugh. Sometimes this action is accompanied by a backward shuffle. This action — the cupped hand in front of the mouth — is common among West Africans. The non-verbal message is that the audience has acknowledged the particularly witty statement of the speaker.

The above description of Black group discussion always applies to a topic being discussed that is not serious. When a serious topic is being discussed, these behavioral patterns are not present in the group's behavior. Thus, we know that the topic is light when the group is "jiving" or "styling" or just playing verbal games. (Blacks play a verbal game of using language in a unique, creative, humorous way for the purpose of seeing how they can "mess up" the English language for comical effects.)

The Black walk is also carried over into the "rapping stance" of young Black males. A "rapping stance" is the stance a young Black male takes when talking romantically to a young Black female. (The word "rap" originally referred only to romantic talk to a female. When it was adopted by the young white population, the word took on an added meaning to refer to any kind of aggressive talk on any topic.) The "rapping stance" of young Black males is a kind of stationary "pimp strut". When young Black males are talking romantically to young Black females — particularly when they are making the initial "hit", or when they are making the initial romantic overtures to a Black female that preludes a romantic relationship — they stand a certain way that non-verbally communicates: "Look at me. I am somebody you can really 'dig' because I am beautiful and I am about to lay my 'heavy rap' on you and you can't resist it. Now, listen to my 'rap' and respond."

The "rapping stance" is as follows: first, the Black male does not stand directly in front of the Black female but at a slight angle; the head is slightly elevated and tipped to the side (toward the female); the eyes are about three-fourths open; sometimes, the head very slowly nods as the "rap" is delivered; the arms conform to the "pimp strut" pattern — one hand may be half-way in the pocket, while the other arm hangs free; finally, the weight of the body is concentrated on the back heel (in the "rapping stance" the feet are not together but are positioned in a kind of frozen step). The Black female will listen to this "rap" nonchalantly with one hand on her hip.

The young white male "rapping stance" is different: the female is backed up against the wall, while the young white male extends one arm, extends the fingers and places his palm against the wall to support himself as he leans toward the female with all his weight placed on the foot that is closest to the female. Sometimes, both arms are extended to support his weight, thus trapping the female between his two extended arms.

It has been pointed out that Black males often turn their backs to another participant in a communication situation. This action always communicates a very friendly intimate message. This action — turning one's back to another — can be observed when Black males greet each other. One of the most friendly greetings that can be given to another Black is to walk up to him and verbally greet him with a warm statement (often, this verbal statement is delivered in a falsetto voice, the friendly level or "game" level) and then, after the verbal greeting is delivered, one (or both) of the participants will turn his back to the other and walk away for a few steps. This is probably the friendliest greeting Black males can give to each other. The non-verbal message is probably: "Look, I trust you so much that I unhesitatingly place myself in a vulnerable position in greeting you."

Another pattern that is common when Black males greet each other is for one to approach the other person, verbally greet him, and then stand during the initial stages of the greeting with the one hand cupped over the genitals. This stance is sometimes maintained throughout the subsequent conversation, particularly if the subsequent conversation pertains to sexual exploits or some kind of behavior which is particularly masculine.

This stance — the cupped hand over the genitals — can even be observed, sometimes, when the young Black male is in his "rapping stance". The non-verbal message here is not clear; perhaps, the young Black male is communicating non-verbally that he is so sexually potent that he must subdue or "rein in" his sexual potential.

The action of turning one's back on another person in a group discussion or greeting always non-verbally communicates trust or friendliness. It also non-verbally communicates confirmation of what another Black has stated. For example, when one Black makes a statement that another Black particularly confirms, the Black who wants to non-verbally communicate his confirmation will turn his back to the other. Often, this action is preceded by a "slap" handshake — that is, both Blacks will execute the "soul" handshake that consists of one Black holding his palm in an upward position while the other Black slaps the palm with his own, usually in a vigorous manner.

Turning the back can often be seen in a Black audience. When listening to a speaker (a preacher, teacher etc.), members of the Black audience will often shift their positions in their seats to slightly turn their backs to the speaker to non-verbally communicate confirmation and agreement with the speaker's remarks (before this action, members of the Black audience will slightly bend forward in their seats to non-verbally communicate that they are concerned about or perhaps not quite sure of what the speaker is saying. At that moment when they understand what the speaker is saying or they agree with the speaker, they will shift in their seats to slightly expose their backs).

It was indicated that when listening to a "rap" of a Black male a Black female will often stand with one hand on her hip. Whenever a Black female places one hand on her hip, it non-verbally communicates an intense involvement with or concern about the situation. But the hand-on-hip stance non-verbally communicates a more specific meaning in other communication situations: it usually communicates intense aggression, anger, disgust or other hostile negative feelings toward the speaker.

In a conflict situation, or when a Black female delivers a hostile verbal message, the verbal message is often accompanied by the hand-on-hip stance. This is the most aggressive stance that Black females take, and it is executed in the following manner: first, the feet are placed firmly in a stationary step, with the body weight concentrated on the heel of the rear foot; the buttocks are protruded; and, one hand is placed on the extended hip (the hip is extended because of the weight concentration on the rear foot and the protrusion of the buttocks); the hand either rests on the hip supported by the fingers being spread, or it is supported by making the hand into a fist and resting the knuckles against the hip. Sometimes, the body of the Black female will slowly rock to and fro during the stance, particularly while she is listening to the other person. If the stance is not taken while the Black female is listening, it is quickly taken when she delivers her hostile verbal message. The stance can also be accompanied by a rolling of the eyes and a twitching of the nose to further punctuate the hostility of the Black female. (Flip Wilson, in his Geraldine characterization, often assumes this stance. In fact, Flip Wilson is a very good illustrator of Black female non-verbal aggressive behavior because the behavior is distorted for comical effects and easily noticed.)

Most Black people know to "cool it" when Black women take this stance. The non-verbal message communicated when a Black female takes this stance is: "I'm really mad, now. You better quit messing with me." (Chicano females often stand with both hands on their hips with their feet spread wide and their heads slightly raised to non-verbally communicate a similar message.)

The non-verbal behavior described in this paper provides some illustrations of the non-verbal communication patterns of Black people that are different from those of white people and other cultural groups in this country. WHY they are different is a question that must be answered by research. The purpose here, again, has not been to explain the WHY, but to describe some of these patterns that are different. Hypotheses were presented to provide a basis on which this research can be conducted.

It is important (particularly, for people who work with Blacks — school teachers, social workers, industry personnel) to recognize these patterns and the messages they convey because it helps one to better understand the communications of Black people. In some ways, non-verbal communication patterns are more important than verbal communication patterns because they are often unconscious — a person cannot easily hide his true feelings when this is the case. The importance of non-verbal communication is indicated in the adage: "Your actions speak so loudly, I can hardly hear what you say."

University of California, Berkeley

Section IV: Black English and Psycholinguistics

INTRODUCTION TO SECTION IV

Psychologists in general have a dismal record with respect to Black English. In fact, Baratz (1973:1), citing Labov (1969a) and Sroufe (1970) has objected to "the psychologist's faulty knowledge about language as well as his methodological inadequacies". For a field that, like psychology, has prided itself on its methodology, those are harsh words. For the followers of Skinner (1957) in verbal behavior (Horner and Gussow 1972; see also Dell Hymes's Introduction in *Functions of Language in the Classroom*, 1972), who claim some extra-special perceptions as embodied in the concepts of mands and tacts, they may be equally harsh. Yet the value of the Skinnerean approach has been accepted by few linguists since Chomsky's review (1959).

The linguists who have gone into psycholinguistics (like Labov and Houston, articles by whom are reprinted in this section) have followed the lead of Chomsky (1968:4), who called for a richer psychological theory, beyond

... a system of stimulus-response connections, a network of associations, a repertoire of behavioral items, a habit hierarchy, or a system of dispositions to respond in a particular way under specifiable stimulus conditions ...

In fact, Chomsky insisted

What is involved is not a matter of degree of complexity but rather quality of complexity (1968:4).

As is now well known, such considerations led him to argue for the existence of mind in the Cartesian sense (Chomsky 1966).

Very few linguists disagree with Chomsky in these attitudes. In spite of the limitations of its methods, even pre-Chomsky linguistics would have preferred his infinite creativity model to its segregation-of-corpus procedures if its techniques had been able to actualize such a theory. But there has been a kind of post-Chomskyean revolution in the last few years. Although no linguist now makes the "Avoid Process Statements" restrictions which were often profferred before Chomsky (1957), and although the "upward" approach which sought to build as much of a grammar as possible on phonology was effectively dead soon after that time, many linguists, like Chafe (1970), are no longer following the early Chomskyean model in which syntax is the generative element and both phonology and semantics are conceived as interpretative elements (Katz and Postal 1964).

With the somewhat diminished emphasis on syntactic deep structure as the creative part of language, and its concomitant emphasis on the essential universality of syntax, there may come a change in the somewhat peripheral notion that dialect variation must involve phonology and lexicon alone, never syntax (Fasold 1972). The discussion by Loflin (section I) seems especially relevant here. Probably along with this belief will have to go the thesis, not specifically Chomskyean but often held by his followers, that historical change must be basically phonological.[1] This belief, obviously unacceptable to the creolists (see section II), has colored a great deal of writing about Black English.[2]

But, no matter how directly or indirectly Chomskyean they may have been, linguists interested in psychology have rejected what has come to be called deficit theory. (Not all of them, unfortunately, have had restraint enough to refrain from stigmatizing a colleague who holds a substantively different view as a deficit theorist.) In fact, the psychologists' preoccupation with individual differences has largely conflicted with the uniformitarian and relativistic bent of linguistics. Chomsky quite early stressed the independence of language acquisition from intelligence differences (whether or not expressed in "IQ"), a fact which has endeared him very slightly to more conventional psychologists. Linguists in general have been virtually unanimous in rejecting Jensen (1969), as have many other social scientists (Baratz and Baratz 1969). Apart from language those who have looked at Black cultural traits as healthful wholes rather than as pathologies have been anthropologists, folklorists, and musicologists.[3] (For a partial discussion, see Introduction to section III.)

[1]   This point of view is apparently not that of Chomsky and Halle (1968:250).
[2]   Houston, who has contributed an article to this section (see below), stresses phonological differences rather than syntactic differences between Black English and other varieties (*genera*, in her terminology) of English. In fairness to Houston, it should be made clear that she does not subscribe to many of the statements made in this collection, especially in the Introduction to section II.
[3]   At one time even the area of motor coordination was involved in deficit theories. Cf. Cohen (1969:92-93):

It should be admitted, however, that psychologists like Jensen (1969) and Shuey (1966) deserve some credit for confronting an issue which had been generally taboo in the academic world. One can make such a statement without approving either of their methods or of their results. Furthermore, the educational psychologists often outpaced the dialectologists in discovering Black dialect data (see section I), although they did not know what to do with those data. For example, Bereiter and Engelmann (1966:113) heard

Me got juice

even though his knowledge of selectional and subcategorization rules (Chomsky 1965) was hardly great enough to allow him to see that the interpretation

*Juice has me

is not a possible one, whereas

I have juice

is. For that matter, the dialect geographers were unable to relate such structures as the invariant pronoun to English Creole, although they generally had enough training in general linguistics to make them wary of talk of language deficits or of slowness in language acquisition. Bereiter heard

They mine

before the debate over the "zero copula" began, although he made the blunder of considering it "a series of badly connected words or phrases" (1966:113). The educational psychologists can not be held entirely to blame because conventional dialectology did not provide a rational interpretation for the data which they were collecting among ghetto children.[4]

"Table 6 reveals a shockingly lower PQ [Perceptual Quotient] among Puerto Rican and black children compared to white and Chinese. The curve for Puerto Rican and black compared to white and Chinese shows a much higher incidence of severe perceptual dysfunctions. Table 7 gives a finer analysis showing for example that all groups are retarded in eye-motor coordination ...".

Since the equal, even superior, motor coordination of Blacks would be suggested by their present dominance in professional sports, it seems very likely that what has been tested is some kind of culturally variable eye-motor behavior rather than ability to coordinate as such. The need for a good kinesic description of Black motor behavior, and a comparison with other groups, seems, then, to be a glaring need of psychology. See Johnson's article in section III for a start in describing the Black system.

[4] For psychologists, especially behaviorists and particularly the disciples of Skinner, it was extremely unfortunate that Skinner (1957) dealt with some pidgin-like ("broken English") structures in his treatment of "autoclitics". Skinner wrote that "Some simple sentences are generated simply by adding autoclitics to available verbal operants"

Fortunately, even though some psychologically-oriented researchers in language were led astray into deficit theory, linguistics itself, under the influence of the transformational-generativists, was headed in the other direction. The Chomskyean revolution brought, in its nativism, withering criticism of the notion of direct environmental influence on language. The strange theory of C. Deutsch (1964) about ghetto noise volume having an adverse effect on the hearing of the children was never acceptable to any major body of linguists.

The answer to the notion of "impaired auditory discrimination" was, obviously, in terms of the different phonological system of Black English (especially "uneducated Child Black English", in Houston's terms). Houston (reprinted in this section) and Labov (Labov et al., 1968) as well as Luelsdorff (section I) and Stewart (all references) argued from a presentation of a different phonological system for Black English and theorized that, in terms of what is known about language contact, presentation in a non-native phonological system must provide bias in the experiment. These structural arguments now have experimental verification in Politzer and McMahon (1970). Those researchers found that the regularly used discrimination test (Wepman 1958)

... contains phonemic discriminations which are simply not found in Negro dialects or in other dialects usually associated with lower socioeconomic status. An examination of the Wepman test reveals at least seven such discriminations on each of the two forms of the test (Politzer and McMahon 1970:17-18).

Extending the domain of the formal, statistically-oriented test beyond the deficit concept, Politzer and his associates found special abilities of Black children which other investigators had not suspected.

Black children scored better in discriminating Black Nonstandard English and Black Standard English (Politzer and Hoover 1972:11).

And they found significant correlations with other notorious scores like those of ghetto children on national reading achievement tests.

For Black children, by contrast, making the distinction between standard and nonstandard English is related to reading achievement from the very beginning of their school career .... The Black child must become highly skilled in recognizing the standard/nonstandard distinction in order to succeed in a Standard English reading program. The white child does not face a comparable task (Politzer and Hoover 1972:12).

(p. 345) and that "In broken English the speaker may simply say *hungry man* or *man hungry* ... as a rudimentary predication" (*Ibid.*).

Further, he made the value judgment that "The complete form *The man is hungry* is optimally effective on the assumed listener" (*Ibid.*). Since he also included the form *Man, he hungry* (said to be characteristic of a speaker "less practiced in English"), Skinner provided considerable bias and confusion for psychologists who would observe a rather similar structure in the language of ghetto children.

Insofar as reading is concerned, Politzer and his associates are obviously performing experiments on a much higher level of sophistication than Rystrom (1970). In view of the announced policy of this collection not to deal with pedagogical matters, however, it will be necessary to drop the subject with no more than a reference to Baratz and Shuy (1969).

If psychologists in general have always been better at examining attitudes and personality traits than in dealing with language, there have been some few, like Lambert and Tucker, who have been at home not only in psychology but in almost all phases of language study. Their famous indirect method of judging language attitudes (Lambert et al., 1965) is known to virtually all social scientists. Their Tougaloo University experiment (reprinted here) was the first of many listeners' tests which showed that Black and White speakers could be distinguished from tape-recorded cues only. Other such tests have been performed by Baratz (1969), Labov et al. (1968), Buck (1968), and Baratz, Shuy, and Wolfram (1969). So far, however, no one has followed up such aspects of the Lambert-Tucker investigation in Mississippi as the test of attitudes toward another important American social dialect, Network Standard.

The work of William Labov and his associates with Black English is of course very well known (see Introductions above, all sections). It seems really unfair to limit Labov to the field of psycholinguistics, even by implication, but he is now a member of a Department of Psychology (University of Pennsylvania), and his work had to be placed somewhere. Further, his widely acclaimed sophistication in elicitation tasks and his use of statistical method gives his work certain methodological similarities to the best of more conventional psychologists. From the 1968 Office of Education report by Labov and his associates, the Vernacular Correction Test and the Classroom Correction Test were selected because they show beautifully the contrast between the natural language behavior of informants in the peer group situation and their language use in those situations where middle-class persons, including professionals, are most likely to encounter them.

Susan Houston was trained as a psycholinguist and has produced a book on the subject (Houston 1972). She is, furthermore, very much concerned with formal criteria in elicitation and with the relationship of language differences to academic accomplishment. Even those who see slight differences between Black English and the school dialect, like Houston and Labov, have pointed out how the discomfort of operating in their second-most-effective language system may impose unfair handicaps on Black English-speaking children.

From the viewpoint of an increasing number of linguists, IQ testing, which may have the famous "self-fulfilling prophecy" effect on the child's school performance, is biased against the Black, Nonstandard English-speaking youngster:

High performance on this test [the Wechsler Preschool Intelligence Test] entails nothing less than full socialization into the culture of speakers of the dominant dialect of English, in addition to some degree of competence in their dialect (Roberts 1969, quoted in Baratz 1973: 27).

Thus the work of linguists (Labov 1969a, Stewart all references) directly contradicts that of many educational psychologists, whose point of view has tended to be more nearly:

The effect of the father-in-home variable on IQ for this sample has been shown in the data presented here. What is less measurable, but may nonetheless exist, is the potential systematic lowering of Negro children's IQ by the greater prevalence of broken homes in Negro SES groups I and II (Deutsch and Brown 1967: 305).

What has been overlooked, obviously, is that the low grade on the IQ test may represent cultural bias on the test. The prevalence of "broken homes" for Negro children may be a cultural fact which relates more directly with Black life style (see section III) than with intelligence. Whatever it does to his "IQ", there is no real evidence that the home environment restricts the Black child's ability to think or to use language.

But the cause is not lost for educational psychology, and its methods can still be used for useful research on the language of poor Black children, provided the investigators have some linguistic training. Stuart H. Silverman, a section of whose dissertation is reprinted here, is not only a psychologist but an educational psychologist — and proud of it; but he was more specifically a member of a Language and Behavior Program whose professors included Joshua Fishman and Beryl Bailey. Since he was also a student of mine, it is a great pleasure to present his article — as it was to work with him on his dissertation and to argue with him in an (unsuccessful) attempt to dissuade him from an essentially Skinnerian orientation. But his dissertation impresses me as a good piece of research from any viewpoint, and it does show the importance of social factors for language change in a very interesting way. That Puerto Ricans in the New York ghettos have been picking up Black English may have seemed obvious to some observers, but Silverman provides objective proof and detailed the conditions under which such influence takes place. It is interesting to note that Wolfram, Shiels, and Fasold (1971), who work with formal linguistic rules rather than with the more characteristic statistics of the psychologist, recapitulate his results in many particulars. By some coincidence, apparently, they have found, as did Silverman, that Puerto Rican boys who play basketball associate on a peer basis with Blacks and pick up more Black English than those who do not.

WILLIAM LABOV, CLARENCE ROBINS, PAUL COHEN, and
JOHN LEWIS

CLASSROOM CORRECTION TESTS

4.4.   In this and the following three sections we will turn to the results
of certain formal tests which were given to our subjects in single interviews. Like any tests, they create context which is appropriate for formal
speech; the sociolinguistic frame of reference for any test situation will
inevitably resemble that of the classroom. In these investigations, we
examined the subject's subjective reactions to variable linguistic forms —
we are concerned with whether or not he can perceive differences between
standard English and the non-standard Negro English form, what value
he assigns to these forms (conscious or unconscious) and whether he can
identify the social and ethnic background of speakers by their use of
language. This subjective evaluation of linguistic behavior falls under
the general topic of this volume — these are the social and psychological
factors which lie behind rules for the use of language. The last three
sections have considered the ways in which the value system of the NNE
community explains their use of language: in this and the following three
sections we will be examining the ways in which values have been embedded in particular linguistic forms themselves. The forms that we will
be concerned with are those generated by the most characteristic grammatical and phonological rules of NNE as discussed in chapter III.

The purpose of the Classroom Correction Tests was to discover which
of the NNE features that do in fact differ from the corresponding SE
forms were perceived as non-standard by NNE speakers. In other words,
we wished to know how successful the school had been in tagging certain

Reprinted with permission from Labov *et al.*, *A Study of the Non-Standard English of
Negro and Puerto Rican Speakers in New York City* (New York, U.S. Office of Education, Cooperative Research Project No. 3288).

forms as wrong — in bringing them to the forefront of consciousness of the pre-adolescents and adolescents we have been dealing with. The results give us clear answers to this question on the forms tested. Furthermore, they show us the gradual acquisition of these standard norms as the child grows up in the non-standard Negro English culture. Finally, the results discriminate sharply between lames and peer group members — more sharply than the indices of linguistic behavior itself. In speaking of characteristic NNE reactions, we are fortunate to have available comparisons with the white Inwood group, which allows us to differentiate general WNS reactions from NNE reactions.

4.4.1. *Form of the Classroom Correction Tests.* The Classroom Correction (CC) test was administered at the end of all pre-adolescent and adolescent interviews, except for the older Oscar Brothers. The instructions for the pre-adolescents read as follows:

Here's some sentences that are a little different. These are the kind that teachers like to correct in school. What if a friend came to you, and said, "Are these O.K. for school?" I'd like you to take a pencil and circle the places that you think have to be fixed, if there are any.

The subject was then handed a piece of $8\frac{1}{2} \times 11$ paper, with the following sentences printed in large (24-point) widely-spaced type.

a. I ate four apple.
b. I met three mens.
1. He pick me.
2. He ain't gone yet.
3. I've pass my test.
4. He don't know nobody.
5. He never play no more, man.
6. The man from U.N.C.L.E. hate the guys from Thrush.
7. Last week I kick Donald in the mouth, so the teacher throwed me out the class.

The interviewer circled the end of the word *apple* in the first example, and the -*s* on the word *men* in the second example. He then said, "Now you do the rest. How would you say each of these after you'd fixed them?" We thus were able to compare the subject's ability to perceive the non-standard form, with his own formal version of the sentences. The large type and the simple form of most of the sentences helped to overcome the fact that most of the subjects are very bad readers. But for many, the problem of bad reading is inextricably mixed with the problem of perception of non-standard forms, so that the contribution of one skill to the other is not clearly separated here. In this discussion, we will be concerned only with the simplest form of the data: whether or not the subjects perceived the non-standard element and corrected it by one means or

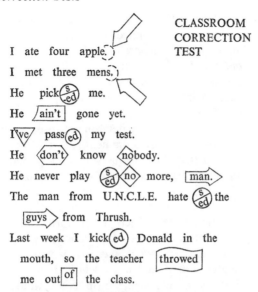

CLASSROOM
CORRECTION
TEST

I ate four apple.

I met three mens.

He pick(s)(-ed) me.

He /ain't| gone yet.

I've/ pass(ed) my test.

He ⟨don't⟩ know ⟨nobody⟩.

He never play ⟨(s)(ed)⟩⟨no⟩ more, [man.⟩

The man from U.N.C.L.E. hate (s)(ed) the

|guys⟩ from Thrush.

Last week I kick(ed) Donald in the

mouth, so the teacher |throwed|

me out|of| the class.

another. This material is very rich in itself; an analysis of the actual corrections made will be undertaken in a later study.

The non-standard forms which we placed in the list are indicated below: The variables which we were examining can be grouped as follows: (a) THIRD SINGULAR ZERO: the absence of an -*ed* or -*s* inflection on the verb in sentences 1, 5, 6, and 7. Sentence 1 is the simplest example since this is the only non-standard element in this short sentence. Sentences 5 and 6 are more difficult because the sentences are longer; number 5 also contains another non-standard form — negative concord — and the word *man* as a form of address, which draws considerable attention. We believed that 7 would be even harder because this sentence is the longest; there are two other non-standard forms, and the -*ed* comes in a phonetic context where it is hard to hear it. Numbers 1, 5 and 6 would normally be corrected by adding either -*ed* or -*s* after the verb, but 5 could be corrected by inserting *will* after *he*, and 6 could be corrected by changing *man* to *men*. In 7, the addition of -*ed* is the only way to change it to standard English. (b) *Have* WITHOUT -*ed*. Sentence 3 has *I've* without an -*ed* following the verb. There are many ways that this NNE form might be corrected to SE, but any one of these should reflect the speaker's understanding of the contracted form of *have* coupled with -*ed*. It has been observed above that the *have* is often deleted in this position, and when it is present the -*ed* will very often be missing. We are here concerned with the perception that standard English requires both forms. (c) NEGATIVE CONCORD. Sentences 4 and 5 show negative concord with the underlying *any*. (d) IRREGULAR PRETERIT. Sentence 7 contains the non-standard preterit *throwed* instead of *threw*. (e) *Ain't*. Sentence 2 contains the non-standard form *ain't*, which may be interpreted as equivalent to either standard English *isn't* or standard English *hasn't*. (f) *Out of*. In sentence 7, the non-standard form *out the class* is used instead of standard *out of the class*. (g) SLANG. Two lexical items were used which are normally considered slang from the standpoint of classroom behavior — *man* as a term of address in sentence 5, and *guys* in sentence 6.

In estimating the difficulty of these items in advance, we felt that wholly stigmatized forms would be most prominent and most easily recognized. Secondly, we expected that those forms which are phonologically most different from standard English would be easily recognized; thirdly, we believed that embedding the item in a longer sentence with other non-standard forms would make it more difficult to perceive. The main focus of classroom correction is on inflection and forms of the verb; since prepositional phrases are not of as much concern, we believe that the correction of *out the class* to *out of the class* would be least likely to be brought to the attention of students in school. Finally, we argued that the grammatical status of the elements in NNE would be the most important factor — whether or not the non-standard form was produced in speech by a rigid rule or optional variant. To sum up the factors involved in performance on a CC test would be:

(1) Social stereotypes.
(2) Phonetic substance.
(3) Number of competing items.
(4) Phonetic context.
(5) Grammatical status in NNE.

It is obvious that a short test such as this would not allow us to factor out all of these inferences; no one could weigh them all in advance or predict their interaction. However, we set up the following provisional prediction, from least difficult to most difficult.

		Sentence
1.	ain't	2
2.	throwed	7
3.	nobody	4
4.	no more	5
5.	don't	4
6.	pick-	1
7.	hate-	6
8.	play-	5
9.	I've pass-	3
10.	kick-	7
11.	out the class	7

More importantly, we felt that the lames would score much higher on the CC tests than the peer group members, since they were plainly more open to the influence of the classroom culture. If we were right in thinking that close attachment to peer group membership was not consistent with easy acceptance of schoolroom culture, it would follow that those who were detached from the peer groups would necessarily perceive the NNE forms in the light of standard English judgment. At the same time, we have seen that there is some learning of middle-class norms throughout adolescence. The previous work in New York City shows that the acquisition of standard English norms and behavior followed an upward slope with increasing age for all social groups — even though lower social classes operated at a lower level throughout this process (Labov 1965).[1] We would therefore expect to see a general rise in the scores of the CC tests with age, still preserving the difference between lames and peer group members at each age.

4.4.2. *Results*. The over all results of the CC tests confirm these views of the acquisition of standard English norms; the patterns were, however, much clearer than expected. Figure 4-11 shows the average scores on the CC tests, combining all items into a single index. The vertical axis is the percentage of non-standard forms which the subjects identified. The eleven items listed above are here given equal weight. A total of 123 pre-adolescent and adolescent boys are tested here, divided into 10 groups:

(a) *Junior Thunderbirds*. 4 younger brothers of Thunderbirds from 1390 5th Avenue, age 8-9.
(b) *Thunderbirds*. 11 boys, age 10-13.
(c) *Aces*. 4 boys, age 10-13. (The Aces are a group quite comparable to the Thunderbirds in a neighboring lower income project.)
(d) 1390 *Lames*. 5 boys age 10-12, living in 1390 5th Avenue, but not members of the Thunderbirds.
(e) *All PA lames*. 52 pre-adolescent boys age 10-12 interviewed in Vacation Day Camps, plus the 1390 Lames.
(f) *Jets*. 24 boys, age 12-17.
(g) *Cobras*. 11 boys, age 12-17.
(h) *TA lames*. 5 adolescent boys, age 15-17, interviewed in the Jet area but not members of the Jets.
(i) *Inwood PA*. 4 Inwood pre-adolescent boys, age 10-13.
(j) *Inwood TA*. 3 Inwood adolescents, age 15-17.

Figure 4-11 shows that these groups follow a pattern of age stratification, if we associate each group with the corresponding group of the same culture background. The lowest scores are shown by the pre-pre-adolescent

---

[1] See references for the introductions. [Ed.]

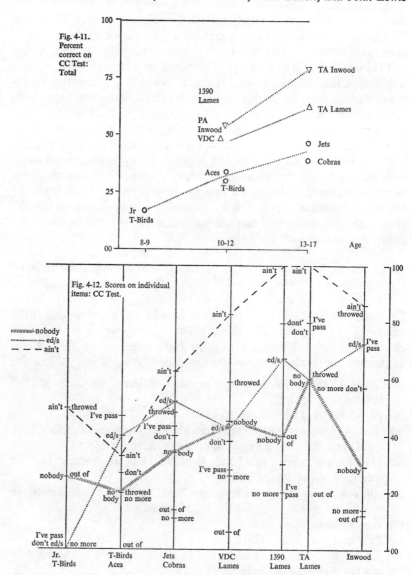

Fig. 4-11. Percent correct on CC Test: Total

Fig. 4-12. Scores on individual items: CC Test.

Junior Thunderbirds, the pre-adolescent Aces and Thunderbirds and the adolescent Jets and Cobras. Note that the scores for the Aces and Thunderbirds are very close together, and the scores for the Jets and the Cobras are also quite close. The scores for the Junior Thunderbirds start at a very low level at 0.13, rise to about 0.33 for the pre-adolescents and to about 0.45 for the adolescents. All the other groups start at a much higher level. There is not only age stratification, but there is a regular pattern of cultural stratification here.

The next level of stratification is that of the isolated individuals who were selected without regard to membership in peer groups. For the pre-adolescents, we have the PA Lames and for the adolescents, the five TA Lames interviewed in the Jet area. It must be remembered that not all of these boys are true lames in the sense of being outside the main stream of the street culture. Some are members of other peer groups, but the majority are not. The Vacation Day Camp series tended to select boys who were somewhat detached from this culture, and most of the TA Lames knew of the Jets but were not members. Their scores on the CC test are well above the peer group members, but not as high as white Inwood groups, which are located one step higher on the graph. Both the lames and the Inwood groups show increasing scores with age. Finally, the 1390 Lames are located above the corresponding Inwood pre-adolescents, at 0.64. If the connection with NNE non-standard grammar were the only factor involved here, it would be surprising that the 1390 Lames had higher scores than the Inwood group, but a number of the test items were also common in the WNS vernacular. The Inwood group show some of the same resistance to the school language, and adherence to their own vernacular, which we observe in the NNE peer group members.

This will be more evident when we note that some of the groups shown on Figure 4-11 are quite small in number, but they nevertheless fall into a regular array when their "social address" as well as their ages are taken into consideration. The pattern of dual stratification we see here is a familiar one. The scores of the younger VDC series are on a level with those of the older peer group members, around 0.46; the scores of the younger 1390 Lames are on a level with those of the older TA Lames. If one does not analyze these groups by their membership as well as their age, this regular stratification would be lost.

When we examine answers to the particular items on the CC tests, some of the numbers involved become dangerously small. However, a number of general tendencies become clearly visible, which indicate which of the factors listed above are most important in determining the perception of the SE norms.

4.4.3. *Reaction to individual items.* When we examine the figures on particular items on the CC test, we find that some of the totals are quite small and the ordering is not always significant. But there are a number of regular tendencies which throw more light on the relation of NNE grammar to the perception of the standard norms.

In general, there is considerable agreement with the original prediction of order of difficulty given above. The biggest exceptions are *nobody* and *no more*, which were marked less often than predicted. This low position of the negative concord items must be due in part to the fact that they are embedded in sentences with other competing items. For all groups, *nobody* was marked much more often than *no more* — one reason is obviously that *nobody* occurs in sentence 5 with one other item, while *no more* occurs in sentence 6 competing with two other items. But the low scores for *nobody* and *no more* are also due to the fact that negative concord is used so regularly as part of a semi-categorical rule by NNE members (3.6.3).

The absolute number of corrections in sentence 3, *I pass my test*, was much higher than predicted. But in the corrections made by the subjects 40% simply show the *'ve* deleted. Although this results in a correct SE sentence, *I pass my test*, it does not demonstrate any recognition of *have...ed* as a possible choice in SE. The ranking of *I've pass* given below is based on a corrected figure in which these deletions of *'ve* are subtracted from the total responses. There were ten others who did not give any correction; undoubtedly many of these would also have simply deleted the auxiliary.

The predicted ranking is shown below against that actually found, with the percentages of correct markings:

	Predicted	Found	%
1.	ain't	ain't	72
2.	throwed	pick-	61
3.	nobody	throwed	49
4.	no more	hate-	44
5.	don't	don't	41
6.	pick-	play-	40
7.	hate-	kick-	40
8.	play	nobody	38
9.	I've pass	I've pass	33
10.	kick-	no more	21
11.	out of	out of	13

The four items with zero inflection followed the expected order, but at a higher level than anticipated. Part of the reason is the salient position of *pick-* in sentence 1, *He pick me*. In other respects, the order of the items reflects the influence of social stereotypes as expected. *Ain't* is the highest, and *out of* is the lowest; these items are respectively the most and the least subject to overt social correction.

Figure 4-12 shows the position of the various items for the groups studied. Here the number for individual items can become dangerously small; several of the groups which react in a similar manner have been combined. For the pre-adolescent peer groups, the Thunderbirds and Aces have been shown together. For the adolescent groups, the Jets and Cobras are combined. The 1390 Lames show approximately the same responses as the adolescent TA Lames and are shown as one set, and finally the two white Inwood groups are given on a single scale.

The stereotype *ain't* is the most sensitive marker of group receptivity to the standard norms. The solid line in Figure 4-12 traces the gradual rise of responses to *ain't*, from the low point of the pre-adolescent groups to the 100% responses of the lames. The responses to the zero inflections show a similar upward path (dotted line on Figure 4-12) but by no means as steep; there seems to be a closer correlation with age than with *ain't*, for the curve dips slightly for the PA Lames before going up. On the other hand, the least learning is shown for *nobody* and *no more*, which move up at the lowest rate; the double line shows the path of *nobody*.

The responses to the CC test clearly mirror the position of the non-standard form in the grammar of the subjects taking the test. The responses of the Inwood group differ from those of the corresponding NNE groups in ways that can be predicted from the use of these items in their own speech.

(a) The Inwood groups use *ain't* but much less (and in a narrower range) than the Jets and Cobras. Accordingly, the Inwood response to *ain't* is higher than the Jets and Cobras, but lower than for the lames of the Negro community.

(b) The Inwood groups do not use the preterit *throwed* for *threw*, and reacted more sharply to this than the NNE members.

(c) The Inwood groups rarely lose the *-ed* inflection and never drop the *-s*; reactions to all of these items were higher than for any of the Negro groups.

(d) The Inwood groups use *don't* with third singular subjects (see Table 4-8); response to this item is about the same as for the Jets and Cobras, and lower than for the lames.

(e) The Inwood groups do use negative concord and responses to these items are approximately the same as for the Jets and Cobras.

For items (d) or (e) the Inwood groups do not show the same semi-categorical rule as the NNE groups do, and therefore their responses would not be expected to dip as low as that of the pre-adolescent NNE group, the Thunderbirds and Aces.

4.4.4. *The corrections made.* We have already noted that the actual corrections used for sentence 3 show the marginal status of the *have...ed* form for NNE members, especially when the *have* is written in contracted form as *'ve*. Of 61 corrections by NNE members, 23 were made by deleting the '*ve* — that is, by indicating that the trouble with the sentence was the presence of this auxiliary rather than the absence of the -*ed* ending. For a comparison with the white Inwood groups, we have only six corrections — but only one of these deleted the '*ve*.

There is some rich information available on subjective evaluation of the *ain't* form in the actual corrections made by subjects taking the test. The non-standard character of *ain't* was clearly marked by the PA Lames, but of the 44 who noted it, only 21 corrected it to *isn't* and one to *hasn't*. There were two corrections to *haven't*, which is understandable in the light of the fact that *have* is the invariant form for this verb in NNE. The use of *ain't* for *didn't* is reflected in the fact that three of the PA Lames corrected to *didn't*, and one to *don't*. It was noted in chapter III that another negative form in the present is *not* (which represents the negative with deleted copula); two of the PA Lames corrected *ain't* to *not*, giving *He not gone yet*. The other NNE peer groups showed a similar sprinkling of non-standard corrections, including such forms as *He ain't go yet*. On the other hand, the Inwood groups simply corrected to *isn't* or *hasn't* in accordance with their own grammar.

Finally, it is worth noting that the sensitivity to the non-standard preterit *throwed* in sentence 7 was not coupled with a comparable ability to give the corrected form *threw*.

Of the 60 Negro subjects who marked this form, only 35 gave the correct form *threw*. On the other hand, all six of the Inwood speakers who marked the form *throwed* as incorrect gave the right form for the preterit (although two spelled it as *through*). Again, it is clear that the underlying grammar of the subjects determined their response to a large extent.

Classroom correction tests appear to be a valuable diagnostic tool in assessing the extent of dialect interference with the writing of standard English. If a student does not recognize the non-standard form when it appears in a test of this sort, it seems unlikely that he will hesitate to use it in his own writing. That does not mean that this necessarily interferes with his ability to read and understand the standard form, since most of the NNE subjects have asymmetrical systems of perception and production; they understand the standard forms even when they automatically produce their own non-standard forms in speaking or writing.

It should be noted that adolescent responses to a CC Test are the reverse of adult responses to a Subjective Reaction Test. When adults have been fully sensitized to a social marker, we find that those who use this feature the most are quick to stigmatize it in the speech of others. But adolescents have not developed sensitivity to such linguistic variables, and their ability to perceive the items that have been stigmatized in school is in direct proportion to their use of them — that is, to the strength of the non-standard rule.

4.5 *Vernacular Correction (VC) Tests*

The converse of a classroom correction test is a "Vernacular Correction Test", in which the subjects are asked to identify SE forms wrongly embedded in the vernacular. Given the fact that the test situation is necessarily a formal one, which directs the subjects' attention to speech, it follows that the SE form will be brought to the forefront of social consciousness. When attention is directed to speech, it is difficult for speakers of a subordinate dialect to perceive their own forms. When they consciously repeat forms in the test situation, their knowledge of SE forms — however slight — inevitably but unpredictably intervenes. For most speakers, there are no clear intuitions (open to introspection) which discriminate between the underlying vernacular and the superposed dialect.

Full support for these observations can be obtained from the "Self Report" tests carried out in the Lower East Side study of the white community. Subjects were asked to select which of four pronunciations came closest to their own. The results reflected their recognition of the prestige norms much more clearly than their actual usage — that is, the self report tests are only another way of reflecting the subject's perception of the prevailing normative pattern, and give us no direct information about the vernacular (Labov 1966:460-74). For example, of those who use more than 30% constricted [r] in final and pre-consonantal position, 79% report themselves as using this form. But for those who use less than 30% [r], most of whom were essentially [r]-less in connected speech, 62% still reported themselves as using [r]. This illustrates the fact that subjects' self report of a prestige feature merely reflects their perception of the norm. The same holds true for stigmatized features such as the pronunciation [əɪ] in *first, hurt*, etc. Thirty-two subjects used this form; but only 10 out of the 32 reported themselves as using it. The distribution of those who did so reflects the relative perceptions of the social norm in the social classes concerned. In the lower class group, 44% of those who used this form said that they did so; of the working class 28%, and of the lower middle class, only 20%. This runs counter to the general observation that the higher social classes pay more attention to speech and should therefore be more perceptive. We can say instead that the higher social classes pay more attention to social norms and perceive them more clearly.

The considerations just given are the basic motivation for the mode of research in this study. If vernacular correction tests did in fact give reliable results, it would be unnecessary to do long and painstaking field studies. Participant observation methods would be quite unnecessary. Instead of the investigator entering the social situation of the informant, it would be possible to take the informant into the social domain of the investigator. It would then be quite possible to sit down with an informant and study the structure of NNE. Attempts of this sort have been made but the results have been untrustworthy in the extreme. In extended face-to-face interviewing between a standard and a non-standard speaker the latter shifts in the direction of the standard language. Attempts on his part to fight this normal and natural tendency will result in reverse hyper-correction — that is, he will automatically select any form which is different from the standard, since he no longer has any means of discriminating between standard norms and his own usage, as long as he is in a situation which is dominated by the standard language and the standard culture.

In the course of this study, we continually tested and retested our original findings on this question. Despite our reservations, it would be a tremendous advantage to locate a speaker who could accurately report on the vernacular. But given our knowledge of sociolinguistic factors, it is obviously necessary to know the vernacular in advance in order to determine whether someone is accurately reporting on it. The circularity of this situation can be circumvented perhaps by calibrating the speaker's reactions against a set of known items. If a speaker could score 100 % on a list of items where we were already certain of the vernacular form, then we could begin to test his information on unknown items. This is particularly important because many syntactic forms of crucial interest for investigating underlying structure are quite rare. In the case of the peer groups we have studied we already have accurate data on a great many non-standard forms, which had been used as calibrating items. There are of course a vast number of items such as tag questions, nominalizations, multiple embeddings, and negative concord to following sentences, where our data are inadequate.

4.5.1. *Construction and trial of a VC test.* We therefore constructed a VC Test in the following form:

The sentences given below were taken from a book that was supposed to be about Harlem, and to show how ordinary people talk. But some of them are wrong, because the writer didn't know Harlem very well. Can you fix these up with as little change as you need to make them sound right, the most natural way that cats who hang out in Harlem would say them?

Example: a. It don't make me any difference.
              should be
              It don't make me NO difference.

          b. He-all and you-all owe me a lotta cashes.
              should be
              You-all and him owe me a lotta cash.

1. There isn't no difference.
2. He rap too stupidly to be the leader.
3. Us don't do that no more.
4. That's Nick's boy.
5. You are boss, man.
6. This fella is down.
7. She is real stab bitch.
8. Why he do that?
9. How be you today?
10. Don't you jum' onta him no more.
11. Ain't no such thing as a good police.
12. I don't use too much slang.
13. That can't be true.
14. I know can he do that.
15. Hardly have I seen anyone like you, sugar.
16. I dig over the Supremes, man.

This test must of course be administered orally. We first administered it to L.J., a Negro man 23 years old, who we thought would have the maximum opportunity to score well. He grew up speaking the vernacular, did not finish high school, and had adjusted his own speech toward the standard no further than most of the young men in our Harlem survey. He was fully aware of our concept of "the vernacular" since we had discussed it with him on many occasions. The results may be summarized in the following item by item account which will also serve to point out the function of the items on the VC test.

(1) Correctly replaced *isn't* by *ain't*; did not replace *there* by *it*.
(2) Incorrectly added -*s* to *rap*. On the second attempt deleted -*s* and replaced *stupidly* by *dumb*. Agreed that *stupid* would be a correct NNE form.
(3) Correctly replaced *us* by *we*.
(4) Incorrectly approved of the possessive -'*s* on *Nick*.
(5) Incorrectly contracted *you are* to *you're*.
(6) Correctly replaced *fellow* by *cat*.
(7) Correctly asked what does *stab* mean (a meaningless item invented by us).
(8) Incorrectly replaced *do* by *does*.
(9) Correctly re-inverted *be* and *you*.
(10) Correctly restored the *p* on *jump*.
(11) Correctly approved.
(12) Incorrectly deleted *too*.
(13) Unnecessarily replaced *can't* by *ain't*.
(14) Correctly inverted *can* and *he*.
(15) Correctly replaced *hardly* by *never* and justified the use of negative

inversion here by saying "Talking to a chick you have to be on your best behavior".

(16) Correctly deleted *over*.

It is clear that the response of L.J. reflects a rich knowledge of the vernacular, but the number of incorrect answers show that we cannot learn anything new from him. Even if he had scored 15 out of 16, then 5 to 10% uncertainty would render his answers useless when it came to more subtle points. On 4 of the 7 items where L.J. is wrong, he is obviously and painfully wrong, as readers of this report will realize — in putting an *-s* on the verb in sentence 2, in preserving the *'s* on *Nick's* in sentence 4, in contracting but not deleting *are* in (5), and in replacing *do* by *does* in (8). Of course L.J. sometimes does use the forms he indicated, but as a report on the basic vernacular, these responses would be terribly misleading. In sentences 12 and 13, L.J. 's responses might be even more confusing, since he is merely replacing one correct form with another. Nevertheless, L.J. did handle this VC test in a perceptive and intelligent manner. He was caught by none of the obvious traps which we laid: *us* for *we*, in 3, *stab* in 7. The less sophisticated members of the peer groups did far worse as we shall see.

4.5.2. *The Thunderbird VC Tests.* In the last group session with the Thunderbirds, following the Memory Tests described in 3.8, a Vernacular Correction Test was conducted with Boot, Money and several other group members we had known for over a year. The test was conducted under the most favorable circumstances for eliciting data: in a discussion with the peer group itself, where the formal situation would be least dominant, and members could correct each other. In this setting, one does obtain accurate information on the ability of each individual member. But the primary interest of VC tests is to explore means of obtaining further data, rather than test the differential capacity of individuals. This session with the Thunderbirds was therefore constructed to give us the maximum chance of getting accurate responses to the VC test cited above. We were much friendlier with the T-Birds than experimenters normally would be in a test situation; we had demonstrated our ability to obtain a large volume of natural and spontaneous speech from them; and we could easily calibrate their responses against what they actually said.

The VC Test was not set up with individual microphones for each speaker — the group was treated as a whole, and the two main speakers identified are Boot and Money. If speakers are not clearly identified, they will simply be introduced by a dash. A staff member first gave a fairly detailed explanation of the goals of the test, following the line in the instructions quoted above. He then read the sentences himself, and obtained responses such as the following:

1. There isn't no difference.
   Money: — There ain't no different.
   Boot: — There's no difference.
   Money: — Ain't no different.

No one replaced *There* by *it*, which would be normal (3.8.1), but Money's last response is solid vernacular (3.6.5). It is clear that there is no difficulty in replacing *isn't* with *ain't*, just as *ain't* is easily identified in the CC test. Items which have been long-standing social stereotypes can be isolated by members, but of course that is of little help in a linguistic investigation.

2. He rap too stupidly to be the leader.
   Boot: — He rap too stupid, man; we don't want him to be the leader.
   Money: — He act too stupid!

These are very high quality responses, as compared to L.J. 's original answers quoted above. The *-ly* on *stupid* is deleted without any hesitation. If all VC answers rose to this level, the test could be considered entirely successful.

3. Us don't do that no more.
   Larry: — We all don't do that no more.
   Boot: — We don't do that any more.

The false *Us* is automatically replaced here, and Larry's *We all* is quite appropriate. But Boot shows the unconscious influence of the test situation by replacing non-standard *no* with standard *any*. Since negative concord is semi-categorical in the vernacular (3.6.3), this is clearly not an accurate response. The memory tests showed that Boot is the member most bound by the vernacular, and it is surprising that he would cross up the VC test in this manner. (It should be noted that the memory tests showed that replacement of *no* by *any* was much easier than *never* by *ever*.)

4. That's Nick's boy.
   Boot: — That's Mr. Nick's son.
   — That's Nick's son right there.
   — That's Nick's son right there.
   — Do you know that's Nick's son?

The interviewer was struck by this response, since the possessive *'s* rarely occurs in the vernacular. (Thus *Nick boy* is actually a quote from D.R. on the telephone — one of our authentic records of spontaneous NNE: see 4.7.) Here are four responses with *Nick's*, an SE form. It is clear that the TEST SITUATION is taking over, and the original instruction to replace SE by NNE is being unconsciously reversed by the subjects. Boot's replacement of *Nick's boy* by *Mr. Nick's son* shows that he is on the wrong track, and the others follow.

Interviewer: — Which would people say more often,
            Tha's Nick's boy or *Tha's Nick boy?*
Boot: — They say, Nick's boy.
            — ... Nick's boy.
Boot: — If he say boys that means more than one.

7. She is real stab bitch.
    Money: — [laughs]
    Boot: — She a real [laughs] — she is a real st— she is a real stab
              bitch.
            — She is a real stab bitch.
    IVer: — What does *stab* mean?
    Boot: — She *bad*.
    IVer: — Is *stab* a word that people use?
            — No. Not that I know of. I ain't — No.
            — Never heard of it till you said said sump'm.

Here we see the copula deleted in the original sentence, but restored in the answer. A completely artificial "hip" word is accepted and repeated as if it was an item in the vernacular. It is easy to see what is going on in this case. But if we had used a real vernacular word which the members did not use themselves, they would have been just as quick to accept it.

8. Why he do that?
    Billy: — Why did you do that, man?
    Boot: — Why did you do that, man?
    IVer: — Don't people say, *Why he do that?*
            — No!
            — No!
    Boot: — Some people that don't speak correc' English do.
            — Calvin little brother! [general laughter].

This sentence is one used many times by Larry of the Jets (see 4.2.4), and follows the most common NNE pattern of simple WH- questions (3.7.2). It is clear that the VC test has become a CC test, and there is little that can be done about it. We do obtain some useful information on the vernacular — especially in the comments that are added at the end of each exchange, like *She bad*, or *Calvin little brother*. We can easily compare the responses to 4 — that no one says *Nick boy* — to this spontaneous utterance, *Calvin little brother*. But the only way that we know which is which, and feel free to discard the responses to 4, is that we already know the vernacular from direct observation. The VC test gives us confirmation of the basic sociolinguistic hypothesis that the most systematic level of linguistic behavior is the vernacular where the minimum attention is paid to speech. As soon as linguistic forms become the focus of attention, the middle class norms begin to intervene. No matter how imperfectly these SE norms are grasped, they are dominant in the test situation.

It is not the case that the Thunderbirds are completely unreliable, and will simply answer anything. If a form alien to both SE and NNE is imposed, no matter how firmly, it will be rejected.

9. How be you today?
       — How are you today?
       — How you feelin' today?
IVer: — Now you talkin' bout the — I don't mean correct him, but — wouldn't a guy say, *How be you today?*
       — No.
       — No.
Boot: — Oh you might — he might say, *How you be today?*

The following example may also show a correct response. The item *I know can he do it* is not acceptable in either NNE or SE, since *know* is not a verb of questioning, and the underlying structure does not contain *Q*.

14. I know can he do that.
       — It know you can't do that.
       — I know you can't do it.
IVer: — Can you say, I know can he do that?
       — No. — that don't sound right.
       — No.

But this ability to distinguish possible from impossible forms is of little use when an SE form is opposed to an NNE form. No matter how hard the interviewer tried to re-insert the test situation, and restore the original sense of the VC test, the responses show that the SE forms are dominant.

IVer: — One thing I wanna ask you guys ... Do fellas on the street say sump'm like — would they be more apt to say ... *He don't know the way how to come?* or *He doesn't know how to come.*
Boot: — He doesn't know how to come.
       — The second one.
Money: — He doesn't know how to come this way.

The second choice contains *He doesn't*, which is certainly alien to the vernacular. Secondly, the adverbial pleonasm *the way how to* is firmly fixed in NNE: again, we are quoting from the telephone conversation of D.R. Nevertheless, the members firmly choose the SE form and attribute it to the vernacular of the street.

This pattern of response to the VC test fits in with the results obtained in the survey of the Lower East Side of New York City (Labov 1966:470-71). When speakers' attention is drawn to a particular linguistic marker, they usually state their firm belief that they use the prestige form — in fact, that they KNOW they use this form because they hear themselves saying it this way in their "inner ear". We can conclude that very early in the acquisition of sociolinguistic norms, the prestige pattern begins to invade the audio-monitoring process. Even the Thunderbirds hear themselves as using any form which has already been established for them as "correct" or "school language". In this sense, the VC test is merely another way of revealing the subjects' grasp of prestige norms, parallel to any other method of self-report.

STUART SILVERMAN

THE LEARNING OF BLACK ENGLISH BY PUERTO RICANS IN NEW YORK CITY

What makes the acquisition of English by Puerto Ricans in New York City a most interesting question is the fact that they, because of economic and housing patterns, learn most of their English from other Puerto Ricans and from lower class Negroes. The Spanish speaking child who enters into peer groups predominantly consisting of other Spanish speaking youngsters might be expected to speak a variety of English characterized by a great deal of Spanish interference while those whose peer group includes a substantial number of Negroes might be expected to speak some form of Negro Non-Standard English (Black English). This simplistic expectation, however, is complicated by the fact that the former group must, on occasion, interact with Negroes and the latter, of course, interacts with Puerto Ricans frequently.

Literature in the area of language acquisition and development indicates that peer group membership is one factor which influences the child's language. Almost no research, however, has been undertaken to empirically demonstrate this point even though there is both theoretical and practical importance attached to it. In terms of the former, if a theory of language development is to be built, then all factors which might be influential must be taken into account. On a more immediately useful level, if one of the goals of our educational system is to teach Standard English to students, then the effects of the peer group on language must be specified.

A review of the literature on the effects of peer group membership on language will not be undertaken here. Interested readers may refer to *The Effects of Peer Group Membership on Puerto Rican English* (Silverman 1971). Suffice it to say, however, that many writers have stated, without experimental evidence, that the peer group exerts significant influence on the language of its members. This paper is a report on an attempt to empirically determine whether a group of Puerto Rican junior high school students with Negro friends speak more like Negroes than a group of Puerto Rican junior high school students who have only Puerto Rican friends.

Measurement of linguistic variables is not simply accomplished by obtaining a corpus of speech and examining that corpus for inter-group differences. Labov (1966) and Ma and Herasimchuk (1968) have empirically demonstrated that speech varies in accordance with the manner in which it is elicited. Different kinds of elicitation procedures will yield speech differing in the degree of formality. That is, a subject reading a list of minimal pairs will speak quite formally, while the same subject engaging in conversation may speak quite informally. Another problem in measuring linguistic variables has to do with the nature of the variables themselves. It is far easier to quantify phonological variables than it is to quantify syntactic variables. What one can do with the former is to determine all of the possible occurrences of that sound, arrange them in a sequence going from most to least standard (for the language in question) and analyze them in terms of parametric statistics. The analysis of variance technique has great usefulness here since one can, at the same time, examine differences across both groups and elicitation procedures.

Phonological Variables

The investigation dealt exclusively with eleven phonological variables which have been shown to differentiate between Standard English and NNE. Each of these variables was quantifiable and had forms of occurrence which could be placed on a continuum going from maximally standard to maximally non-standard. Variables were not chosen (unfortunately) on the basis of discriminating Standard English or NNE from Spanish because of a lack of data relating to the effects of Spanish interference on English. The two major works in this area (Fishman and Herasimchuk 1969, and Jones 1962) dealt with different populations and different variables.

Table 1 summarizes each of the eleven variables, the possible forms of occurrence and the score assigned to each form of occurrence.

TABLE 1

*Phonological Variables, Forms of Occurrence for each
and Scores Assigned to Forms of Occurrence*

Variable	1	2	3	4	5
1. Intervocalic [đ]	*d*	Ø	*v*		
2. Final [θ]	*θ*	Ø	*f*		
3. Medial [ɪ]	*ɪ*	*ɪ·*	*i·*		
4. Final [r]	*r*	Ø			
5. Medial [r]	*r*	Ø			
6. Initial [st]	*st*	*SʔP*	*SØ*		
7. Initial [sk]	*sk*	*SʔP*	*SØ*		
8. Final [sp]	*sp*	Partial or *SʔP* Closure	*SØ*	*ØS* or *ps*	
9. Final [sk]	*sk*	Partial or *SʔP* Closure	*SØ*	*ØS* or *ks*	
10. Final [t]	*t*	Partial or *ʔP* Closure	Ø		
11. Final [d]	*d*	Partial or *ʔP* Closure	Ø		

Materials

It was decided to test for the forms of occurrence of the variables in five elicitation procedures. These were: Minimal Pairs — List, Minimal Pairs — Sentences, Word List, Paragraph Reading and Conversation. By using more than one elicitation procedure, it was possible to insure that each variable occurred several times. Also, Fishman and Herasimchuk (1969), Labov, Cohen, Robins and Lewis (1968) and Labov (1965), all found that results often differ across elicitation procedures.

Nine pairs of words were used for the Minimal Pairs — List procedure. Each pair appeared twice so that each word could occupy both first and second position. The pairs were: *either-even, fourth-ford, tim-team, high-hire, Carol-Carl, went-when, build-bill, scream-stream* and *disk-crisp.*

For the Minimal Pairs — Sentences procedure, the same words were used as for Minimal Pairs — List. To eliminate the possibility of stress and/or intonation as a factor, both words in a pair appeared in the same position in the sentence. The eighteen sentences were: *either of us can do it; even if we go now we'll be late; he was the fourth one; he bought a Ford car; I gave it to Tim; I saw the team; Carol is here; Carl is here; build the house; Bill is here; I saw the stream; I heard the scream; the price is too high; he is the one to hire; yes he went, tell me when; the cookie was crisp; it was round like a disk.*

The word list consisted of twenty-eight words. Each variable appeared three times. Five words contained two variables each. The words used were: *other, father, rather, him, Jim, risk, clasp, wasp, side, had, sight,*

*height, art, dusk, strong, stream, string, both, mouth, fourth, around, Harry,
sorry, scratch, scream, screw, task, desk.*

The passage used for Paragraph Reading was adopted from a book of
short stories, designed for junior high school students reading on the
fifth grade level. The passage was modified to include several instances
of each variable. The story went as follows:

My name is Tim. For most people, except for my mother and father it does
not make much difference that I am Tim. But for me it is a great trouble.

It is different for Harry, my seven year old brother. For Harry, everything is
simple. Almost all the things that Harry wants, he has without much worry.

I wanted to find out how it was with him. One day when we were both in our
private place near the Scrasp River, a stream that goes by our farm. It was
a crisp afternoon, almost dusk. We both sat and leaned against fence posts. I
asked him, "Harry, suppose you could have anything or everything you want.
What kinds of things would you choose?"

He looked up from reaching under a rock in the river. In this way we catch
trout, slowly feeling around in the quiet places underneath big stones. If the fish
comes by, sliding soft against your hand, you can catch him. Harry was just
learning to fish like this. He looked straight up, not wishing to talk. (If you talk
you risk losing the fish.) "Of course I want something, Tim."

"Like what?"

"Like not so much school." He closed his eyes, moving his hand around
slowly in the water, holding his breath, with his tongue between his teeth. He
scratched his head.

All of a sudden he grabbed and screamed. He made a big commotion. But
even before he took his hand out of the water, I knew it was empty.

"A good big trout, that's what I want." Harry looked at me like he was mad
at me, like I spoiled his chance for the fish. I thought it was strange that he
began to cry.

Subjects

The subjects who were utilized in this investigation consisted of two
groups of male Puerto Rican students and one group of male Negro
students drawn from a Special Service[1] junior high school in the Bronx,
New York. "Puerto Rican", as used in this investigation, describes children whose parents (both) were born in Puerto Rico. Further, the subject
himself had to have been born in Puerto Rico or in New York City and
had to have had all of his schooling in the New York City public school
system. Only those Negro children whose parents (both) were born in
the Continental United States were considered for this study. Like the

---

[1] Special Service schools are those schools in New York City which receive Title III
funds from the Office of Educational Opportunity for special programs for disadvantaged children. In general, for a school to receive these funds, the majority of the
students must be minority group members.

Puerto Rican subjects, the Negro subjects had to have had all of their education in the New York City public school system. The population of the school from which the sample was drawn was (for the 1969-1970 academic year) comprised of six hundred and twelve (612) Negro youngsters, six hundred and seventeen (617) Puerto Rican youngsters.

The nature of the school and the neighborhood in which it is located bears some comment at this point. One of the more interesting features of the school is that it is one of few, if any, schools in New York City where the balance between Negroes and Puerto Ricans is so even. This balance, of course, is a result of a neighborhood which is divided along similar lines. However, very few Puerto Ricans had Negro friends and very few Negroes had Puerto Rican friends. Initially this seemed like a strange state of affairs, except that there is, in the neighborhood at large, an apparent struggle going on between Negroes and Puerto Ricans. The area in which this conflict is most apparent is in the Puerto Rican demands that the district school superintendent, who is Negro, be replaced by one who is Puerto Rican. One can readily imagine that at least some of the animosity between adults has transferred to the children.

There is another possible reason for the lack of intermingling of Negroes and Puerto Ricans. Physically, the two groups are quite different; Puerto Ricans are generally smaller than Blacks. (This factor has caused the Puerto Rican community in New York City to complain that the minimum height standard of five feet seven inches for entrance into the police department is discriminatory). This difference in size contributes to other differences between the groups. In terms of sports, Negroes are interested in basketball and football (where, of course, height is an advantage), while Puerto Ricans are interested in baseball. The school's basketball team has no Puerto Ricans and the softball team has only two Negroes. In addition, fighting (where size is advantageous) is more common among the Negroes than the Puerto Ricans.

In order to find the two groups of Puerto Rican students to use in this study, certain criteria in the selection of the sample had to be employed. First, a group of Puerto Ricans, each with at least three Negro friends (out of a prospective subject's ten best friends) had to be chosen. The number "three" was arbitrarily chosen, and, if not for the fact that finding Puerto Ricans with Negro friends was so difficult, would have been higher. A second group of Puerto Ricans, each having no Negro friends also had to be selected. Lastly, a group of youngsters, all Negro, had to be chosen for the study. A decision was made to use only boys as subjects in this study. This was done for one primary reason. Only two Puerto Rican girls were found to have three or more Black friends.

In order to select the sample population from the total school population of twelve hundred and sixty-three (1263), a specially devised questionnaire was administered to three hundred and ninety-two (392) children in thirteen classes. The questionnaire required the student to indicate his name, official class number, date of birth, place of birth and parents' places of birth. It then asked him to list his ten best friends within the school, indicating their respective official class numbers (if this was known). The questionnaire was administered in the students' classes by a teacher who simply stated: "Please fill out the sheet I am giving to you. If there is any imformation asked for that you don't know, leave the space blank. Your doing this will be appreciated, but it is not required." No student refused to fill out the questionnaire.

In order to independently verify the information given on the questionnaires, the responses of each potential subject were shown to two of his teachers. They were asked to indicate whether or not they have observed the child in social situations and, if so, to confirm the list of friends. If there was no close correspondence between teacher and pupil ratings, that student was not used in to sample population. To further verify the accuracy of the students' responses, the questionnaires of all the respondents were compared to determine whether their stated friendships were mutual. For example, if Raymond Lopez indicated that David Jones was one of his ten best friends, then David Jones' questionnaire was consulted to see if Raymond Lopez appeared on his list of ten friends. As a result, thirty-six subjects were chosen. There were twelve in each of the three previously described groups.

The mean age for the Puerto Ricans with Negro friends was 164.83 months. The subjects ranged from a low of 156 months to a high of 179 months. Three of the subjects were in the seventh grade, five were in the eighth grade and four were in the ninth grade. For the Puerto Ricans without Negro friends, the mean age was 161.17 months with a range of 147 months to 183 months. Nine of the twelve subjects in this group were in grade seven, two were in grade eight and one was in grade nine. Finally, the mean age in months for the group of Negro youngsters was 164.75. They ranged in age from 149 months to 183 months. Seven members of this group were in the seventh grade, two were in the eighth grade and three were in the ninth grade.

Reading grades for the subjects were unavailable. However, all of them were able to read the specially prepared materials. Further all classes from which the subjects came were among the upper third in each grade.

Experimental Design and Statistical Treatment

As previously described, the subjects used in this investigation were divided into three equal groups of twelve each. Group I consisted of twelve Puerto Ricans each with three or more Black friends. Group II was comprised of twelve Puerto Ricans, each having no Black friends. Group III consisted of twelve Black youngsters.

The actual design for the study called for the subjects to be tested in pairs. Group I subjects were paired with each other as well as with subjects from Groups II and III. Group II subjects were paired with others in Group II and with members of Group I and Group III. Finally, subjects who were members of the third group were paired with each other and with those in the other two groups. The purpose of the pairing was an attempt to lessen expected tension at the interview, especially for the elicitation of Conversation speech.

Table 2 presents the experimental design which was used in this investigation. In each of the cells the number shown in the center represents the number of pairs of subjects under that condition while the number in the upper left hand corner of the cell represents an identification of that cell.

TABLE 2

Number and Distribution of Pairs of Subjects

Group	I	II	III
I	1 2	2 4	3 4
II		4 2	5 4
III			6 2

Cell #1 indicates that two pairs of Puerto Ricans with Negro friends were interviewed together in this study. In Cell #2 there are four Puerto Ricans with Negro friends, each paired with a Puerto Rican without Negro friends. Cell #3 shows that four Negro subjects were paired with four Puerto Ricans with Negro friends. As noted in Cell #4, two Puerto Rican subjects without Negro friends were paired with two other subjects from the same group. In Cell #5, each of four Puerto Rican students without Negro friends was paired with a Negro student. Finally, in Cell #6, there were two pairs of Negro students. In total, there were eighteen pairs of subjects.

To as great an extent as possible, subjects were paired on the basis of stated friendships; i.e. students who claim, on the questionnaires, to be friends were paired together. This was done to attempt to maximize the possibility of the Conversation Elicitation Procedure being as informal as possible. In Cell #5, however, this was not possible since Puerto Ricans without Negro friends, by definition, have no Negro friends.

Where stated friendships could not determine the pairings, a random selection was utilized.

The specific statistical design by means of which the data was analyzed was a series of two factor analyses of variance referred to by Bruning and Kintz (1968) as a "Two-Factor Mixed Design: Repeated Measures on One Factor" (p. 68). This design "...is basically a combination of the completely randomized design and the treatments-by-subjects design. Not only does this design permit comparison of the differences in the overall performance of the subjects in the several experimental groups, but it also permits evaluation of the changes in performance shown by the subjects during the experimental session" (Bruning and Kintz 1968: 68). In terms of the present problem, this design was able to determine whether the three groups of subjects differed in terms of their production of each of the eleven phonological variables and whether or not there were differences in production which could be attributed to the five elicitation procedures.

The first factor, Peer Group Membership (B), has three mutually exclusive levels. That is, a subject can belong to one, and only one, of the three groups. He could be a Puerto Rican with Negro friends, a Puerto Rican without Negro friends or he could be a Negro youngster. The second factor, Elicitation Procedure (A), has five levels (Conversation, Paragraph Reading, Word List, Minimal Pairs-Sentences and Minimal Pairs-List). This is the repeated measurement. Each subject was tested under each of the five Elicitation Procedures.

The raw data (tape recordings of the forms of occurrence of the variables) was transcribed by the investigator. Scoring was done in the following manner. Each of the eleven phonological variables was broken down into its possible forms of occurrence. Each of these forms was then placed on a scale which went from Standard English on one end to Negro Non-Standard English on the other. Each form was given a point value. (See Table 1 page 333.) Thus, each subject received a score for each occurrence of each variable in each of the five elicitation contexts. Since each context contained a different number of occurrences of any given variable, mean scores were used. Thus, for example, if a subject on the Word List Elicitation Procedure got scores of 5, 5 and 2 on the three occurrences of the words containing final [t] he would receive a mean score of 12/3 or 4. Each subject, then, received five scores for each of the eleven variables.

All of the transcribing and scoring was done by this investigator. Another graduate student, however, was asked to transcribe the tapes of six of the subjects (chosen at random). A correlation of 0.928 was obtained between the two raters. In addition, a linguist, on this investigator's doctoral dissertation committee, analyzed parts of the tapes of two or more subjects. A correlation of 0.964 was obtained between this investigator and the second rater. Finally, the investigator analyzed three of the subjects' tapes twice. The reliability established via a correlation coefficient here was 0.989.

For each of the phonological variables, a single two factor analysis of variance (described earlier) was performed to test for differences in forms of occurrence between the three peer groups and between the five elicitation procedures. Each analysis showed, via the F ratio, whether one or more of the three peer groups was significantly more non-standard (or, conversely, standard) than the other(s) or if the three were statistically equal. In addition, each analysis showed, regardless of peer group affiliation, whether any of the contexts elicited significantly more non-standard (or standard) forms of the variable than did the others. Finally, each analysis showed whether any particular combinations of peer group membership and elicitation procedure yielded significantly more (or less) non-standard forms than any other such combination.

If any of the analyses of variance showed a significant F ratio for the main effects of Peer Group Membership or Elicitation Procedure, or if a significant F ratio was obtained for the Peer Group Membership — Elicitation Procedure interaction, the F test for simple effects (as outlined by Bruning and Kintz 1968) was utilized to test for significant differences between specific means.

Procedure

Because of a lack of interviewing facilities in the school which the subjects attended, all interviews were conducted in this investigator's home. Comfortable chairs were used in an attempt to make the subjects feel at ease. A Uher 4400 four track stereo tape recorder was utilized to record each of the interviews. Both subjects had individual microphones which were worn around their necks. Thus, each subject's voice was recorded on a separate track of the tape in order to maximize the recording fidelity of each subject and to simplify the transcription of the linguistic variables.

In order to get the subjects to participate in this study, each pair was approached three or four days before the interview by a teacher whom he knows. The teacher told them that a new junior high school textbook was being written and that they had been chosen to help in its preparation. They were told that the session would last about an hour and that they would receive two dollars for their participation. If the students agreed, they were given a date, time and place for meeting the teacher who drove them to the place of the interview. If one or both of the subjects did not agree, an alternate student(s) was contacted. There was very little problem with students refusing to participate since two dollars was considered a fair amount of money by the children.

When the students entered the investigator's home they were met by his wife, a teacher in the school. This was done in an effort to have him relate to someone familiar in strange surroundings. The subjects were seated in the living room. They were then again told that they were specially selected to aid in the preparation of a new book. At this time they were shown the tape recorder and the microphones as well as a demonstration of how each works. Each subject was told that the recording is being made only because it is easier than taking notes. He was assured that no one but the interviewer would hear the tapes and that the tape would be erased after the information on it was reviewed.

After these preliminaries had been completed, the actual testing began. Both subjects in a given pair were presented with the tasks in the same order. However, the order of presentation of each pair was determined randomly. In all cases, however, Conversation procedure was elicited after the other four tasks had been completed. The first subject was asked to read the first of four pages. After he finished, the second subject read the same page. Following this the subject who read the first page second read the second page first and so forth, until both subjects completed their four tasks. (Thus, each subject was the first to perform on two of the tasks and the last to perform on two tasks.)

After each subject had performed on all four of the reading tasks, refreshments consisting of soda and candy were served in order to relax the subjects for the Conversation procedure. This technique was found to be effective, for younger children, by Labov (1969b). During the few minutes that the experimenter left the room to get the refreshments, the tape recorder was left on on the chance that the subjects might talk to each other. Following a short rest period, during which the subjects had the refreshments and were given their two dollars, elicitation of the Conversation speech ensued. The teacher who accompanied the students was brought into the room in further attempting to relax the students. The subjects were told that the reading passage (Paragraph Reading) does not seem very interesting and that an exciting, "real-life" story would be better. They were asked whether or not they have ever been very afraid or angry and, if so, to tell about the experiences which made them feel that way. If the subject responded negatively, the teacher reminded him of a specific incident of which he (the teacher) was aware and asked the subject to recount it. If the subject was still quiet, the experimenter told a story about a time when he was very angry or afraid and then asked the subject, again, to tell a story.

When the experimental session ended, the subjects were thanked and driven home. They were asked not to discuss the session with other students (since some might be potential subjects).

HYPOTHESES

The investigation which was conducted was concerned with answering three principal questions. The first of these was, perhaps, the most important. The question was whether or not Puerto Rican youngsters who have Negro friends speak more like Negroes than Puerto Ricans without Negro friends. It was hypothesized that:

if a group of Puerto Rican junior high school students (all male), each having among his ten best friends at least three Negroes, and a group of Puerto Rican junior high school students (all male), having no Negroes among their ten best friends, are compared in terms of spoken English with respect to the occurrence of Standard English and Negro Non-Standard English forms of a set of previously selected phonological variables, then the Puerto Ricans with Negro friends will evidence a greater degree of Negro Non-Standard English than the Puerto Ricans without Negro friends.

The second question dealt with a comparison of the speech of Negroes and Puerto Ricans (both with and without Negro friends). It was predicted that:

if two groups of Puerto Rican junior high school students (all male), one comprised of youngsters with Negro friends and the other of children without Negro friends, are compared with a group of Negro junior high students (all male), in terms of spoken English with respect to the occurrence of Standard English and Negro Non-Standard English forms of a set of previously selected phonological variables, then the Negro youngsters will evidence a greater degree of Negro Non-Standard English than either of the two groups of Puerto Rican children.

The final question was concerned with the way in which the spoken English was to be elicited. It was predicted that:

if a group of Puerto Rican and Negro junior high school students' spoken English is examined with respect to the occurrence of Standard English and Negro Non-Standard English forms of a set of previously selected phonological variables, and if these variables are elicited using the following procedures: Conversation, Paragraph Reading, Word List, Minimal Pairs-Sentences and Minimal Pairs-List, then the highest degree of Negro Non-Standard English will occur when the Conversation procedure is utilized and the lowest degree of Negro Non-Standard English will occur when the Minimal Pairs-List procedure is used.

RESULTS

1. *Quantitative Analysis*

As described earlier, a two factor analysis of variance was performed for each of the phonological variables to test for differences between the three peer groups and the five elicitation procedures. Where main effect differences were found, F tests for simple effects were employed to test for differences between specific means. The cut-off point for accepting differences as being statistically significant was the 0.05 level of confidence.

The first hypothesis had predicted that Puerto Ricans with Negro friends would evidence a greater degree of Negro Non-Standard English than Puerto Ricans without Negro friends. Table 3 presents these results. It should be noted that the higher the score, the greater the amount of Negro Non-Standard English.

TABLE 3

Mean Scores on Eleven Variables for Puerto Ricans with Black Friends and Puerto Ricans without Black Friends

Variable	Puerto Ricans With Negro Friends	Puerto Ricans Without Negro Friends
1. Intervocalic [ð]	1.23*	1.08
2. Final [θ]	1.77*	1.20
3. Medial [ɪ]	2.15*	1.66
4. Final [r]	1.79*	1.53
5. Medial [r]	1.27*	1.06
6. Final [t]	2.73*	2.18
7. Final [d]	2.87*	2.22
8. Final [sp]	2.50*	1.92
9. Final [sk]	3.33*	1.89
10. Initial [str]	No analysis of variance performed	
11. Initial [skr]	No analysis of variance performed	

* Significantly higher at the 0.05, or better, level of confidence

The table indicates that for nine of the eleven phonological variables, the Puerto Ricans with Negro friends evidenced significantly more Negro Non-Standard English than the Puerto Ricans without Negro friends. For two variables, initial /str/ and initial /skr/, no analyses were performed since, for both groups, all occurrences of these variables were in the Standard English form.

The second hypothesis had predicted that the Negro subjects would evidence a greater amount of Negro Non-Standard English than either of the two groups of Puerto Rican subjects. Table 4 presents these results.

Again, the higher the mean score, the greater the amount of Negro Non-Standard English.

TABLE 4

Mean Scores on Eleven Variables for Puerto Ricans and Negro Subjects

Variable	Puerto Ricans With Negro Friends	Puerto Ricans Without Negro Friends	Negroes
1. Intervocalic [ð]	1.23	1.08	1.25**
2. Final [θ]	1.77	1.20	1.79**
3. Medial [ɪ]	2.15	1.66	2.19**
4. Final [r]	1.79	1.53	1.82**
5. Medial [r]	1.27*	1.06	1.11
6. Final [t]	2.73	2.18	2.93**
7. Final [d]	2.87*	2.22	2.71
8. Final [sp]	2.50**	1.92	2.42
9. Final [sk]	3.33*	1.89	2.91
10. Initial [str]	No analysis of variance performed		
11. Initial [skr]	No analysis of variance performed		

*   highest-significantly.
** highest-not significantly.

The results indicated that for five of the eleven variables, the Negro subjects evidenced a greater amount of Negro Non-Standard English than either of the two groups of Puerto Ricans. In all five cases the mean scores for the Negroes were significantly higher than the mean scores for the Puerto Ricans without Negro friends, but not significantly higher than for the Puerto Ricans with Negro friends. (Two stars were given since the hypothesis had predicted that the Negroes would be more non-standard than both of the Puerto Rican groups.) In four instances, the mean scores for the Negroes were lower than the mean scores for the Puerto Ricans with Negro friends. For initial [str] and initial [skr] no analyses of variance were performed as all occurrences of these variables were in the Standard English form.

The third, and final hypothesis had predicted that of the five elicitation procedures, the lowest degree of Negro Non-Standard English would occur when the Minimal Pairs-Test procedure was employed. Table 5 presents these results. Again, the higher the score, the greater the amount of Negro Non-Standard English.

The results indicate that for one variable, intervocalic [ð], Conversation yielded significantly more Negro Non-Standard English than the other four procedures. In three instances, final [θ], final [r] and final [t], Minimal Pairs-List yielded a significantly lower degree of Negro Non-Standard English than the other four procedures. In two instances, final [sp] and

TABLE 5

Mean Scores on Eleven Variables for Five Elicitation Procedures:
Conversation, Paragraph Reading, Word List, Minimal
Pairs-Sentences, Minimal Pairs-List

Variable	Conversation	Paragraph Reading	Word List	Minimal Pairs Sentences	Minimal Pairs List
1. Intervocalic [ð]	1.49*	1.17	1.06	1.08	1.12
2. Final [θ]	1.88	1.68	1.60	1.56	1.22**
3. Medial [ɪ]	2.39	1.96	2.10	2.06	1.84
4. Final [r]	1.77	1.76	1.76	1.72	1.56**
5. Medial [r]	1.19	1.09	1.06	1.22	1.17
6. Final [t]	2.89	2.69	2.75	2.69	2.07**
7. Final [d]	2.85	2.87	2.53	2.25	2.49
8. Final [sp]	no data	2.46	2.71	2.50	2.34
9. Final [sk]	no data	2.89	2.81	2.48	2.66
10. Initial [str]	no analysis of variance performed				
11. Initial [skr]	no analysis of variance performed				

* Conversation procedure elicited significantly more Negro Non-Standard English than the other four procedures.
** Minimal Pairs elicited significantly less Negro Non-Standard English than the other four procedures.

final [sk], no occurrences of the variable were found in Conversation. For initial [skr] and initial [str] no analyses of variance were performed since all occurrences of these variables were in Standard English form.

2. *Protocol Presentation*

In order to give a better idea of the speech (relative to the phonological variables) of the three groups of subjects, one from each group was selected at random. These three protocols will be presented here, side by side. Only the variable in question was transcribed. This was done, again, because of great difficulty in getting raters to agree on the forms of occurrence of many of the non-variable sounds. Protocols for each of the contexts will be presented separately.

As can be seen in table 6, the Negro speaker appears to be the most non-standard of the three speakers and the Puerto Rican without Negro friends appears to be the most standard. There are, however, instances where the Negro speaker is quite standard and where the Puerto Rican without Negro friends is non-standard. In many instances, a speaker's production on the first presentation of the stimulus word is very different from that on the second presentation.

TABLE 6

Transcription of Eleven Phonological Variables for Three
Subjects in the Minimal Pairs-List Procedure

Variable	Context (Word)	Puerto Rican With Negro Friends	Puerto Rican Without Negro Friends	Negro
1. Intervocalic [ð]	*either*	Ø	ð	Ø
2. Final [θ]	*fourth*	Ø	Ø	θ
3. Medial [ɪ]	*Tim*	ɪ	ɪ	i
4. Final [r]	*here*	Ø	Ø	Ø
5. Intervocalic [r]	*Carol*	r	r	r
6. Final [t]	*went*	ʔ	closure	Ø
7. Final [d]	*build*	ʔ	partial	Ø
8. Initial [str]	*stream*	str	str	str
9. Initial [skr]	*scream*	skr	skr	skr
10. Final [sk]	*disk*	sØ	s	sØ
11. Final [sp]	*crisp*	sØ	s	sØ
12. Intervocalic [ð]	*either*	Ø	Ø	v
13. Final [θ]	*fourth*	θ	θ	Ø
14. Medial [ɪ]	*Tim*	ɪ	ɪ	ɪ
15. Final [r]	*here*	Ø	r	Ø
16. Intervocalic [r]	*Carol*	r	r	Ø
17. Final [t]	*went*	Ø	partial	Ø
18. Final [d]	*build*	Ø	d	Ø
19. Initial [skr]	*scream*	skr	skr	skr
20. Initial [str]	*stream*	str	str	str
21. Final [sp]	*crisp*	sØ	sp	sØ
22. Final [sk]	*disk*	sk	s	sØ

TABLE 7

Transcription of Eleven Phonological Variables for Three Subjects
in the Minimal Pairs-Sentences Procedure

Variable	Context (Word)	Puerto Rican With Negro Friends	Puerto Rican Without Negro Friends	Negro
1. Intervocalic [ð]	*either*	ð	ð	Ø
2. Final [θ]	*fourth*	f	θ	f
3. Medial [ɪ]	*Tim*	ɪ	ɪ	i
4. Intervocalic [r]	*Carol*	r	r	r
5. Final [d]	*build*	ʔ	closure	ʔ
6. Initial [str]	*stream*	str	str	str
7. Initial [skr]	*scream*	skr	skr	skr
8. Final [r]	*here*	Ø	r	Ø
9. Final [t]	*went*	Ø	t	Ø
10. Final [sp]	*crisp*	s	s	s
11. Final [sk]	*disk*	s	partial *s*	sØ

TABLE 8

Transcription of Eleven Phonological Variables for Three
Subjects in the Word List Procedure

Variable	Context (Word)	Puerto Rican With Negro Friends	Puerto Rican Without Negro Friends	Negro
1. Intervocalic [ð]	other	ð	ð	ð
2. Intervocalic [ð]	father	v	ð	v
3. Intervocalic [ð]	rather	ð	Ø	v
4. Final [r]	other	Ø	r	Ø
5. Final [r]	father	Ø	r	r
6. Final [r]	rather	Ø	r	Ø
7. Medial [ɪ]	Jim	ɪ	ɪ	i
8. Medial [ɪ]	him	ɪ	ɪ	i
9. Medial [ɪ]	risk	ɪ	ɪ	ɪ
10. Final [θ]	both	Ø	θ	Ø
11. Final [θ]	mouth	Ø	θ	Ø
12. Final [θ]	fourth	Ø	θ	f
13. Final [sk]	risk	s	s closure	sØ
14. Final [sk]	task	s	s closure	sØ
15. Final [sk]	dusk	s	sk	sØ
16. Final [sp]	clasp	s partial	s partial	s
17. Final [sp]	wasp	s partial	s	s
18. Final [t]	sight	Ø	Ø	ʔ
19. Final [t]	height	Ø	partial	ʔ
20. Final [t]	art	ʔ	partial	Ø
21. Final [d]	side	d	ʔ	Ø
22. Final [d]	had	d	d	ʔ
23. Final [d]	around	ʔ	ʔ	ʔ
24. Intervocalic [r]	around	r	r	Ø
25. Intervocalic [r]	Harry	r	r	r
26. Intervocalic [r]	sorry	Ø	r	r
27. Initial [str]	strong	str	str	str
28. Initial [str]	straw	str	str	str
29. Initial [str]	string	str	str	str
30. Initial [skr]	scratch	skr	skr	skr
31. Initial [skr]	scream	skr	skr	skr
32. Initial [skr]	screw	skr	skr	skr

As in the presentation for the Minimal Pairs-List procedures, the tables for the Minimal Pairs-Sentences and World List procedures show that, in general, the Negro speaker is the most non-standard, while the Puerto Rican without Negro friends is the closest to the standard variety of English. Further, for any given variable, any of the three speakers might be the most standard or non-standard. A subject often differs, within one procedure, on his production of a single variable (which appears more than once).

The data for the Paragraph Reading and Conversation procedures will not be presented as they do not essentially differ from the other three procedures.

DISCUSSION

The first of the three hypotheses of this investigation had predicted that:

if a group of Puerto Rican junior high school students (all male), each having among his ten best friends at least three Negroes, and a group of Puerto Rican junior high school students (all male), having no Negroes among their ten best friends, are compared in terms of spoken English with respect to the occurrence of Standard English and Negro Non-Standard English forms of a set of previously selected phonological variables, then the Puerto Ricans with Negro friends will evidence a greater degree of Negro Non-Standard English than the Puerto Ricans without Negro friends.

The results of the study confirmed this hypothesis. For nine of the eleven phonological variables, the Puerto Ricans with Negro friends were significantly more (Negro) non-standard in their spoken English than the Puerto Ricans without Negro friends. The other two variables, initial [str] and initial [skr], were not analyzed since all of their occurrences were in Standard English form.

The fact that the peer group seems to have such a great effect on one's spoken English is of more than passing interest to those involved in the education of speakers of languages and/or varieties other than Standard English. Certainly all of the attempts at setting up T.E.S.O.L.[2] programs and bilingual schools is evidence that non-English speakers (many of these programs include Black children) are not learning to speak the kind of English teachers want them to speak. Bailey (1968) has indicated that the more traditional techniques of teaching English, both where the goals are directed towards refining a speaker's skill and where they are directed toward providing a second language to those who don't speak English in the home, have not proven effective for those speakers whose basic language system differs greatly enough from the standard variety of English to cause problems on the classroom level. Brainin (1964) also recognizes that the school has failed to teach Standard English to speakers of other varieties. She finds that lower-class children come to school with a rich language which the middle-class teacher doesn't understand. The teacher, thinking the child speaks English poorly, and cannot learn to speak correctly, encourages the child to fulfill her low expectations by

[2]   Teaching English to Speakers of Other Languages.

neither learning to speak nor being receptive to the formal middle-class language which is, by and large, foreign to him. Deutsch (1963) points out that "...the lower-class child enters the school situation so poorly prepared to produce what the school demands that initial failures are almost inevitable, and the school experience becomes negatively rather than positively reinforced" (p.164). John (1967) is most to the point when she states that "the schools are not educating anyone adequately" (p. 2). She further indicates that when compared to middle-class children, lower-class children, who are totally dependent on skills taught in the classroom, do less well on all kinds of language tests. These researchers, in asserting that the schools are, for the most part, ineffective in teaching the standard variety of English to speakers of non-standard varieties of English, are representative of the majority of the workers in the field.

The primary question, of course, is to determine what behaviors the Negro peer group reinforces; it is not initially, for the Puerto Rican boy, language. The Puerto Rican speaks a variety of English characterized by a good deal of Spanish interference. This fact has been documented by Fishman and Herasimchuk (1969) and Jones (1962). In looking at the Puerto Ricans with Negro friends in this study, and contrasting them with the Puerto Ricans without Negro friends, several differences are immediately apparent. The former group is, first of all, physically bigger and stronger than the latter. (School health records indicate that the difference in height is, on the average, four inches.) In addition, in informal situations the Puerto Ricans with Negro friends are more aggressive and verbal than the Puerto Ricans without Negro friends. (One need only listen to the tapes of the interview situations to realize this.) Finally, the Puerto Ricans with Negro friends are all interested in basketball, something which few in the other group care about. These three things may well be important in terms of entering a group comprised mainly of Negroes. Firstly, basketball is the dominant sport for Negro children in the city, while baseball is the major sport for Puerto Rican children. (The school from which the subjects came has no Puerto Ricans on its basketball team and two Negroes on its softball team.) Physical prowess and aggressiveness seem to be important in the Negro peer group as evidenced by the great number of fights (both in and out of school) involving Negroes as opposed to very few fights involving Puerto Ricans. (The above observations are independently suggested by several members of the school's staff who are in close contact with those used as subjects in the present investigation and who were asked to comment on the three groups.) Part of the interest in basketball by the Puerto Ricans with Negro friends is probably as a result (and not a cause) of their membership in the Negro peer group. This holds true also for their aggressiveness and verbalness. On the other hand, part of these factors might well have been involved in making for the mutual attraction between the Negroes and Puerto Ricans. Peer group pressure and reinforcement would have then increased the aggressivity, interest in basketball and amounts of verbal behavior. In other words, certain Puerto Ricans, for whatever reasons, have interests, abilities and characteristics which are reinforced more by the Negro peer group than by the Puerto Rican peer group. They are thus drawn towards the former group where these abilities and interests are maintained and further shaped.

It was thought, before this investigation began, that one of the characteristics of those Puerto Rican children whose best friends included Negroes would be that they would look, in terms of coloring and hair texture, like the Negro subjects. This, however, was not the case (as subjectively judged by this writer). There seemed to be no essential difference in coloring between the two groups of Puerto Ricans. None of the twenty-four subjects in Groups I and II could be mistaken for being Negro. Another characteristic which it was thought might possibly differentiate the two groups of Puerto Ricans was their ability to speak Spanish. In fact, however, all twenty-four boys were fluent speakers of the language. A third possibility considered was that the group classified as Puerto Rican with Negro friends live in areas dominated by Negroes, while Puerto Ricans without Negro friends live in areas dominated by other Puerto Ricans. The neighborhood from which the school population is drawn, however, is fully integrated (in terms of Puerto Ricans and Negroes). This applies to whole blocks as well as apartment houses.

Thus far, it has been posited that the main reason why the Puerto Ricans with Negro friends have so great a degree of Negro Non-Standard English forms of occurrence of the phonological variables in their speech is that this represents the influence of the peer group as a reinforcing agent. There is, however, an alternative explanation to account for the results. It might be that the Puerto Ricans with Negro friends learned the Negro Non-Standard English at home from parents, siblings, or relatives who have substantial numbers of Negro friends. In order to demonstrate this, several things would have been necessary. First, information as to the friendship patterns of those people with whom the subject verbally interacts at home would have to have been obtained. Second, those same people's language would have had to be measured with respect to their production of Negro Non-Standard English forms of occurrence of the eleven phonological variables. Unfortunately, these two pieces of information were unavailable to this investigator. The school authorities allowed the children to be used as subjects somewhat reluctantly. There was a fear, because of the decentralization issue in New York, of angering the parents in the community. Because of this, it was felt that a non-Board of Education research effort should be as inconspicuous as possible. Some of this information might have been obtained from the subjects. There would be, however, a question as to the reliability of such data. In addition, the possible importance of these data was not recognized at the time of the data gathering.

The second hypothesis had predicted that:

if two groups of Puerto Rican junior high school students (all male), one comprised of youngsters with Negro friends and the other of children without Negro friends, are compared with a group of Negro junior high school students (all male) in terms of spoken English with respect to the occurrence of Standard English and Negro Non-Standard English forms of a set of previously selected phonological variables, then the Negro youngsters will evidence a greater degree of Negro Non-Standard English than either of the two groups of Puerto Ricans.

The results showed that for nine of the phonological variables, the Negro subjects were more non-standard than the Puerto Ricans without Negro friends. In one case this difference was not statistically significant. When the Negroes were compared with the Puerto Ricans with Negro friends, highly interesting results were obtained. For five of the eleven variables, the Negroes were significantly more non-standard than the Puerto Ricans with Negro friends. In three cases, however, the reverse was true; Puerto Ricans with Negro friends were more non-standard than the Negroes. In one case, the Puerto Ricans with Negro friends were more non-standard than the Negro subjects, but not significantly so. These results certainly warrant further discussion at this time since they did not confirm the hypothesis.

If it is accepted that certain characteristics of the school situation force the child to seek reinforcement outside of it, and if it is accepted that characteristics of some Puerto Rican youngsters lead them to associate primarily with Negro children rather than other Puerto Rican children, and, finally, if one accepts the role of reinforcement in shaping and maintaining behavior, then it is no surprise that for verbal behavior, Puerto Ricans with Negro friends begin to speak Negro Non-Standard English. What is surprising, however, is the finding that on three of the phonological variables, the Puerto Ricans with Negro friends were significantly more non-standard in their speech than the Negro youngsters. (These variables were: final [d], medial [r], and final [sk].) The answer may be, in fact, that the forms of occurrence for these variables for the Puerto Ricans with Negro friends may be hypercorrections. Labov (1966) found this phenomenon in his groups (which were based upon socioeconomic criteria). The variable [oh], for example, follows a pattern wherein, for the more formal styles, the lower-class speakers are more formal than the middle-class speakers. This, according to Labov (1966), shows that the lower-class, in attempting to rise to the middle-class, over adopts some of their language patterns. A similar phenomenon may be at work here (except that acceptance by the peer group and not social class is the critical variable). In trying to assimilate into the Negro peer group, the Puerto Rican adopts the behaviors of that group and, in some instances, adopts them to an extreme degree. As in Labov's (1966) study, this happened in some, but not all, of the linguistic measures. It should be pointed out that in its usual sense, hypercorrection refers to excessive movement towards the standard variety. In this instance, the term is applied because to the Puerto Rican trying to get into the Negro peer group, Negro Non-Standard English is, in a sense, the standard variety (or the most desirable one) for him. However, since the term "hypercorrection" is usually associated with the relation of the non-standard variety to the standard, the term 'hyper-non-standardization' will be substituted.

The question of why the hyper-non-standardizations appeared for final [d], medial [r] and final [sk] must go unanswered at this point. The three seem to have little in common. One is a cluster ([sk]) while two are not; one is found in medial position while two are found in final position; one is extremely common in English (final [d]) while two are not. It is, however, somewhat easier to explain why the groups did not differ significantly in their production of either initial [str] or [skr]. First of all, these are the only variables which appeared in initial position. It may be that subjects are more careful (or formal) in their speech production of initial consonantal sounds. This is attested to by the finding that one of these variables in final position ([sk]) did differentiate among the groups (with Puerto Ricans with Negro friends being significantly more non-standard than Puerto Ricans without Negro friends and Negroes being significantly more non-standard than Puerto Ricans without Negro friends). It seems as if initial [str] and [skr] were difficult clusters for the subjects. That is, there appeared to be a good deal of hesitation preceding their production. This led to slower and more careful production than for the other variables. What happened was that subjects would "sound out" the cluster in much the same way as a youngster who is first learning to read sounds out an unfamiliar word. There would often be a very long [s] followed by a [t] or [k] and then an [r]. It should be pointed out in addition, that Stewart (1964) has indicated that the non-standard occurrence of [skr] where standard [str] appears is an age graded phenomenon which disappears at around age ten. The present subjects were all older than twelve.

For the remaining six variables, the results showed that the Puerto Ricans with Negro friends and the Negroes were significantly more non-standard than the Puerto Ricans without Negro friends (but not significantly so). These findings appear to be logical in that one would expect that the Negro children, having utilized Negro Non-Standard English for a much longer period of time than the other two groups, would be more non-standard than the Puerto Ricans (of either of the two groups). This, in fact, was what the hypothesis of this investigation predicted.

The third, and final hypothesis had predicted that:

if a group of Puerto Rican and Negro junior high school students' spoken English is examined with respect to the occurrence of Standard English and Negro Non-Standard English forms of a set of previously selected phonological variables, and if these variables are elicited using the following procedures: Conversation, Paragraph Reading, Word List, Minimal Pairs-Sentences and Minimal Pairs-List, then the highest degree of Negro Non-Standard English will occur when the Conversation procedure is utilized and the lowest degree of Negro Non-Standard English will occur when the Minimal Pairs-List procedure is used.

The obtained results did not support this hypothesis. In only one instance did the Conversation procedure yield the greatest amount of Negro Non-Standard English. In four cases the Minimal Pairs-List procedure elicited the lowest amount of Negro Non-Standard English. These findings go counter to the results of Labov (1966), Fishman and Herasmichuck (1969) and Labov, Cohen, Robins and Lewis (1968). Labov (1966), in fact, postulated that contextual changes are the most important determinants of linguistic shift. The results of this study indicate that for this population, at least, linguistic shift is influenced greatly by peer group affiliation but little by contextual change. There is a further possibility that the repertoire ranges of the subjects in this study are not as wide as those of subjects in the investigations mentioned above. This, however, must await further investigation since the subjects were tested in what was probably a formal situation (in a teacher's home and by a stranger). It should be noted that the situation in which the subjects found themselves may well have been quite formal and may have greatly reduced the amount of variability that is contained in their verbal repertoires. If, in fact, this is the case, then the findings in this study were biased in two ways. First of all, there would be a strong possibility that if the subjects had been more at ease, variations in speech as a function of elicitation procedure would have been found. Secondly, there may well have been a greater degree of Negro Non-Standard English produced by the Negro subjects and by the Puerto Ricans with Negro friends, and a greater degree of forms characterized by Spanish interference produced by each of the two groups of Puerto Ricans.

The last statement raises some interesting questions. In all of the tapes of the Puerto Ricans, there were no occurrences of Spanish interference (on the eleven variables examined). Several of the variables were the same as those used by Fishman and Herasimchuk (1969) and Jones (1962). These researchers found, for example, that Puerto Rican speakers often have an [ɛ] preceding the production of initial [s]. This was not found for either initial [str] or initial [skr] in the present study. In addition, both of the studies cited above found that Puerto Ricans often produced [r] (trilled r) in words like *worry* and *sorry*. This phenomenon did not occur in the present study. One reason for this might be the formality of the situation. If less formal English had been elicited, then, perhaps, more Spanish interference would have occurred. Another possible explanation for the lack of Spanish interference in the speech of the Puerto Rican subjects is that the variables chosen did not adequately sample their verbal repertoires.

A small sub-study, not originally a part of this investigation, was carried out to determine whether the differences found between the three groups on the basis of the phonological variables were correlated with what people not trained in the area of language could perceive. Two tapes from each of the three groups were selected at random and played to ten middle-class, white college educated adults. (The sample of subjects is by no means representative of all middle-class, white college educated adults since all were friends or relatives of this investigator.) The adults were asked to rate the speakers on the tapes as being Negro or Puerto Rican. All of the subjects rated the first of the Puerto Ricans without Negro friends to be Puerto Rican. Nine of the adult subjects identified the second Puerto Rican without Negro friends to be a Puerto Rican and one subject incorrectly identified him as being Negro. Seven of the subjects identified the first Puerto Rican with Negro friends as being Negro and three judged him to be Puerto Rican. Eight of the adults rated the second Puerto Rican with Negro friends as being Negro and two correctly rated him as being Puerto Rican. (Because of the in-informalness of this study, no statistics were performed on the data.) Obviously, then, the differences found by the phonological analysis take on added importance since the distinction between the two groups of Puerto Rican speakers is not simply an artifact of a linguist's orthographic transcription system. What happened, in fact, was that naive informants confirmed the data obtained in this investigation.

BIBLIOGRAPHY

Asch, Solomon
　1952　*Social Psychology* (New York: Prentice-Hall).
Bailey, Beryl
　1965　"A New Perspective on American Negro Dialectology", *American Speech* 40:171-77.
　1968　"Some Aspects of the Impact of Linguistics on Language Teaching in Disadvantaged Communities", *Elementary English* 45:570-77.
Barker, George
　1947　"Social Functions of Language in a Mexican American Community", *Acta Americana* 5:185-202.

1951 "Growing Up in a Bilingual Community", *The Kiva* 17:17-32.
Boehm, L.
1957 "The Development of Independence: A Comparative Study", *Child Development* 28:85-102.
Bossard, J. H. S.
1945a "Family Modes of Expression", *American Sociological Review* 10:226-37.
1945b "The Bilingual Individual as a Person — Linguistic Identification with States", *American Sociological Review* 10:699-709.
Brainin, Sema
1964 *Language Skills, Formal Education and the Lower Class Child* (New York: Mobilization for Youth).
Brooks, Charlotte K.
1964 "Some Approaches to Teaching English as a Second Language", in William A. Stewart (ed.), *Non-Standard Speech and the Teaching of English* (Washington, D.C.: Center for Applied Linguistics).
Bruning, James L. and B. L. Kintz
1968 *Computational Handbook of Statistics* (Glenview: Scott, Foresman and Company).
Campbell, John
1964 "Peer Relations in Childhood", in Martin L. Hoffman and Lois W. Hoffman (eds.), *Review of Child Development Research: VI* (New York: Russell Sage Foundation).
Cartwright, Dorwin and Alvin Zandler (eds.)
1953 *Group Dynamics: Research and Theory* (Evanston, Ill.: Row, Peterson).
Coleman, J. S.
1961 *The Adolescent Society* (New York: Free Press of Glencoe).
DeCamp, David
1958 "Pronunciation of English in San Francisco", *Orbis* 7:372-91.
Deutsch, Martin
1963 "The Disadvantaged Child and the Learning Process", in A. Passon (ed.), *Education in Depressed Areas* (New York: Columbia University, Teachers College).
Dillard, J. L.
1967a "The English Teacher and the Language of the Newly Integrated Student", *Teachers College Record* 69:115-20.
1967b "Negro Children's Dialect in the Inner City", *Florida FL Reporter* 5.
1968 "Non-Standard Negro Dialects: Convergence or Divergence", *Florida FL Reporter* 6:9-12.
1972 *Black English, Its History and Usage in the United States* (New York: Random House).
Ervin-Tripp, Susan
1964 "Interaction of Language, Topic and Listener", in John Gumperz and Dell Hymes (eds.), *Ethnography of Communication, American Anthropologist* 66:86-102.
Ferguson, Charles
1964 "Teaching Standard Languages to Dialect Speakers", in Roger A. Shuy (ed.), *Social Dialects in Language Learning* (Champaign: National Conference of Teachers of English).
Fishman, Joshua A.
1965 "Who Speaks What Language to Whom and When", *Linguistics* 2:67-88.
Fishman, Joshua A. and Eleanor Herasimchuk
1969 "The Multiple Prediction of Phonological Variables in Bilingual Speech", *American Anthropologist* 71:648-57.

Garrison, K., A. Kingston and A. McDonald
  1964 *Educational Psychology* (New York: Appleton-Century-Crofts).
Hannerz, Ulf
  1969 *Soulside: Inquiries into Ghetto Culture and Community* (New York: Columbia University Press).
Havighurst, R.
  1953 *Human Development and Education* (New York: Longmans, Green).
Hayes, William
  1963 *Statistics for Psychologists* (New York: Holt, Rinehart and Winston).
Hicks, David
  1965 "Imitation and Retention of Film-Mediated Aggressive Peer and Adult Models", *Journal of Personality and Social Psychology* 2:97-100.
Hockett, Charles F.
  1950 "Age Grading and Linguistic Continuity", *Language* 26:449-57.
Horner, Vivian and Joan Gussow
  1972 "John and Mary: A Pilot Study in Linguistic Ecology", in Cazden, Hymes, and John (eds.), *Functions of Language in the Classroom* (New York).
Horrocks, J. E.
  1962 *Psychology of Adolescents* (New York: Houghton Mifflin).
Hymes, Dell
  1967 "Models on Interaction of Language and Social Setting", *Journal of Social Issues* 23:8-28.
Iscoe, I. and J. A. Carden
  1961 "Field Dependence, Manifest Anxiety and Sociometric Status in Children", *Journal of Consulting Psychology* 25:181.
John, Vera P.
  1967 "Communicative Competence of Low-Income Children: Assumptions and Programs", unpublished manuscript prepared for language study group, Ford Foundation.
Jones, Morgan E.
  1962 "A Phonological Study of English as Spoken by Puerto Ricans Contrasted with Puerto Rican Spanish and American English" (University of Michigan Dissertation).
Joos, Martin
  1968 "The Isolation of Styles", in Joshua A. Fishman (ed.), *Readings in the Sociology of Language* (The Hague: Mouton).
Labov, William
  1964a "Phonological Correlates of Social Stratification", *American Anthropologist* 66:164-76.
  1964b "Stages in the Acquisition of Standard English", in Roger A. Shuy (ed.), *Social Dialects in Language Learning* (Champaign: National Council of Teachers of English).
  1966 *The Social Stratification of English in New York City* (Washington, D.C.: Center for Applied Linguistics).
  1969a "The Logic of Non-Standard English", *Florida FL Reporter* 7:60-74.
  1969b *The Study of Non-Standard English* (Washington, D.C.: Center for Applied Linguistics).
Labov, William and Paul Cohen
  1967 "Systematic Relations of Standard and Non-Standard Rules in the Grammars of Negro Speakers", in *Project Literacy Reports*, no. 8 (Ithaca).
Labov, William, Paul Cohen, Clarence Robins and John Lewis
  1968 *A Study of the Non-Standard English of Negro and Puerto Rican Speakers in*

   New York City (New York: Columbia University).
Levine, Lewis and Harry Crockett
   1967   "Friends Influence on Speech", *Sociological Inquiry* 37:109-28.
Lewin, Kurt A., Ralph White and Ronald Lippitt
   1939   "Patterns of Aggressive Behavior in Experimentally Created 'Social Cli-
          mates'", *Journal of Social Psychology* 10:271-99.
Lindquist, E. F.
   1956   *Design and Analysis of Experiments in Psychology and Education* (Boston,
          Houghton Mifflin Company).
Ma, Roxana and Eleanor Herasimchuk
   1968   "Linguistic Dimensions of a Bilingual Neighborhood", in Joshua A. Fishman,
          Robert L. Cooper, Roxana Ma, *et al.* (eds.), *Bilingualism in the Barrio* (New
          York: Yeshiva University).
Newton, Eunke
   1965   "Planning for the Language Development of Disadvantaged Children and
          Youth", *Journal of Negro Education* 34:167-77.
Ojeman, R. H.
   1969   *The Child's Society — Clubs, Gangs and Cliques* (Chicago: Brooks/Cole).
Opie, Iona and Peter Opie
   1959   *The Lore and Language of School Children* (Oxford: Clarendon Press).
Pederson, Lee A.
   1964a "Non-Standard Speech in Chicago", in William A. Stewart (ed.), *Non-
          Standard Speech and the Teaching of English* (Washington, D.C.: Center
          for Applied Linguistics).
   1964b "Some Structural Differences in the Speech of Chicago Negroes", in Roger
          A. Shuy (ed.), *Social Dialects in Language Learning* (Champaign: National
          Council of Teachers of English).
Reissman, Frank
   1964   "The Overlooked Positives of Disadvantaged Groups", *Journal of Negro
          Education* 33:225-31.
Rogers, Dorothy
   1969   *Child Psychology* (Belmont, California: Brooks/Cole).
Silverman, Stuart H.
   1969   "The Evaluation of Language Varieties", *The Modern Language Journal*
          53:241-44.
Skinner, B. F.
   1963   *Verbal Behavior* (New York: Appleton-Century-Crofts).
Stanfield, R. E.
   1966   "The Interaction of Family Variables and Gang Variables in the Aetiology of
          Delinquency", *Social Problems* 13:411-17.
Stewart, William A.
   1964   "Foreign Language Teaching Methods in Quasi-Foreign Language Situa-
          tions", in William A. Stewart (ed.), *Non-Standard Speech and the Teaching
          of English* (Washington, D.C.: Center for Applied Linguistics).
   1965   "Urban Negro Speech: Sociolinguistic Factors Affecting English Teaching",
          Center for Applied Linguistics, Washington, D.C.
   1967   "Sociolinguistic Factors in the History of American Negro Dialects", *Florida
          FL Reporter* 5:11-29.
Thasher, Frederic M.
   1955   "The Gang", in Paul Hare, Edgar Borgatta and Robert Bales (eds.), *Small
          Groups: Studies in Social Interaction* (New York: Alfred A. Knopf).
Williamson, Juanita

1964   "Report on a Proposed Study of the Speech of Negro High School Students in Memphis", in Roger A. Shuy (ed.), *Social Dialects in Language Learning* (Champaign: National Council of Teachers of English).

Winer, B. J.
1962   *Statistical Principles in Experimental Design* (New York: McGraw Hill).

SUSAN H. HOUSTON

A SOCIOLINGUISTIC CONSIDERATION OF THE
BLACK ENGLISH OF CHILDREN IN NORTHERN FLORIDA

Non-standard English, especially those varieties spoken by socalled disadvantaged children, has been examined by recent researchers in two main ways. Linguistic attention has most often concentrated on descriptions of these forms of language from the viewpoint of a dialect atlas (e.g. Kurath and McDavid 1961) or of technical linguistics (e.g. Labov 1966, 1969; Wolfram 1969; Fasold and Wolfram 1970). Work in other fields, chiefly education and social science, has been oriented toward studying these children's communication problems and putative linguistic-cognitive deficiencies (e.g. Bereiter and Engelmann 1966; Bernstein 1961; Blank and Solomon 1968). Since linguists have only relatively recently become involved with such studies, most examinations of the language of disadvantaged children have been undertaken without much linguistic sophistication. But both the linguistic and the social-science viewpoints are useful, and they can be combined. It is the intent of this paper to synthesize the two approaches, in a way which hopefully may prove helpful to both technical linguists and educators working with dialect-contact situations.

The present study is a pilot investigation of the language of children in one country of rural northern Florida. The research was carried out under the auspices of the Southeastern Education Laboratory in Atlanta, a regional laboratory of the Office of Education; the report was originally designed to provide descriptive information on which to base linguistic retraining or "remediation" programs. The subjects were between the ages of 9 and 11, with a modal age of about 11; there were 22 of them,

Reprinted by permission of the author and publisher from *Language* 45(1969): 599-607.

of whom 5 were boys, and all were black. The children spoke what I term Uneducated Child Black English (hereafter CBE). The following remarks will explain this terminology.

The form of language which I have called Black English has traditionally been considered a "dialect". However, this term is used in a number of senses, some of them tending towards opprobrium (cf. Malmstrom 1967: 1), and therefore is ambiguous: the term "dialect" is probably best used to refer only to regional variants of language, rather than to social, situational or racial linguistic types. In this sense, Black English and White English are not dialects, although to be sure they have dialects or alternative forms characteristic of geographic areas. Instead, they may be called GENERA of American English. Black English is a genus of English, and so is White English (among others).

In this study and elsewhere, we presume that BE and WE can be regarded as separate entities for the purposes of formal linguistic description. This working hypothesis is based on the datum that a number of specifiable linguistic characteristics appear exclusively in one or the other genus. The sociolinguistic situation is comparable to the linguistic one: there are perceptual differences between these genera in most or all regions of the US, such that a black or white speaker from a particular region can usually, although not always, identify another speaker of that region as black or white on the basis of speech alone. In one study (Shuy 1968) respondents were able to make this judgment with about 80% accuracy. That such judgments are not infallible is not especially significant, since BE and WE subsume different ranges of linguistic features even though the ranges overlap. For instance, the difference between BE and WE in the Southeast is perhaps less than in the North because of demographic and linguistic history (cf. Stewart 1968), but even in the South the differences are considerable, and it is of course incorrect to propose that BE is equivalent to general Southern English (cf. also Houston 1970b, 1972).

The language of the children in the present study is termed Uneducated CBE, since each genus of English may be considered as including two subtypes, Educated and Uneducated. Educated varieties of language are those spoken by educated, often urban speakers of the relevant genus, and accorded prestige and maximum acceptance in typical educated and integrated environments. Both Educated BE and Educated WE are markedly different from their corresponding Uneducated variants. It is presumably the Uneducated form of language, Black or White, which serves as a hindrance to educational, social, economic and other success because of its hearers' attitudes towards it (rather than from any inherent deficiency of the language, it should be noted); and thus it should logically be the goal of school language programs to make child speakers of

Uneducated White English into speakers of Educated White English, and to make child speakers of Uneducated Black English into speakers of Educated Black English.

A final term to be explained here is "register". As I use it, a register is a range of styles of language, which have in common their utilization in a given unified situation or environment. For example, the children in this study speak and behave differently with friends and family than they do in school, as will be shown subsequently. They have, in other words, (at least) a School register and a Nonschool register. With each, there is usually much variation in actual features of language, or even several distinct styles, but each is nevertheless considered a single register since it contains features which appear in that situation and no other. Characteristic registral features are extralinguistic and behavioral as well as purely linguistic.

The data on which this study is based consist of about 25 hours of taped material, culled from some three times that much field observation. It was collected during field sessions originally planned for one to two hours each, with from one to four children per session. However, the actual recording circumstances were considerably modified, for reasons important to the sociolinguistic aspects of CBE studies and therefore described below.

Prior to this project, I viewed a number of videotapes of Southeastern children in school settings in order to familiarize myself with their speech. All these tapes were characterized by a distinctive set of linguistic and extralinguistic features which I tentatively labeled as a specific School register since it differed markedly from the usual language of children of this age. Utterances in this register were quite short; rate of speech was slower than in the Non-school register; the prevalence of strong stress, and of mid-high and high pitch, was increased. In addition, the content expressed in this register seemed limited and nonrevelatory of the speakers' personality and feelings (cf. also Houston 1972).

In the early recording sessions in the present study, it became clear that the children were speaking in this same School register. Since this was a definite impediment to the gathering of free-text material, or in fact of any quantity of data, it became necessary to elicit the Non-school register instead. One way of doing this turned out to be working with the children in larger, unstructured and open-ended group sessions. In addition, use of the Non-school register was encouraged by general unthreatening behavior on the part of the investigator, including allowing the children to say and record anything they chose; by lack of formal scheduling or routine, letting the children come and go as they pleased; and in sum, by reinforcement of behavioral concomitants of the Non-school register (cf. Houston f.c.).

Register is important because it accounts for many common observations about the language of the disadvantaged or minority child. The School register is used with a variety of persons and in a variety of situations not all of which involve school *per se*. In general it is likely to be used with adults and persons in authority over the children, and with persons not well known to them, especially if much older; and in situations which are formal, constrained and school-like or threatening to the children, or in which their behavior is clearly being tested or observed. It may also occur in any situation involving gross change of routine. Obviously, most studies and researches with which these children come into contact do involve these circumstances, including, of course, the present study, in which they were being investigated by an unknown adult white female teacher who furthermore speaks a different dialect, genus and subtype of language from theirs. At any rate, the School register is that form of language almost certain to be observed by researchers or teachers studying CBE or its speakers. The highly limiting characteristics of this register's form and content are very probably in large measure responsible for the frequent statement that disadvantaged children are linguistically and perhaps cognitively deprived: the School register does at first give this mistaken impression to the unprepared observer. Both the children and their teachers may regard the School register as the children's "best" language, since it seems to represent careful speech; but the children use the Non-school register with more ease, naturalness of expression, and creative fluency.

Once the Non-school register is elicited, the picture of the children's communicative competence changes completely. Far from being non-verbal, they are, as the linguist might expect, beautifully creative and imaginative in their use of language. The children I studied engaged in constant verbal play, storytelling and language games, some of them gratifyingly consistent with traditions of verbal art and folklore (for instance, their ritualized insult game). Their linguistic creativity is highly valued by their peers (cf. Houston f.c.), and many have developed remarkable talent in spontaneous narration and improvisation on traditional tales. Southeastern rural black children are often quite poor, and are further usually engaged in some task such as working in the fields or tending small siblings; the resulting lack of play-time and of material playthings contributes to the joy these children find in the creative use of language and to their readiness to use words as toys.

One of the few areas in which reports of nonfluency have some basis occurs in the School register, in reading (cf. Riessman 1962:115-17). The Oral-reading style commonly used by those Uneducated CBE speakers whom I observed is "word calling", or reading each word in a sentence with strong stress, high pitch, and list intonation, as though it were written in a foreign language (for a text in this style, cf. Houston 1972). Although oral reading in this manner does not necessarily preclude understanding of the target text, it contributes neither to reading speed nor to the reader's enjoyment of the task, and leads the observer to question the general relevance of oral reading as a classroom exercise. Probably the method by which the children learn to read is partly at fault: this is usually the sight-reading or whole-word method rather than one based on phonological segmentation (cf. Chall 1967). The whole-word method seems to prevent rational attack on newly-encountered lexicon; and since much of the lexicon the children encounter outside of school in newspapers etc. is in fact new to them, the method by and large is inadequate. The problem appears to be in part caused by misconceptions about the relationship of English (or any other) orthography to phonology, leading to the erroneous conclusion that phonologically-oriented methods of reading instruction such as traditional phonics are unsuited to children who speak dialectal or generic variants of General Shared English. There are, of course, further contributory factors in formation of the reading style; these include the nature of reading-instructional material (cf. Riessman 1962:30-31), which often tends in the Southeast to be of the "Dick-and-Jane" variety, as well as teachers' unawareness that the children's Oral-reading style is not universal and should not be condoned. This is clearly a problem, or series of problems, deserving much further study.

It has been proposed above that the frequent reports of disadvantaged children's "non-verbalness" may stem from observation of the School register only. Register also enters into another often misunderstood facet of BE sociolinguistics, namely that often termed "bidialectism". By this is generally meant control by black speakers of both Black and White English (cf. Cheyney 1967:59-61; Baratz 1970). Although this is the goal of most remedial language programs for CBE speakers, bidialectism in this sense has never been observed by this writer in the Southeast or elsewhere, including in children cited by teachers as prototypic examples of bidialectal speakers. Though the situation may perhaps be different among speakers of Educated variants of language, it appears that bidialectism per se does not exist. Instead, the linguistic switching usually mistaken for it might better be called "biregistralism" or the possession of two or more linguistic registers, common among speakers of Uneducated BE and possibly also WE. In almost all cases which I have observed, registers controlled by a single speaker belonged to the same linguistic genus i.e. BE or WE; control of both Educated and Uneducated variants of a genus is also a strong possibility, of course, and a more realistic and useful goal of language programs than socalled "bidialectism". Most remedial language programs now extant achieve only building up of the School register, and it is this register to which new forms are added and in which phonological alterations occur. But typically, neither register of the young Uneducated CBE speaker's natural or untaught language represents a good approximation to Educated BE, in which the distinction between registers is either lessened or nonexistent (i.e. replaced by stylistic distinctions).

A major problem of dialect and genus research obtains in linguistic analysis of CBE, namely the assignment of particular features to phonology or to syntax. For example, educators of CBE speakers often comment on the lack of regular past tense forms or noun plurals which are purportedly features of the children's syntax. However, such items may also be treated on the phonological level: roughly one can say either that regular past tense markers do not appear in CBE, or else that final stops which appear in WE do not appear in BE. The two explanations are equally valid in regard to past tense; the choice between them is made on the grounds of their relative generality in the language as a whole, and the importance of their grammatical claims. There are usually unambiguous decision procedures in such cases. It is preferable, other things being equal, to treat such differences between Black and White English as phonological where possible. One expects variants of a language to differ in surface- rather than in deep-structure features; phonological divergence involves a less sweeping claim than syntactic. Additionally, further evidence can frequently decide the issue in that a few general phonological rules may solve not only the particular problem in question but also other dubious items. For instance, there actually is a marked past tense in CBE, appearing with strong verbs, *have* and *be* etc. — as well as upon occasion with regularly marked verbs in the School register, where overcorrection reduces the number of simplified consonant clusters and unrealized final consonants (cf. Houston 1970b). It is the conclusion of the present study that Black and White English, in principle, differ chiefly in phonology ("in principle" because an actual CBE speaker may analogize from a phonologically-determined form such as /wɔk/ 'walked' to a syntactically-determined one e.g. #gow# for 'went'). Very few major morphosyntactic differences between BE and WE have appeared so far, unsurprisingly since these variants of English no doubt share a linguistic competence and diverge only at low-level performance strata.

Following is a phonological feature chart of Southeastern CBE and a set of descriptive rules, demonstrating the derivation of CBE Systematic Performance (as contrasted to Actualized Performance; cf. Houston 1970b) from General Shared English Competence; in other words, the rules output the main theoretical level of linguistic divergence between CBE and other genera of English, although they do not produce actual phonation (any more than the rules in, say, *Sound pattern of English* [Chomsky and Halle 1968]). The description is of the Non-school

FIGURE 1

The features of CBE

	i	i	ī	u	e	ē	ö	ō	æ	a	ā	e	y	w	r	l	p	b	f	v	m	t	d	θ	ð	n	s	z	š	ž	č	j	k	g	ŋ	h
Cons.	−	−	−	−	−	−	−	−	−	−	−	−	−	−	+	+	+	+	+	+	+	+	+	+	+	+	+	+	+	+	+	+	+	+	+	−
Voc.	+	+	+	+	+	+	+	+	+	+	+	+	−	−	+	+	−	−	−	−	−	−	−	−	−	−	−	−	−	−	−	−	−	−	−	−
High	+	+	+	+	−	−	−	−	−	−	−	−	+	+	−	−	−	−	−	−	−	−	−	−	−	−	−	−	+	+	+	+	+	+	+	−
Back	−	−	−	+	−	−	−	+	−	+	+	−	−	+	−	−	−	−	−	−	−	−	−	−	−	−	−	−	−	−	−	−	+	+	+	−
Mid	−	−	−	−	+	+	+	+	−	−	−	+																								
Low	−	−	−	−	−	−	−	−	+	+	+	−																								
Anter.															+	+	+	+	+	+	+	+	+	+	+	+	+	+	−	−	−	−	−	−	−	
Coron.															+	+	−	−	−	−	−	+	+	+	+	+	+	+	+	+	+	+	−	−	−	
Tense	+	−	+	+	−	+	−	+	−	−	+	−																								
Voice	+	+	+	+	+	+	+	+	+	+	+	+	+	+	+	+	−	+	−	+	+	−	+	−	+	+	−	+	−	+	−	+	−	+	+	−
Contin.																	−	−	+	+	−	−	−	+	+	−	+	+	+	+	−	−	−	−	−	+
Nasal																	−	−	−	−	+	−	−	−	−	+	−	−	−	−	−	−	−	−	+	
Strid.																	−	−	+	+	−	−	−	−	−	−	+	+	+	+	+	+	−	−	−	

FIGURE 2

Some phonological rules of CBE/Fla

1.
$$\begin{bmatrix} -\text{cons} \\ -\text{voc} \\ +\text{back} \\ -\text{mid} \\ +\text{tense} \end{bmatrix} \rightarrow \begin{bmatrix} +\text{voc} \\ -\text{back} \\ +\text{mid} \\ -\text{tense} \end{bmatrix} / \begin{bmatrix} +\text{cons} \\ -\text{voc} \\ +\text{hi} \\ -\text{back} \\ -\text{anter} \\ +\text{coron} \\ +\text{contin} \\ +\text{strid} \end{bmatrix}$$
(Sample output: *braš → breš*
həš → heš)

2.
SD: $\# \begin{bmatrix} -\text{cons} \\ +\text{voc} \\ -\text{tense} \end{bmatrix} \begin{bmatrix} +\text{cons} \\ -\text{voc} \end{bmatrix}$
$\qquad\quad 1 \qquad\qquad\quad 2$

SC: $1 \rightarrow [+\text{tense}] \begin{bmatrix} -\text{cons} \\ -\text{voc} \\ -\text{lo} \end{bmatrix}$ *Dipthongization*
(Sample output: *eg → ēəg*
pig → pi͜ig)

3.
$$\begin{bmatrix} +\text{cons} \\ +\text{voc} \\ \langle +\text{anter} \rangle \end{bmatrix} \rightarrow \begin{bmatrix} -\text{cons} \\ -\text{voc} \\ -\text{lo} \end{bmatrix} / \begin{bmatrix} -\text{cons} \\ +\text{voc} \end{bmatrix} \underline{\quad\quad} \left\{ \begin{matrix} C_0 \\ \# \langle C_1 \rangle C_0 V_0 \end{matrix} \right\}$$
Liquid loss
(Sample output:
pɔrt → pɔət
hərz → hə:z)

4.
$$\begin{bmatrix} +\text{cons} \\ -\text{voc} \\ -\text{hi} \\ -\text{back} \\ +\text{anter} \\ +\text{coron} \\ -\text{contin} \end{bmatrix} \rightarrow \begin{bmatrix} +\text{hi} \\ +\text{back} \\ -\text{anter} \\ -\text{coron} \end{bmatrix} / \underline{\quad\quad} \begin{bmatrix} +\text{cons} \\ +\text{voc} \\ -\text{anter} \end{bmatrix}$$
(Sample output:
driym → griym
trəbəl → krəbəl)

(Note: This rule is rare.)

5.
$$\begin{bmatrix} +\text{cons} \\ -\text{voc} \end{bmatrix} \rightarrow \emptyset / \begin{bmatrix} +\text{cons} \\ -\text{voc} \end{bmatrix} \left\{ \begin{matrix} \underline{\quad\quad} \# \\ \begin{bmatrix} -\text{strid} \end{bmatrix} \# \end{matrix} \right\}^{***}$$
Cluster simplification
(Sample output:
kihst → kihs
dahmz → dahm)

(Note: The portion of this process labeled *** may repeat twice, with somewhat lower
probability for the second cycle.)

6. (a)
$$\begin{bmatrix} -\text{cons} \\ +\text{voc} \end{bmatrix} \rightarrow [+\text{nasal}] / \underline{\quad\quad} \begin{bmatrix} +\text{cons} \\ -\text{voc} \\ +\text{nasal} \end{bmatrix}$$
Nasal loss
(Sample output: *brawn → brãw*
kænt → kæht)

(b)
SD: $\begin{bmatrix} -\text{cons} \\ +\text{voc} \\ +\text{nasal} \end{bmatrix} \begin{bmatrix} +\text{cons} \\ -\text{voc} \\ +\text{nasal} \end{bmatrix} \left\{ \begin{matrix} \#V \\ \#C \\ C\#C_0 V_0 \end{matrix} \right\}^{***}$
$\qquad\quad 1 \qquad\qquad\quad 2 \qquad\qquad\quad 3$

SC: $1 \rightarrow [1] \begin{bmatrix} -\text{cons} \\ -\text{voc} \\ -\text{lo} \end{bmatrix}$

SC: $2 \rightarrow \emptyset$

(Note: This rule has a lower probability of occurrence in the context labeled ***).

7.

$$\text{SD:} \begin{bmatrix} +\text{cons} \\ -\text{voc} \\ -\text{back} \\ +\text{coron} \\ +\text{contin} \\ +\text{strid} \end{bmatrix} \# \begin{bmatrix} -\text{cons} \\ -\text{voc} \\ -\text{mid} \\ -\text{lo} \end{bmatrix} \begin{bmatrix} +\text{cons} \\ -\text{voc} \\ -\text{hi} \\ -\text{back} \\ +\text{anter} \\ +\text{coron} \\ +\text{voice} \\ +\text{contin} \end{bmatrix}$$

/−əz/ *loss*
(Sample output:
hawzəz → haws
bušəz → buš)

1   2   3

SC: 1 → [+voice]
SC: 2 3 → Ø

(Note: The rule has a low probability. Its phonological status is dubious; it is treated here as a phonological process because it is almost certainly a very low-level rule caused by surface analogy from instances of final sibilant-loss.)

8.

$$\begin{bmatrix} +\text{cons} \\ -\text{voc} \\ -\text{voice} \\ -\text{contin} \end{bmatrix} \rightarrow \begin{bmatrix} -\text{cons} \\ -\text{voc} \\ -\text{lo} \end{bmatrix} / \text{V} \underline{\quad} \#$$

(Sample output: *kæht → kæh*
leyt → ley)

9.

$$\begin{bmatrix} -\text{cons} \\ -\text{voc} \\ +\text{hi} \\ -\text{back} \end{bmatrix} \rightarrow \varnothing / \begin{bmatrix} -\text{cons} \\ +\text{voc} \\ -\text{hi} \\ -\text{back} \\ -\text{mid} \\ -\text{lo} \end{bmatrix} \underline{\quad} \text{(C)}$$

Monophthongization
(Sample output: *tray → trah*)

10.

$$\begin{bmatrix} +\text{cons} \\ -\text{voc} \\ +\text{strid} \end{bmatrix} \rightarrow \varnothing / \text{V} \underline{\quad} \# \begin{Bmatrix} \begin{bmatrix} +\text{cons} \\ -\text{voc} \end{bmatrix} \\ [+\text{sonor}] \\ \varnothing \end{Bmatrix} {}^{***}$$

(Sample output:
kihs → kih
pliyz livy → pliy liyv)

(Note: The rule has a higher probability of occurrence in the context labeled ***).

11.

$$\text{SD:} \begin{bmatrix} -\text{cons} \\ +\text{voc} \\ \alpha \text{ tense} \\ \langle +\text{hi} \rangle \\ \langle -\text{back} \rangle \end{bmatrix} \begin{bmatrix} -\text{cons} \\ -\text{voc} \\ -\text{lo} \end{bmatrix}$$

1   2

SC: 1 → [−αlong]

$$\text{SC: } 2 \rightarrow \begin{bmatrix} -\alpha \text{seg} \\ -\alpha \begin{bmatrix} \langle +\text{hi} \rangle \\ \langle -\text{back} \rangle \end{bmatrix} \end{bmatrix}$$

(Note: This rule provides the form of the glide: Ø following tense V; *i* following *hi* non-back V; *ə* elsewhere.)

register of CBE. The rules are presented as ordered, although the ordering is only partial, necessitated by the final glide-realization processes and by subrule-ordering in the nasal-loss series. It should be carefully noted that these rules do not derive any form of BE from any form of WE, nor *vice versa*; rather, they show the development of BE from a linguistic competence common to both.

The rules above, which are all phonological processes, account for nearly all the typical differences between CBE and General Shared English. There are only four major exceptions, of which two concern syntactic forms peculiar to CBE alone, and two, processes characteristic of Uneducated English in general. These syntactic differences between CBE and GSE are as follows:

(1) CBE's characteristic disinverted WH-question form, resulting in such utterances as e.g. #why he said that# (phonologically /hwa hiy sey dæh/) for GSE 'why did he say that'.

(2) Either omission of the copula in present-tense contexts (cf. Labov 1969); or omission of the copula contrasted with its presence (in the invariant form /biy/) as an aspect marker. The situation in regard to this feature of CBE, its origin, distribution and function, is far from clear; this author suspects the aspectual use of 'be' to be characteristic of only certain dialects of BE, of which, by and large, Southeastern CBE is not one.

(3) Use of *ain't* and the socalled "double negative", approximately as in other variants of Uneducated English.

(4) Use of epenthetic pronouns (e.g. in such constructions as #my brother he at school# for GSE 'my brother is at school'), again as is typically observable in general Uneducated English (cf. Smith 1968).

Further syntax of CBE speakers is what one would expect from children of this age; it includes use of noun clauses, a full tense system, descriptive adjectives and so forth (cf. Williams 1969), and it is in no way impoverished or deficient. It is also not a different language from General Shared English, so that, as one need hardly add, teaching methods such as those employed in English as a Foreign Language are not appropriate in "correcting" it.

The attempt of this study was to give an account of the language and communication of Southeastern CBE speakers from as eclectic a viewpoint as possible. The study was unfortunately relatively brief and so not comprehensive; but I hope it may help to dispel some current misconceptions connected with the sociolinguistic aspects of Child Black English, and to suggest avenues for further explorations.

Northwestern University

REFERENCES

Baratz, J.
1970 "Educational considerations for teaching Standard English to Negro children", in R. W. Fasold and R. W. Shuy (eds.), *Teaching Standard English in the inner city* (Washington, D.C.: CAL): 20-40.

Bereiter, C. and S. Engelman
   1966   *Teaching disadvantaged children in the preschool* (Englewood Cliffs, N.J.: Prentice-Hall).
Bernstein, B.
   1961   "Social structure, language, and learning", *Ed. Research* 3:163-76.
Blank, M. and F. Solomon
   1968   "A tutorial language program to develop abstract thinking in socially disadvantaged preschool children", *Child Devel.* 39, 2:379-89.
Chall, J.
   1967   *Learning to read: The great debate* (New York: McGraw Hill).
Cheyney, A. B.
   1967   *Teaching culturally disadvantaged in the elementary school* (Columbus, Ohio: Merrill).
Chomsky, N. and M. Halle
   1968   *The sound pattern of English* (New York: Harper & Row).
Fasold, R. W. and W. Wolfram
   1970   "Some linguistic features of Negro dialect", in R. W. Fasold and R. W. Shuy (eds.), *Teaching Standard English in the inner city* (Washington, D.C.: CAL): 41-86.
Houston, S. H.
   1970a "Competence and performance in Child Black English", *Lang. Sci.* 12, Oct.: 9-14.
   1970b "Contingency Grammar: Introduction to a general theory of competence and performance", paper presented to the 45th Annual Meeting of the Linguistic Society of America.
   1972   "Child Black English: The School register", *Linguistics* 90, Oct.: 20-34.
   f.c.   "Syntactic complexity and information transmission in 1st-graders: A cross-cultural study".
Kurath, H. and R. I. McDavid Jr.
   1961   *The pronunciation of English in the Atlantic states* (Ann Arbor: Univ. of Michigan Press).
Labov, W.
   1966   *The social stratification of English in New York City* (Washington, D.C.: CAL).
   1969   "Contraction, deletion and inherent variability of the English copula", *Lang.* 45, 4, Dec.: 715-62.
Malmstrom, J.
   1967   "Dialects", *Florida FL Reporter*, Winter: 1-3.
Riessman, F.
   1962   *The culturally deprived child* (New York: Harper & Row).
Shuy, R.
   1968   "A preliminary investigation of language attitudes in Detroit", paper presented to the American Dialect Society.
Smith, R.
   1968   "The interrelatedness of certain deviant grammatical structures in Negro Nonstandard Dialect", paper presented to the American Dialect Society.
Stewart, W. A.
   1968   "Continuity and change in American Negro dialects", *Florida FL Reporter* Spring: 1-6.
Williams, C. E.
   1969   "On the contribution of the linguist to institutionalized racism", paper presented to the 44th Annual Meeting of the Linguistic Society of America.
Wolfram, W. A.
   1969   *A sociolinguistic description of Detroit Negro speech* (Washington, D.C.: CAL).

G. RICHARD TUCKER and WALLACE E. LAMBERT

WHITE AND NEGRO LISTENERS' REACTIONS
TO VARIOUS AMERICAN-ENGLISH DIALECTS

In recent years, a useful technique has been developed at McGill University to measure, in an indirect fashion, the views that members of one social group have of representatives of some other contrasting group. Described briefly, a sample of "judges" is asked to listen to a series of taped recordings of different speakers reading a standard passage, and to evaluate relevant personality characteristics of each speaker, using only voice characteristics and speech style as cues. The technique appears to expose the listeners' more private feelings and stereotyped attitudes toward a contrasting group or groups whose language, accent, or dialect is distinctive, and it appears to be reliable in that the same profile of reactions emerges on repeated sampling from a particular social group. The procedure has been used to compare the reactions of judges listening to the two guises of bilingual speakers presenting (a) contrasting languages, (b) contrasting dialects, or (c) contrasting accents.[1]

An earlier version of this study was presented at the E.P.A. meetings in Boston, 1967. This research was financed in part by research grants from the Canadian Defense Research Board and from The Canada Council, and by a grant from the Rockefeller Foundation to W. N. Francis at Brown University. Reprinted with permission from *Social Forces* 47 (1969).
[1] M. Anisfeld, N. Bogo, and W. E. Lambert, "Evaluational Reactions to Accented English Speech", *Journal of Abnormal and Social Psychology* 65 (1962): 223-31; Elizabeth Anisfeld and W. E. Lambert, "Evaluational Reactions of Bilingual and Monolingual Children to Spoken Languages", *Journal of Abnormal and Social Psychology* 69 (1964): 89-97; W. E. Lambert, R. C. Hodgson, R. C. Gardner, and S. Fillenbaum, "Evaluational Reactions to Spoken Languages", *Journal of Abnormal and Social Psychology* 60 (1960): 44-51; W. E. Lambert, M. Anisfeld, and Grace Yeni-Komshian, "Evaluational Reactions of Jewish and Arab Adolescents to Dialect

370   *G. Richard Tucker and Wallace E. Lambert*

The present research extends the basic technique and focuses on the reactions of white and Negro college students to various exemplars of white and Negro American-English speech. The study was guided by the practical and theoretical significance of two questions: (1) Are both white and Negro subjects sensitive enough to dialect variations to make reliable differentiations? (2) If so, will there emerge a meaningful pattern of dialect preferences i.e. some particularly favored and others disfavored?

METHOD

Development of Rating Scales

To be most useful, the rating scales provided listeners for evaluating speakers should be developed specifically for the samples of subjects to be examined. In this case,[2] scales were chosen with two ends in mind: (a) positive rating should indicate that the listener believes the speakers could attain or have already attained "success", and (b) that speakers are "friendly". Thus, success should not imply separation from or mobility out of the group represented by the speaker.

With this purpose in mind, students from a small southern Negro college were asked to indicate those traits which they considered important for friendship and those important for success. Their responses were tabulated and the traits ranked in order of popularity. They were then asked to give free associations to and synonyms for some of the trait names, and finally to choose, from a larger list of traits drawn from previous research using the same technique, those they considered important for friendship and those important for success. The rating scales finally used were selected on the basis of this initial survey. Bipolar rating scales were constructed by pairing a positive and a negative adjective with each trait (e.g. good upbringing, poor upbringing; good disposition, bad disposition; considerate, inconsiderate). Two of the traits, speaking ability and good upbringing, were not spontaneously suggested by the students, but were added because we believed they were appropriate for our purposes. Similar pilot work with traits suggested by

and Language Variations", *Journal of Personality and Social Psychology* 2 (1965): 84-90; W. E. Lambert, Hannah Frankel, and G. R. Tucker, "Judging Personality Through Speech: A French-Canadian Example", *The Journal of Communications* 4 (1966): 305-21; N. N. Markel, R. M. Eisler, and H. W. Reese, "Judging Personality From Dialect", *Journal of Verbal Learning and Verbal Behavior* 6 (1967): 33-35; and M. S. Preston, "Evaluational Reactions to English, Canadian French and European French Voices", unpublished M.A. thesis, McGill University (1963).
[2] Miss Marilen Picard, now a graduate student at the University of Western Ontario, assisted us in this phase of the study.

white college students permitted us to decide on a set of scales useful for all three groups.

Selection of Stimulus Voices

The dialect samples were selected by trained dialectologists, specialized in variations in American speech styles. Recordings were made of 4 representatives of each of 6 dialect groups: (1) speakers of *Network* English (the typical mode of speaking of national newscasters); (2) college-*Educated White Southern* speakers; (3) college-*Educated Negro Southern* speakers; (4) college-Educated Negro speakers from Mississippi presently attending *Howard University* in Washington, D.C.; (5) southern Negro students, referred to as the *Mississippi Peer* group, who spoke a dialect similar to that used by most students at the Negro college where the actual testing was carried out; and (6) alumni from this college who have since lived for several years in New York City — *New York Alumni.* All speakers in groups 1 and 2 were white, while those in groups 3, 4, 5 and 6 were Negro.

Each speaker read aloud the same passage, a short one requiring about forty-five seconds to read. The context of the passage was simple and neutral as to emotional value. Both male and female speakers were chosen to represent each dialect group except for the Educated White Southern group which, because of an oversight, included only males. The 24 recordings (6 dialects and 4 representatives of each) were placed on two separate tapes, making two groups of 12 recordings each, with each dialect group represented by two voices on each tape. A "practice" voice was also added at the beginning of each tape.

Subjects

The subjects were 150 male and female freshmen from a southern Negro college, 40 white male and female students from a New England university, and 68 white male and female students from a southern university.

Experimental Procedure

The testing was carried out on the three campuses, and the procedure was the same for all groups. The students serving as "judges" were asked to listen to the voices on one of the two tapes and to evaluate each speaker in terms of the traits listed in Table 1. A separate rating sheet was provided for the evaluation of each speaker, and the order of adjective placement on the sheet was alternated. Standard instructions and examples were given to explain the testing procedure and the use of the 8-point rating scales.

TABLE 1

Mean Ratings[a] and Ranks of Mean Ratings[b] of each Dialect Type by Northern White University Students

Dialect Groups	Traits															Sum
	Upbringing	Intelligent	Friendly	Educated	Disposition	Speech	Trustworthy	Ambitious	Faith-God	Talented	Character	Determination	Honest	Personality	Considerate	
Network	6.8 [1]	6.7 [1]	5.8 [2]	7.2 [1]	6.0 [1]	6.7 [1]	6.3 [1]	5.8 [1]	5.3 [2]	6.1 [1]	6.4 [1]	5.9 [2]	6.2 [1]	6.1 [1]	6.3 [1]	[18]
Educated Negro Southern	5.4 [3]	5.5 [3]	5.7 [3]	5.1 [3]	5.4 [4]	4.7 [3]	5.8 [2]	5.6 [2]	5.8 [1]	5.2 [3]	6.0 [2]	6.0 [1]	5.9 [2]	5.3 [4]	5.7 [2]	[39]
Educated White Southern	6.0 [2]	5.8 [2]	5.6 [4]	5.7 [2]	5.5 [3]	5.5 [2]	5.6 [3]	5.2 [3]	5.2 [3]	5.3 [2]	5.7 [4]	5.5 [3]	5.6 [4]	5.5 [3]	5.6 [3]	[44]
Howard University	5.2 [4]	5.4 [4]	6.0 [1]	4.6 [4]	5.9 [2]	4.6 [4]	5.6 [3]	5.1 [4]	5.2 [4]	5.1 [4]	5.9 [3]	5.2 [4]	5.8 [3]	5.9 [2]	5.6 [4]	[48]
New York Alumni	4.6 [5]	4.5 [6]	5.3 [5]	3.5 [6]	5.0 [5]	3.1 [6]	5.2 [5]	4.5 [5]	5.1 [5]	3.9 [6]	5.2 [5]	4.9 [5]	5.5 [5]	5.0 [6]	5.3 [5]	[80]
Mississippi Peer	4.3 [6]	5.0 [5]	5.1 [6]	3.9 [5]	5.0 [6]	3.3 [5]	4.9 [6]	4.4 [6]	4.9 [6]	4.1 [5]	5.0 [6]	4.5 [6]	5.1 [6]	5.1 [5]	4.8 [6]	[85]
Dialect difference, F ratios: ($df = 5,175$)[c]	22.5	14.3	2.0	35.1	4.9	35.7	6.5	5.5	3.0	14.5	6.1	7.3	4.6	3.4	3.9	

[a] Mean ratings are rounded to one decimal place.
[b] Ranks of mean ratings are set in brackets.
[c] All F ratios except that for the trait "Friendly" are significant at or beyond the 0.05 level of confidence.

TABLE 2

Mean Ratings[a] and Ranks of Mean Ratings[b] of each Dialect Type by Southern Negro College Students

Dialect Groups	Traits															Sum
	Upbringing	Intelligent	Friendly	Educated	Disposition	Speech	Trustworthy	Ambitious	Faith-God	Talented	Character	Determination	Honest	Personality	Considerate	
Network	6.4 [1]	6.5 [1]	6.2 [1]	6.6 [1]	6.2 [1]	6.3 [1]	6.3 [1]	6.0 [1]	6.0 [1]	6.0 [1]	6.4 [1]	5.9 [1]	6.3 [1]	6.4 [1]	6.3 [1]	[15]
Educated Negro Southern	5.8 [2]	5.8 [2]	5.5 [3]	5.8 [2]	5.2 [3]	5.1 [2]	5.7 [3]	5.4 [2]	5.6 [2]	5.3 [2]	5.5 [3]	5.4 [2]	5.6 [3]	5.4 [3]	5.3 [3]	[37]
Howard University	5.3 [3]	5.4 [3]	5.7 [2]	5.2 [3]	5.6 [2]	4.2 [3]	5.7 [2]	5.0 [3]	5.4 [3]	4.7 [3]	5.8 [2]	4.9 [3]	5.8 [2]	5.8 [2]	5.7 [2]	[38]
Mississippi Peer	4.9 [4]	4.8 [4]	5.4 [4]	4.4 [4]	4.9 [4]	3.4 [4]	5.2 [4]	4.6 [4]	5.2 [4]	4.1 [4]	5.0 [4]	4.4 [4]	5.4 [4]	5.0 [4]	4.7 [4]	[60]
New York Alumni	4.9 [5]	4.8 [5]	5.0 [5]	4.3 [5]	4.6 [5]	3.4 [5]	5.0 [5]	4.6 [5]	4.9 [5]	3.9 [5]	4.8 [5]	4.2 [5]	5.2 [5]	4.7 [5]	4.4 [5]	[74]
Educated White Southern	4.4 [6]	4.4 [6]	4.2 [6]	4.2 [6]	4.1 [6]	3.3 [6]	4.6 [6]	4.0 [6]	4.8 [6]	3.7 [6]	4.4 [6]	4.0 [6]	5.1 [6]	4.1 [6]	4.2 [6]	[90]
Dialect differences, F ratios: ($df = 5,720$)[c]	42.7	56.2	26.6	77.7	39.3	107.7	29.5	32.2	14.6	60.9	38.1	41.0	16.7	37.9	37.8	

[a] Mean ratings are rounded to one decimal place.

[b] Ranks of mean ratings are set in brackets.

[c] All these F ratios are significant beyond the 0.01 level of significance.

TABLE 3

Mean Ratings[a] and Ranks[b] of Mean Ratings of each Dialect Type by Southern White College Students

Dialect Groups	Upbringing	Intelligent	Friendly	Educated	Disposition	Speech	Trustworthy	Ambitious	Faith-God	Talented	Character	Determination	Honest	Personality	Considerate	Sum
												Traits				
Network	6.7 [1]	6.6 [1]	5.9 [1]	7.0 [1]	6.1 [1]	6.8 [1]	6.2 [1]	6.3 [1]	5.4 [1]	6.3 [1]	6.4 [1]	6.0 [1]	6.2 [1]	6.1 [1]	6.2 [1]	[15]
Educated White Southern	6.2 [2]	6.2 [2]	5.8 [2]	6.5 [2]	5.9 [2]	5.4 [2]	6.1 [2]	5.8 [3]	5.1 [3]	5.6 [2]	6.0 [2]	5.6 [3]	6.0 [2]	5.8 [2]	5.8 [2]	[33]
Educated Negro Southern	5.9 [3]	5.9 [3]	5.5 [4]	6.1 [3]	5.5 [4]	5.2 [3]	5.6 [3]	5.9 [2]	5.3 [2]	5.3 [3]	5.8 [3]	5.7 [2]	5.9 [3]	5.6 [3]	5.7 [3]	[44]
Howard University	4.9 [4]	5.0 [4]	5.6 [3]	4.8 [4]	5.6 [3]	3.8 [4]	5.4 [4]	5.1 [4]	5.1 [5]	4.4 [4]	5.4 [4]	4.7 [5]	5.4 [4]	5.5 [4]	5.6 [4]	[60]
New York Alumni	4.6 [5]	4.5 [5]	4.8 [6]	4.2 [5]	4.8 [6]	3.0 [5]	5.0 [5]	4.6 [5]	5.1 [4]	3.8 [6]	5.3 [5]	4.7 [4]	5.3 [5]	4.7 [6]	4.8 [6]	[78]
Mississippi Peer	4.0 [6]	4.2 [6]	5.2 [5]	3.9 [6]	4.9 [5]	−3.0 [6]	4.8 [6]	4.3 [6]	4.8 [6]	3.9 [5]	4.9 [6]	4.4 [6]	5.0 [6]	5.0 [5]	4.8 [5]	[84]
Dialect differences, F ratios: (df = 5,63)[c]	53.1	40.8	7.6	65.1	12.6	78.2	15.6	26.7	1.3	41.1	16.7	17.4	10.4	12.3	16.1	

[a] Mean ratings are rounded to one decimal place.
[b] Ranks of mean ratings are set in brackets.
[c] All these F ratios are reliable at or beyond the 0.05 level of significance except that for the trait Faith in God.

First, the practice voice was played and the judges made their ratings. All questions were answered and the formal testing session began. Each speaker's taped passage was played twice, separated by a five-second pause, and thirty seconds were given for judges to complete their evaluations before the next speaker's recording was played. Each judge evaluated 12 speakers in addition to the practice voice.

Method of Data Analysis

A number from 1 to 8 was assigned to each rating. The positive end of each scale was arbitrarily given the value 8, and the negative end the value 1. The ratings produced by the two groups of male judges were combined as were those of the female judges. This was done for each of the dialect groups and for each of the 15 traits, making it possible to determine, for instance, how favorably the southern Negro male in contrast to the female judges rated any one of the 6 dialect groups on any particular trait.

A three-way analysis of variance, repeated-measures design with corrections for unequal sample size,[3] was performed separately on the responses of the southern Negro and northern white judging groups for each of the 15 traits. A separate analysis was performed for the responses of the southern white group of judges. This statistical analysis indicates (1) whether the dialects were rated differentially (e.g. whether different ratings were given to the Network speakers than to the Howard University speakers), (2) whether male and female judges responded differently, and (3) whether there were differences in the reactions to the members of the dialect groups separated on the two tapes.

RESULTS AND DISCUSSION

The results are summarized in Tables 1, 2, and 3 where the ratings by each group of judges for the 15 traits are presented. The column marked "total" provides an index of the overall ranking of each group over all traits. In these comparisons, the ratings of male and female judges are combined since there were, for the most part, no sex differences in patterns of response. In the few instances where sex differences in responding did occur, the females tended to rate the speakers slightly more favorably.

The statistical analyses show that each group of judges clearly differentiates the various dialects. The most pronounced trend noted for all

³ B. J. Winer, *Statistical Principles in Experimental Design* (New York: McGraw-Hill Book Co., 1962).

three groups of judges was the nearly unanimous perception of the Network speakers as having the most favorable profile of traits. This dialect group was considered as most favorable by the Negro judges AND by the southern white judges on every trait, and by the northern white judges on 12 of the 15 traits.

The dialect group rated next most favorably by both northern white and southern Negro judges was the Educated Negro Southern. In fact, the northern white judges thought that the Educated Negro Southern speakers had slightly more "faith in God" and were more "determined" than the Network speakers. The Negro judges, however, rated these speakers only slightly more favorably than the Howard University group. The southern white judges, on the other hand, rated speakers belonging to their own peer group (i.e. Southern Educated White) in the second position followed by the Educated Negro Southern speakers.

A very interesting contrast emerges in the choice of the least favored group. The Negro judges rated the Educated White Southern speakers least favorably on every one of the 15 traits, whereas the white judges, both northern and southern, rated the Mississippi Peer speakers least favorably, and the New York Alumni speakers only slightly higher.

The two groups of white judges were also asked to indicate what they thought the race of each speaker was.[4] The following percentages indicate the northern white judges' estimates of the race of the speakers representing each dialect group: Network, 95 percent white; Educated White Southern, 87 percent white; New York Alumni, 49 percent Negro; Educated Negro Southern, 49 percent Negro; Howard University, 84 percent Negro; and Mississippi Peer, 94 percent Negro. The following percentages indicate the southern white judges' estimates: Network, 98 percent white; Educated White Southern, 96 percent white; Educated Negro Southern, 47 percent Negro; New York Alumni, 54 percent Negro; Howard University, 70 percent Negro; and Mississippi Peer, 89 percent Negro.

Although incidental to the central theme of this study, these results indicate that further research on judges' estimates of a speaker's race would be valuable. There is here an interesting relation between the perceived favorableness of a speaker and his perceived race. From a consideration of the extreme cases, e.g. the Network in contrast to the Mississippi Peer group, it might appear that speakers thought of as being white are judged favorably while those perceived as Negro are judged relatively unfavorably. But this generalization doesn't hold since the New York Alumni group is seen as being more likely white than is the Howard University group, and yet the New York Alumni group is less

---

[4] In the context of the experiment, it would have been inappropriate to ask this question of the Negro students.

favorably rated. One might then argue that the New York Alumni group is looked on suspiciously because racial background is not clear from speech style in this case, but this explanation doesn't hold since the Negro Educated Southern group is also ambiguous as to race and yet it is clearly regarded more favorably than the New York Alumni by both groups of white judges.

In summary, several instructive results have come to light. First, subjects were able to reliably differentiate the dialect groups and they clearly favored the Network style of spoken English in comparison with the other styles. There are, of course, limits to the generalizability of this finding because of the sampling of stimulus voices. Many speakers could have been selected for each of the 6 dialect groups, and we used only small samples. Thus, the reliability of these results can only be determined through repeat studies, using new samples of stimulus speakers.

The second noteworthy finding concerns the different perspectives of the white and Negro judges regarding the least favorable of the dialects. These differences in views likely reflect basic comparisons in affectively-toned attitudes that representatives of America's major ethnic groups hold toward one another. The contrasts also make it evident that speech styles which are pleasing to one social group will not necessarily be so perceived by another.

In the third place, the results indicate that white judges can, in certain instances at least, distinguish white from Negro speakers. Much more research is needed, of course, to examine this question in depth. This finding, however, suggests some interesting next steps in research, calling for cooperation of dialectologists and psychologists. For instance, certain COMBINATIONS of dialect features might enhance or depress the perceived pleasantness of speech styles. A fusion of Network and Educated Southern White characteristics might be particularly attractive for certain listeners, say southern whites, whereas Network-Educated Southern Negro mixtures might be most appealing to southern and northern Negro listeners.

McGill University

REFERENCES FOR THE INTRODUCTIONS

Abrahams, Roger D.
1962 "Playing the dozens", *Journal of American Folklore* XXV:209-220.
1964 *Deep Down in the Jungle* (Hatsboro, Pennsylvania).
1968 "Public drama and common values in two Caribbean islands", *Trans-Action* July-August: 62-71.
Aguirre Beltrán, Gonzalo
1958 *Cuijla, Esbozo Etnográfico de un Pueblo Negro* (Mexico).
Alleyne, Mervyn
1971 "Acculturation and the cultural matrix of creolization", in Hymes (ed.), *Pidginization and Creolization of Language* (London).
Álvarez Nazario, Manuel
1961 *El Elemento Afronegroïde en el Español de Puerto Rico* (San Juan).
Atkins, John
1732 *A Voyage to Guinea, Brazil, and the West Indies* (London).
Atwood, E. Bagby
1953 *A Survey of Verb Forms in the Eastern United States* (Ann Arbor, Michigan).
Bailey, Beryl Loftman
1965 "A new perspective on American Negro dialectology", *American Speech* XI:171-77.
Baratz, Joan C.
1969 "A bi-dialectical task for determining language proficiency in economically disadvantaged Negro children", *Child Development* 40, 3:889-900.
1973 "Language abilities of Black Americans, Review of Research: 1966-70", in Miller and Dreger, *Comparative Studies of Negroes and Whites in the United States* (Basic Books).
Baratz, Joan C. and Roger W. Shuy (eds.)
1969 *Teaching Black Children to Read* (Washington, D.C.).
Baratz, Joan C., Roger W. Shuy and Walter Wolfram
1969 "Sociolinguistic Factors in Speech Identification", Final Report, NIMH Grant no. 15048.

Baratz, Joan C. and Stephen
1969 "Early childhood intervention: The social science basis of institutional racism", *Harvard Educational Review*.
Bascom, W. R. and Melville J. Herskovits
1962 *Continuity and Change in African Cultures* (Chicago).
Baumann, Heinrich
1877 *Londinismen (Slang and Cant) Wörterbuch der Londoner Volkssprache* (Berlin-Schöneberg).
Bereiter, Carl and Sigfried Engelmann
1966 *Teaching Disadvantaged Children in the Pre-School* (Englewood Cliffs, N.J.).
Bereiter, Carl, Sigfried Engelmann, Jean Osborn, and P. A. Reidford
1966 "An academically oriented preschool for culturally deprived children", in Hechinger (ed.), *Pre-School Education Today* (New York).
Bernard, J. R. L-B.
1969 "On the uniformity of spoken Australian English", *Orbis* XVIII:63-73.
Berreman, Gerald D.
1961 "Caste in India and the United States", *American Journal of Sociology* 66:120-27.
Bickerton, Derek and Aquilas Escalante
1970 "Palenquero: A Spanish-based creole of Northern Columbia", *Lingua* 24: 254-67.
Blanc, Haim
1964 *Communal Dialects of Baghdad Arabic* (Harvard University Press).
Bloomfield, Leonard
1933 *Language* (New York).
Brewer, J. Mason
1947 "Afro-American Folklore", *Journal of American Folklore* 60:372-83.
1958 *Dog Ghosts and Other Texas Folk Tales* (Austin).
1968 *American Negro Folklore* (Chicago).
Brooks, Cleanth
1935 *The Relation of the Alabama- Georgia Dialect to the Provincial Dialects of Great Britain* (Baton Rouge, Louisiana).
Buck, Joyce
1968 "The effects of Negro and white dialectical variations upon attitudes of college students", *Speech Monographs*: 181-86.
Cabrera, Lydia
1957 *Anagó; Vocabulario Lucumí (el Yoruba que se habla en Cuba)* (Havana).
1959 *La Sociedad Secreta Abakuá, Narrada por Viejos Adeptos* (Havana).
1968 *El Monte, Igbo, Finda, Ewe Orishi, Vititi Nfinda* (Miami).
Campbell, Duncan
1873 *Nova Scotia in Its Historical, Mercantile, and Industrial Relations* (Montreal).
Cassidy, Frederic G.
1961 *Jamaica Talk* (London).
1962 "Toward the recovery of early English-African pidgin", Symposium on Multilingualism (Brazzaville).
1971 "Tracing the pidgin element in Jamaican Creole", in Hymes (ed.), *Pidginization and Creolization of Language* (London).
Catalán, Diego
1958 "Génesis del españo atlántico", *Revista de Historia Canaria* XXIV, núms. 123-124.
Chafe, Wallace L.
1970 *Meaning and the Structure of Language* (Chicago).

Chomsky, Noam
  1957 *Syntactic Structures* (The Hague).
  1959 "Review of B. F. Skinner, *Verbal Behavior*", *Language*.
  1965 *Aspects of the Theory of Syntax* (Cambridge, Massachusetts).
  1966 *Cartesian Linguistics: A Chapter in the History of Rationalist Thought* (New York).
  1968 *Language and Mind* (New York).
Chomsky, Noam and Morris Halle
  1968 *The Sound Pattern of English* (New York).
Cohen, Hennig
  1952 "A Southern colonial word list: Addenda to the DA", *American Speech* XXVII:282-84.
Cohen, S. Allen
  1969 *Teach Them All to Read: Theory, Methods, and Materials for Teaching the Disadvantaged* (New York).
Courlander, Harold
  1963 *Negro Folk Music, U.S.A.* (New York).
Crum, Mason
  1940 *Gullah: Negro Life in the Carolina Sea Islands* (Durham, North Carolina).
Dalby, David
  1969 *Black Through White: Patterns of Communication in Africa and the New World* (Bloomington, Indiana).
  1972 "The African element in Black American English", in Thomas Kochman (ed.), *Rappin' and Stylin' Out; Communication in Urban Black America* (Champaign, Illinois).
Davis, Lawrence M.
  1969 "Dialect research: Mythology and reality", *Orbis*.
  1971 "Social dialectology in America: A critical survey", *Journal of English Linguistics*.
DeCamp, David
  1967 "African day names in Jamaica", *Language* 43:139-47.
  1971 "Toward a generative analysis of a post-creole speech continuum", in Dell Hymes (ed.), *Pidginization and Creolization of Language* (London).
De Granda, German
  1968a *Materiales para el estudio sociohistórico de los elementos lingüísticos afro-americanos en el área hispánica* (Bogotá, Instituto Caro y Cuervo).
  1968b *Sobre el estudio de las hablas "criollas" en el área hispánica* (Bogotá, Instituto Caro y Cuervo).
Deutsch, Cynthia
  1964 "Auditory discrimination and learning: Social factors", *Merrill-Palmer Quarterly* 10:277-96.
Deutsch, Martin
  1965 "The role of social class in language development and cognition", *American Journal of Orthopsychiatry* 35:24-35.
Deutsch, Martin and Bert R. Brown
  1967 "Social influences in Negro-white intelligence differences", in Deutsch and associates, *The Disadvantaged Child* (New York).
Dickinson, Jonathan
  1697 *Jonathan Dickinson's Journal; or, God's Protecting Providence, Being the Narrative of a Journey from Port Royal in Jamaica to Philadelphia Between August 20, 1696 and April 1, 1697* (reprinted 1945, New Haven, Conn.).
Dillard, J. L.
  1968 "On the grammar of Afro-American naming practices", *Names*.

1969a "The DARE-ing old men on their flying isoglosses", *Florida FL Reporter*.
1969b "Standard average foreign in Puerto Rican Spanish", in Atwood and Hill (eds.), *Studies in Language, Literature and Culture of the Middle Ages and Later* (Austin, Texas).
1971 "Black English in New York", *The English Record* (Anthology on Language Issue).
1972 *Black English, Its History and Usage in the United States* (New York).
1973 "The History of Black English in Nova Scotia: A first step. *Inter American Review* II, 4.

Dollard, John
1937 *Class and Caste in a Southern Town* (New Haven, Conn.).

Dorson, Richard
1959 *American Folklore* (Chicago).

Drake, Samuel G.
1866 *The Witchcraft Delusion in New England* (Roxbury, Massachusetts).

Fasold, Ralph W.
1972 *Tense Marking in Black English, A Linguistic and Social Analysis* (*Urban Language Series* 8) (Washington, D.C.).

Fauset, Arthur Huff
1927 "Negro folk tales from the South", *Journal of American Folklore* 4.

Fickett, Joan G.
1970 *Aspects of Morphemics, Syntax, and Semology of an Inner-City Dialect, "Merican"* (West Rush, N.Y.).

Fisher, Miles Mark
1953 *Negro Slave Songs in the United States* (New York).

Fisher, Ruth
n.d. *Extracts from the Records of the African Companies* (Washington, D.C.).

Frazier, E. Franklin
1957 *Black Bourgeoisie* (New York).

Furman, Gabriel
1875 *Antiquities of Long Island* (New York).

Goeje, C. H. de
1906 "Bijdrage tot de Ethnographie de Surinaamsche Indianen", *Supplement zu Internationales Archiv für Ethnographie*, Band XVII.

Gold, Robert S.
1964 *A Jazz Lexicon* (New York).

Goodman, Morris
1964 *A Comparative Study of French Creole Dialects* (New York).

Goveia, Else V.
1964 *Slave Society in the British Leeward Islands at the End of the Eighteenth Century* (= *Institute of Caribbean Studies*, 8).

Greaves, Ida
1930 "The Negro in Canada", *McGill Economic Studies*.

Greene, Lorenzo Johnston
1942 "The Negro in Colonial New England, 1620-1776", *Columbia University Studies in History, Economics and Public Law*, 494.

Gumperz, John
1958 "Dialect differences and social stratification in a North Indian Village", *American Anthropologist*.

Hall, Robert A., Jr.
1966 *Pidgin and Creole Languages* (Ithaca, New York).

Hancock, Ian F.
1969 "A provisional comparison of the English-based Atlantic Creoles", *African Language Review* VII:7-72.
1971 "A survey of the pidgins and creoles of the world", in Dell Hymes (ed.), *Pidginization and Creolization of Language* (London).
1972 "A domestic origin for the English-derived Atlantic Creoles", *Florida FL Reporter*.
Hattori, Shiro
1964 "A special language of the older generations among the Ainu", *Linguistics* 6:43-58.
Herskovits, Melville J.
1941 *The Myth of the Negro Past* (Boston).
Herskovits, Melville J. and Frances S. Herskovits
1936 "Suriname Folk-Lore", *Columbia University Contributions in Anthropology* XXVII.
Hesseling, D. C.
1905 *Het Negerhollands der Deense Antillen, Bijdrage tot de Geschiedenis der Nederlandse Taal in Amerika* (Leiden).
Hoetink, Hermannus
1962 "Americans in Samaná", *Caribbean Studies* II:3-22.
Horner, Vivian and Joan D. Gussow
1972 "John and Mary: A pilot study in linguistic ecology", in Cazden, Hymes, and John (eds.), *Functions of Language in the Classroom* (New York).
Horsmanden, Daniel
1744 *The New York Conspiracy, or a History of the Negro Plot, with the Journal of the Proceedings Against the Conspirators at New York in the Years 1741-42* (New York).
Houston, Susan
1972 *Psycholinguistics* (The Hague).
Jackson, Bruce
1967 *The Negro and His Folklore in Nineteenth Century Periodicals* (Austin, Texas).
Jensen, Arthur R.
1969 "How much can we boost IQ and scholastic achievement?" *Harvard Educational Review*.
John, Vera P.
1963 "The intellectual development of slum children", *American Journal of Orthopsychiatry* 33:813-22.
Jones, E.
1962 "Mid-nineteenth century evidences of a Sierra Leone patois", *Sierra Leone Language Review* 1:19-26.
Jones, LeRoi
1963 *Blues People* (New York).
Jones, Morgan E.
1962 "A Phonological Study of English as Spoken by Puerto Ricans Contrasted with Puerto Rican Spanish and American English", University of Michigan dissertation.
Josselin de Jong, J. P. B. de
1924 *Het Negerhollandsch van St. Thomas en St. Jan* (Amsterdam).
Katz, Jerrold J. and Paul M. Postal
1964 *An Integrated Theory of Linguistic Descriptions* (Cambridge, Mass.).
Keil, Charles
1966 *Urban Blues* (Chicago).

Kloeke, G. G.
1927   *De Hollandsche Expansie* (= *Noord- en Zuidhollandsche Dialectbibliotheek*, 2) (The Hague).
Kochman, Thomas
1969   "Rapping in the Black Ghetto", *Transaction*.
Krapp, George Philip
1924   "The English of the Negro", *American Mercury* II:190-95.
1925   *The English Language in America* (New York).
Kurath, Hans
1928   "The origin of dialectical differences in spoken American English", *Modern Philology* XXV.
1936   "The Linguistic Atlas of the United States and Canada", in Daniel Jones and D. B. Frey (eds.), *Proceedings of the Second International Congress of Phonetic Sciences* (Cambridge, Mass.).
1965   "Some aspects of Atlantic seaboard English considered in connection with British English", *Communication et Rapports, Troisième Partie* (Louvain).
Labov, William
1966   *The Social Stratification of English in New York City* (Washington, D.C..)
1969a "The logic of nonstandard English", in Alatis (ed.), *Monograph* 22 (Georgetown University School of Languages and Linguistics, Washington, D.C.).
1969b "Contraction, deletion, and inherent variability of the English copula", *Language* 45:715-62.
Labov, William, Paul Cohen, Clarence Robins, and John Lewis
1968   "A Study of the Non-standard English of Negro and Puerto Rican Speakers in New York City", *U.S. Office of Education, Cooperative Research Project* no. 3288.
Lambert, W. E., M. Anisfeld, and G. Yeni-Komsian
1965   "Evaluational reactions of Jewish and Arab adolescents to dialect and language variations", *Journal of Personality and Social Psychology* 2.
Lambert, Wallace and G. Richard Tucker
1969   "White and Negro listener's reactions to various American-English dialects", *Social Forces* 47:463-68.
Leechman, Douglas and Robert A. Hall, Jr.
1955   "American Indian Pidgin English: Attestations and grammatical peculiarities", *America Speech* 30:163-71.
LePage, Robert
1971   "Review of Arne Zettersten, The English of Tristan da Cunha", *Lingua*.
Loban, Walter
1967   *Problems in Oral English: Kindergarten through Grade Nine* (Champaign, Illinois, NCTE).
Loflin, Marvin D.
1967   "A note on the deep structure of non-standard English in Washington, D.C.", *Glossa* I:26-32.
1969   "Negro non-standard and standard English: Same or different deep structure?", *Orbis* XVIII:74-91.
1970   "On the structure of the verb in a dialect of American Negro English", *Linguistics* 59:14-28.
Loman, Bengt
1968   *Conversations in a Negro American Dialect* (= *Urban Language Series* 2) (Washington, D.C.).
Lomax, Alan
1950   *Mister Jelly Roll* (New York).

1968   "Folk Song Style and Culture", *American Association for the Advancement of Science*, Publication no. 88.
Loon, L. G. van
1938   *Crumbs from an Old Dutch Closet; the Dutch Dialect of Old New York* (The Hague).
Luelsdorff, Philip A.
f.c.   *Segmental Phonology of Black English* (The Hague).
Mason, Julian
1960   "The etymology of *buckaroo*", *American Speech* XXXV:51-55.
Matthews, W.
1935   "Sailors' pronunciation in the second half of the seventeenth century", *Anglia* LIX:192-251.
McDavid, Raven I, Jr. and Virginia Glenn McDavid
1951   "The relationship of the speech of American Negroes to the speech of whites", *American Speech* XXVI:3-16.
Miller, Mary Rita
1967   "Attestations of American Indian Pidgin English in fiction and non-fiction", *American Speech* XLII:142-47.
Morgan, Raleigh
1959   "Structural sketch of Saint Martin Creole", *Anthropological Linguistics* I:20-24.
1960   "The lexicon of Saint Martin Creole", *Anthropological Linguistics* II:7-29.
Nathan, Hans
1962   *Dan Emmett and the Rise of Early Negro Minstrelsy* (Norman, Oklahoma).
Neto, Serafim da Silva
1950   "Falares Crioulos", *Brasilia* 5:1-28.
Nida, Eugene and Harold Fehdereau
1970   "Indigenous pidgins and koinés", *International Journal of American Linguistics*.
Oliver, Paul
1963   *The Meaning of the Blues* (New York).
Olmsted, Frederick Law
1861   *The Cotton Kingdom: A Traveler's Observation on Cotton and Slavery in the American Southern States* (New York).
Ottley, Roi and William J. Weatherby
1967   *The Negro in New York* (New York).
Owen, Mary Alicia
1893   *Old Rabbit the Voodoo, And Other Sorcerers* (London) (Also published as *Voodoo Tales, As Told Among the Negroes of the Southwest, Collected from Original Sources* [New York, 1893]).
Pfaff, C.
1971   *Historical and Structural Aspects of Sociolinguistic Variations: The Copula in Black English* (Inglewood, Calif.).
Pierson, Donald
1967   *Negroes in Brazil: A Study of Race Contact at Bahia* (Carbondale, Illinois).
Politzer, Robert L.
1971   "Developmental Aspects of the Awareness of the Standard/Non-standard Dialect Contrast", *Stanford Center for Research and Development in Teaching*. Memorandum no. 72.
Politzer, Robert L. and Mary R. Hoover
1972   "The Development of Awareness of the Black Standard/Black Non-standard Dialectic Contrast Among Primary School Children: A Pilot Study", *Stanford Center for Research and Development in Teaching*. Memorandum no. 83.

Politzer, Robert L. and Sheila McMahon
 1970 "Auditory discrimination performance of pupils from English- and Spanish-speaking homes", *Stanford Center for Research and Development in Teaching*, Memorandum no. 67.

Pompilus, Pradel
 1961 *La Langue Française en Haiti* (Paris).

Prince, J. Dyneley
 1910 "The Jersey Dutch Dialect", *Dialect Notes* III:459-69.

Puckett, Niles Newbell
 1937 "Names of American Negro Slaves, in George P. Murdoch (ed.), *Studies in the Science of Society* (New Haven, Connecticut).

Raimundo, Jacques
 1933 *O Elemento Afro-Negro na Lingua Portuguesa* (Rio de Janeiro).

Ramsey, Frederic and Charles Edward Smith
 1939 *Jazzmen* (New York).

Read, Allen Walker
 1933 "British recognition of American speech in the eighteenth century", *Dialect Notes* VI:313-34.
 1935 "Amphi-Atlantic English", *English Studies* 17:161-78.

Reinecke, John
 1970 *Language and Dialect in Hawaii* (Honolulu).

Resnick, Melvin
 1968 "The Coordination and Tabulation of Phonological Data in American Spanish Dialectology", University of Rochester dissertation.

Roberts, Elsa
 1969 "An Evaluation of Standardized Tests as Tools for the Measurement of Language Development", Language Research Foundation (Cambridge, Massachusetts).

Rystrom, Richard
 1970 "Dialect training and reading: A further look", *Reading Research Quarterly* 5:583-99.

Schneider, Gilbert D.
 1966 "West African Pidgin English", Hartford Seminary Foundation dissertation.
 1967 "West African Pidgin English: An Historical Overview", *Ohio University Papers in International Studies*, no. 8.

Shuey, Audrey M.
 1966² *The Testing of Negro Intelligence* (New York).

Shuy, Roger W., Joan C. Baratz, and Walter A. Wolfram
 1969 "Sociolinguistic Factors in Speech Identification", *NIMH Research Project* no. MH 15048-01 (Washington, D.C.).

Shuy, Roger W., Walter A. Wolfram, and William C. Riley
 1968 *Field Techniques in an Urban Language Study* (Urban Languages Series 3) (Washington, D.C.).

Skinner, B. F.
 1957 *Verbal Behavior* (New York).

Sroufe, A.
 1970 "A methodological and philosophical critique of intervention oriented research", mimeograph (Minneapolis).

Stearns, Marshal D.
 1956 *The Story of Jazz* (New York).
 1968 *Jazz Dance: The Story of American Vernacular Dance* (New York).

386   *References for the Introductions*

Stewart, William A.
1962a "Creole languages in the Caribbean", in F. A. Rice (ed.), *Study of the Role of Second Languages in Asia, Africa, and Latin America* (Washington, D.C.).
1962b "The functional distribution of Creole and French in Haiti", in E.D. Woodworth and R. J. Di Pietro (eds.), *Linguistics and Language Study* (13th Georgetown Round Table Meeting).
1964 "Urban Negro speech: Sociolinguistic factors affecting English teaching", in Shuy (ed.), *Social Dialects and Language Learning*, NCTE.
1965 "Foreign language teaching methods in quasi-foreign language situations", in Stewart (ed.), *Non-Standard Speech and the Teaching of English* (Washington, D.C.).
1968 "A sociolinguistic typology for describing national multilingualism", in Joshua Fishman (ed.), *Readings in the Sociology of Language* (The Hague).
1969 "On the use of Negro dialect in the teaching of reading", in Baratz and Shuy (eds.), *Teaching Black Children to Read* (Washington, D.C.).
1970 "Sociopolitical issues in the linguistic treatment of Negro dialect", Report of the 20th Round Table, Georgetown University.
f.c. "Acculturation processes and the language of the American Negro", in William W. Gage (ed.), *Language in its Social Setting* (Washington, D.C.).
Stockton, Eric
1964 "Poe's use of Negro dialect in 'The Gold Bug'", in *Studies in Language and Linguistics in Honor of Charles C. Fries* (Ann Arbor, Michigan).
Taylor, Douglas McRae
1951 *The Black Carib of British Honduras* (New York).
1961 "New languages for old in the West Indies", *Comparative Studies in Society and History* 3:277-88.
i.p. *Languages of the West Indies* (New Haven, Connecticut).
Toscano Mateus, Humberto
1953 *El Español en el Ecuador* (Madrid).
Turner, Lorenzo Dow
1949 *Africanisms in the Gullah Dialect* (Chicago).
Vanderbilt, Gertrude Lott
1881 *The Social History of Flatbush, and Manners and Customs of the Dutch Settlers in Kings County* (New York).
Voorhoeve, Jan
1961 "A Project for the Study of Creole Language History in Surinam", in R. B. LePage (ed.), *Proceedings of the Conference in Creole Language Studies* (= *Creole Language Studies* 2) (London).
1973 "Historical and linguistic evidence in favor of the relexification theory in the formation of Creoles", *Language in Society* II, No. 1:133-46.
Wagner, Max Leopold
1949 *Lingua e Dialetti dell' America Spagnola* (Firenze).
Wepman, J. M.
1958 *Auditory Discrimination Test, Manual of Directions* (Chicago).
Whinnom, Keith
1965 "The origin of the European-based pidgins and creoles", *Orbis* XIV: 509-26.
Whitten, Norman and John Szwed (eds.)
1970 *Afro-American Anthropology: Contemporary Perspectives* (New York, Free Press).
Williams, Frederic (ed.).
1970 *Language and Poverty: Perspectives on a Theme* (Chicago).

Williamson, Juanita V.
   1961   "A Phonological and Morphological Study of the Speech of the Negro of Memphis, Tennessee", University of Michigan dissertation.
   1968   "The Speech of Negro High School Students in Memphis, Tennessee", U.S. Office of Education OEC-6-10-207, Final Report.
Winks, Robin
   1971   *The Blacks in Canada* (Montreal).
Wolfram, Walter A.
   1969   *A Sociolinguistic Description of Detroit Negro Speech* (= *Urban Language Series* 5), (Washington, D.C.).
Wolfram, Walter and Nona H. Clarke
   1971   *Black-White Speech Relationships* (= *Urban Language Series* 7), (Washington, D.C.).
Wolfram, Walter, Marie Shiels and Ralph W. Fasold
   1971   "Overlapping Influence in the English of Second Generation Puerto Rican Teenagers in Harlem", Office of Education Grant no. 3-70-033(508) Final Report.
Work, John Wesley
   1940   *American Negro Folk Songs* (New York).
Zettersten, Arne
   1969   *The English of Tristan da Cunha* (Lund).

Index